My Vue

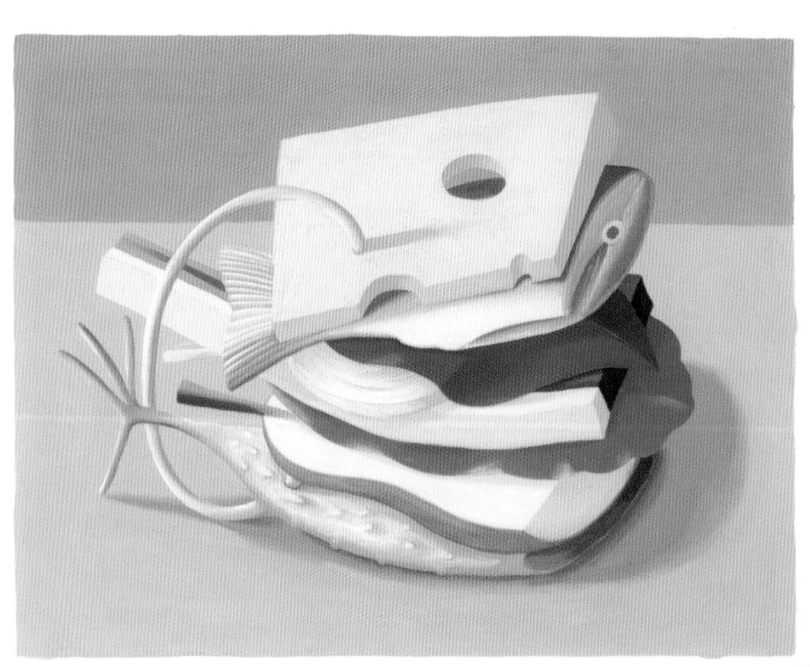

My Vue

Modern French Cookery

Shannon Bennett

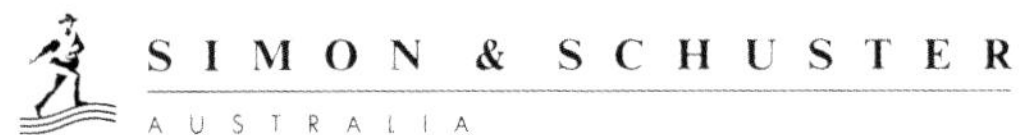

For assistance regarding ingredients and recipes
visit the interative My Vue web site:
www.myvue.com.au

MY VUE
First published in Australia in 2004 by
Simon & Schuster (Australia) Pty Limited
Suite 2, Lower Ground Floor
14–16 Suakin Street
Pymble, NSW 2073

A Viacom Company
Sydney New York London Toronto

Visit our website at www.simonsaysaustralia.com

Copyright © Shannon Bennett 2004

All rights reserved. No part of this publication may be reproduced, stored in a retrieval system, or transmitted, in any form or by any means, electronic, mechanical, photocopying, recording or otherwise, without the prior permission of the publisher in writing.

Cataloguing-in-Publication data:

Bennett, Shannon
My Vue: modern French cookery.
Includes index.
ISBN 0 7318 1236 0.
1. Vue de monde (Restaurant: Melbourne, Vic.).
2. Cookery, French. I. Title.
641.5944

Cover and internal design by Tou-can Design
Photography by Dean Cambray
Illustrations by Tom Samek
Back cover photograph by Dean Cambray
Front cover illustration by Tom Samek
Typeset in Perpetua by Kirby Jones
Printed in China by SNP Leefung Printers

10 9 8 7 6 5 4 3 2 1

Contents

Foreword by Paul Bocuse • *vii*
Preface • *ix*
Acknowledgments • *xi*
My Story • *1*
The Grain, the Flour and the Bread • *47*
The Tomato • *77*
The Potato • *91*
The Mushroom • *107*
The Truffle • *127*
The Market Garden • *137*
The Foie Gras • *169*
The Scallop • *187*
The Oyster • *199*
The Caviar • *215*
The Freshwater Fish • *225*
The Deep Sea • *241*
The Wilderness • *267*
The Pasture • *291*
The Dessert • *317*
The Chocolate • *345*
The Cheese • *359*
Foundation Recipes • *369*
Glossary • *398*
Index • *408*

by

PAUL BOCUSE

JE PARCOURS LE MANUSCRIT de Shannon BENNETT et me surprends à penser que décidément, il y a des jeunes qui ont bien du talent. Nous les croisons malheureusement trop vite.

Mais des garçons de la qualité de ce chef BENNETT sauront marquer leur passage dans le monde de la cuisine et plus particulièrement Shannon, qui riche d'expériences multiples sait à travers son ouvrage My Vue, dont il est l'auteur, nous faire partager ses découvertes tout en nous suggérant des recettes à la portée de tous, ne reniant en rien l'enseignement de ses maîtres.

Félicitations et tous mes voeux de succès l'accompagnent.

[WHILE READING THROUGH Shannon Bennett's manuscript, it has surprised me to discover that there are definitely young people with such a wealth of talent. Unfortunately, sometimes, they cross our paths too briefly.

But men of the quality of this chef, Bennett, know how to leave their mark on the world of cuisine. Shannon particularly, enriched by numerous experiences, shows through this book, *My Vue*, how to make us share his discoveries, simultaneously suggesting recipes within everyone's reach while never disowning his masters' teaching. Congratulations and all my best wishes of success go with him.]

Preface

IT WOULD BE A big mistake to generalise when talking about Australia — you can't expect uniformity in a country of 6.7 million square kilometres (2.5 million square miles)! In order to understand this land, which is both a country and a continent, you have to make a trip around and through it. Situated below the equator, Australia, a country of extremes, is the oldest — as well as the flattest and driest — island of Oceania. When it is 30°C (85°F) in Darwin in the north, the temperature can dip to 5°C (40°F) in Hobart in Tasmania.

In the land down under, summer happens in the winter, the wine grapes are harvested in February and Christmas falls on a midsummer day. Australians used to begin their day with a cup of tea and bacon and eggs, at least that is the myth. We tended to see ourselves as a southern branch of the great Anglo-Saxon tree, with a lingering Victorian influence, weather-beaten from the open air, raising sheep, hunting crocs and pursuing kangaroos. Surprise! Today you're more likely to find an Australian starting the day in French or Italian style, with a cappuccino or an espresso, a brioche or a croissant.

Since the end of the Second World War, the British archetype has become increasingly diluted in this melting pot of cultures. Australian cuisine eagerly embraces new international flavours. The food scene exploding across the country is inventive, daring and built on European foundations that increasingly incorporate traditional Aussie and Asian influences. One unchanging fact remains: the cooking here is based on a respect for the great Australian products issuing from the country's expansive rich soil and seemingly endless shorelines.

Acknowledgments

THE APPRECIATED SUPPORT, friendship and encouragement of all who helped make this book a reality, including Gavan Disney, the team at Vue de monde and particularly Anna Curry, Ryan Clift and the VDM kitchen boys, Tom Samek, Dean Cambray, Serge Thomann, Phillipe Mouchel, Megan Johnston, Jon Attenborough, Julia Collingwood and the team at Simon & Schuster, and finally Paul Bocuse who gave his support by writing the Foreword.

In a modern world it is encouraged and not to be frowned upon to accept help from a vast array of family, friends, customers and even strangers to whom I will always be indebted. As they all know who they are: thank you.

My Story

WESTMEADOWS — A SMALL suburb 25 kilometres (15 miles) north of Melbourne, Australia with a mixture of lower- to middle-income earners — is where I spent most of my childhood. I have many great memories of an innocent and uninterrupted childhood with very few complications and an enormous amount of adventure. My early years were spent playing Aussie Rules Football for the Westmeadows' Tigers in winter and cricket for the same team in summer. The immediate surrounding world was full of excitement. Watching Mum bake in the kitchen on a cold Sunday afternoon while listening to BBC radio family favourites on long-wave fired in me an insatiable curiosity and an interest in food.

As a child, I collected pets — everything from stray dogs to turtles, geese to poisonous snakes. Their innocence and purpose in life was so simple. I have as much respect for animals as any vegetarian, but I also maintain that we should make the most of what the earth has given us. My attraction to nature drew me to the conclusion that, as humans, we are incredibly complicated, from our minds to our

palates, and we have a responsibility to protect the things around us that are vulnerable and precious. Food produce is as complex as we are. Appreciation for what is put on the table is, in my opinion, a quality worth cultivating.

In Westmeadows, going to a restaurant meant visiting Papa Gina's Pizza Parlour or the Dragonfly for Chinese and BYO soft drinks. At the time, Melbourne had a nationwide reputation for fine dining: only 25 kilometres (15 miles) away, we were 25 years away.

Like all the other children from the area, I attended the local Westmeadows Primary School. It had a bad reputation because of its proximity to Broadmeadows with its less than desirable streets. Nonetheless, I learned to hold my own against thugs and drugs, which became an advantage to me later in my career. Most of my friends spent their weekends of boredom hanging around with older brothers. I felt uneasy with the lack of adventure and spirit my young mates and I were experiencing. I now look back, as we all do, and blame everything that didn't seem right in my life on the first confusing stages of adolescence.

I started to escape the long boring weekends by visiting my grandmother on my father's side who lived close by. She spoilt me, taking me on trips to the city. We went to the cinema or the theatre, and nice restaurants.

I was captivated by the atmosphere of places like the historic Florentino and the Cliveden dining room at the Hilton. My grandmother, who lived by herself after the death of my grandfather, Gordon Bennett, cooked every weekend. She would prepare and store enough food for the week. The Depression had taught her the skills of preservation and an appreciation for the food that is laid on the table.

My Story

My grandfather, after surviving the war — I can proudly say he was one of the famous Rats of Tobruk — decided on a career in politics. This took my grandparents to all corners of Australia, especially parts of the outback. In these bush and outback areas my grandmother was introduced to slower methods of cooking, such as braising and slow roasting, with cuts of meat such as shanks, trotters, pork belly, wild rabbits, mutton and, of course, kangaroo. Nan passed this knowledge on to me when I stayed with her. I had a great introduction to the basics of baking: making damper, fresh bread, pumpkin scones and different types of biscuit and shortbread — recipes I still use to this day.

The quote below from my father encapsulates my determination to succeed in this industry and to make my grandfather proud.

Thrust doggedly onwards: starting again, failing again, implacably thrusting towards success. For success, even if it is only the success of knowing that one has tried to the utmost and never surrendered, is the target of every battler.

My mother, from Dublin, was also a great cook, making much more complicated recipes and dishes that confused me. Measurements in recipes confuse me to this day — I believe that feel and technique are more important. Nevertheless, I loved to watch and absorb the old-fashioned cooking in pokey ordinary kitchens with the two most important women of my childhood. I loved tasting and smelling, but not eating. I became, and still do now, too excited to eat. I have more fun pleasing the hungry than being one of them. A chef always performs better on an empty stomach! I say this to my kitchen team now: never trust a fat chef! If you are hungry your senses and instincts are much sharper, just like an animal hunting. I use this sense when I taste. If I love what I just tasted, so will nine out of ten people I cook for. The tenth person must have spoilt their appetite before dinner.

Wild rabbit stew à la bourguignonne

[serves 8]

THIS IS AN ADAPTATION of my Nan's recipe. It is a great Sunday lunch dish served with garlic and rosemary roasted potatoes or Parmesan-flavoured polenta and a crispy watercress salad.

2 x 1.2 kg (2 lb 5½ oz) wild rabbits
2 onions, roughly chopped
2 carrots, roughly chopped
2 sticks of celery, roughly chopped
1 leek, roughly chopped
1 head of garlic, cut in half
3 sprigs of thyme
3 cups red wine
100 g (3½ oz) plain (all-purpose) flour
*100 g (3½ oz) goose fat**
4 cups veal stock (see page 294)

GARNISH

100 g (3½ oz) small button mushrooms
100 g (3½ oz) butter
Squeeze of lemon juice
1 tablespoon goose fat
*100 g (3½ oz) pancetta lardons**
100 g (3½ oz) baby pickling onions, peeled

Chop the rabbits into four with a heavy cleaver, then in half again, separating the front legs, ribs, loins and hind legs • Combine the rabbit, vegetables, garlic, thyme and red wine in a large container and marinate in the refrigerator for 24 hours • Preheat the oven to 180°C (350°F) • Sprinkle the flour into an ovenproof frying pan and toast in the oven for 15 minutes, or until light golden brown with a lovely nutty smell • Remove the vegetables and rabbit from the marinade and strain, reserving the red wine • Preheat the oven to 140°C (275°F) • Heat the goose fat in a large heavy-based saucepan, add the vegetables and rabbit and cook until golden. Season with salt and pepper and deglaze with the reserved marinade. Cook until reduced by two-thirds • Add the veal stock, bring to the boil, cover with aluminium (aluminum) foil and a lid, and place in the oven for 2–3 hours • Remove the braising vegetables before serving. (You may ask the inevitable question why? Well, the vegetables have transferred all their flavour into the braise and the texture of overcooked vegetables can be quite unappealing.) Serve at your own leisure over the next few days, as the flavour will improve • To make the traditional garnish of Burgundy, place the button mushrooms with the butter and a generous squeeze of lemon juice in boiling salted water until tender. (You can also add the onions to the mushrooms and blanch for 15 minutes, or until tender, then drain and cook in olive oil or goose fat over medium heat until golden and caramelised)

• Melt the goose fat in a frying pan, add the pancetta, mushrooms and onions and warm over low heat • Transfer the braised rabbit and vegetables to a large warmed serving bowl. Spoon over the garnish and serve. To add an extra dimension, serve with parsley leaves that have been deep fried for a couple of seconds until they are crisp.

Ingredients marked with a * are discussed in more detail in the glossary.

AT THE AGE OF TWELVE, it was time to grow up. My parents were excited that I had been accepted at the private boys' school, Essendon Grammar. A new experience was about to hit me: strict, passionate, eccentric teachers; a mixture of students, geniuses and smart middle-class kids with bright futures in corporate middle management; rich, spoilt brats with brains stored in the heels of their shoes. I became fond of both sides of this social division; there was a little bit of me in each. I never felt that I fitted in at school. I was a dreamer. I was starting to see the whole world as an exciting place, where I believed something special would happen for me.

The year I started at Essendon Grammar the Principal had decided to integrate a home economics course for boys at the girls' division of the school, Penleigh. This involved a half day every week, where a few unrealistically eager boys would look forward to home economics with the girls. I signed up straight away.

A French teacher by the name of Janik Jarnet inspired me. Monsieur Jarnet told me about how people in Europe would follow a chef's progression from restaurant to restaurant as if he were a movie star. How the French treated food religiously. He used to mention the *Michelin Guide* and Michelin Stars and how much they meant to a chef and his restaurant's reputation. Monsieur Jarnet is now one of my most valued customers at Vue de monde.

About this time, Marco Pierre White had his own cooking show on SBS TV called *Cooking with Marco*. The show so interested me that I watched all eight episodes without skipping a beat. How could I have known that one day I would work with him? He created a dream in me that I knew would become a reality. I wondered if it was his awe-inspiring skill, his technique, his knowledge, or his unquestionable leadership? It was all these things, but foremost it was his energy, optimism and youth that inspired me.

Scared, yet drawn to Marco at the same time, I don't believe any chef on the planet will ever have what he had at Harvey's, his first restaurant in Wandsworth.

He once said, memorably, on the show, 'Cooking is difficult for the ignorant and easy for the vulnerable'. I often think about it and wonder. I have found that it reverses from day to day in my life.

'One day I will be Marco!' I proclaimed to my parents. I now understand that was a fantasy — that there will only ever be one Marco Pierre White.

THERE IS A BIG-BONED teacher standing in front of the chalkboard before a home-economics class of twenty. She is elegant, and has a definite presence in the room. She eyes the room looking for troublemakers and finds twenty of them. We sit up dead straight. Mrs Malcolm's goal was to teach at least a couple of us to fend for ourselves. She saw something in me and quickly reined me in. By the end of our time together she had become the most approachable teacher for me.

With her enthusiasm and belief in me, our interaction blossomed into a successful student-teacher relationship. I quickly developed a passion for absorbing techniques and methods. It was my first step to becoming a chef. I started to use the home kitchen as a laboratory and my family as guinea pigs.

A dish derived from my lessons with Mrs Malcolm was crêpes Suzette. This recipe is used in my restaurant today in two forms: as it is or by adding a Grand Marnier flavoured soufflé mix inside. To finish, the crêpe is folded in half, icing (confectioners') sugar is sprinkled over the top, then it goes into a 200°C (400°F) oven for 5 minutes. Serve the same way as the recipe which follows and the result is worth the extra effort.

Crêpes suzettes

[serves 6]

CRÊPE MIX

125 g (4 oz) plain (all-purpose) flour
80 g (2¾ oz) ground almonds
2 eggs
1 teaspoon salt
*25 g (1 oz) vanilla sugar**
200 ml (7 fl oz) milk
2½ tablespoons rum
2 tablespoons melted butter
100 g (3½ oz) butter

SAUCE

200 ml (7 fl oz) freshly squeezed orange juice
100 ml (3½ fl oz) Grand Marnier
2 tablespoons soft brown sugar
2 Seville oranges, segmented
2 cups vanilla ice cream

Combine the flour, ground almonds, eggs, salt, sugar and milk in a large mixing bowl • Beat until the batter is smooth and the consistency of single cream. A little more milk may be needed to achieve the right consistency • Add the rum and melted butter and set aside for 2–3 hours • To make the crêpes, heat 1 tablespoon of butter in a non-stick frying pan over low to medium heat • Ladle the batter into the centre of the pan and tilt to evenly spread the batter into a round flat crepe • After 2–3 minutes, when golden brown, gently flip and cook for a further 1–2 minutes, or until golden on both sides. The more crêpes you make the better you will get at it! • Fold the crêpes into quarters. Arrange 2–3 crêpes in the centre of each serving plate • Combine the orange juice, Grand Marnier and brown sugar in a saucepan and bring to the boil. Add the orange segments in the last second. Pour the sauce over the crêpes. Serve with a scoop of vanilla ice cream • If time allows, you could jazz up the dish for an extra special effect. Take the zest of 4–5 oranges, blanch in cold water brought to the boil 2–3 times, then slowly cook in a standard sugar syrup (see page 393) for 10 minutes. Sprinkle over the final dish.

After a year Mrs Malcolm suggested that I should get a feel for the industry. This led me to fib that I was a year older than I was to obtain a position at the local McDonald's cooking burgers. It was great for a while. I learnt about hard work and discipline, and most of all organisation and cleanliness. McDonald's gave me confidence. They promoted hard work and saw training as a vital element in a consistent, successful business. Working a few nights a week from 5 pm to midnight then up for school at 7 am the next morning was the perfect learning process for a life in the kitchen.

The psyching-up period at around 5 pm, when it is full steam ahead getting organised for the first order, that's a buzz I was hooked on — something too hard to explain; only another chef would know. The adrenaline of service; cooking with the immense heat radiating from the stove, the sweat, noise, panic and the overwhelming feeling that you are out of your depth — that there is no light at the end of the tunnel. Five hours of burns, sore feet, no voice and intense concentration all packed into two intense hours of service. The biggest bonus of all is that you can't do it by yourself; you're part of a team. You make a mistake and everyone goes down. Stirred together, being a chef is more than a job, more than just cooking; in a way the food is just a by-product.

It is a great feeling when you know what you're going to do with your life! This was further enhanced for me when I was given the opportunity to visit family in London and Dublin for the school holidays. At fourteen I stayed with my Uncle Tom. Fifty-something, never-married, Uncle Tom had trained as a chef, but was swept away when he had the chance to become the rhythm guitarist in a 1960s band called The Kings. Well respected in the music industry, he was playing a few nights a week at the Dorchester, London when I was with him. He owned two pubs around Regents Park, West London, and a winter villa retreat in the Costa de Sol. His pubs always had great food and a warm comfortable feeling, reflecting his own persona.

I looked up to Tom and his way of life. I found it exciting being with a man who was responsible only for himself. I was able to see him for who he was — a complete individual with great expression. On my last night before heading back to Melbourne, he took me out to the dining room in the Ritz Hotel on Piccadilly. I was overawed and inspired by the grandeur and elegance. Women with the sparkle of fame in their eyes, dressed with beauty and finesse; men in suits, blending in with the evening; young and old, out for an evening of splendour and refinement.

The thing that made it great was this could be anyone's experience — once a week, once a year, an anniversary, a birthday or a once-in-a-lifetime celebration. It wasn't just the food that made the night, it was the wine, the service, the decor, and the atmosphere. At every moment during that evening a professional was in charge of my experience; all I had to do was to sit back and watch the show. It made me realise that being a chef would take years of training.

My night was topped off when Uncle Tom snuck me into the famous Stork Club, just off Regent Street, for a nightcap. If you've been to the Stork Club, don't think anything less of me. It's a topless cabaret club with some of the most glamorous dancers this side of the Moulin Rouge. Crystal and Dom Perignon. Sorry Mum!

Upon returning from London I felt very restless and eager to explore what I had discovered that night at the Ritz. Mrs Malcolm could sense I was getting itchy feet. It didn't look good for my future at Essendon Grammar. So one evening, feeling excited and fearful, I told Dad of my intention to leave school to pursue a career in cooking. I had never been close to my father; we didn't share any common interests, but I need not have worried as both he and my mother approved of my decision. I think it is everyone's goal to make their parents proud. It was then, and still is, a motivation that got me through some very tough and lonely times. Fortunately my parents were happy for me; they believed in me.

I took the initiative and wrote to the top ten hotels in and around Melbourne requesting an apprenticeship. A month or so passed and I received only one positive reply, from the Grand Hyatt. At the time it was the most modern hotel in Melbourne with a great reputation for its food. It was recognised in the industry as being a tough, organised, profitable and efficient business due to the man at the top, Swiss chef Roger Lienhard.

I turned up for the initial interview full of confidence, thinking it would be a breeze. A human resources officer — who didn't really care that I wanted to have my own restaurant one day — interviewed me. Getting through all the questions was tough. Two weeks later I had a second interview with the man that mattered,

Lienhard. At the time he was in charge of more than 100 kitchen personnel. We hit it off straight away. He could see the passion in my eyes. We discussed how food was only one aspect of a chef's career.

It was a great interview. We talked for over an hour about the pros and cons of giving up my private school education and the issues to be faced in committing myself to a life in the kitchen: the alcoholism, the drug abuse, the antisocial hours, the failed relationships, the constant fatigue — and an overwhelming sense of satisfaction.

At the end of the interview I was told to arrange a date for a trial in the kitchen. A chance, if you will, to confirm that it was what I wanted — and that I was what they wanted. As I left his office I thanked him for the opportunity and told him I wouldn't let him down, to which he replied, 'Oh yes you will!'.

MY FIRST DAY AT the Hyatt didn't go entirely well. Half an hour into cutting up some red capsicum (sweet pepper) I sliced through my thumb. Not wanting to make a big deal of it, I patched it with a little help from a kitchen hand. It woke me up, got rid of the nerves, and made me realise I was only human, the same as everyone else around me.

The place was huge, and I was the youngest, the bottom of the pecking order. Time went on, I gained confidence and skill. My communication with the Chef became very professional and at times it felt impersonal and distant. Nonetheless, the message remained: no matter what my future held, I still had to get there the hard way, by myself. He kept asking me 'When are you going to let me down?'.

My Story

No matter how you earn a living, there is always a first bollocking and you will always remember it. When it comes from a 203-centimetre (6-foot 8-inch) 130-kilogram (286-pound) Swiss fanatic, it hurts the ego. My day came one Thursday morning when I was the assistant breakfast chef. I was in charge of making French toast and pancakes. All I had to do to prepare the mix was to add a few eggs and milk, simple. But on that particular morning the mix wasn't rising to its normal fluffiness. I could hear all 130-odd kilograms of the Chef in his wooden clogs coming up the kitchen ramp to begin his morning rounds starting with an espresso in the breakfast kitchen. The call came for a pancake and in my naivety and innocence I ladled the mixture onto the flat grill. In a few minutes I passed the poor excuse for a fluffy pancake to be plated — and that's when the explosion happened.

The big man screamed at a pitch I had never heard before. The feeling of panic and adrenaline rushing through my body was a new sensation. I didn't realise the body could feel such extremes.

In order to survive the gruelling years ahead every top chef's nervous system has built up an immunity to such bollockings from the man wearing the top hat, the Chef! The pancake in question ended up against a kitchen wall.

I was told before starting the arduous journey of my apprenticeship that I would only ever hear from him directly if I were doing a bad job. I received a few more bollockings over the next twelve months to keep me on my toes.

I was now seventeen years old with close to two years' cooking under my belt. As part of my apprenticeship I was also studying at college. I had to do seven weeks a year at the college.

I felt the world was my oyster. During the monthly chefs' meetings, where the Chef would brief the 100-plus strong team on costs and staff movements (the usual boring bureaucracy of a big hotel), something he was saying came to my attention.

'A competition . . . something called a "Salon Culinaire". Today is the deadline for signing up.'

There were two categories, apprentice or open; I accidentally signed up in the 'open' category, choosing the 'classical four course set menu'. Without knowing it, I had stacked the odds against me. I had only four months to train in any spare time I had. As the competition got closer I started to become noticed around the different departments by the senior chefs. Perhaps I caught their imagination.

I kept my menu simple. Possibly the greatest modern chef of the last thirty years, Allain Chapel, believed simplicity created perfection. I had heard this on a cooking program when I was a kid and it has lived with me ever since.

The last day before the competition was manic: last-minute practice sessions and new ideas filled me with anxiety. At around 11:30 that night, I was getting some last-minute help from the Chef and his German assistant Dieter. The Chef offered me a room for the night at his place, which was close to the hotel. I felt honoured and privileged. He drove me home in his brand new German sports car. His place was trendy, modern and big. He probably spent only a few hours a week there, but that's the life of a chef.

MENU

Salon Culinaire

SEPTEMBER 1991,

EXHIBITION BUILDINGS, MELBOURNE

Terrine of scallop and Atlantic salmon, pulses and braised pippis

Butternut pumpkin consommé served in its own shell, ravioli of goat's cheese

Roulade of venison and polenta, braised baby vegetables, morel jus

Trio of fruit mousses, chocolate trellis served with their own sauces

That night I couldn't sleep. The phone rang and Roger (his name outside of work) answered it. It was his ex-girlfriend. The talk was friendly; no anger nor heated exchange. He spoke softly. He said he was sorry he worked so hard. The conversation seemed sad. I understood that night that the life of a chef is filled with a mixture of tumultuous emotion and passion.

The next day I didn't let Chef down. I won. It was my fifteen minutes of fame. I beat other well-known chefs. Me, a young apprentice with competitors twice my age had won with a score of 98/100. I still have that gold medal in a shoebox under my bed. It was a great step in my career.

I went through my apprenticeship winning many more competitions. The greatest highlight and disappointment at the same time was winning a bronze medal at Hotel Asia in Singapore. It is one of the largest cooking competitions with over 3000 competitors from all over the world. I lapsed in a few basic skill areas in my dessert that ironically I had practised for months, but when it came to the real pressure I folded. The lesson learnt from this was facing the adversity of failure and knowing it rested on my own shoulders, and to motivate me never to repeat the same mistake.

Roger was annoyed with me; he knew I could have been the first Australian individual to win gold there. I was still only eighteen, but I started to feel addicted to pressure; it was becoming a need in my life.

THE OPPORTUNITY OF spending a well-earned three-week break in Europe arose. I was suffering from the travel bug and working a lot had enabled me to save my wages; I travelled to Europe on my allocated leave, catching up again with my uncles, including Tom. The attraction of eating at Marco Pierre White's then Michelin three-star The Restaurant at the Hyde Park Hotel was too hard to resist, even though it set me back $250. I was dressed in a shabby second-hand suit borrowed from Uncle Tom, who had made the booking for 9 pm.

We were greeted by flawless perfection in a bow tie and seated in the lounge for a pre-dinner drink. A class of society surrounded me to which I was not accustomed; it added to the atmosphere of inaccessibility that was dangerous because I got a buzz out of it.

The menu was long, and very foreign. I felt pressured to order and chose anything, but what came to the table was everything. Perfect diced carrot, fennel, celery, zucchini (courgette), and celeriac filled the custom-designed Villeroy & Boch bowl like paint on a canvas. I felt compelled to count the dice. Sitting on top, five types of shellfish, all cooked differently. Steamed, poached, boiled and roasted, embodied in their own stock and tastefully called Mariniere of Shellfish. It blew me away. By the time we had finished, we were the last in the restaurant.

Marco walked into the dining room late, but with a purpose. He had a presence about him. He sat at the table next to me, sipped a short black, signed my menu and left. He spoke with silence. At this point I had broken into a cold sweat. I was thinking about what I was missing out on, not being in Marco's kitchen.

I FOUND COLLEGE A sterile place with little inspiration. Most of the teachers were ex-chefs who couldn't hack the industry. You could sense the negativity in them. It's unfair of me to categorise all cookery teachers in this way — I know there is passion and commitment out there and I did experience it, but only from the occasional teacher. How does an institution place passion alongside academic standards, tradition, and techniques, and control it across all sectors and types of students, to achieve a product that strives for and produces excellence?

My time as an apprentice at the Grand Hyatt was coming to completion and I was ready. Reflecting back, my basic training could not have been better, especially with twelve months in pastry and bakery where I learned the art of making bread, tempering chocolate, sugar work, and general baking. The most important message I took from the pastry section was that I didn't want to devote myself to being a pastry cook. I saw three different bakers pass through the section while I was there. They all had their own spots in the flour bins to hide their stash of beer and whisky for when things got a little lonely at 3 am.

During the last six months of my four-year apprenticeship I would go to the famous Hill of Content bookshop and slowly read my way through a collection of English food guides and the *Age Good Food Guide* and the *Michelin Guide*. I researched around fifteen restaurants that I believed I could commit to. But first I wrote to Marco Pierre White, begging him to employ me. With a month gone and no reply I phoned him, managing to speak to him by pretending to be older. I said I was looking for a chef de partie position. He abruptly told me I was 'just an Aussie drifter' and he had had Aussie chefs before me who had let him down . . . so I should work in at least two three-star restaurants before I even bothered knocking on his door again.

I was in shock that my hero had shut the door on me, but I was energised even more. Knowing that to succeed takes energy and perseverance, I now wrote individual letters to the other fifteen restaurants telling the chef why I wanted to work with him in particular. I received ony two replies, but I was elated; I had been expecting none.

One reply was from John Burton Race, owner-chef of two-Michelin starred L'Ortolan in country Berkshire, 100 kilometres (60 miles) west of London. The other reply was from Gordon Ramsay, who at the time was the up and coming owner-chef of the one-Michelin star Aubergine in London's fashionable Chelsea. That was all I really knew about him, apart from his youth, ambition and an excellent pedigree of training. Both letters were very typical replies from top class chefs with few human relation skills. They basically informed me of a position at the lowest rank with very little pay, seventeen hours a day, six days a week.

The decision was not an easy one. Most of the senior chefs with whom I had worked had tremendous respect for John Burton Race's kitchen as being the hardest in England and one of the toughest in Europe. Many of them suggested that I would not even last one month in his kitchen. That spurred me on to work with Burton Race at his acclaimed restaurant, L'Ortolan.

The offer of £220 a week sounded like good money for a country restaurant. However, shaving off accommodation expenses and tax, I was left with ten pints of Guinness and £40 in the bank.

FOUR WEEKS AFTER receiving the reply I was walking up the old church road in the English country village of Shinfield with knives and chef's jacket in hand and the naivety of the casual Australian approach to life and work.

The restaurant was housed in a seventeenth-century vicarage perched on a hill surrounded by winding country lanes and green fields. It was hard to imagine that 50 metres (55 yards) up the road was a kitchen so tough it could compare with a vicious, unforgiving military training ground. Entombed inside the old brick walls was a group of chefs with enough energy, fire and passion to propel the restaurant to another planet. So weird a planet, it inspired Lenny Henry to produce the award-winning comedy, *Chef*, based on the antics in the L'Ortolan kitchen.

As I walked into the kitchen, most of the chefs were already hard at work; admittedly it was 7:45 am. In my letter I had been told to start at 8 am. I approached Burton Race to introduce myself. The reply was swift.

'Who the fuck are you? Oh, you're the Aussie. Okay, get changed in the cottage and start work with Alisha over there.'

That was my wake-up call. For the first three months it was a shit-fight. I struggled, but I stuck it out. I didn't know what foie gras was, let alone mange-tout, or pousse epinarde. Every week I saw someone new start and finish; either they were sacked or they just couldn't hack it.

The kitchen was split up into five sections: pastry; meat and sauce; fish; hot entrée and larder (cold entrée); and of course the garnish or vegetable section. This is how most European-style kitchens are organised. The only thing that varied was the number of chefs in each section. Traditionally a French kitchen has two chefs per section, one senior and a commis or a trainee. Pastry had a minimum of three, as the workload was immense (all the breads, canapés, petits fours and desserts came from this vital section of the kitchen). There was also a full-time pot washer/kitchen-hand, second chef (sous chef), and of course the leader of the team, John Burton Race.

Most top-class Melbourne restaurants have a maximum of five chefs in the entire kitchen, and — if they are lucky — one kitchen-hand. They are nevertheless expected to give an unforgettable experience. They would probably serve four times as many customers as a two-star Michelin restaurant in Europe. One of the many businessmen pretending to be a restaurateur would say that this is common sense: 'There's no way you could make money with so many staff, without even considering the front of house costs; which are double again'. This is a widespread misunderstanding for many who can't grasp what it's all about: it's about the food, the service and the overall product — making an experience that cannot be forgotten. Inevitably the customers will walk out to spread word about the restaurant. Slowly but surely it will become busier and eventually it will be full every night, thus justifying the labour costs and keeping the quality and consistency that should be expected in a top-class restaurant.

L'Ortolan was a busy, frantic, yet focused kitchen. In the end, when all that hype was over, it was also an empty and lonely place. Not many workplaces where colleagues work together for 90 hours a week have such little personal communication. I found out I didn't even know the man next to me at all. No one dared to have any friendly banter; there was no time. We were all too busy trying to survive; there was no room to strike up a friendly relationship. I had hit the wall in a fantastic and disturbing way. I was getting a buzz from this lifestyle.

One evening, after about three months, I got to know an Irish guy named Paddy. He was quiet, professional and became a big help in my survival of Michelin-star cuisine. He had already had five years' more experience of working with food and, being twenty-five, he had more experience of life than I had. He was also a Manchester United supporter, which I was to find out later is his only real downfall!

The house I boarded at was in the middle of a very poor government housing estate on the other side of Shinfield. It was beyond the busy M4 motorway, which acted like a class divide. The area was rough and not unlike Westmeadows in its looks, atmosphere and dwellers. The restaurant was a 30-minute walk over the M4 walkway, past the Six Bell's pub, through some countryside and up the old Vicarage Road.

The most interesting part of living there was the landlord, a 60-year-old closet gay undertaker who had false teeth. His favourite trick was to leave his teeth in the bathroom and then to conveniently retrieve them while I was in the shower.

I finally moved out after three months when the landlord started putting a pregnant cat under my bed every night. Inevitably, the cat had her kittens there and he would come and check on them every morning . . . at around 3 am. I couldn't hack it, so I packed my bags, complained briefly to the administration at L'Ortolan (to make sure no one else would be bunked up with the undertaker) and left for the other side of Shinfield. It was £20 more, but you get what you pay for, right?

Burton Race was a mad genius, my friend and my boss. It was a strange combination, but it worked. The motivation I received from his energy and confidence made me feel that I could do and achieve anything. I worked so hard for him and to this day regret not a minute of it. My first real bollocking from him made Roger's look like a compliment.

It happened on a cold February evening. The restaurant was quiet and I had been moved to the fish section for a few weeks to cover for someone who had been sacked the week before for not making the grade. I actually felt relieved, as we had started on the same day so I knew the 'Gaffer' had rated me above him. It meant a lot. It sounds sad, but it is a dog-eat-dog world.

My chef de partie (head of section) had the night off. There were only four bookings, as all the roads were snowed in. However, we started to take a lot of late bookings around 7 pm and I was in panic mode. I knew all the garnishes and sauces that went with each particular fish, but taking fish off the bone to order as Burton Race demanded (to keep the fish as fresh as possible) was an immense task.

Ça Marche! ('To order' in French) *Deux St Jacques, un rouget, deux ravioli*. No problem. The orders kept coming through and I was 'gunning it' until I passed the master a piece of wild Scottish salmon wrapped in ventrèche bacon* to impart a smoked, salty flavour through the delicate, pale, beautifully cooked fish. It was to be steamed for five minutes and rested for another five minutes before serving.

Well, that tray and its contents flew past me into a kitchen tile, smashing its contents and the tile. The explanation? The bacon was too thick, therefore imparting too strong a flavour to the flesh of the salmon. He was right but for the fact that it wasn't me who had wrapped it. My chef de partie had. The point was that we are a team, and I should have taken responsibility and rectified it.

Then came the verbal onslaught. Everything else I sent up to him that night was wrong and sent back with violent disgust. Sweat was cold, nerves were needles and concentration was instinct. The kitchen had stopped and was waiting on me for every table we sent. Customers were waiting. Nightmares don't get worse than this. Everything I was producing was of excellent standard and he knew that, but he wanted more. He got more. The customers and the food were tools; he wanted my commitment. It was a test to see if I could weather the storm without breaking.

I was in an adrenaline-packed world of artistic craziness that only the audience of diners had a front-row seat to appreciate. I passed the test and witnessed quite a few others come and go during my time at this madhouse.

Lightly steamed salmon infused with pancetta

[serves 4]

THIS RECIPE IS great for those nights when you need something quick. It is easy and versatile, relying on the juices and flavour of the fish.

If you do not have a steamer, buy a Chinese steam basket suitable for a conventional saucepan. Just remember to place a strip of aluminium (aluminum) foil around the rim of the saucepan to prevent any steam escaping through the gap where the basket and saucepan meet.

1 spring cabbage
*1 tablespoon duck/goose fat**
100 g (3½ oz) chopped shallots
1 clove of garlic, crushed
*50 g (1¾ oz) cultured butter**
2 tablespoons finely chopped curly-leaf parsley
Salt and freshly ground pepper
*8 slices flat pancetta**
4 x 200 g (6 ½ oz) Atlantic salmon fillets
100 ml (3½ fl oz) olive oil
Juice of ½ lemon

Remove the cabbage leaves from the stem. Use only the medium to light green leaves. The dark leaves are too bitter • Blanch the cabbage for 2 minutes in boiling salted water. Refresh in iced water. Remove the leaves and pat dry with paper towel • Cut the cabbage into ribbon size strips • Heat the duck fat in a frying pan and sauté the shallots and garlic until transparent. Add the cabbage, sauté for 2 minutes, then toss through 2 tablespoons of the butter. Add the parsley and season with salt and pepper • Wrap 2 slices of pancetta around each salmon fillet. Season with salt and pepper. Place on a plate, then transfer to a steamer and cook for 6 minutes. To test if the fish is cooked, place a toothpick through a raw fillet of fish; you will feel a slight resistance as you push. Now try it with a cooked piece of fish, there should be no resistance. Overcooked fish is easy to spot by the appearance of a white substance that resembles cooked egg white weeping from the fish. This is protein and is a sign that the fish will be dry and limited in flavour • Whisk the juices left on the plate from cooking the salmon with the olive oil and season with a little lemon juice • To serve, place the sautéed cabbage in the centre of a serving dish, top with the salmon and the sauce.

TWELVE MONTHS PASSED like one big service. Before I knew it, I was promoted to chef de partie — head of a section — at the age of twenty. I was pretty proud of this promotion as L'Ortolan was ranked in the top ten restaurants in the UK. It gave me the energy to continue with new goals, to further myself in the tunnel before I needed to look for some light. I was working hard at developing my cooking skills, learning recipes that were all of a French classical mould developed by chefs more than a century before me.

Burton Race's food is easily described as New World classical. If a dish required cream, he would add whipped cream, using half the amount of cream to produce a lighter, frothier sauce. The use of butter was minimal, and all fish was cooked in olive oil. The cuisine reflected the changing trends of a more health-conscious society.

My favourite dishes at L'Ortolan were anything Burton Race cooked with mushrooms, morels, cèpes (similar to porcini), girolles, chanterelles or Trumpet de Bleau ... always fresh. Autumn was fantastic for these delicacies. All the trimmings would go into a stock with Madeira or white wine and cook for an hour or so. The flavours and aromas extracted from these trimmings, which most chefs would throw in the bin, was amazing. Combine this style of sauce with a freshly roasted fillet of John Dory seasoned with lemon and tarragon and garnished with watercress, and you have a flavour match that cannot be surpassed. He was undoubtedly the best fish cook in Britain and one of the best in Europe — and he made it look so easy.

In Shinfield, I also took on the art of wine appreciation. Jerome was a middle-aged, cheeky Norman. I've heard him jokingly say he would have preferred to marry a magnum of 1990 Chave Hermitage than his current wife Olga, who was also the restaurant manager. Jerome, the sommelier, would travel constantly to France for testing and purchasing trips, bringing back different samples of wine. We were all encouraged to express our thoughts on what we tasted and to think of characteristics of the wine that would harmonise with a particular ingredient.

The theory behind this relies on the sauce being the bridge between the wine and food. This makes it possible for a red wine sauce to complement a fillet of fish, which then in turn could be matched with a red wine such as a pinot noir or a dolcetto. The fish needs to be thought about: to hold up against such a rich sauce it would need to be a heavier, densely flavoured fish, such as salmon, tuna, or mullet. If that doesn't suffice and you crave for a pure white-fleshed fish, try to bring out the flavour more by roasting, which will give a caramelised flavour, linking it to the heavier flavours of the sauce.

A lighter sauce with a heavier flavoured protein works in the opposite way. For example, use the cooking method to lessen the interruption between the pure flavour of the meat and sauce by using a lighter style, such as steaming, poaching or baking, then matching with a sauce that is delicate. The possibilities are endless, a warm dressing like sauce vierge or, it being a cold Sunday afternoon, mushroom essence lightly finished with a dash of whipped cream would be a real winner. Once you have chosen the right combination of flavours for the dish, you can now look for a wine with some similar characteristics to the flavours of the meat or poultry. I recommend the dish be paired with a heavier style of white wine such as a wood aged chardonnay or chenin blanc, even possibly a viognier that has been aged in oak to bring out the caramel and rich honey characteristics. Lighter grape varieties are too delicate for poultry and meat unless you try some of the sweeter, heavier style Alsatian wines. In good vintages they have great viscosity and stronger fruit characteristics, such as apples, cider and even hints of spice. Remember to add a touch of sweetness to your sauce.

I'm not sure if it is true that chefs don't have a long life expectancy but what I saw at L'Ortolan certainly bears this out.

The summer of 1998 was coming to an end. The restaurant was busy and building up to a full-on 'silly season'. Working alongside Burton Race you could see extra sweat on his brow and less colour in his complexion. One minute he was calling out an order and screaming, 'Let's do it boys'. The next moment I couldn't see him over the top of the fish grill. I walked around to check the fish presuming he had walked into the restaurant and there he was on his knees holding his chest. The boys knew he wasn't well. It had been building up. That night, he was placed in hospital for two weeks. Eventually the doctors decided to implant a pacemaker. It shocked us all, but we were determined to keep the kitchen running smoothly while he was recovering. To let the 'Gaffer' down was to let ourselves down — why work this damn hard, then spoil it all with a few sloppy services?

Burton Race was back at work in less than a month. He raced through the back door smoking his favourite Silk Cuts. Here's a guy who had been sponsored by Porsche, BMW, Audi. He had written off two Audi A8s travelling at more than 160 kilometres (100 miles) per hour down the M4, while I had been at the restaurant. I hate to imagine the capabilities of this lunatic in his twenties! The scary thought is he would occasionally drive me to London in 40 minutes — a trip that would usually take over an hour — after we had finished work for the week. He was, in no uncertain terms, a maniac . . . and I somehow aspired to be just like him.

After nearly two years at the stoves in this intense house of madness, restlessness was coming on again. I gathered my courage and headed to London to see Marco — Marco Pierre White, that is.

Through Paddy, my best mate, I had made some great contacts who were working in Marco's kitchens. Knocking on Marco's door, I was welcomed as a friend. We talked for three hours in a cramped, disorganised office. Most of his questions were in regard to my time at L'Ortolan. I could see his interest in and respect for Burton Race. At the end he muttered about my old salary at L'Ortolan.

'Oh, ahhh . . . let me see . . . £900 per month in your hand.'

That was not acceptable.

'Okay, you can start on £1,100 clear, how does that sound?'

'Fine, that's absolutely fine, Marco. Thanks, Marco.'

'See you next Monday.'

'Yes, Marco, next Monday.'

On the way home, I thought about Marco's hypnotic way with speech, and how I could use it on Burton Race when I told him that I was leaving to take up work with his arch-rival.

I approached Burton Race after service the next day and happily his reaction was one of encouragement. He had a sense of satisfaction; he had taken 'an Aussie fucker' who didn't even know what mange-tout meant, to a level of being one of the hardest-working chefs at L'Ortolan.

SHAVED HEADS, TATTOOS, white T-shirts and Caterpillar boots, intense heat and humidity were my first impressions of Marco Pierre White at The Restaurant, at Hyde Park Hotel, Knightsbridge. Boy, this will be tough. The chefs wore an expression of determination; at no cost would they crumble.

However, I knew from the moment I walked in that I was going to enjoy it. The boys in the kitchen had seen it all. They had been through the regime of Harvey's; they had been Marco's platform for success. Surprisingly, these guys were all very helpful and seemed interested in my story.

My future in this kitchen depended on my approach in the first few days. I had only a small amount of time to prove my worth. I was under immense pressure. The survival rate of new chefs in this kitchen was, on average, two weeks.

Utilising the skills I had learnt from L'Ortolan, I kept my mouth shut and simply repeated to myself: 'Don't panic, work hard'. Marco, with his immense presence of 183-centimetre (6-foot) plus frame and voice to match, appeared every evening like clockwork in the upstairs kitchen an hour before service, without a noise or word. The feel of the kitchen immediately changed into a sweaty pressure-cooker environment, which would continue to build until the first order arrived.

Conversation always started with Marco talking to Lee, the head chef of the sauce section. The questions asked and answered were more or less routine but I always listened carefully. As the service progressed, conversation flowed to Bunny, Lee's assistant. Opportunities would arise to be involved in the humorous stage of the friendly talk, but — showing that my mind was on the job at hand — I would occasionally ignore or brush off any questions asked, eager to show Marco I was focused. At the same time I knew the importance of being involved — wanting Marco to like me, I suppose.

Lee had worked for Marco since day one, eleven years before. His seemingly effortless technique of roasting, steaming, poêleing and sautéing, then reducing, seasoning and finishing each sauce was like an artist putting the final touches to a sculpture. The big man relied on Lee's expertise and consistency, seeing each service until the end, venturing out to the dining room at different times during the night. Names such as Andrew Lloyd Webber, Lord Archer, Sting, Sir Elton John — even the occasional member of the royal family — came to watch the show.

I did my job and I did it well. Working on the vegetable and garnish section gave me great scope to take note of the more technically demanding sections such as the fish. The work required of me at The Restaurant was in some ways easier than that at L'Ortolan. Whatever I cooked and presented had to be 100 per cent every time. Not 120 per cent one minute and 90 per cent the next. L'Ortolan was perceived as the underdog, while The Restaurant was number one. It had glamour, a lot of press and three stars. The pressure was also different, it was calmer and more co-ordinated. There were fewer menu changes and less flamboyancy in the dishes, this was the negative side of pursuing consistency.

All the potato dishes, as well as most vegetables, were assembled and then cooked to order. My favourite potato recipe is the simplest, pommes mousseline; the silky smooth texture of butter and puréed potatoes is one of life's great pleasures.

The Hyatt and L'Ortolan had provided me with a solid training for discipline, but The Restaurant at Hyde Park Hotel was to take me to another level. After four years of eating food and sitting in surroundings that were a blurry dream, I was now living in a world where the service was faster and gutsier. I would love to go back and relive it occasionally; it would be like a fantastic dream. I felt then as if I was in a first class football team going out to play an important match every day. Everyone was with Marco to the end. In a way so was I.

Marco had accumulated, over five years, some of the world's best chefs. They all had the training that involved immense sacrifice. If you also include the chefs who had followed Marco from the start, the result was a machine capable of producing food that is incomparable.

Marco's bollockings were unlike anyone else's. They would start as a rational discussion about how your mistake had been made, and then slowly turn into a full-blooded scalding. He would walk away only to return and start the scalding again until finally he would throw items around the kitchen. The experience would turn you into a complete psychological mess: would I be sacked, hurt, humiliated? At the next service, he would thank you for your humility, as he had compelled you to apologise for your weak performance. It was a most mentally draining experience.

London was treating me well. With the milder weather it was much easier to tackle the early starts and late walks home from a tough day. The vibrant atmosphere was at my front door and I was finding a balance with a small window of social life. For the first time since leaving Australia I had a regular string of girlfriends, including a mad Scottish flight attendant and a Swedish model who spoke four languages, with whom I was quickly becoming infatuated. I was working and playing hard. Life was great!

The job made me use all my senses and refine them. While I was in the kitchen they didn't belong to me — they belonged to Marco. There was no panic, but rather a simple atmosphere of confidence, encompassed by precision and technique. Every dish was cooked to order. I realised that sometimes people would wait 40 to 50 minutes for each course. The customers were fully aware of the waiting times — they weren't dining because of hunger. They were there to experience the precision and discipline of the highest quality food and service. It would all start with the amuse-bouche, then go to the entrée, main, pre-dessert (the most unbelievable crème caramel I have ever tasted, so smooth, no sign that it had entered an oven, simplicity turned into perfection) followed by the dessert. Roasted pineapple with vanilla and chilli topped with milk ice cream, Valrhona chocolate truffe, soufflé Rothschild. In all, the dessert menu comprised twelve different dishes, six petits fours and six different chocolates. Thierry Busset was nicknamed the 'Angel of the Kitchen'. He was so quiet and there was never a mark on his perfectly white, pressed Bragard Jacket and Gucci jeans.

By now, the kitchen was absorbing me and my cooking had reached a new level. I thanked my solid training for this. I was finding a senior role, still learning, but at the point where I would be able to teach others. My good mate Paddy had joined the team. He was given the heavy role of head of the fish section. It was tough for him; he was copping a lot from Marco. The pace and consistency of the service was leaving Paddy behind. We were fully booked every night; compared to L'Ortolan where we held only three busy services per week.

Around this period, Marco implemented quite a few changes, one being that everyone had to wear a chef's jacket and skullcap during service. A week or so into this new rule, I had forgotten to iron my jacket and it had more wrinkles than usual. Marco walked in and didn't say a word. His mood told me I might cop it. The section was fully set, ready for a busy lunch. As the orders trickled through, Marco turned around and told me to leave the kitchen and iron my jacket.

'Don't come back until it is presentable. If you can't do that, then don't come back at all.'

He then politely asked Robert Reid, the Head Chef, to take over my section. He was the most talented chef I have ever had the privilege to work with. His training included five years in Paris as the protégé of chefs like Joel Robuchon and Roger Vergé. I was furious. I vowed never to go back again. He was not the man I had seen on TV only a few years before.

Leaving the restaurant that beautiful Monday morning in May, I saw blue skies, smiling faces, busy London streets. I felt a part of it. I felt like I was a teenager again.

Beautiful women, tourists of all nationalities, men in pinstriped suits hurrying to their next appointments, traffic horns ricocheting off the gorgeous historic buildings. The streets were drenched in a vibrant atmosphere. The feeling was so unlike home. It had all the enthusiasm and worldly culture that Westmeadows did not.

After walking around the West End for half a day feeling free and alive, a cloud of guilt began building up. Someone else was copping all my bollockings from Marco. It made me feel compelled to return — to swallow my pride. I also realised after spending that night at my local Kensington Tavern, watching what people do after their nine-to-five day; that it wasn't for me.

The next morning I walked into the kitchen as if nothing had happened. Marco called me into his office as soon as he noticed I was back. He thanked me for showing humility; I apologised and said my jacket would always be ironed. I think we both knew that it would never be perfect but I would give it my best shot. I received a generous pay rise of £50 a week, and nothing else was said. I had heard stories of this going on in the kitchen quite regularly; so I had a feeling that I was now one of Marco's boys.

Service after service, the team became very united. What could be better than to form a soccer team at the same time? We played on Friday afternoons in Hyde Park. Almost a cross between Australian Rules and rugby, it was a brutal affair that left us exhausted, bruised and battered. We would finish at the Paxton's Head for a quick pint before promptly returning to the kitchen ready for the big man's arrival at 6 pm. It didn't matter if the restaurant was full for lunch and dinner on a Friday, we had to have that game and be back and ready in time; we always were.

I had never heard of the Oak Room before, but it was to become the most important development for my career as a future restaurateur. Marco's ambition was to move there — his final resting place, so to speak. Then one week in 1998 he told everyone he had signed a deal with Granada, a huge multinational company covering everything from media to roadhouses and cleaning services. Granada owned Hotel Le Meridian in which the historic Oak Room was situated.

Granada and Marco became partners; in return Marco became a very wealthy man. In fact he was listed as being one of the top 400 richest men in Britain. Moving all the kitchen equipment, wine cellar, staff and personal belongings to the Oak Room was a huge job. It took a whole week to set it up. The dining room looked as though it was from the eighteenth century. It was fitted with oak panelling, chandeliers, and superb green velvet chairs with matching table light shades. The tables were set with Christofle silverware, the crystal glassware was the full sommelier (wine waiter) range. The wine list was in a different hemisphere compared to other three-Michelin star restaurants in Britain. The sommelier had total freedom to buy any wine necessary. He stocked every vintage of d'Yquem from the late 1800s to the more recent vintages of 1945.

That first service in the huge kitchen launched us into unchartered territory. The bollocking yaps from Marco would drop you to your knees, piercing your heart and making you beg for forgiveness. In all honesty, we didn't miss a beat. Andrew Lloyd Webber was reported in the *Guardian* as saying the transitional move from the Hyde Park Hotel to Le Meridian was like clockwork. The food went out with that same constant flair and was as hypnotising at it ever was.

IT WAS WHILE I WAS working for Marco that I was approached by an agency to do some modelling. I had been modelling for a little while when in October 1998 I received a phone call from the editor of the magazine *Company*. Each year they published *Britain's 50 Most Eligible Bachelors* and I was asked if I wanted to be included. I took a few days to think about it. I was being compared with footballers, actors, models and doctors. I felt it was a touch silly, that I would look a bit out of place — that it wasn't my thing. In the end I thought, 'Bollocks! It will be a laugh!' I didn't want Marco or (heaven forbid) any of the boys in the kitchen to know.

On the day of *Company*'s launch of Britain's 50 Most Eligible Bachelors (held at Café de Paris in Leicester Square), the *Evening Standard* ran a huge photo article on me

modelling some clothes for the retail chain Next. During the interview I had mentioned a lot about the kitchen and my favourite dishes. I also stressed to the journalist my undying respect for Marco. They didn't print that bit, so the whole thing came out as though I was blowing my own trumpet. Marco was not impressed. I had made a mistake not asking his permission to be involved.

That evening at the launch just after I had been presented — cameras flashing, celebrities everywhere and champagne glasses clinking — I noticed Marco's greengrocer, Richard, staring at me. In his true London Cockney accent, he told me to get back to the restaurant, that Marco wanted to see me. He said if I didn't go back Marco wouldn't get any vegetables from him ever again. Marco knew I was fond of all my suppliers, so with this in mind I hurried back. Marco was furious, accusing me of not asking permission for the night off. He huffed and told me he would deal with it tomorrow.

Marco didn't deal with it the next day — he just ignored me. It was like being back on my first day at L'Ortolan, standing on the edge of the Grand Canyon, waiting to be pushed.

A week later my new commis chef made an error in the preparation of the cabbage purée. The cabbage is cooked in cream, puréed and seasoned. Butter is added, then it is quenelled with a small spoon onto a plate and served with an intricate stuffed lamb cutlet. The commis had used way too much cream. As Murphy's Law would have it, Marco walked past and sacked me on the spot for not doing my job properly. This time it was a Friday, so I managed to get the whole weekend off. I gave Marco a call on Monday and told him, 'This is my life, I want to come back'.

Once again it was great to be back. I wouldn't be without all those hard-arsed bastards who had become my mates (such as Thierry, Lee, Bunny, Charlie and Robert)

Wild rabbitt stew à la bourguignonne

Crêpes suzettes

Lightly steamed salmon infused with pancetta

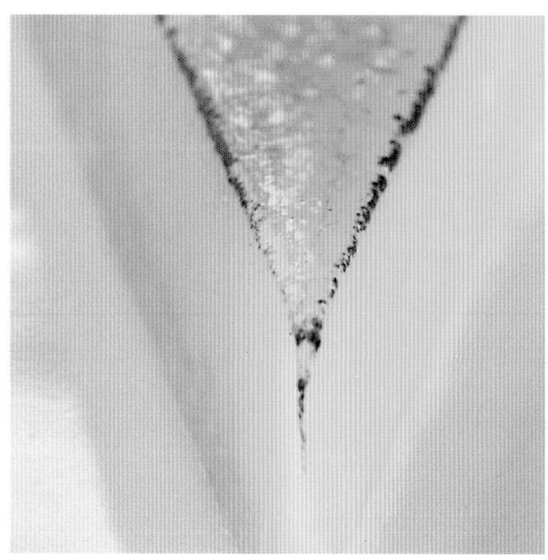

Lemon tart

Sable biscuit

for the world. My relationship with Marco was very strong. I trusted him and he trusted me, but I started to feel restless. So a month or so later I took up an offer of a 12-month contract with a reputable modelling and casting agency. I believed I could balance both careers but I didn't enjoy the modelling palaver. The money and the travelling were good, but I belonged in the kitchen. It did nothing but distract me for a short period.

Times had changed at Hotel Le Meridian. It had been great for two years, but the Oak Room just wasn't the same. The food wasn't any different; the same guys were working front and back of house, but there was no Marco. There was no adrenaline, no rush, no fighting to survive. Marco had seemingly resigned from the kitchen to pursue other business interests in and around London. Robert had taken over, but it didn't suit him — he needed his own front door.

The two goals I achieved working with Marco were in fact the simplest of goals: to survive and to leave better than when I started.

THE NEXT STOP ON the journey was six months working for Albert Roux. Taking a step back, I worked as a commis chef in his pastry kitchen, which provided pâtisserie for many large European hotels and restaurants. The work was very mundane, but important for my development in becoming a complete chef. Everyday work involved the large deep creamy lemon tarts so much loved by the French palate and almond frangipane tarts, baked golden, cooled, then filled with crème diplomat, a vanilla custard lightened with whipped cream, spread over the tart and topped with fresh berries.

Lemon tart

[serves 16]

THIS RECIPE WILL become an all-time favourite in your household. It is by no means foolproof and will take some practice. The biggest problem I had when learning this was rushing the construction of the pastry case, leaving cracks and holes for the lemon mix to escape through. If you find any such cracks patch them up with some raw dough and place back in the oven for a few minutes to harden the patches.

250 g (8 oz) unsalted butter
160 g ($5\frac{1}{4}$ oz) icing (confectioners') sugar
1 egg
$2\frac{1}{2}$ tablespoons milk
180 g (6 oz) plain (all-purpose) flour

FILLING

500 g (1 lb) sugar
4 cups freshly squeezed lemon juice
5 eggs
7 egg yolks
2 cups lightly whipped cream

Cream the butter and sugar until light and fluffy. This should take about 5 minutes on high speed • I sometimes like to add a dash of rum or vanilla extract at this stage, especially if I have decided to serve the tart as a single item dessert • Add the egg and milk. Place mixer on low and slowly add the flour, beating until the mixture just comes together • Wrap the dough in plastic wrap and refrigerate for at least 1 hour. The dough can be refrigerated for over a week or frozen for much longer • Preheat the oven to 180°C (350°F) • Roll out the pastry on a lightly floured work surface until 6 mm ($\frac{1}{4}$ in) thick • Place the dough in the tart tin, gently easing into the corners, letting the pastry overhang the edge of the tin. Trim the excess pastry. Tightly wrap the remaining dough in plastic wrap and store in the freezer for up to 1 month • Place the tart tin in the freezer for 10–15 minutes to firm up. Line the pastry with baking paper and fill with baking pulses • Place in the oven for 15 minutes. Remove the baking paper and bake for a further 10 minutes, or until golden. Remove and allow to cool. Patch any holes in the baked shell with some raw dough, then return to the oven for a few minutes • To make the filling, slowly blend the sugar with the lemon juice • At the same speed add the eggs and egg yolks, beating until well incorporated. Gently fold in the lightly whipped cream. Cover and refrigerate the lemon custard for at least 6 hours • Preheat the oven to 120°C (250°F) • Remove the pastry case from the tin and place on a baking tray. Using a cup, pour the lemon custard into the pastry case until it is full. Carefully slide the tart into the oven • Bake for 2 hours, or until the lemon custard is set, but slightly wobbly. Serve at room temperature with whipped cream and raspberry coulis.

THE MOST IMPORTANT benefit I picked up during this period was learning and appreciating the art of chocolate; the love that is involved in producing that crisp shiny finish encasing a rich but not heavy ganache. Transforming a thick, boring, brown, over-sweet mass into shiny, crisp delicate art forms was a great ego trip, something you couldn't share with the boys down at the pub; nonetheless it made me happy, and still does to this day. I did not have a lot to do with Albert Roux. He and his brother were masters at transforming English cuisine from dull, boring and terribly clichéd and training some of England's finest chefs and restaurateurs. His wife Madame Roux and their son Michel Roux were lovely people who were passionate about food and were both a support on some tough days. I used the arduous time to network as much as possible with the predominantly French kitchen team, managing to gather some great connections for my plans to move to France, the holy grail of cuisine. During this stage I started to understand the simplicity required to produce outstanding food. Two components are necessary: technique and ingredients of the highest quality. Many great examples of this long-lived theory exist, but Thierry's pâte sable biscuit comes to mind as a favourite. In French, pâte sable simply means 'sand dough' — the texture should crumble like sand in your mouth. To achieve this you need butter of the highest quality and then a good hard flour that has been carefully milled. Then technique takes over as you carefully combine the butter and flour to a dough without activating the gluten, which would make the dough elastic and chewy with disastrous results.

Sable biscuit

[makes 50]

450 g (14 oz) plain (all-purpose) flour
50 g ($1^{3}/_{4}$ oz) cornflour (cornstarch)
400 g (13 oz) butter, chopped into dice, at room temperature
200 g ($6\ ^{1}/_{2}$ oz) icing (confectioners') sugar
4 egg yolks
Pinch of salt

Preheat the oven to 160°C (325°F) • Sift the flour and cornflour into a mixing bowl • Make a well in the centre of the flour mixture and add the butter and sugar, work together with your fingertips until no hard lumps remain • Add the egg yolks and salt, drawing in the flour. Work until the dough resembles coarse breadcrumbs. Do not overwork. Roll the pastry into a log and refrigerate for several hours • Cut the dough into 6 mm ($^{1}/_{4}$ in) slices and briefly knead each slice. Roll each slice out to a thickness of 3 mm ($^{1}/_{8}$ in); they will be extremely delicate. Place on a greaseproof paper-lined baking tray, allowing space for spreading. Bake for 10 minutes, or until just golden on the edges.

Travelling through France, particularly Monaco, and working in some of the most renowned kitchens in France wasn't as interesting as it should have been. It was sometimes intimidating and at other times boring and pretentious. I kept dreaming of the day when I would have my own kitchen. I had even devised a name: Vue de monde. Looking out of the train window approaching the French Pyrénées with a friend, I quietly said, 'View of the world; what a great name, and a good way to describe my cooking.' I immediately wrote it down. My Swedish girlfriend Linda later told me it was spelt incorrectly, but I wanted to keep it as I first remembered and saw it.

I made a decision to take a holiday in Australia, to show Linda what the place was all about and to recharge my focus. What a mistake. Linda, whom I was quite fond of, fell in love with Melbourne and wanted to stay permanently. I also found another challenge: no one was interested in what I had been doing overseas, and I hated that. Now, I felt, I had something greater to prove. Chefs in Melbourne felt the training abroad had little relevance to their cause. This worried me greatly, as with no head chef experience I would have to work for one of these people, who to me were ignorant losers.

I quickly headed back to Europe, handed in my resignation at Hôtel de Paris, said a few goodbyes and returned to Melbourne. Before I knew it I was once again knocking on restaurant doors looking for work. It was a different feeling this time: nobody knew me; nobody wanted to know me. Testing the water around Melbourne restaurants to see whether anyone would take me on in a senior role in the kitchen was a daunting task. Most chefs either felt threatened or didn't have a clue about the places where I had worked. This really put me down in the dumps, and other options started to come into my head. One of them was buying my own place where I could express what I do best without the issue of dodgy owners with no real respect for the industry or me.

Five years after it all began, I was back where I had started. It felt easier and less frightening to conquer Melbourne dining than to attempt the feat of feeding the experienced, cultured palates of Europe, but a part of me had been left behind in Europe. However, I vowed that once I had completed this challenge I would go back to take on the kitchen mates I had made in those top Michelin kitchens.

Another problem had arisen: Linda was not enjoying Melbourne, realising that it was not 30°C (85°F) all year round and that there weren't the same job opportunities for her in Australia. To keep the peace and soften a little bit of the homesickness, we bought a Siberian husky rightly named Buck.

Ignoring all problems, I began to search for a site I could afford, one that I could sustain with my philosophy of food. You won't believe the feeling of frustration I have had, but guess what? At last I've found it.

The day finally came when I found what I believed was the restaurant of my dreams. It was a place in Carlton running as a simple café/pasta restaurant called Sicilian Vespers. The owners had had it for only 14 months and had spent over $300,000 on the project. Not feeling sorry for them, I offered them $70,000 plus extra for stock. They rejected the offer through their broker, so I kept looking over the next five to six days but to no avail. Finally the agent came back with an answer that the owners would sell for $75,000. I accepted knowing that it was a fair deal. It was a quick 14-day takeover. The next thing I knew I was negotiating a lease and a contract of sale, and watching every cent.

Getting the money together was the next step. How much would I need?

It is so funny when you approach people to invest in you and what you do best. I believe schools should have a subject dedicated to how to sell yourself. This was my biggest problem. Every person I knew and approached saw how personal it was to me and walked away, knowing there wasn't an investment there — just a twenty-four-year-old trying desperately to gain some recognition.

My final attempt at persuading someone to invest in my restaurant was such a surprise. I didn't even know George all that well, but he had been a family friend long before I was even thought of. He was German and he ran his own business called Steger Engineering. On the day I went to see him and tell him the dream I wanted to make reality, he simply wrote me out a personal cheque for $70,000 and said he wanted it back within three years. That was it. No contract, no signatures, just eye contact, a smile and a firm handshake.

I estimated I needed around $150,000 to start up my dream.

Did I know what I was doing? I was signing guarantees against my only asset (the house I had bought with my modelling money a few years before), employing staff, setting up bank accounts with no money, running up debt, and already spending long hours thinking and devising, but in the end I had to just go for it. I thought, who cares if I go broke? It doesn't mean I failed; it just means I have to start again.

By this time Linda had left and gone back to the high fashion world in the UK.

SUNDAY, 9 MAY 2000 was a quiet night; the handover was scheduled for the following morning at 8 am. I was down to my last $9000. The menu had been written: eight entrées, nine mains, six desserts and four cheeses, and a very ordinary wine list. I had packed into three cardboard boxes all my restaurant belongings, including cookbooks, knives and moulds. All this was going to get me through the next few months; I was saving every dollar I could until I got on my feet.

The next morning, in front of a team of besuited lawyers and accountants, I signed all the documents and contracts in my chef's uniform. Something came across at the meeting that I will never forget, something my very expensive lawyer had overlooked: the three-month bond required to secure the lease. It added up to over $10,000. Without a blink I signed a cheque for that amount, thinking I would deal with it later. Convincing the bank the next day was a tough one, but I managed to get the cheque cleared — bank charges included, of course.

The place was a mess, and I had 24 hours to clean it up, prepare the menu and start trading. I had employed two apprentices and two casual waiters, and had talked my brother into washing the pots while he was at flying school. I don't know how I did it, but that first day I cleaned, prepped and hosted and turned my misspelled dream name, Vue de monde, into reality.

The two boys and I worked through the night. It was close to 10 pm and we were starting to feel a little tired. Sitting on the bench with a beer and a slice of pizza I devised my first dish; my own combination of flavours, technique and presentation. The dish was twice-cooked pig's ears with crispy prawns, truffles and seasonal salad leaves. With the dish in hand and my mind back on it I worked for another five hours that night while the two apprentices, Jason and Adrian, slept upstairs. I eventually slept in the back seat of my car parked out the front of the restaurant, and awoke to find I had been given a parking ticket. It was only 7:30 am — my running battle with parking inspectors had just begun.

We ended up pushing through 20 covers on my first lunch. It was a great feeling. I met some fantastic people that day who still dine with me on a regular basis — including Dr Gleeson, the first ever patron of Vue de monde.

I slowly transformed the basic tiny cramped space of a kitchen into a productive working environment designed to fit a team of up to ten chefs and kitchen hands. With any extra cash I made, I would go out on a Monday and buy second-hand kitchen equipment which I got my mechanically-minded brother to fit into the restaurant. We

both spent a whole weekend reconditioning a flat-top stove, then removing the front door and its frame to fit it through the space. By the end of the year I had a kitchen fit for any top establishment in Europe.

Over the next month the restaurant got busier and tougher. I struggled to understand the front-of-house mentality. They didn't seem to work as hard or the same hours as the back-of-house staff. My naivety and lack of knowledge in this area let me down greatly. I can even recall one night when, after sacking the only full-time waiter I had because he ordered some food incorrectly and then hid the fact from both the kitchen and customer, I ended up changing into a suit and waiting on tables myself. Desperate times call for desperate measures, as the saying goes. That moment was a great learning experience. I had fun that night; I love wine and food matching, and felt a great interaction with the customers.

Word spread among the industry pretty quickly that I was achieving something very different from where the rest of the Melbourne food scene was heading. Food critics started to roll in, with pretty good results, most ignoring the generic décor and the lack of direction from the front-of-house team and concentrating on the idea. In a way they put their own reputations on the line by giving the restaurant a positive report. People were giving me a chance you might say.

Three months into my career as restaurateur/chef, new dishes were developing and I was maturing and earning respect. *The Age Good Food Guide* was due for release and I was hoping anxiously that I would win a chef's hat, the local equivalent of the Michelin star.

The following week Vue de monde won its first chef's hat. It was a good feeling.

LET ME DIGRESS for a moment and give you some of my thoughts on wine and food matching, which I believe is an important element to Vue de monde's success. If there is one rule that I have learned about wine and food matching it is that there are no rules. It's all about intuition. Experiment, enjoy the journey and discover taste sensations you never knew existed.

Escoffier followed the guidelines set out by the celebrated nineteenth-century chef Viard, author and collector of recipes entitled *Le Cuisiner Imperial*, published in 1806. Used as a reference book by chefs throughout the nineteenth century, I have expanded on his philosophy and am using it in the twenty-first century:

- Madeira or sherry, or a similar wine, with soup, melon or hors d'oeuvre.
- White wine, dry demi-sec or sweet (Chablis, Meursault, Pouilly, Graves, Sauternes, Rhine, Moselle) with oysters or fish.
- To quench thirst: ordinary table wine during the entire meal.
- For entrées: high-quality Bordeaux.
- To accompany the roast: first-vintage Burgundy.
- To accompany sweet desserts: Champagne or sometimes port or wine from haut-Sauternes.

With cheese and wine matching, I usually go with the harder the cheese, the richer the wine. Soft cheese tends to sit well with sweet wine. Good-quality chocolate does not need to be matched with black sherry or Australian muscat (possibly poor quality chocolate that cloys to the roof of your mouth may need it!). Go for it and have fun. What you like somebody else will, too.

ONE YEAR INTO Vue de monde's short life and I had experienced so much. Life support was still needed financially for the restaurant, due to the lack of cash flow and my ignorance of business rules. When struck with a creative flash, I would go out and buy $10,000 worth of Villeroy & Boch crockery for the new dishes that were being conjured up or Perigord truffles at $3000 a kilogram (2 pounds), then surprise loyal customers and friends with a generous risotto or soup strategically placed between courses. I knew that in a way this was a marketing ploy, but it was very costly and inefficient and it would be my demise unless Vue de monde was consistently busy or I found another source of income to supplement these moments of joy.

Then I was approached by a management company to represent me for any media opportunities and endorsement deals that might come my way, this proved to be a godsend a little further down the track. I had started to pay George back his loan, another great feeling. One downside was that I was still living off the restaurant and not able to afford to pay myself. I found this frustrating, especially when employees took advantage of me by not caring or by stealing wine or cash. No one, not even my family, could understand the emotional feeling of not knowing whether failure or success was around the corner. I moved into the house I had bought while overseas instead of renting it out for extra income. This was a release and a sort of safe haven from the pressures and constant thinking involved with trying to build Vue de monde into a top-flight restaurant. Like Roger Lienhard, I spent 40 hours a week in this humble abode, but this chill-out time recharged the batteries for another big week.

Building my team was the most important goal then and still is now. It comes before any pay rise to myself. Without these individuals, investing mind, body and soul in the pursuit of excellence, Vue de monde is nothing. The most important piece of advice I can give when employing staff is to always check references and never panic or employ someone hastily. To recognise a valuable employee is a lengthy process and, no matter what, all your staff will let you down at some stage. It is the reaction of the employee after the event that shows their true character. Everyone enjoys their work when everything is going their way, what the inferior employee doesn't realise is it takes hard work, a lot of bad days and some not so enjoyable moments to get there.

Taking the next step was even harder. Just as I had started to make money, I started to spend it or, as I like to put it, invest it back into my original investment. We closed for two weeks for renovations, and $100,000 later there was not a lot to show for it — a coat of paint, new blinds and bar stools, some banquette seating and new lights.

The investment turned out to be a good one, however. It brought the critics back, and new reviews and our second chef's hat, along with numerous other awards. These included best French restaurant, best dessert, and dish of the year for my pig's trotter stuffed with langoustines.

THIS RECOGNITION, HOWEVER, attracted a new type of customer. The lack of knowledge or appreciation demonstrated by my newfound clientele soon became frustrating and demoralising. For a while I was an angry, negative person, asking a lot of people to leave. Some found my behaviour amusing. Others found it offensive and the rest embarrassing. Unfortunately, I found it addictive.

One rule was obeyed by all of them: my way or no way. People were walking in wanting to change my sauces, wanting the meat roasted instead of steamed, asking for side salads. 'Do you do snails, straight up?' 'Where are the frogs' legs?'

The war with culinary and cultural mentality is not over. Every seat of the forty-five at Vue de monde is intended for someone who would like to journey through an eating experience that cannot be produced at home. I'm certainly not here for convenience or to be perceived as a quick fix for a bite to eat or a subservient chophouse for the middle rich.

I desperately searched for a solution to the issue of the anger within me. I eventually realised that if I didn't find a new direction for my frustration I would lose it and permanently affect my reputation and business. Burnout was inevitable. I turned to my agent/manager and created a way of letting the public know who I was and where I was coming from. We did this by increasing my profile through cooking demonstrations, advertisements for cooking equipment, and promotions in restaurants overseas and interstate. Not only was the extra money good, but so was the reflective thinking time it gave me. It made me realise that I was either a maverick chef with a limited shelf life or a businessman. Sitting on a British Airways flight on my way to promote myself at a five-day stint at the Singapore Hilton, I realised I wanted to be both. With careful planning it could be done.

The trip to Singapore was very self-motivating. I returned to Melbourne with new vigour and vitality and a real plan to attack the magical world of success. One by one I called in all my key employees — everyone from my full-time kitchen hand to my accountant — and told them the direction I wanted to go in, and that I needed them to travel with me.

It was a new beginning. I devised plans to stay true to the philosophy of my cuisine — that is, classical recipes modernly presented, but keeping in mind our attitude towards healthy food.

THROUGH ALL THE distractions, the laughter and occasional tears, my thoughts continued to relate to food and little else. I had responsibility for the welfare and development of the young team working for me. I didn't know how my staff perceived me. Did they respect me? Did they like me as a person? Do they want to be like me?

Screaming, swearing, staring, sweating, the smell of roast seafood, grilled foie gras, freshly shaved truffles, simmering chicken stock. *Ça marche*. Twenty covers walking through the door in ten minutes. Burning your hands. Cutting your fingers, patching them up. What else is there to care about? Pondering these questions, I knew the answers lay within me. My life was a lonely one outside the realm of the restaurant. No real school friends to keep in touch with, no girlfriend or casual relationship. I suspect a large part of me was starving, wasting away at the expense of striving to excel at the only thing I'm good at: cooking.

NOW ALL THOSE worries — money problems, the sacking of useless staff, good staff members walking out on me, high food costs — have all but disappeared. I don't think I would have made it without positive thinking and the constant reminder to myself of zero tolerance for self-pity or complacency.

By late 2002 the team around me was starting to blossom. I owe much of the support and success of the restaurant to the ongoing relationship I built up with my suppliers — everyone from Joe, my truffle importer and supplier, to George, Nick, Con and James, my fishmongers.

In particular, my coffee suppliers, John and Nina Frisco, are very enjoyable to work with and learn from. They are the importers of Illy coffee. Illy is known in America and Europe as a premium brand coffee, consisting of carefully selected and roasted 100 per cent Arabica beans, but not in Australia. The Friscos took the brave step in the early 1990s to start importing Illy and charging double any other coffee company. They made the brand exclusive, turning away more requests than they accepted. I liked their policy: 'You make and serve Illy coffee our way or no way.' It reflected my policy at Vue de monde.

The Grain, the Flour and the Bread

I WANT TO START with a few basic rules; I use only the best flours and grains in my bread recipes. I don't believe in top restaurants getting outside help to make their bread, unless it has a story behind it, as is the case with many small village restaurants in south-west France where a brother may own the local bakery while the father owns the bistro next door. Chefs these days seem to like to deploy their energy elsewhere rather than organise space and time into bread that reflects their style and place. I see bread in a restaurant much like grapes in a vineyard, both reflect their environment by releasing a certain characteristic common to the area.

Organic to me is about protecting the tradition of humane, healthy non-chemical farming practices and producing seasonal produce that celebrates the fact that we are what we eat. It is a positive step towards our future well-being.

Three commonly available flours that will cover all your baking needs are spelt, wholemeal spelt and kamut. All are organic and are favourable with people who are wheat intolerant because they are lower in gluten; however, they are not suitable for people who have an extreme gluten allergy. High in protein, vitamin B and magnesium, kamut flour, especially, is great for homemade pasta.

Humans have harvested these particular varieties for thousands of years; yet since the outbreak of World War II we have gone into shock mode, forcing the production of genetically modified (GM) goods. America and Canada seem to be leading the way in genetically modified products with Europe and Australia resisting such practices in farming and cropping.

The world is seeing massive problems with genetic contamination from neighbouring farms with genetically modified corn, soybeans and canola. Most of the soybean supply in the US is already contaminated with genetically modified seeds. Many organic and conventional corn farmers are losing markets because their crops are testing positive for GM traits. Many experts have said that it is next to impossible to find non-GM canola in Canada because of this genetic trespass. Wheat pollen is even more pervasive than that of canola.

I love cultured butter. You may ask what is cultured butter? Very simply, it is a natural product relying on bacteria to act as a preservative. The process starts with culture being added to cream in a maturation tank. Everyday butter has a synthetic preservative added to act in the same way as a natural culture. I find the taste of this style of butter unappealing, I also find the preservative brings out the inconsistencies caused by producing butter from poor-quality milk. Cultured butter has a pale colour compared to the nearly carotene colour of the average supermarket butter.

My favourite butter is the famous Echire, with Lescure and d'Isigny Sainte-mère good substitutes. I prefer the salted variety with fresh hot bread. These butters are available worldwide from good delicatessens and purveyors of fine foods.

I don't find there is much difference between dried and fresh yeast with the resulting final product. I do find fresh yeast is easier to work with. There is no need

to dissolve fresh yeast in warm water, just add to the dry ingredients in the mixing stage of the recipe. Dried yeast is convenient if you do not bake a lot; fresh yeast only has a limited shelf life of around two weeks. When converting recipes from fresh yeast to dry: 10 grams (1/3 ounce) of dried is the equivalent to 50 grams (1 3/4 ounces) of fresh.

What is proving or rising and why do we need it? is one question pondered by many. Proving or rising is the result of a fermentation process known as leavening. A successful result depends on many factors: one, no draughts; two, warm atmosphere (25–30°C [77–85°F] — try the top shelf in the cupboard above the oven or the bench closest to the oven); and three, time (which the yeast needs to feed on the sugar — 15 grams [1/2 ounce] of fresh yeast, 30 grams [1 ounce] of sugar and 500 grams [1 pound] of plain [all-purpose] flour takes at least 2 hours to double in size). Why do we go to all this trouble? Ever tried brioche without yeast, ever overproved white bread, baked, then consumed it at the dinner table? No? Hopefully, this chapter will ensure you never have such an experience.

The golden crusty look you see on breads and pastries in your favourite magazines and books is easily achieved. Simply combine 1 egg yolk and 2 1/2 tablespoons of milk, then gently brush over the dough before baking.

Soda bread

[makes 2 loaves]

I WAS AN EIGHT-YEAR-OLD the first time my Grandma fed me a slice of freshly baked soda bread from Jerry the local baker on the Hoath Road, North Dublin. I had just been on my first ever periwinkle hunt with my grandfather, Tom Fitzpatrick. He used to call me the 'Feckon Poet' because of my long hair and obscure outlook on life. The bread tasted tart, nearly acidic. I hated it! Five years later Grandma Fitzpatrick finally converted me. The soft texture with the dusty taste has so much character it reminds me of my grandparents. If there had been more times spent enjoying eating warm bread spread with garlic mayonnaise and boiled periwinkles, I suppose I could have ended up being a 'Feckon Poet'!

In the past it was common in parts of rural Ireland to make bread using baking soda rather than yeast — hence Irish soda bread. Yeast won't make dough rise unless the baker uses 'strong' flour, which was scarce in parts of Ireland. Baking soda, however, could be counted on to leaven bread. The baking soda has to be combined with something acidic in order to do its magic. In this case, I have used buttermilk.

So, not only is this a historic and tasty recipe; it's pretty foolproof, too. I put a cross on the top of the bread, which traditionally was to warn off the devil.

800 g (1lb 10 oz) organic spelt flour, sifted

½ cup sugar

2 teaspoons baking soda

1 teaspoon salt

100 g (3½ oz) butter, chilled and chopped into fine dice

300 ml (10 fl oz) buttermilk or plain yoghurt

Preheat the oven to 180°C (350°F). • Combine the dry ingredients in a large mixing bowl • Add the butter and mix using a dough hook until the mixture resembles coarse breadcrumbs • Add the buttermilk or yoghurt and mix for 2–3 minutes or until the dough is smooth and elastic. Turn the dough onto a floured work surface, knead for 1 minute, then shape into two round balls. Press the balls slightly flat • Dust the top of each ball with some flour • Cut an 'X' in the top and bake on a greased baking sheet for 45–50 minutes • Allow to cool for 20 minutes before serving.

Brown dinner rollls

[makes 20 rolls]

THE SIMPLICTY OF this recipe is a reflection of Vue de monde's resolve to bake fresh bread twice daily in the restaurant.

100 g (3½ oz) organic spelt flour, sifted
300 g (10 oz) organic wholemeal spelt flour, sifted
*15 g (½ oz) gluten**
2 tablespoons salt
45 g (1½ oz) butter, softened
45 g (1½ oz) fresh yeast
1 cup tepid water

Combine the dry ingredients in a large mixing bowl. Add the butter, yeast and water. Using a mixer with the dough hook attached, start mixing on low gradually increasing the speed to high • Mix for at least 10 minutes, the more the gluten works, the better the texture will be after baking. The dough should be firm, smooth and in one large ball • Place the ball of dough on a lightly oiled tray, cover loosely with plastic wrap, and stand in a warm spot in the kitchen for 1 hour or until doubled in size • Knead and knock out the air from the dough • Divide the dough into golf ball-sized rounds using the palms of your hands. Alternatively roll out long strips of the dough and cut 5 cm (2 in) logs to create an elongated shape • Transfer to a greased baking tray. Sprinkle over enough sifted flour to cover the top of each roll. Cover with plastic wrap • Preheat the oven to 200°C (400°F) • Return to the warm place. Prove until doubled in size, around 30 minutes • Place the baking trays in the oven. Throw a cup of water into the bottom of the oven to create some steam. Shut the door immediately. Bake for 10–15 minutes or until crisp and golden • Allow the rolls to cool in a basket or on a cake rack to prevent condensation. They can be successfully frozen.

Sourdough

[makes 2 loaves]

To create the perfect sourdough you first need to know what it is. Normally bread is leavened by yeast. Sourdough requires a starter, which gives the bread a sour taste. All fruits and vegetables contain some natural yeast. I prefer to use bananas, grapes or potatoes to extract the natural yeast.

To create a starter, combine 500 g (1 lb) of plain (all-purpose) flour, 250 g (8 oz) of overripe red grapes puréed in a blender, 300 ml (10 fl oz) of warm water and 7 g (1/4 oz) of dried yeast in a mixing bowl. Cover in an airtight container. Leave on the kitchen bench for 5 days. On the fifth day feed the starter by stirring in 1 cup of water and 1 cup of flour. Transfer to the fridge for at least 6 days. Every few days add 1 cup of water and 1 cup of flour. Three weeks from starting your mix it is ready to use. I use the rule one-third of the recipe weight should be made of the starter. Always replace what you take from the starter with the same amount of flour.

400 g (13 oz) rye flour, sifted
200 g (6 1/2 oz) organic spelt flour, sifted
20 g (3/4 oz) salt
20 g (3/4 oz) cocoa powder
300 g (10 oz) sourdough starter
40 g (1 1/3 oz) butter
400 ml (13 fl oz) tepid water
2 tablespoons polenta

Combine the dry ingredients with the starter, butter and water in a large mixing bowl. Using a mixer with the dough hook attached, start mixing on low gradually increasing the speed to high • Mix for at least 10 minutes, the more the gluten works the better the texture will be after baking • Place the ball of dough on a lightly oiled tray, cover loosely with plastic wrap, and stand in a warm spot in the kitchen for 2 hours or until the dough has doubled in size • Knead and knock out the air in the dough. Shape the dough into one large round loaf • Place the dough on a greased baking tray. Cut a deep cross in the top of the loaf • Dust over some polenta with a sieve • Cover the tray with plastic wrap • Preheat the oven to 200°C (400°F) • Return to the warm place, allow to prove until doubled in size, around 50 minutes • Place the loaf in the oven • Throw a cup of water into the bottom of the oven to create some steam. Shut the door immediately. Bake for 30–35 minutes or until crisp and golden. Tap the loaf with your fingertips, it should sound hollow • Allow to cool in a basket or cake rack to prevent condensation. The loaf can be successfully frozen.

White dinner rolls

[makes 20 rolls]

400 g (13 oz) organic spelt flour, sifted
*15 g (½ oz) gluten**
20 g (¾ oz) salt
2 tablespoons olive oil
25 g (1 oz) fresh yeast
220 ml (7¾ fl oz) tepid water
2 tablespoons poppy seeds

Combine the dry ingredients with the olive oil, yeast and tepid water in a large mixing bowl. Using a mixer with the dough hook attached, start mixing on low speed, gradually increasing to high • Mix for at least 10 minutes, the more the gluten works the better the texture will be after baking • Place the ball of dough on a lightly oiled tray, cover loosely with plastic wrap, and stand in a warm spot in the kitchen for 1 hour or until doubled in size • Knead and knock out the air in the dough • Divide the dough into golf ball-sized rounds using the palms of your hands. Place on a greased baking tray • With a sharp knife or a pair of scissors make a decorative cut on top of each roll • Gently brush each roll with a wet pastry brush; sprinkle over the poppy seeds. Cover with plastic wrap • Preheat the oven to 200°C (400°F) • Return to the warm place. Prove until doubled in size, around 30 minutes • Place the trays in the oven. Throw a cup of water into the bottom of the oven to create some steam. Shut the door immediately. Bake for 10–15 minutes or until crisp and golden • Cool the rolls on a cake rack to prevent condensation. They can be successfully frozen.

Melba toast

Melba toast was inspired by Madame Marie Ritz, who frequently commented to her husband that her toast was too thick and as a result she was too full to finish her meal. Monsieur Ritz asked Escoffier to produce a lighter and thinner toast to be served to ladies during their hors d'oeuvres and savouries course. After the bread had been toasted it would be sliced in half and re-toasted until beautifully golden and crisp. The result was well received, but Madame Ritz was too shy to accept the honour of a dish in her name. A few years later in 1905 at the Carlton Hotel in Melbourne Nellie Melba had arrived from New York and was said to be on a diet, she was served the toast and subsequently it was crowned Melba toast.

Puff pastry

The results and praise you will receive from making your own puff pastry will spur you on to attempting recipes in this book you thought were for an impromptu performance by Paul Bocuse on his day off. The process of puff pastry rising is all in the lamination: the butter and flour mixture which is folded inside the basic dough to form layers upon which, after eight subsequent folds, a thousand layers are created.

Puff pastry has been around for hundreds of years, but was reinvented by the famous pastry chef Claude Lorrain in the seventeenth century. These days a good restaurant can easily be judged by its commitment to producing its own puff pastry.

1.5 kg (3 lb) butter, softened

2.2 kg (4 lb 6½ oz) plain (all-purpose) flour, sifted

50 g (1¾ oz) salt

2½ tablespoons lemon juice

250 g (8 oz) butter, melted

1.2 litres (2 pt) tepid water

To make the lamination, beat the butter with 200 g (6½ oz) of the flour until combined • Line a shallow baking tray 20 x 30 cm (8 x 12 in) with greaseproof paper, spread out the butter and flour mixture to a thickness of 2.5 cm (1 in). Cover with a layer of plastic wrap and place in the refrigerator until it starts to harden, around 90 minutes • Combine the remaining ingredients in a large mixing bowl. Using a mixer with the dough hook attached, mix to form a firm dough • On a floured work surface, roll out the dough into a long rectangle three times the length of the lamination • Allow the lamination to come to a workable temperature. This will take 10 minutes. Place it in the middle of the dough • Fold the excess dough on either side over the lamination into the middle, then fold in half so that four layers have been formed • Roll out the dough to the original length • Brush the pastry with a soft brush to remove any excess flour • Fold the dough again into four layers. Place on a plastic wrap-lined baking tray and cover with a tea towel • Rest for 30 minutes in a cool place. I do not recommend the fridge • Repeat the rolling out and resting process once more • Cover and refrigerate on the plastic wrap-lined tray for 20–30 minutes to rest and firm up • Roll out the dough and repeat the folding and resting process three times in total. Refrigerate for 30 minutes to 1 hour to rest and firm up between each fold • Repeat the rolling out process once more. It is ready to use! • Portion the block of dough into eight evenly sized pieces. Wrap individually with plastic wrap and store in the freezer • Roll out on a lightly floured surface to the required thickness when needed.

Soda bread

Brown dinner rolls

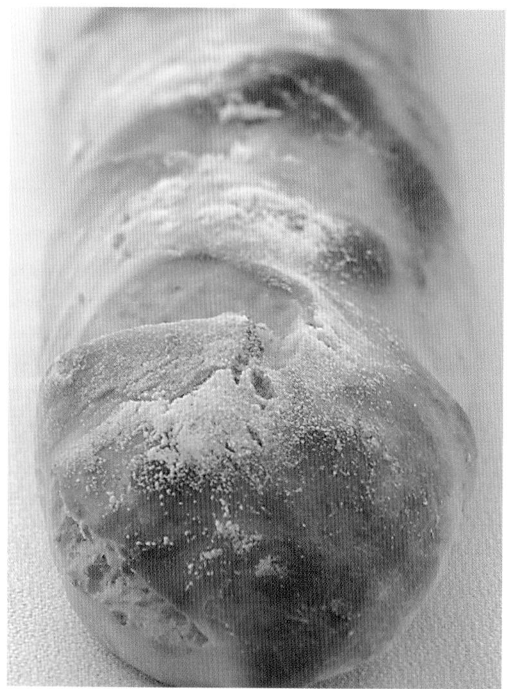
Sourdough

White dinner rolls

Melba toast

Puff pastry

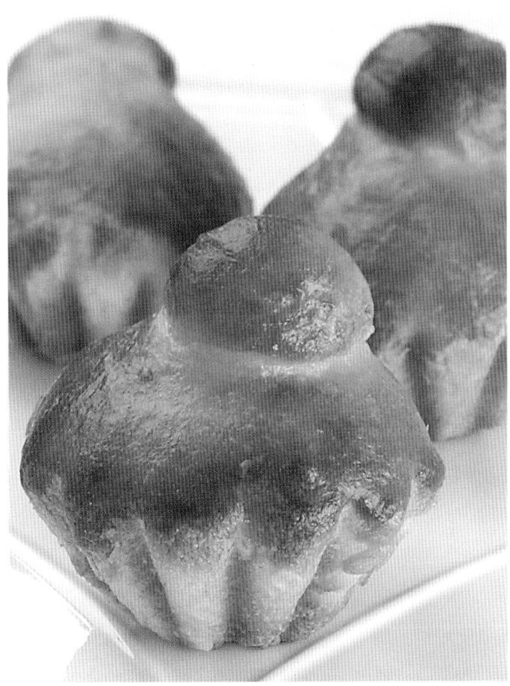

Brioche

Miniature zopf dinner rolls

Brioche

[makes 3 loaves]

MANY FIRST-TIME diners at Vue de monde are embarrassed when they do not recognise the word brioche. In fact brioche is served in many different forms around the world, from America, home of the hamburger bun, to France, where this sweet soft bread is served traditionally with foie gras, terrine and pâté. Store the loaves in the freezer and serve lightly toasted with parfait of chicken livers.

*1 kg (2 lb) bakers' flour**
*20 g (3/4 oz) gluten**
20 g (3/4 oz) salt
50 g (1 3/4 oz) fresh yeast
1/2 cup sugar
3 1/2 tablespoons milk
12 eggs
700 g (1 lb 6 oz) softened butter, chopped into rough dice
*2 1/2 tablespoons egg wash**

Combine the flour, gluten, salt, yeast, sugar and milk in a large mixing bowl. Using a mixer with the dough hook attached, mix to form a firm dough • Add the eggs one at a time, beating well between each addition • Slowly add the butter in four stages to ensure the mixture does not split • Transfer to a lightly oiled container twice the size of the mixture. Cover with plastic wrap and rest in the fridge for 24 hours. The dough will double in size • Place the dough on a floured work surface and knead for 1 minute. Remember the dough is made with a lot of butter, work quickly or it will start to melt • Divide the dough into three equal amounts of 600 g (1 1/4 lb) • Shape the portions into elongated barrels. Place in three greased cake tins 30 x 10 cm (12 x 4 in). Cover with plastic wrap • Preheat the oven to 200°C (400°F) • Place the cake tins in a warm spot in the kitchen until doubled in size, about 90 minutes • Brush the loaves gently with the egg wash • Bake in the oven for 15 minutes or until golden brown • Reduce the oven temperature to 170°C (335°F) • Carefully turn the loaves in the tins onto the unexposed side and bake upside-down for 30 minutes. This process will shape the brioche into perfect square loaves • Tap the top of the brioche; if it sounds hollow, it's ready • Remove the loaves from the tins and allow to cool on a wire rack.

It is advisable not to wash the tins, simply wipe clean with a paper towel as washing the tins can cause the dough to stick when used again.

Miniature zopf dinner rolls

[makes 24 rolls]

My first ever bread recipe was this particular sweet Austrian dough similar to brioche that I learnt from Eric, a consummate professional baker. I recommend presenting this delicate dinner roll as a plait. Weigh each plait to 10 g (1/3 oz), the resulting bread roll will weigh 30 g (1 oz).

These rolls are a great accompaniment to barbecued hamburgers.

2 cups water
70 g (2½ oz) powdered milk
¼ cup sugar
15 g (½ oz) salt
40 g (1⅓ oz) fresh yeast
100 g (3½ oz) butter
900 g (1¾ lb) kamut flour, sifted
*100 ml (3½ fl oz) egg wash**

Combine the water, powdered milk, sugar, salt, yeast, butter and flour in a large mixing bowl. Using a mixer with the dough hook attached, beat on a medium speed for 10–15 minutes or until the dough is smooth and shiny in appearance but somewhat sticky in texture • Transfer to a lightly oiled container that will accommodate the dough when it has doubled in size. Cover with a large plastic bag, set aside to prove in a warm place for 2 hours or until doubled in size • Knock the dough down releasing all the carbon dioxide. Divide the dough into 40-g (1⅓-oz) portions and roll into balls using the palms of your hands • Place on a greased baking tray. Cover the tray with the plastic bag • Preheat the oven to 220°C (425°F) • Set aside to prove for 30 minutes or until doubled in size • Gently brush with the egg wash • Place in the oven and bake for 10 minutes or until golden and slightly crusted • Cool on a wire rack. These rolls freeze well.

Rum babas

[makes 6 cakes]

Named after Ali Baba of Arabian Nights fame, this recipe is steeped in history. Originally attributed to the Polish King Lesczyinski, who greedily and masterfully soaked his stale kugelhopf in rum, the dish was eventually claimed by the French and renamed Savarin after the famous eighteenth-century gastronome Brillat-Savarin. The dough can be formed into one large cake or individual cakes for a nice simple dessert with fresh or poached fruit and ice cream.

500 g (1 lb) spelt flour, sifted
Pinch of salt
15 g (½ oz) fresh yeast
20 g (¾ oz) caster (superfine) sugar
200 ml (7 fl oz) warm milk
6 eggs
150 g (5 oz) softened butter, chopped into rough dice

SOAKING SYRUP

3 tablespoons rum liqueur
100 g (3½ oz) caster (superfine) sugar
300 ml (10 fl oz) water
1 cinnamon quill
5 juniper berries, crushed
Pinch of saffron

Combine the flour, salt, yeast, sugar and 100 ml (3½ fl oz) of the milk and mix until an elastic dough is formed. The dough will be quite wet • Add the eggs one at a time, beating well after each addition, to prevent the mixture from curdling • Slowly add the butter in four stages to ensure the mixture does not split • Mix in the remaining milk to form a shiny elastic batter • Cover the bowl with plastic wrap, and leave in a warm place to rise for 1 hour • Preheat the oven to 200°C (400°F) • Knock out the air in the dough using a wooden spoon • Place the dough in a non-stick Savarin mould, filling to the top • Bake in the oven for 15 minutes • Turn the mould upside down and bake for a further 5 minutes • Test the cake to determine whether it is cooked by inserting a metal skewer, if it comes away clean it is ready • Unmould and place on a cake rack to cool for 1 hour • To make the soaking syrup, combine the rum, sugar, water, cinnamon, juniper berries and saffron in a saucepan. Bring to the boil and cook for 5 minutes. Remove from the heat and allow to infuse for 10 minutes • Strain the syrup into a large bowl and discard the flavouring ingredients • Dip the cake in the syrup and soak for 5 minutes. Turn the cake over and soak for another 5 minutes • Carefully remove the cake from the syrup with a spatula. Place the cake in the centre of a serving plate. Serve with poached raspberries or blueberries and whipped cream or caramelised bananas with vanilla ice cream.

Crêpes

[makes 24]

I MUCH PREFER TO see crêpes in the dessert section of a menu, rather than as an hors d'oeuvre. Try Calvados, cinnamon, apple and vanilla ice cream as accompaniments.

500 g (1 lb) plain (all-purpose) flour
5 eggs
Pinch of salt
900 ml (1½ pt) milk
40 g (1⅓ oz) butter, melted
120 g (4 oz) butter

Sift the flour into a large mixing bowl. Make a well in the centre, add the eggs and salt, and gradually pour in the milk, mixing to a smooth batter • Beat in the melted butter • Cover the bowl with plastic wrap and set aside for 30 minutes • Melt a teaspoon of the remaining butter over a medium heat in a non-stick frying pan. When the butter starts to bubble, add a ladleful of the batter. Tilt the pan to spread the batter into a thin round crêpe. Turn the crêpe over when bubbles start to form on the surface. The second side will take only a minute to cook. Repeat until all the batter is used • Layer the crêpes with greaseproof paper between each one on an upside down plate to help keep their shape and to make it easier to peel off when required. The crêpes can be kept warm in the oven while you finish cooking the rest • Serve as soon as possible.

Profiteroles

[makes 25 medium buns]

The real name of this particular recipe is choux paste — the best known derivative is profiteroles. Once you have mastered this recipe, practise your piping skills, let your imagination run wild and you will have found a new profession, choux sculpting. Swans, éclairs, gâteau Saint-Honoré and even croquembouches will be a walk in the park.

100 g (3½ oz) butter, chopped into rough dice
½ cup milk
½ cup water
Pinch of salt
150 g (5 oz) plain (all-purpose) flour, sifted
3 eggs
*1½ tablespoons egg wash**

Combine the butter, milk, water and salt in a heavy-based saucepan. Bring to the boil • Remove from the heat. With one hand add the flour and with the other incorporate the flour with a whisk, mixing until smooth • Return to the stove and cook on a medium heat, stirring constantly with a wooden spoon until the mixture bubbles. This is called the drying out stage • Remove from the heat immediately. Continue to beat until the mixture starts to come away from the sides • Beat in the eggs one at a time, beating well after each addition • Allow the mixture to rest for 30 minutes. Cover with plastic wrap to prevent a skin forming • Preheat the oven to 200°C (400°F) • Using a medium piping nozzle and a piping bag, pipe 2-cm (¾-in) discs onto a greaseproof paper-lined baking tray. Brush gently with egg wash and bake for 5 minutes • Reduce the oven temperature to 120°C (250°F) and bake for 15 minutes or until golden and hollow inside. They should be light to pick up • Remove the profiteroles from the tray and allow to cool on a wire rack • Store in an airtight container or in the freezer. Reheat before using.

Rum baba

Crêpes

Profiteroles

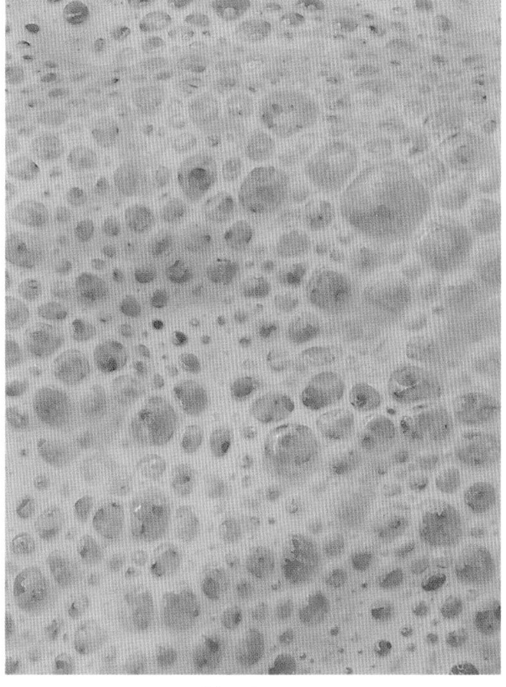

Blini batter

Blini

[makes 24]

THESE TINY LEAVENED pancakes are traditionally served with smoked salmon, caviar and crème fraîche.

15 g (1/2 oz) fresh yeast
1 cup lukewarm milk
150 g (5 oz) wholemeal (wholewheat) flour
2 eggs, separated
2 pinches of salt
100 g (3 1/2 oz) clarified butter (see page 381)

Dissolve the yeast in 2 1/2 tablespoons of the milk • Combine the flour, eggs yolks, a pinch of salt and the remaining milk in a mixing bowl. Whisk until smooth • Mix in the dissolved yeast mixture • Whisk the egg whites with a pinch of salt in an electric mixer until they form stiff peaks • Fold the egg whites into the batter to form a very light pancake-style mix • Cover with plastic wrap and leave in a warm part of the kitchen for 30 minutes • If you don't have a blini pan use a non-stick frying pan. Over a very low heat, warm 1 teaspoon of the clarified butter. Spoon the batter into the pan forming small miniature pancakes about 4 cm (1 1/2 in) in diameter. Turn when bubbles start to form on the surface. Cook until golden on each side. Repeat until you have 24.

Samosa dough

[makes 40 serves]

300 g (10 oz) plain (all-purpose) flour
2 tablespoons melted butter
5 g (1/4 oz) salt

Combine all of the ingredients in a mixing bowl. Beat until the dough has formed a complete ball • Wrap the dough tightly in plastic wrap, then transfer to the fridge for a few hours • The dough has a shelf life of 2–3 days. It does not freeze well.

Yeast batter

[makes 8 serves]

THIS VERY VERSATILE batter can replace any of your existing recipes which include the word fritter. Serving suggestions range from pineapple and banana to snails and duck confit.

Remember the rules when deep-frying: clean oil, 180°C (350°F) and close supervision. Use a paper towel to drain the food and serve immediately. Cottonseed oil is a good option for deep-frying as it is accepted by most allergy sufferers. Peanut oil always produces great results with its tolerance to high temperature and clean flavour. The best and most expensive way to deep-fry is in olive oil, it has the highest temperature capacity and cleanest flavour.

This particular batter can be a little awkward when dipping, use a toothpick and always dip the item into the flour before the batter, this helps the batter adhere.

You might find a sugar thermometer handy for this recipe.

2 tablespoons fresh yeast
1 cup beer
200 g (6½ oz) plain (all-purpose) flour, sifted
Pinch of salt and pepper

Dissolve the yeast in 2½ tablespoons of warm beer. Don't heat the beer over 30°C (85°F) as it will kill the yeast • Make a well in the centre of the flour, and whisk in the remaining beer and the beer/yeast mix. Season • Cover with plastic wrap and leave in a warm place for 30 minutes. This will allow the yeast to activate. The batter is now ready to use.

Croissants

[makes 24]

There are two types of croissant in this world: the good crusty golden and soft, slightly chewy croissant and then there is bad. I don't want to go into these but let's just say the bad are unfortunately very common. Albert Roux taught me to make the ultimate croissant. Yes, there is work involved but there is no such thing as a free lunch. Croissants were first made in Budapest to celebrate the repulsion of Turkish invaders in 1686; the shape depicts the crescent on the Turkish flag.

Try filling fresh croissants with anything you desire; my favourite is smoked salmon and rocket.

500 g (1 lb) spelt flour
2 teaspoons salt
2 tablespoons sugar
17 g (½ oz) fresh yeast
25 g (1 oz) powdered milk
300 ml (10 fl oz) water
300 g (10 oz) cultured butter, at room temperature*
*100 ml (3½ fl oz) egg wash**

Combine the flour, salt, sugar, yeast, powdered milk, and water in a large mixing bowl. Using a mixer with a dough hook attachment, mix on a low speed until a dough has formed. Do not overwork. This whole process should take around 2 minutes • Place the dough in a lightly oiled bowl large enough to accommodate the dough when it has doubled in size. Cover with plastic wrap and set aside in a warm spot in the kitchen for 1 hour or until the dough has doubled in size • Knock the dough down quickly on a clean, cold working surface • Return the dough to the container and place in the refrigerator for 8–12 hours • Roll out the butter between two sheets of greaseproof paper to form a rectangle 20 x 30 cm (8 x 12 in) • Roll out the dough on a lightly floured work surface to form a rectangle 40 x 60 cm (16 x 24 in). Place the butter in the centre of the dough and fold over the dough to resemble an envelope. Make sure the butter is completely enclosed • Roll out the dough to roughly 40 x 70 cm (16 x 28 in). Fold the dough into three, bringing the top third down and the bottom third up. Wrap in plastic wrap, then refrigerate for

30 minutes. Repeat this process twice always rolling the opposite way from the fold to ensure a build up of even layers • Again roll out the dough to 40 x 70 cm (16 x 28 in) • Cut the dough lengthwise into three equal strips approximately 13 cm ($5^1/_3$ in) wide. Make sure the sides are straight, trimming away any excess dough • Cut even triangles, shaped 10 x 15 cm (4 x 6 in) from the strips. There should be no wastage because each triangle should fit into the other • Place the triangles onto a greaseproof paper-lined tray then transfer to the refrigerator for 10 minutes • Place the triangles on a clean cold work surface with the singular point facing you. With your fingertips firmly grasping the two points further away from you, roll the pastry towards you forming a tight scroll. Then curve the tips of the scroll towards the single point to form a crescent shape. Place each croissant on the paper-lined baking tray spaced well apart. Repeat until you have completed the process for all 18 triangles. Brush the croissants with egg wash ensuring you brush from the inside out to prevent the pastry losing its shape • Leave to rise in a warm part of the kitchen for $1^1/_2$ hours or until doubled in size • Preheat the oven to 200°C (400°F) • Lightly brush the croissants with the egg wash again and bake in the oven for 15 minutes. Place on a wire rack to cool. Croissants freeze well.

Samosa dough

Deep fried beignets (yeast batter)

Croissants

Chocolate croissant

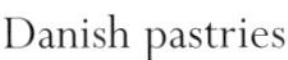

Danish pastries

Pizza

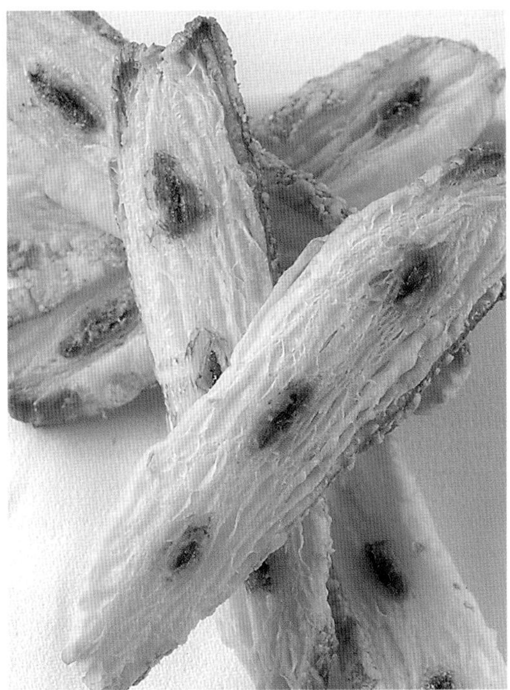

Anchovy sticks

Quiche Lorraine using pâte sel

Chocolate croissants

[makes 24]

A GOOD QUALITY couverture chocolate is going to be wasted here; it will simply burn and go bitter. Use good-quality baker's chocolate sticks instead. This sort of chocolate is found only in good providores.

1 recipe of croissant dough (see page 66)

24 x 8 g (1/4 oz) dark cooking chocolate sticks

*100 ml (3 1/2 fl oz) egg wash**

Cut the rolled dough into 24 rectangles 8 x 15 cm (3 x 6 in) • Place a stick of chocolate in the centre of each rectangle. Roll the pastry towards you forming a tight scroll. Place each croissant onto a greaseproof paper-lined baking tray spaced well apart. Repeat until you have completed the process for all 24 rectangles. Brush the croissants with egg wash ensuring you brush from the inside out to prevent the pastry losing its shape • Leave to rise in a warm part of the kitchen for 1 1/2 hours or until doubled in size • Preheat the oven to 200°C (400°F) • Lightly brush the croissants with the egg wash again and bake in the oven for 15 minutes. Place on a wire rack to cool • Miniature versions of these delicious pastries make great teacakes. Cut the dough into rectangles 9 x 25 cm (3 1/2 x 10 in). Place a chocolate stick one-third of its original size at the top of the dough. Roll up using your fingertips, starting from the top, to make one large scroll. Cut through the scroll at 2.5-cm (1-in) intervals. Follow the procedure above for cooking. They are easily stored in the freezer and reheated in a matter of minutes at 160°C (325°F). Serve crisp and hot with an espresso or hot chocolate.

Danish pastries

[makes 24]

WRITING THIS RECIPE brings back memories of my apprenticeship days in the basement of the Grand Hyatt Hotel bakery. At 3 am while slaving away rolling out Danish pastries and trying to block out conversations regarding Austrian politics from Eric the baker next to me, I could hear the sounds of the nightclub above and imagined all my mates getting down on the dance floor. But still I wouldn't have swapped it for the world. There is nothing better than sitting down, having just finished work, with a cup of Mariage Frères tea and a fresh blueberry Danish — and the rest of the day ahead of you.

50 g (1¾ oz) cultured butter, softened*
350 g (11 oz) plain (all-purpose) flour, sifted
540 g (1 lb 1¾ oz) spelt flour, sifted
¼ cup sugar
20 g (¾ oz) fresh yeast
2 teaspoons salt
*180 g (6 oz) cultured butter**
100 ml (3½ fl oz) milk
4 eggs, lightly beaten
*100 ml (3½ fl oz) egg wash**
Crème pâtissière (see page 335)
24 poached apricot halves
200 g (6½ oz) apricot jam, warmed

To make the lamination, beat the softened butter with the plain (all-purpose) flour until combined • Line a shallow baking tray 10 x 15 cm (4 x 6 in) with greaseproof paper, spread out the butter and flour mixture to the same size as the lined tray to a thickness of 2.5-cm (1-in). Cover with a layer of plastic wrap and place in the refrigerator until it starts to harden, about 90 minutes • Combine the spelt flour, sugar, yeast and salt in a large mixing bowl. Add the butter, milk and eggs, and using a mixer with a dough hook attachment, mix on a low speed until a firm dough has formed. This process should take no more than 3 minutes. Do not overwork the dough • Cover with a tea towel and leave to rise in a warm place for approximately 40 minutes or until doubled in size • On a floured work surface, knock the air out of the dough. Place the dough into a plastic bag and store in the fridge for 8–10 hours • On a floured work surface, cut a cross in the top of the dough and roll out into a rectangle double the size of the butter lamination • Allow the butter lamination to come to a workable temperature. If it is too hard it will pierce the dough causing the butter to ooze out later • Place the butter lamination in the middle of the rolled out dough • Wrap the dough around the butter. Roll out the dough away from you into a rectangle approximately 40 x 75 cm (16 x 29 in). Brush off any excess flour, then fold the dough into three. Wrap the dough in a plastic bag and refrigerate for 20 minutes. Repeat this process three times • Roll out the dough on a lightly floured work surface into a 40 x 75 cm (16 x 29 in) rectangle. Cut into three equal strips lengthwise. Cut these strips into equal sized squares • Brush the squares gently with the egg wash • Place a generous teaspoon of crème pâtissière into the centre of each square; place an apricot half on top of the crème pâtissière. Fold over two opposite corners of the pastry and join in the middle of the pastry • Preheat the oven to 180° (350°F) • Place the pastries onto a greaseproof paper-lined baking tray. Rest in a warm place to prove for 30 minutes • Transfer to the oven and bake for 15 minutes or until golden • Glaze the top with the apricot jam while the pastries are hot. Yes, Danish pastries can be stored in the freezer.

Pizza dough

(makes 1 large pizza)

THIS DOUGH IS GOING to be your best friend; it takes only an hour or so to prove unlike other bread recipes that require twice that. I have used this dough for bread rolls, flat bread, calzone and tomato and garlic pizza. Good pizza should always be thin and crisp with a good tomato base, such as the tomato fondue on page 81, and good-quality toppings. The best I have ever tasted was a zucchini (courgette) and tarragon pizza in Rome. Don't forget salt and pepper when adding the finishing touches.

1.1 kg (2 lb $3\frac{1}{2}$ oz) spelt flour, sifted
50 g ($1\frac{3}{4}$ oz) olive oil
2 tablespoons fresh yeast
25 g (1 oz) salt
2 teaspoons sugar
*5 g ($\frac{1}{4}$ oz) improver**
*5 g ($\frac{1}{4}$ oz) gluten**
560 ml (18 fl oz) water

Combine all of the ingredients in a large mixing bowl. Using a mixer with a dough hook, work the dough for at least 15 minutes. The more elastic the dough, the better • Transfer the dough to a lightly oiled container that will provide enough room for it to double in size. Cover the container with plastic wrap and set aside in a warm part of the kitchen for 40 minutes or until doubled in size • Place onto a floured work surface and knead for 5 minutes. Roll out the dough thinly and use immediately.

Anchovy sticks

[makes 60]

Anchovies are great crushed and added to any stew containing tomatoes, and fantastic dipped in beer batter and deep-fried. Serve these while hot, no sauce is needed.

500 g (1 lb) puff pastry (see page 54)
*30 Ortiz anchovies**
1 egg, lightly beaten
250 g (8 oz) Parmesan cheese, grated

Roll out two sheets of puff pastry 20 x 40 cm (8 x 16 in) to 3 mm ($\frac{1}{8}$ in) thick. Place one sheet on a greaseproof paper-lined baking tray • Brush with the beaten egg and make several puncture marks with a fork • Place the anchovy fillets head to tail in two lines, leaving 2 cm ($\frac{3}{4}$ in) from the side and 5 cm (2 in) on either side of the centre line • Place the other sheet of pastry on top and press to define the lines of anchovies • Brush the top with the egg, then sprinkle with cheese • Freeze for 30 minutes until firm enough to cut • Preheat the oven to 180°C (350°F) • Using a large sharp knife, cut down the centre line, then slice across in 5 mm ($\frac{1}{4}$ in) strips to show a cross section of the anchovies. The sticks should be 10 cm (4 in) in length • Place the strips on a greaseproof paper-lined baking tray and cook for 10–15minutes or until golden brown and crispy.

Pâte sel (short crust pastry)

[Makes enough for 2 large tarts]

This dough is essential for such recipes as beef pies, egg tartlets, quiche, flans and crème pâtissière mille-feuilles. The key tip is don't overwork the flour. The end product should be light and delicate.

150 g (5 oz) butter
1 egg
250 g (8 oz) kamut flour, sifted
1 teaspoon salt
Pinch of sugar
2 tablespoons milk

Cream the butter in a mixing bowl. Add the egg and mix well • Add the flour and beat on a very low speed until incorporated, 2–3 minutes. Add the salt, mix for 1 minute, then add the sugar • Add the milk and stir to combine. Cover with plastic wrap and rest in the refrigerator for at least 1 hour • When required, roll out the pastry to a thickness of 1.5 cm (1/2 in) on a cold lightly floured work surface then carefully place into the desired baking case. Yes, the dough does freeze well.

Quiche Lorraine

[serves 8]

THE ORIGINAL QUICHE Lorraine was an open pie with an egg, cream and bacon filling. It was only later that cheese was added. (If you add onions, then you have a quiche Alsacienne.) The bottom crust was originally made from bread dough, but now is made with shortening-type crusts or puff pastry crusts.

Keep with the theme of Alsace and serve with a refreshing glass of crisp pinot blanc.

Pâte sel dough (see page 74)
200 g (6½ oz) smoked bacon, chopped
1 cup thinly sliced spring onions
1 cup grated Gruyere cheese
1¼ cups double cream
4 large eggs
Pinch of ground nutmeg
Salt and freshly ground pepper
10 g (⅓ oz) cultured butter, finely chopped*

Roll out the pâte sel dough on a lightly floured work surface until 6 mm (¼ in) thick • Lift the dough onto the rolling pin and drape over a 23-cm (9-in) tart tin. Press into the bottom and ease into the edges, letting the pastry overhang the rim of the tin. Trim excess dough • Transfer to the freezer for 10–15 minutes to firm up. Line the pastry shell with baking paper and fill with baking pulses • Preheat the oven to 180°C (350°F) • Place in the oven for 15 minutes. Remove the baking paper and bake for a further 10 minutes or until golden. Patch any holes in the baked shell with some raw dough, then return to the oven for a few minutes. Remove and allow to cool • Cook the bacon in its own fat in a heavy-based frying pan over medium heat for 2–3 minutes or until lightly coloured. Scatter the bacon over the piecrust • Combine the spring onions, cheese, cream, eggs, nutmeg, salt and pepper in a large bowl, and pour into the piecrust. Scatter the butter over the top of the pie • Place in the oven on a middle rack and bake for 35–45 minutes or until the top is browned and a knife inserted in the centre comes out clean • Cool for 15 minutes and serve with lightly dressed seasonal salad leaves.

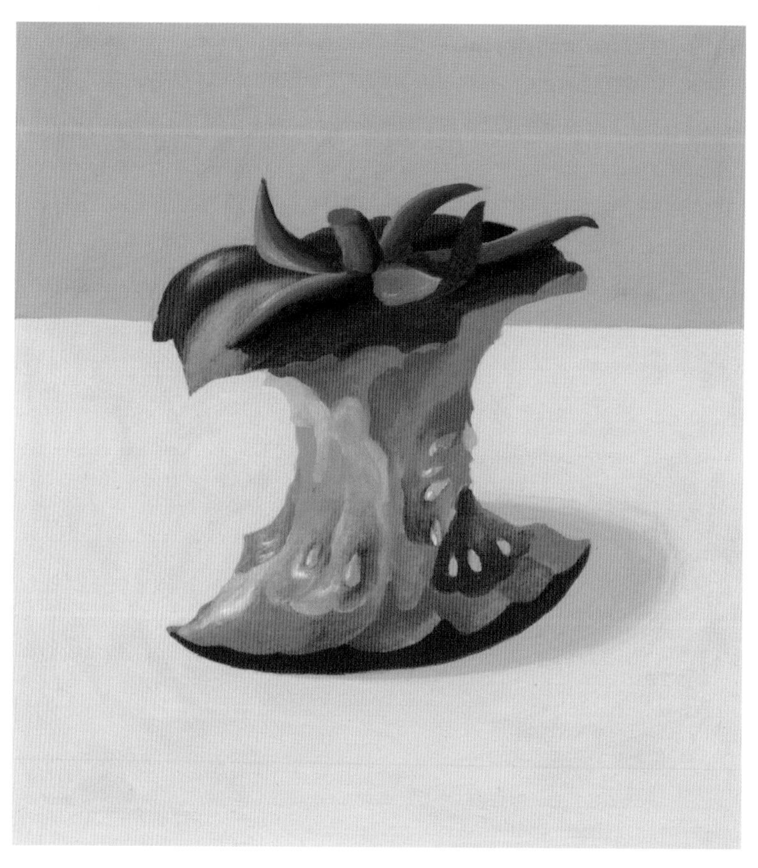

The Tomato

MEDITERRANEAN COOKERY IS unimaginable without this slightly acidic, bright red, shiny, fleshy fruit that is used, cooked or raw, in salads, garnishes and sauces. The tomato, which originates from Peru and whose name derives from the Aztec word *tomatl*, was considered poisonous up until the early eighteenth century.

The marmande or beef tomato, the largest of the tomato family, is available from late-spring to mid-autumn. Like all tomatoes, it ripens well off the vine in a warm dry part of the kitchen and will last for up to 10 days. Montfavet hybrid or vine tomato is the newest of the tomato varieties, closely related to the beef tomato but smaller, it is perfect for stuffing and serving as a light healthy entrée or simply sliced and served in a salad or on freshly toasted bread. The skin of the tomato is not as thick as other varieties, so there is less need to remove it before use. This tomato is grown hydroponically all over the world with mixed results, as a consequence it is available all year round. The Roma (plum) is the egg-shaped variety that is most commonly used in Mediterranean cooking. Sweet, succulent and rich in Vitamins A, B and C, it is

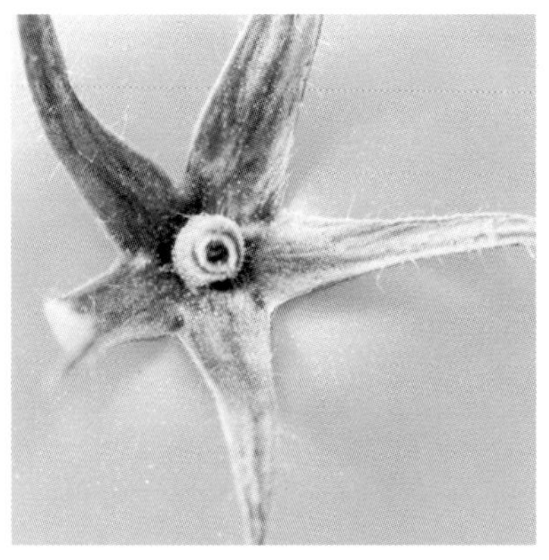

easily scalded and skinned for preparation in sauces, salsas and purées. Its association with garlic, basil, olives, capsicums (sweet peppers) and eggplants (aubergines) is classical and famous in every sense.

The tomato means a lot to me — it is a bridge between new and old. There is a relationship and understanding of any recipe from a bygone era that contained tomatoes. I can understand what the chef was trying to achieve by adding tomato to the recipe. Its sweet and sour characteristic gives the flavours of other ingredients a lift and visually it is appealing with its bright red colour. It is a common factor in all cuisines apart from Chinese cookery where its discovery was too late for it to be included in the repertoire of a cuisine so rich in belief, culture and history.

Sauvignon blanc, especially when fermented and aged in oak, is a good match for tomato dishes. Good examples are the wines of Sancerre and in particular Didier Dagueneau. His Silex and Pur Sang wines are hard to find, but are worth tracking down.

Squeezing the tomato pulp out of the fruit before use is a good way to free the palate of the difficult and strong acid found in the tomato.

Cold-pressed tomato soup with fromage blanc and profiteroles

[serves 8]

THIS SIGNATURE DISH of the restaurant is used for its refreshing qualities to cleanse the palate before the main course. Alternatively, serve with cold poached seafood mixed with a crisp julienne of very lightly dressed root vegetables or as an hors d'oeuvre in a chilled espresso cup.

1 kg (2 lb) ripe Roma (plum) tomatoes
25 g (1 oz) sugar
25 ml (1 fl oz) Champagne vinegar
1 cup cold water
½ bunch of basil
4 cloves of garlic
1½ teaspoons Worcestershire sauce
5 drops Tabasco sauce
Salt and freshly ground pepper
1 tablespoon finely chopped curly-leaf parsley
½ tablespoon finely chopped chives
24 profiteroles (see page 62)
200 g (6½ oz) fromage blanc mixture (see page 366)

Deseed and juice the tomatoes by squeezing them in the palm of your hand over a plastic bag • Combine the sugar and vinegar in a saucepan and bring to the boil. Reduce heat to low and simmer until reduced by two-thirds or until you have a thick syrup that coats the back of a spoon • Purée the tomatoes, water, basil and garlic in a food processor. Add the Worcestershire, Tabasco and salt and pepper. Transfer to a cheesecloth-lined strainer placed over a bowl. Place in the refrigerator for 12 hours to filter through. The liquid should be clear. If it is cloudy, try a finer filter. It will take only 10–15 minutes to filter through the second time • Place eight serving bowls in the refrigerator 1 hour before serving • Place the herbs in the chilled serving bowls • Preheat the oven to 180°C (350°F) • Heat the profiteroles in the oven. Hollow out the profiteroles from the bottom with a small paring knife, making the hole no bigger than 3 mm (⅛ in). Spoon in the fromage blanc. Do not be concerned that the fromage blanc will fall out of the profiteroles, it is thick enough to adhere to the pastry. Place three profiteroles in the centre of each serving bowl • Transfer the chilled soup to a jug and, at the table, pour around the crispy profiteroles.

Tomato jelly with sea urchin and basil velouté

[serves 8]

The sea urchin or *herisson de mer* as it is nicknamed in France fascinated me the first time I came to use it. How could something so surreal be eaten? Sea urchins lurk around shallow bays and inlets where fishermen normally pick them off mussel ropes and cray pot lines. The weather needs to be very calm to create the still water needed to pluck them out. The spines should be firm and the mouth of the sea urchin should not appear sunken when fresh. Fresh sea urchins are hard to buy as they have a very limited shelf life of around two days. Most large cities have a Japanese quarter or shopping district, much in the same way as a Chinatown, this is the best place to look for this alluring creature. If you are on good terms with your fishmonger, ask him nicely to open the sea urchins for you, it will save a good amount of trial and error. Sea urchin meat is more readily available in its frozen form. Make the dish the same way substituting ramekins 7 cm (2¾ in) in diameter for the shells.

*2 leaves of gelatin**

8 x 90 g (3 oz) fresh sea urchins in the shell

300 ml (10 fl oz) cold-pressed tomato soup (see page 79)

1½ cups basil leaves

200 ml (7 fl oz) mussel velouté (see page 244)

Salt

Soak the gelatin in enough cold water for it to be well submerged • Wearing heavy rubber gloves and being very careful not to spike yourself, open the sea urchin shells carefully with a serrated knife or a sharp pair of scissors by removing the top to create a clean opening in the same way a boiled egg is opened. The top is easy to identify, it has a white opening or mouth. Place the sea urchin on its side, run the knife carefully around the inside of the shell. A substantial amount of liquid will run out. Do not be alarmed it is simply seawater. Alternatively a good fishmonger may be able to open the sea urchins for you • The sea urchin meat is a pale orange colour. Using a teaspoon, scoop everything but the orange roe out of the shell and discard. Repeat for all eight shells • Place the shells onto a tray and rest in the refrigerator for 10 minutes • Remove the gelatin from the water and squeeze out any excess moisture • Warm the tomato soup, add the gelatin and stir to dissolve • Pour the soup into the sea urchin shells, return to the refrigerator and allow to set for 1 hour • In boiling salted water, cook the basil leaves for 5 minutes or until they start to break up when pressed between two fingers. Refresh in iced water, remove and strain. Transfer to a blender and purée until smooth • Combine the mussel velouté and the basil purée in a saucepan and gently heat until just warm. Taste and season with a little salt • Froth the velouté by placing the saucepan on a slight angle and froth using a hand blender • Place each sea urchin on a serving plate. Spoon the froth into and over the shell of the sea urchin and serve.

Tomato fondue

[makes 500 g (1 lb)]

Once you have tasted the intensity and purity of this concentrated tomato paste, you will understand why this is called a fondue. Toss through pasta, spread over steamed fish, use on pizza bases and add to flavour stews and braises.

1 kg (2 lb) tomatoes, roughly chopped
4 cloves of garlic, crushed
2 teaspoons white peppercorns, finely crushed
2½ tablespoons extra virgin olive oil
2 tablespoons sea salt
2 bay leaves
¼ bunch of thyme

Preheat the oven to 120°C (250°F) • Purée the tomatoes in a food processor. Add the garlic, pepper, olive oil and salt. Pour into a deep-sided baking tray • Tie the bay leaves and thyme together with some kitchen twine to form a bouquet. Add to the purée • Bake in the oven for 2 hours or until the tomato fondue is deep red in colour and void of moisture • Discard the bouquet. Push the tomato fondue through a fine sieve. Store in an airtight container in the refrigerator for up to 2 weeks. Suitable for freezing.

Tomato stuffed with crab and avocado

[serves 10]

THE FRESH APPROACH to this dish relies on choosing the reddest sweetest tomatoes you can find. The crabmeat will also need to be on the sweet side. I recommend blue swimmer crabs or any other shallow water variety. Correct presentation of this dish is essential, so don't rush it.

Serve with a luscious viognier or French Condrieu with good acidity and rich complexity to match the array of flavours. Try Petaluma from the Coonawarra region in Australia or the French Rhone Valley producer Gilles Barge.

10 vine-ripened medium beef tomatoes, stems attached

2 ripe avocados

Juice of 1 lime

1 continental cucumber, peeled and finely diced

3 shallots, finely chopped

2 red capsicums (sweet peppers), roasted, peeled, blanched and diced

2 Granny Smith apples, peeled and finely diced

200 g (6½ oz) white crabmeat

200 ml (7 fl oz) Mary Rose sauce (see page 388)

Salt and freshly ground pepper

1 tablespoon finely chopped chives

1 tablespoon extra virgin olive oil

1½ tablespoons green mayonnaise (see page 388)

Scald the tomatoes in boiling water, then refresh in iced water • Carefully slice 1 cm (⅓ in) off the top of each tomato. Reserve the lids. Peel and hollow out the tomatoes using a teaspoon • Finely dice the avocados, then squeeze over some of the lime juice to prevent discolouring • In a large bowl, combine the avocado, cucumber, shallot, capsicum and apple. Add the crabmeat and 2 tablespoons of the Mary Rose sauce, season with salt and pepper and the remaining lime juice. Mix in the chives, spoon into the tomatoes and place the lids on top • Season and brush the stuffed tomatoes with the olive oil • Place a large round cutter (a take away container cut into a ring will suffice) in the centre of each serving plate and spoon around the remaining Mary Rose sauce to create a near perfect circle • Place the green mayonnaise into a piping bag or a small squeezeable sauce bottle. Pipe dots of mayonnaise around the Mary Rose sauce • Place a tomato in the centre of each circle and serve.

CLASSIC TOMATO GAZPACHO

[serves 10]

CONFUSION REIGNS OVER the origin and authenticity of gazpacho. My research has led me to many different ingredients and methods. However, I can tell you that the Arabic translation for the name is soaked bread, the soup should always contain bread and garlic; and it should always be served cold.

Tomatoes are not a compulsary ingredient, but in this recipe they are the backbone. I draw inspiration from a Madrilène version that includes orange juice. This led me to the idea of pairing it with seafood: garnish the soup with a mixture of crispy and grilled squid or use it as a sauce to go with roast scallops. At Vue de monde this recipe is served as a garnish with deep-fried cherry tomatoes and poached seafood. Once you have perfected the technique of gazpacho give this presentation a go, it is bound to impress.

600 g (1¼ lb) ripe Roma (plum) tomatoes
2 red capsicums (sweet peppers)
1 cucumber
1 large red onion, diced
4 cloves of garlic, peeled
Juice of 2 oranges
2 ½ tablespoons Champagne vinegar
2 tablespoons sherry vinegar
100 ml (3½ fl oz) tomato ketchup
300 ml (10 fl oz) virgin olive oil
5 thick slices of sourdough bread, crusts removed and chopped into 1 cm (⅓ in) cubes
2½ tablespoons extra virgin olive oil
Salt and freshly ground pepper

Squeeze the seeds from the tomatoes and roughly chop • Cut the capsicums and cucumber in half, remove the seeds and roughly chop • Purée the tomatoes, capsicum, cucumber, red onion, and 3 cloves of garlic until fine. Pass through a coarse sieve, then through a fine sieve • Whisk the orange juice, vinegars and ketchup into the purée • Add the virgin olive oil, whisking constantly until all the ingredients are amalgamated • Season to taste and refrigerate for 24 hours • Preheat the oven to 180°C (350°F) • Toss the bread cubes in the extra virgin olive oil and bake for 10 minutes or until golden. Remove and rub with the remaining garlic clove • Refrigerate ten serving bowls • Taste the gazpacho and adjust seasoning. No one particular ingredient should stand out. If you need to sweeten the flavour, add some extra tomato ketchup • To serve, pour into the cold bowls and spoon over the garlic croutons.

Cold pressed tomato soup

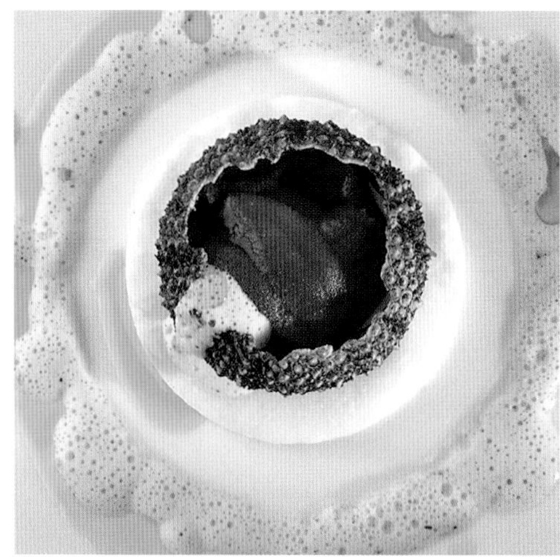

Tomato jelly with sea urchin and basil velouté

Tomato fondue

Tomato stuffed with crab and avocado

Classic tomato gazpacho

Tomato tart

Potato-crusted red mullet with eggplant caviar and tomato butter

Tomato coulis

Tomato tarts with almond gazpacho sorbet and crispy anchovies

[serves 8]

Over the next few years this recipe will evolve and change to become one of my signature dishes. I may replace the tomato confit with pickled green tomatoes, or use a combination of both; I haven't made up my mind. This is a simpler version of what I serve in the restaurant when tomatoes are in full season. The confit of tomato is a real winner; use it as a garnish for roasted meats or fish. Anchovies are a controversial product that I love. The Spanish brand Ortiz is famous for their preserved anchovies. They are not cheap but the quality and consistency are amazing. I have seen them in speciality stores all around the world. I have managed to track down a fisherman, his name is Barry Bonza, who specialises in catching these anonymous creatures of the deep and who now supplies my restaurant with fresh anchovies. The difference is incredible, especially in the texture. A worthy tip is to treat them in the same way as you would a sardine.

Serve with an aged riesling from the Clare Valley or Mount Barker.

CONFIT TOMATOES

10 Roma (plum) tomatoes

3 cloves of garlic, thinly sliced

¼ bunch of thyme

2 tablespoons sea salt

Pinch of freshly ground black pepper

200 ml (7 fl oz) olive oil

ALMOND GAZPACHO SORBET

2 slices of sourdough bread, crusts removed

250 g (8 oz) almond meal

Preheat the oven to 90°C (195°F) • Score the tomatoes by cutting a shallow cross at each end with a sharp paring knife. Blanch the tomatoes in boiling salted water for 20 seconds. Refresh in iced water. From the point where the tomatoes have been scored, peel away the skin. Cut the tomatoes in half and deseed • Place the tomato halves on a large greaseproof paper-lined baking tray. Top each with a slice of garlic. Scatter over the thyme, sea salt, pepper and olive oil • Bake for 1–2 hours, then rest for 1 hour. The end result should be beautiful rich red semi-dried tomatoes • To make the almond gazpacho sorbet, soak the bread in water for 5 minutes, then squeeze out excess water • Combine the almond meal, bread and garlic in a food

2 cloves of garlic, crushed
300 ml (10 fl oz) olive oil
$2^1/_2$ tablespoons grapeseed oil
150 ml (5 fl oz) warm water
2 teaspoons sherry vinegar
Salt

TOMATO TARTS

300 g (10 oz) butter, melted
7 sheets of filo pastry
8 cups vegetable oil
1 bunch of sage

TEMPURA BATTER

100 g ($3^1/_2$ oz) cornflour (cornstarch)
100 g ($3^1/_2$ oz) plain (all-purpose) flour
20 g ($^3/_4$ oz) baking powder
3 tablespoons water

GARNISHES

*8 Ortiz anchovies**
100 g ($3^1/_2$ oz) plain (all-purpose) flour
Juice of $^1/_2$ lemon
*$2^1/_2$ tablespoons herb oil**
*20 Ligurian or Niçoise olives**
8 x 2-cm ($^3/_4$-in) slices of bread

processor. Blend for 4–5 minutes, slowly adding the olive and grapeseed oils through the funnel while the motor is running. The mixture will start to emulsify, resembling a mayonnaise. Add a little warm water to prevent the mix from splitting • Add the sherry vinegar and salt to taste • Transfer to an airtight container and freeze for 2–3 hours. Alternatively, use an ice-cream churner and follow the manufacturer's instructions • Preheat the oven to 180°C (350°F) • To make the tomato tarts, brush the melted butter over each sheet of filo pastry. Carefully place each sheet one on top of the other. Once all the sheets have been used, cover with a damp tea towel and place in the fridge for 10 minutes • With a sharp knife cut out eight rectangles 8 x 5 cm (3 x 2 in) from the pastry • Place on a lightly greased baking tray and bake for 5 minutes or until golden brown • Place 2 semi-dried tomatoes on each pastry base and return to the oven for 3 minutes • Pour the vegetable oil into a deep-fryer and preheat to 180°C (350°F) • Bunch 6 sprigs of sage into 8 bouquets. Deep-fry the sage for 2 minutes or until crispy. Drain on paper towel • To make the tempura batter, combine the cornflour, flour and baking powder in a large mixing bowl. Slowly whisk in the water until the batter is smooth and shiny and the consistency of thickened cream • Lightly dust the anchovies in the flour, spike with a toothpick, then dip into the batter. Deep-fry until crisp and golden. Season with lemon juice. Drain on paper towel • Heat the herb oil in a frying pan, add the olives and warm gently • To serve, place each tomato tart on the left side of a serving plate. To the right of the tart, quenelle the sorbet onto one slice of the bread (this prevents it from sliding). Lean a crispy sage bouquet and an anchovy against the tart. Arrange the olives and drizzle over the herb oil.

Potato-crusted red mullet with eggplant caviar and tomato butter

[serves 4]

This is a tricky recipe, but the effort is worth it! Pinot noir is always a favourite with red mullet.

4 x 500 g (1 lb) red mullet (goatfish) fillets
4 large sebago potatoes
2½ tablespoons olive oil
Salt and freshly ground pepper

TOMATO BUTTER

250 g (8 oz) cherry tomatoes
100 ml (3½ fl oz) tomato ketchup
2½ tablespoons sherry vinegar
1½ tablespoons Champagne vinegar
3 tablespoons extra virgin olive oil
100 g (3½ oz) cultured butter, chopped into rough dice*
200 g (6½ oz) eggplant (aubergine) caviar (see page 153)
½ tablespoon olive oil
*50 g (1¾ oz) goose fat**
Saffron potatoes (see page 93)

Pick out the bones from each fillet with a pair of fine tweezers. Dip the tweezers in cold water after removing each bone • Shape the potatoes into cylinders, then slice into thin discs using a mandoline • Heat the olive oil in a frying pan over low heat; add the potato discs and toss until they become sticky, about 2 minutes. Drain on paper towel • Place the fish fillets on a tray, skin side up, season with salt and pepper. Starting at the thicker end of each fillet, overlap the potato discs on the skin to resemble large fish scales • To make the tomato butter, combine the cherry tomatoes, ketchup and vinegars in a food processor. Blend until smooth. Pass through a fine sieve, pushing all the pulp through • Rest in the fridge for 1 hour. The tomato purée may be stored in a covered container in the fridge for up to 2 days • Gently warm the tomato purée over a low heat, whisk in the olive oil and butter. Taste and season with a little salt • Warm the eggplant caviar in a saucepan with the olive oil. Season with salt and pepper • Heat the goose fat in a heavy non-stick frying pan over high heat. Lay the fish fillet potato-side down and cook for 3 minutes or until golden. Turn over gently using a fish slice and cook for 1 minute • Place each fish fillet onto a warmed serving plate. Quenelle the eggplant caviar alongside. Spoon a small amount of the tomato butter on the other side of the fillet. Season the potato crust and serve with the saffron potatoes.

TOMATO COULIS

[makes 8 cups]

THIS RECIPE ACTS AS a two-in-one dish: it makes a lovely delicate sauce for pasta, steamed fish, crustaceans, vegetable stews and hot pots; and it also makes a delicious soup paired with a goat's cheese ravioli or minced (ground) veal tortellini. Simply drizzle some herb oil over the top of the finished soup, add a few shavings of Grana Padano Parmesan cheese and top with crispy sage.

30 Roma (plum) tomatoes
2½ tablespoons olive oil
1 carrot, diced
1 stick of celery, diced
1 bulb of fennel, diced
1 leek, diced
2 onions, diced
1 head of garlic, cut in half
10 fennel seeds
10 black peppercorns, crushed
1 bay leaf
4 sprigs of thyme
300 g (10 oz) tomato paste
3 cups dry white wine
8 cups chicken stock (see page 378)
1 ham bone
*100 ml (3½ fl oz) herb oil**
½ bunch of basil
Salt and freshly ground pepper

Preheat the oven to 160°C (325°F) • Squeeze the tomatoes free of seeds and juice • Heat the olive oil in a large heavy-based flameproof casserole dish. Add the carrot, celery, fennel, leek and onion and cook, stirring constantly, over medium heat for 8 minutes or until soft and tender • Add the garlic, fennel seeds, peppercorns, bay leaf and thyme and cook for 2 minutes • Add the tomatoes and tomato paste. Cook for 5 minutes or until the skin starts to separate from the tomatoes • Deglaze with the white wine and cook until reduced by half • Add the chicken stock and bring to the boil. Add the ham bone, herb oil and basil • Seal tightly with aluminium (aluminum) foil, cover with the lid, and place in the oven for 2 hours • Remove the ham bone, then strain the vegetables through a coarse sieve. Push the strained liquid through a fine sieve • Transfer the coulis to a saucepan and reduce over low heat to the consistency required. The great diversity of this dish is in by how much you reduce the coulis. Season and serve.

The Potato

IN 1733, THE ENGLISHMAN Stephen Switzer echoed popular opinion of the potato as 'that which was heretofore reckon'd a food fit only for Irishmen and clowns'.

It took Frenchman Antoine August Parmentier four years in a German jail during the Seven Years War, with nothing to eat but boiled potato, to realise the worth of today's second most consumed food in the world, behind the rice grain. A skilful public relations man, he convinced high society in France to accept the potato flower as an accessory for women's hairpieces. He then proceeded to convince King Louis XVI to plant potatoes on the outskirts of Paris. He had the plot heavily guarded during the day, but by night it was left without supervision. Ingeniously planned, he predicted the peasants would assume anything guarded was of value, so they stole the plants by night. Potatoes quickly sprouted up all over France, then spread throughout Europe.

Native to the Americas, the potato was once considered 'too poor' to be recorded in the French repertoire. Now the potato is the king of vegetables.

I break the potato down to two categories, frying and mashing. Powdery new-season potatoes from warmer climates with low seasonal rainfall provide the best means to make a good crisp golden fried chip. Waxy yellow small potatoes, such as kipflers or rattes, made famous by Joel Robuchon's pommes mousseline, are excellent for puréed or steamed dishes.

As consumers we have become very complacent regarding the availability of potatoes. The harvest runs from mid-spring to late-autumn. The rest of the time farmers have no alternative but to store the harvested potatoes in cool dark sheds to comply with demand. Towards the end of this period the starch can revert to sugar, making the potato sweet, watery and useless for frying.

A good tip for sourcing quality frying potatoes is to try the big supermarket chains. I have found in times of need your best bet is the large generic washed variety known as sebago, which supermarkets always seem to have. I do like the Italian variety spunta, which is available during the height of summer; they are large and full of vibrant flavour. Another tip is to pick large potatoes with good red clay soil still visible, this indicates that the potato has come from rich fertile soil devoid of a lot of moisture. Too much moisture affects the potatoes ability to fry well. In mid-winter try the kipfler or ratte to produce your own perfect roast chips.

Oh and one other thing, you will notice I don't use a lot of pepper with potato; its powerful spiciness is far too strong for a delicate buttery purée or crisp golden French fries.

Saffron potatoes

[serves 6]

Kipfler potatoes are perfect for this dish. Their yellow waxy texture enables the cook to be very versatile with contrasting results: the potatoes keep their shape even when overcooked and, best of all, they can be turned with a small knife to create attractive barrels due to their wonderful elongated shape.

30 kipfler or ratte potatoes, peeled
1 tablespoon olive oil
5 cloves of garlic, thinly sliced
5 shallots, thinly sliced
Pinch of saffron
5 sprigs of thyme
2 bay leaves
1 teaspoon fennel seeds
200 ml (7 fl oz) white wine
2 cups chicken stock (see page 378)
2 teaspoons sea salt
2 ½ tablespoons glace de viande (see page 295)
*5 g (¼ oz) cultured butter**

Preheat the oven to 160°C (325°F) • Turn the potatoes into a barrel shape using a sharp knife • Heat the olive oil in a heavy-based flameproof casserole dish, add the garlic, shallots, saffron, thyme, bay leaves and fennel seeds and cook over medium heat for 6 minutes or until soft and transparent • Deglaze with the white wine and reduce until the liquid has all but evaporated • Pour in the chicken stock, bring to the boil, then add the potatoes and a pinch of salt • Cover and place in the oven for 15 minutes • Test the potatoes with a small pointed knife; they should be bright yellow and soft but firm. Leave to cool in the cooking liquid • To serve, pour the cooking liquid into a saucepan, bring to the boil and cook for 10 minutes or until it coats the back of a spoon. Whisk in the glace de viande and butter until almalgamated, then gently toss the potatoes in the glaze. Place in a serving bowl, season with the remaining salt and serve.

Pommes fondantes

[serves 6]

Many variations of fondant potatoes exist. Let's simplify things. Shape consists of two types: the classic turned potato and the round hockey puck with devilled edges. Butter, thyme, water or stock, and salt, are the only ingredients needed. The idea is for the potato to absorb the butter and turn an appealing golden colour at a very low temperature. Other vegetables, such as turnips, can be cooked in a similar fashion.

6 large sebago potatoes
400 g (13 oz) unsalted butter, diced
200 ml (7 fl oz) water
20 g (¾ oz) salt

Cut the potatoes into cylinders 5 cm (2 in) in size • Spread the diced butter over the base of a shallow straight-sided non-stick frying pan. Push the potatoes into the butter • Add the water and cook over low to medium heat for 15 minutes. The butter and water will emulsify and boil rapidly. Shake the pan to prevent the potatoes from sticking and breaking up • Continue until the butter starts to split. Monitor the potatoes constantly as they will start to colour quickly. Reduce the heat to low and cook for 25 minutes. Check their progress by lifting the potatoes out of the butter at 1-minute intervals. Once they start to colour on the bottom, turn the potatoes over. Remove the pan from the heat, season with the salt and leave in a warm place for about 20 minutes or until the butter is absorbed • Once the residual heat has cooked the potatoes, remove from the pan and brush away any dark impurities. Test the potatoes with a toothpick to see if they are cooked. They are ready if the toothpick slides in and out of the potato without resistance • Preheat the oven to 180°C (350°F) • Transfer the potatoes to the oven for 5 minutes. Brush with a little of the butter from the pan and serve.

Pommes Maxim

[serves 6]

NAMED AFTER THE famous restaurant in Paris, many variations of pommes Maxim exist. Once you have mastered this dish, it will be useful when creating your own menus.

3 large desiree potatoes
Salt and freshly ground pepper
3 tablespoons clarified butter (see page 381)

Preheat the oven to 160°C (325°F) • Wash and cut the potatoes into long cylinders using a serrated bread knife for better control • Using a mandoline, carefully slice the potatoes into 3 mm (1/8 in) discs. Pat dry with a tea towel, season with a small amount of salt and toss in 1 tablespoon of the clarified butter • Layer the discs on a non-stick baking tray in rows two wide and six long • Lightly brush the tops of the potatoes with the clarified butter and season • Place in the oven for 20 minutes or until golden and crisp. Serve hot or at room temperature.

Pommes Anna

[serves 6]

POMMES ANNA IS A fantastic variation of pommes Maxim.

3 large desiree potatoes
3 tablespoons clarified butter (see page 381)

Slice the potatoes into 6 mm (1/4 in) discs, slightly thicker than for pommes Maxim • Heat the clarified butter in a heavy-based frying pan. Place two layers of potato discs into 6 small round non-stick pommes Anna moulds (available from speciality stores) and add to the pan. Cook for 10 minutes or until golden • Turn the potatoes and cook on the other side. Serve immediately or rest on a cake rack. To reheat, place in a deep-fryer at 180°C (350°F) for 1 minute.

Saffron potatoes

Pommes fondantes

Pommes Maxim

Pommes Anna

Pommes soufflées

Kipfler potatoes filled with snails

Pommes Pont Neuf

Potato confit

Pommes Dauphine

Pommes mille-feuille

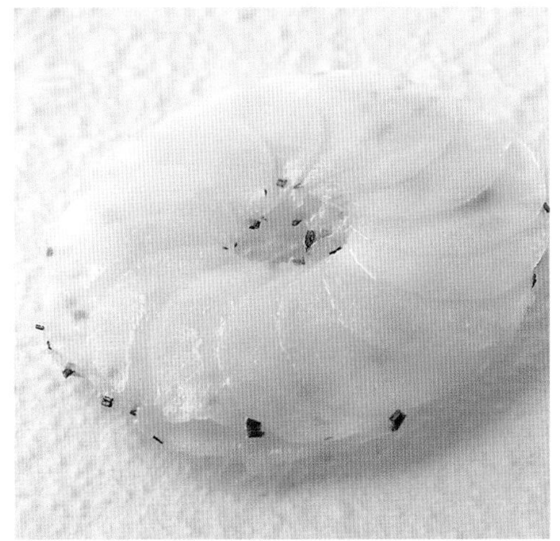
Pommes à la boulangere

Pommes mousseline

Pommes soufflées

[serves 4]

I LIKE TO SURPRISE people; pommes soufflées is certainly the way.

5 large patrone potatoes, peeled
4 cups canola or peanut oil
Sea salt

Using a sharp knife, slice the potatoes into discs 3 mm (1/8 in) thick • Heat the oil in a wide heavy-based saucepan to 120°C (250°F), add the potato slices and continuously swirl the oil to stop the potatoes from crisping. We need the steam within the potatoes to puff them up. As soon as the potatoes show signs of puffing, remove from the oil with a slotted spoon. Drain on paper towel • Reheat the oil to 180°C (350°F), add the potato slices and carefully stir the oil to cause the potatoes to rise to the surface. Fry the slices for 2 minutes or until golden. Season with salt and serve immediately.

Kipfler potatoes filled with snails

[serves 6 as a light entrée]

THIS DISH MAKES a good accompaniment to roast beef or salmon.

18 small rounded kipfler potatoes, washed
*50 g (1 3/4 oz) goose fat**
Sea salt
36 marinated cooked snails (see page 393)*
Peas à la Française (see page 141)
1/2 bunch of chervil

Slice the bottoms off the potatoes to create a sturdy base, cut the top one-fifth off the potatoes to create a flat top. Scoop out a couple of teaspoonfuls from each potato • Place the potatoes in a saucepan of boiling salted water, cook for 15 minutes or until soft. Drain and dry well • Heat the goose fat in a heavy-based frying pan over low to medium heat, add the potatoes and gently cook for 15 minutes or until golden and crisp. Drain and season with the salt • Add the snails and peas and gently warm through. Place two snails and a spoonful of the peas in the cavity of each potato, garnish with a sprig of chervil and serve.

Pommes Pont Neuf

[serves 6]

THE NAME IS SAID to come from the Pont Neuf over the river Seine in Paris because small stands selling French fries sprang up around the capital, the most famous being on the Pont Neuf.

6 large sebago potatoes, peeled
8 cups olive oil
2 tablespoons sea salt

Chop the potatoes into large rectangular chips, about six per potato. Wash under cold running water to remove excess starch • Bring a large saucepan of salted water to the boil, add the chips and cook for 2 minutes or until just soft • Transfer to a tray and freeze for 30 minutes. This stops the chips from breaking up in the deep-fryer • Heat the oil to 180°C (350°F) in a deep-fryer. Drop in the chips and cook for 8–10 minutes. Remove from the oil, let the temperature return to 180°C (350°F) • Drop in the chips and cook for 5 minutes or until golden and crispy. Season with salt and serve.

Potato confit

[serves 4]

THERE IS A CERTAIN amount of difficulty involved with the following recipe but the end result is a garnish that looks great.

2 large desirée potatoes
*2 cups goose fat**
Salt

Preheat a griddle pan over high heat • Using a thin-bladed paring knife, shape each potato into a barrel. Cut the barrels into 1.5-cm (½-in) discs. Rub the discs in 1 tablespoon of warmed goose fat • Place in the griddle pan for 1–2 minutes and turn to form a crisscross pattern. Repeat on the opposite side • Heat the remaining goose fat in a saucepan, add the discs and cook over low heat for 15 minutes. Remove and drain on paper towel • Season with salt. Serve warm or reheat in a 180°C (350°F) oven for 5 minutes.

Pommes Dauphine

[serves 6]

I WAS ALWAYS UNDER the impression that Dauphine was a style named after a queen. The truth is Dauphine is a region covering Savoy to Provence. The wide range and diverse cuisine means just about every ingredient used in French cookery can be called à la Dauphine. These particular croquettes are great as a snack or served with roast meats.

3 large sebago potatoes, washed
Pinch of sea salt
4 cups olive oil
4 sprigs of thyme
50 g (1¾ oz) lean bacon, rind and excess fat removed, finely diced
500 g (1 lb) choux pastry (see page 62)*
2 tablespoons finely chopped curly-leaf parsley
2 shallots, finely chopped
Salt and freshly ground pepper

Preheat the oven to 180°C (350°F) • Season the potatoes with the salt, sprinkle over 2½ tablespoons of the olive oil, add the thyme and wrap in aluminium (aluminum) foil. Bake in the oven for 1 hour or until cooked • Heat 1 tablespoon of the oil in a heavy-based frying pan, add the bacon and cook over medium heat for 2 minutes or until crisp. Drain well on paper towel • Remove the potatoes from their skins while hot • In a large mixing bowl, combine the potatoes and choux pastry, whisking to form a purée • Add the parsley, shallots and bacon. Season well • Heat the remaining oil in a deep-fryer to 180°C (350°F) • Spoon quenelles of the potato mixture into the oil. Cook for 3–4 minutes or until golden and crispy. Season well and serve immediately.

Pommes mille-feuille

[serves 4]

The crucial element to the success of this recipe is, in fact, your local purveyor of kitchen equipment: without non-stick dariole moulds the dish will prove too difficult to produce consistently.

4 large sebago potatoes
250 g (8 oz) butter
½ bunch of thyme
Salt and freshly ground pepper

Preheat the oven to 180°C (350°F) • Place four non-stick dariole moulds in the freezer • With a sharp serrated bread knife, shape the potatoes into a cone resembling the size of the dariole mould • Remove the dariole moulds from the freezer and grease with a generous amount of butter. Place a sprig of thyme in the bottom of each mould • Using a mandoline, thinly slice the potato cones starting from the thinnest end • Place three layers of potato, starting with the thinnest part, in each mould. Every third layer, add another sprig of thyme and a little salt and pepper. As the final layers are placed in the mould, the potato will start to protrude over the top. Cover with more butter, then wrap the open end of the mould with aluminium (aluminum) foil • Transfer to a baking tray and bake in the oven for 25 minutes. Remove the foil, increase the temperature to 200°C (400°F) and bake for 10 minutes or until golden. Unmould and serve.

Pommes à la boulangere

[serves 4]

There are many versions of this recipe and I have found different uses for different recipes. The following version is designed to complement fish dishes.

2 large desiree potatoes
Salt
1 tablespoon finely chopped shallots
1 teaspoon finely chopped tarragon
2 tablespoons fish stock (see page 243)

Using a thin-bladed paring knife, shape each potato into a barrel 4 cm ($1\frac{1}{2}$ in) wide. Cut each barrel into 3-mm ($\frac{1}{8}$-in) thick discs. Season with salt • Combine the potato with the shallots, tarragon and fish stock • Arrange the discs in fanned circles on greaseproof paper-lined plates. Complete two layers on each plate. Cover with plastic wrap and microwave on high for 2 minutes, rest for 30–60 seconds, and cook on high for a further 2 minutes. Alternatively, steam over high heat for 8 minutes. Serve.

Pommes mousseline

[serves 6]

Marco Pierre White's head chef Robert Reid showed me this technique.

3 large sebago potatoes
250 g (8 oz) butter, chopped into fine dice
2 tablespoons warm milk
2 tablespoons sea salt

Cook the potatoes for 25 minutes in boiling salted water. Test with a knife, if it slides in without resistance, they are cooked. Immediately mash with 90 g (3 oz) of the butter. Mix any visible butter into the purée with a wooden spoon • Place the purée in a saucepan, add 1 tablespoon of the milk and whisk on a low heat for 3–4 minutes • Add the remaining butter, a quarter at a time, whisking rapidly. If the butter starts to separate, the purée is too hot. Remove from the heat, beat in 1 tablespoon of milk and whisk like mad to bring it together. When all the butter is incorporated, check the seasoning, add salt if necessary, and serve.

Pommes sauté

[serves 4]

Sautéed potatoes are a great accompaniment to duck leg confit, are easy to prepare and, best of all, taste great.

6 kipfler or ratte potatoes, washed
2 tablespoons olive oil
*1 tablespoon foie gras fat**
1 clove of garlic, crushed
Salt and freshly ground pepper
1 teaspoon roughly chopped curly-leaf parsley

Boil the potatoes in salted water for 10 minutes or until just tender. Drain and leave to cool. Peel and cut into 5-mm (1/4-in) slices • Heat the olive oil and foie gras fat in a heavy-based frying pan over medium heat, add the potatoes and garlic and season with the salt and pepper. Cook for 3–4 minutes or until golden. Drain on paper towel, add the parsley and serve.

Pommes beaucaire

[serves 4]

I love to serve these simple yet extravagant patties with fillet steak and a good hearty red wine sauce or with battered fish and tartare sauce.

6 kipfler or ratte potatoes, washed
2 egg yolks
Pinch of ground nutmeg
Salt and freshly ground pepper
*2 tablespoons goose fat**

Boil the potatoes in salted water for 10 minutes or until just tender. Drain and set aside to cool • Peel the potatoes and crush finely using a hand masher • Transfer to a mixing bowl and add the egg yolks, nutmeg and salt and pepper. Shape the potato mixture into 5-cm (2-in) balls and flatten into 2.5-cm (1-in) patties • Heat the goose fat in a heavy-based frying pan, add the patties and cook, in batches of four, for 3 minutes or until golden. Turn and cook for 3 minutes. Drain on paper towel, season with salt and serve.

Pommes sauté

Pommes beaucaire

Pommes gaufrette

Pommes paille

Pommes gaufrette

[serves 4]

These potatoes can be prepared a few hours in advance and simply rewarmed in a 180°C (350°F) oven.

8 cups canola oil
2 large sebago potatoes, peeled
Sea salt

Heat the canola oil in a deep-fryer to 180°C (350°F) • Using the fluted blade on a mandoline, cut lattice-style slices by turning the potato 180 degrees after every slice • Soak the latticed potatoes in water for 1 minute to remove excess starch. Drain well • Cook the potatoes, in two batches, in the deep-fryer for 2 minutes or until golden. Drain well on paper towel, season with salt and serve.

Pommes paille

[serves 4]

These potato straws may be prepared a few hours in advance and reheated in a 180°C (350°F) oven.

8 cups canola oil
2 large sebago potatoes, peeled
Sea salt

Heat the canola oil in a deep-fryer to 180°C (350°F) • Chop the potatoes into batons 3 mm x 6 cm (1/8 x 2 1/2 in) and soak in cold water for 2–3 minutes to remove excess starch • Cook the potatoes, in two batches, in the deep-fryer for 1–2 minutes or until crisp and golden. Drain on paper towel, season with salt and serve.

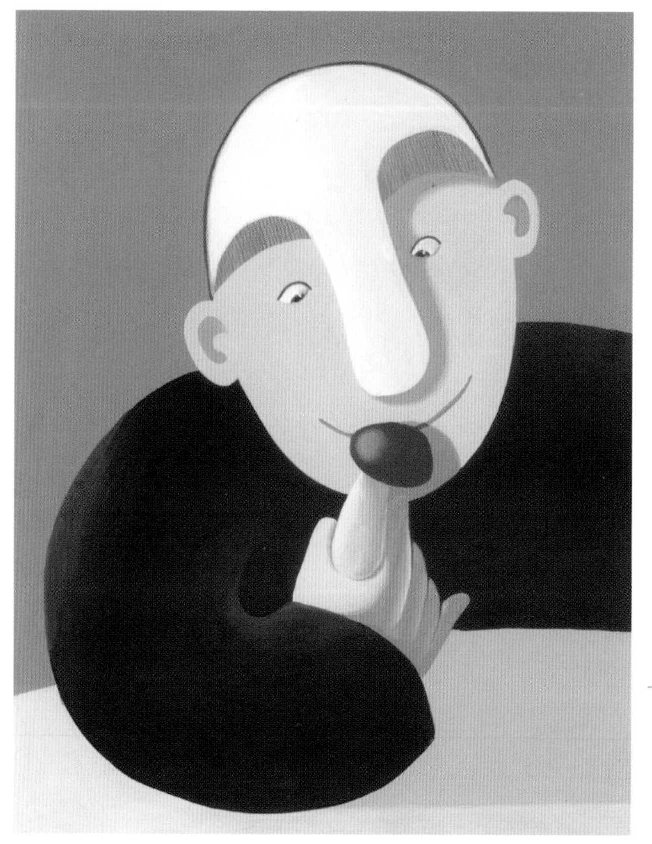

The Mushroom

AT THE LAST COUNT the varieties of edible mushroom lurking in fields and near pine trees around the world numbered over 2000. Favourite cultivated varieties of mine are the common field mushroom, Swiss brown, baby button and shiitake. Girolles, chanterelles, morels (*Morchella elata*), slippery jacks (*Boletus luteus*), pines, truffles and cèpes (*Boletus edulis*) are wild mushrooms that cannot be successfully cultivated, and as a result are much more expensive. All mushrooms are rich in iron, minerals and vitamin B12.

I have found no other fungi to compare with the Swiss brown or Paris, known for its charcoal brown cap and distinct smoky aftertaste, and the king of all mushrooms, the cèpe, with its delicate earthy creaminess. I hear you ask, what about the morel? It is hard to find in the wild, but is readily found on menus all around the world. The dried version is available but it can be very hard to get rid of all the grit, despite soaking and washing the morels.

The easiest way to ensure a mushroom supply is to have on hand dried wild mushrooms stored in an airtight container. Keep a stock of mixed mushrooms, cèpes and morels in your pantry. Porcini are basically the same as cèpes, except the cèpes have a more subtle creaminess.

Many speciality stores around the world now stock different varieties of frozen fresh wild mushrooms. They are not cheap, but the concentrated flavour derived from one wild mushroom is 3–4 times stronger than that of the cultivated variety. I find cèpes and chanterelles the best. They are a great option for those impulsive cooking moments when you decide you need a wild mushroom fricassee to accompany a fillet of John Dory.

Australia is vastly underrated when it comes to our wild harvested mushrooms. My two favourites that I always look out for when taking a stroll through a field or forest are slippery jacks and pine mushrooms. The flavour is not as definite as a morel or cèpe, but they do hold their shape and retain a wonderful amount of moisture. Simply fry in olive oil with crushed garlic, chopped parsley, freshly cracked pepper and a pinch of sea salt. A squeeze of lemon juice is brilliant for bringing out the flavour of mushrooms.

Mushroom stock

[makes 8 cups]

THE BEST MUSHROOMS to use in this versatile stock, which makes a great base for any broth or clear soup, are the button mushrooms that have been left in the fridge for a week. They are more concentrated in flavour; giving a darker colour and better yield. Do not let mushroom trimmings or peelings go to waste; they will enhance the flavour of the stock.

1 kg (2 lb) button or wild Paris mushrooms, thinly sliced

*350 ml (12 fl oz) Madeira**

350 ml (12 fl oz) dry white wine

2 shallots, peeled and sliced

5 cloves of garlic

5 sprigs of thyme

1 bay leaf

5 peppercorns

4 cups chicken stock (see page 378)

Combine all of the ingredients in a stockpot and bring to the boil. Cook rapidly for 1 hour • Taste the stock. If satisfied the mushrooms have imparted enough flavour and colour, remove from the heat and strain • Pour the stock back into the stockpot and reduce by one-third. The stock can be stored in the freezer for future use.

Mushroom sauce

A FEW POINTS TO remember with this sauce: don't add the cream until the last minute — the idea of the whipped cream is to give a light fluffy finish to the sauce — and make sure the sauce is reduced enough, if it isn't, the intensity of your lovely stock will be lost and you will blame me!

200 g (6½ oz) dried cèpes
10 sprigs of tarragon
300 ml (10 fl oz) mushroom stock (see page 109)
100 g (3½ oz) double cream
Salt and freshly ground pepper
Juice of ½ lemon

To make the cèpe powder, place the dried cèpes on a greasproof paper-lined baking tray. Set aside in a dry place for 24 hours until dry and brittle • Use a coffee grinder or mortar and pestle and blitz to a fine powder • Blanch the tarragon in boiling salted water, then refresh in iced water. Allow the tarragon to cool, squeeze out excess moisture by wringing in a tea towel and finely chop • Pour the mushroom stock into a heavy-based saucepan, simmer over medium heat until reduced by two-thirds • Whip the cream to ribbon stage. To test that it has been whipped to the correct consistency, take a spoon and create a figure 8 in the top of the cream, the figure should hold momentarily. If the cream is over-whipped the figure 8 will not disappear; try thinning it with 3 tablespoons of milk • Whisk the cream into the stock until fully incorporated. Bring to the boil and add the tarragon. Remove from the heat, season with salt, pepper and lemon juice and serve immediately.

Wild mushroom purée

[makes 10 quenelles]

I USE THIS VERY adaptable recipe to accompany everything from salads to roast meat. To serve, simply rewarm over a gentle heat. The best form of presentation is to quenelle the mushroom purée onto a plate using two spoons that have been dipped into hot water. My favourite adaptation is to use only cèpes, expensive, I know, but if you practise and perfect this with button mushrooms, then give it a go with cèpes. You will not look back.

1 tablespoon olive oil
1 onion, finely diced
2 cloves of garlic, crushed
200 g (6½ oz) button mushrooms, thinly sliced
100 g (3½ oz) frozen cèpes
200 ml (7 fl oz) mushroom stock *(see page 109)*
Juice of ½ lemon
Salt and freshly ground pepper

Heat the olive oil in a heavy-based saucepan, add the onion and garlic and cook over medium heat for 6 minutes or until soft and transparent • Add the mushrooms and cook, stirring ocassionally with a wooden spoon, for 5 minutes • Add the mushroom stock, a squeeze of lemon juice and salt and pepper. Increase the heat to high, bring to the boil and cook for 2 minutes. Immediately remove from the heat and transfer to a food processor. Blend to a fine purée • Season and add more lemon juice, if necessary. Serve.

Wild mushroom fricassee

[serves 4]

Wild mushrooms show their versatility during the winter months. This recipe can be made in any season, using any type of mushroom you like! For a smart serving suggestion, place the duxelles (finely chopped mushrooms, shallots and herbs cooked in butter) into a ring mould and top with seasonal salad leaves dressed with chopped shallots, garlic croutons and French dressing combined with crispy snails in tempura batter.

*5 g (¼ oz) dried morels**
80 ml (2¾ fl oz) double cream
1 tablespoon olive oil
100 g (3½ oz) button mushrooms, chopped into quarters
50 g (1¾ oz) frozen cèpes, roughly chopped
50 g (1¾ oz) Swiss brown mushrooms, chopped into quarters
*2 tablespoons goose fat**
1 onion, finely diced
2 cloves of garlic, crushed
200 ml (7 fl oz) mushroom stock (see page 109)
Salt and freshly ground pepper
Juice of ½ lemon
3 cups baby spinach
2 tablespoons finely chopped curly-leaf parsley
8 sprigs of watercress

Soak the morels in hot water for 10 minutes • Whip the cream to ribbon stage. To test that it has been whipped to the correct consistency, take a spoon and create a figure 8 in the top of the cream, the figure should hold momentarily. If the cream is over-whipped the figure 8 will not disappear; try thinning it with a tablespoon or two of milk • Heat the olive oil in a frying pan, add the mushrooms and cook over medium heat for 3 minutes or until the mushrooms are tender, but still holding their original shape. Transfer to a colander to drain • In the same pan, reduce the heat to low. Add the goose fat, onion and garlic and cook for 3 minutes or until transparent and tender • Return the mushrooms to the pan, and increase the heat to medium and cook for 2 minutes • Add the mushroom stock, salt and pepper and a squeeze of lemon juice. Simmer rapidly until reduced by two-thirds • When the fricassee just starts to catch on the bottom of the pan, spoon in the cream • Toss through the baby spinach and parsley and garnish with the watercress. Serve immediately.

Mushroom risotto

[serves 8 as a light main course]

Be patient when making risotto, and have a small amount of hot stock reserved to fold through the risotto when serving. The acid butter is stirred into all types of risotto for the lift in flavour it gives to the rice.

A New World dry-style riesling with a little age cuts through the richness of this dish, good examples are Grosset or Pikes from the Clare Valley in South Australia.

$2\frac{1}{2}$ tablespoons olive oil
1 medium onion, finely diced
250 g (8 oz) Arborio rice
350 ml (12 fl oz) dry white wine
1 cup chicken stock (see page 378)

ACID BUTTER

2 tablespoons Champagne vinegar
$\frac{1}{3}$ cup white wine
1 small onion, sliced
5 sprigs of thyme
1 bay leaf
500 g (1 lb) cultured butter, chopped into fine dice*

300 ml (10 fl oz) mushroom stock (see page 109)
50 g ($1\frac{3}{4}$ oz) frozen cèpes, sliced
60 g (2 oz) Grana Padano Parmesan cheese, grated
Salt and freshly ground pepper
$\frac{1}{2}$ tablespoon chopped tarragon

Heat the olive oil in a heavy-based saucepan, add the onion and cook over low heat for 3 minutes or until soft, but not coloured. Add the rice stirring until each grain is coated with oil • Increase the heat to medium, add the wine and deglaze, stirring well. Cook until the wine has evaporated, stirring with a wooden spoon to prevent sticking • Add the chicken stock and cook, stirring occasionally, for 5 minutes or until the stock is absorbed • Lay the rice out on a tray, cover with plastic wrap and refrigerate to set. (I find when the rice is precooked a more consistent product is achieved, especially when under pressure, which may occur during an occasion such as a dinner party. When precooking the rice the finishing process will take only 5 minutes. The rice will last for 3–4 days in the fridge.) • To make the acid butter, combine the vinegar, white wine, onion, thyme and bay leaf in a saucepan and reduce by four-fifths. Only a small amount of liquid should remain in the pan. Gradually whisk in the butter to form a beurre blanc-style butter sauce • Pass through a fine sieve into an airtight container and place in the refrigerator to set until firm, about $1\frac{1}{2}$ hours. The butter lasts for up to 30 days in the fridge • In a small heavy-based saucepan, bring the mushroom stock to the boil, then reduce heat to low • Place the semi-cooked rice in a medium heavy-based saucepan; add enough hot mushroom stock to just cover the rice. Add the cèpes and simmer over medium heat until the rice has absorbed all the stock, occasionally stirring with a wooden spoon. Remove from the heat • Add the acid butter and a good pinch of Parmesan; and gently fold through the risotto. If the risotto appears a little firm, add more stock to loosen the texture • Season with salt and pepper and add the tarragon. Serve immediately.

Potato ravioli with mushroom essence

[serves 8 as an entrée]

JOHN BURTON RACE showed me how to make this dish; I'm indebted to him forever as it has been a major drawcard for loyal vegetarian diners. The whipped cream is added to give the sauce a lovely light, fluffy texture and to complement the mushroom flavour. I know you will enjoy reproducing this.

PASTA DOUGH

10 egg yolks

*250 g (8 oz) Italian 00 flour**

6 large desiree potatoes, peeled

*100 g (3½ oz) cultured butter**

*2½ tablespoons white truffle oil**

Sea salt

1 leek heart, thinly sliced

100 g (3½ oz) fresh peas

2 tablespoons olive oil

To make the pasta dough, combine the egg yolks and flour in a large mixing bowl. Using an electric mixer with a dough hook attachment, mix until a firm dough forms. Wrap the dough in plastic wrap and rest in the refrigerator for 30 minutes • Boil four of the potatoes in salted water for 30 minutes or until cooked. Pass the potatoes through a mouli with the butter and truffle oil, season and rest in a warm place for 10 minutes • Chop the two remaining potatoes into 8-cm (3-in) cubes and boil in salted water for 4 minutes or until just cooked • Lay the potato cubes out on a non-stick baking tray. Pipe the potato purée into cone shapes on top of each potato cube. Set in the refrigerator

½ tablespoon chopped tarragon
300 ml (10 fl oz) double cream
200 ml (7 fl oz) mushroom stock (see page 109)
8 large frozen cèpes, halved lengthwise

for 20 minutes or until firm • Roll out the pasta dough to the second thinnest setting on the pasta machine. Cut the pasta into 10 x 15-cm (4 x 6-in) rectangles for the ravioli top and 5 x 5-cm (2 x 2-in) squares for the ravioli base • Place a ravioli base under each cube of potato then take the ravioli top and wrap around the cone-shaped dome, pressing down around the edges to seal. Trim around the ravioli with a sharp knife to create a square • Cook the leek and peas in boiling salted water for 2 minutes. Drain and toss in 1 tablespoon of the olive oil. Season with a pinch of salt, add the tarragon, and place in the centre of each warmed serving plate • Whip the cream to ribbon stage. To test that it has been whipped to the correct consistency, take a spoon and create a figure 8 in the top of the cream. The figure should hold momentarily. If the cream is over-whipped the figure 8 will not disappear; try thinning it with 2 tablespoons of milk • Combine the mushroom stock and cèpes, and cook over medium heat for 5 minutes or until thickened and reduced to ½ cup • In a large saucepan, cook the ravioli in salted water just under boiling point for 5 minutes. Drain, drizzle over a little olive oil and add a pinch of salt. Arrange the ravioli on top of the leek and peas • Remove the cèpes and arrange on the plate next to the ravioli. Return the sauce to the heat. Whisk in the cream; season and spoon over the ravioli and serve.

Mushroom stock

Mushroom sauce

Wild mushroom purée

Wild mushroom fricassee

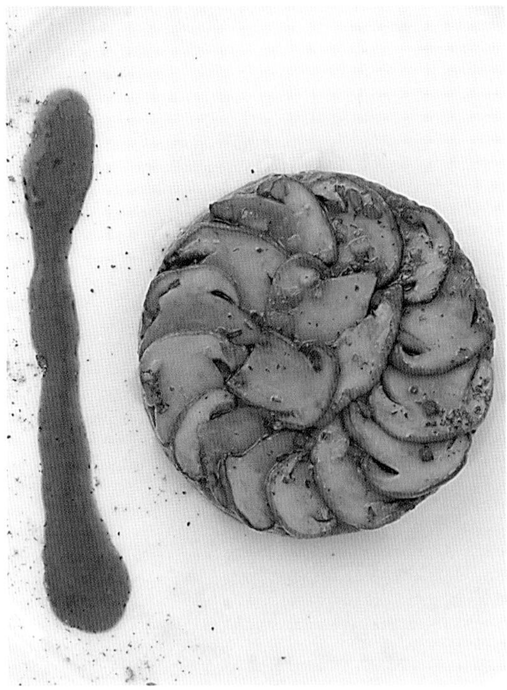

Mushroom risotto

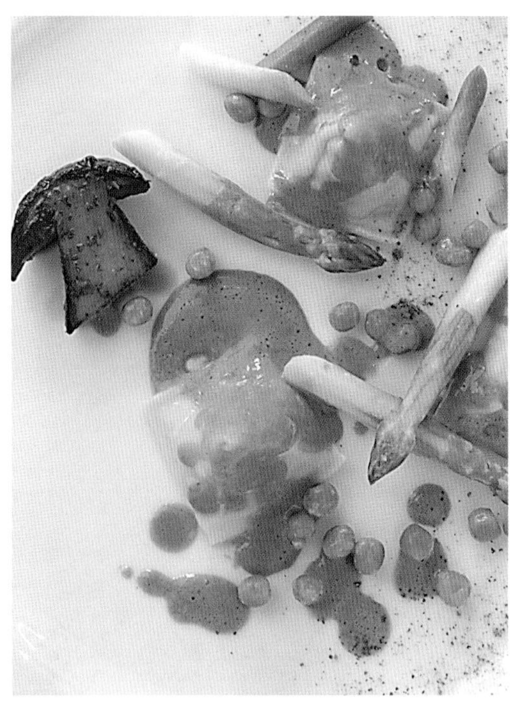

Potato ravioli with mushroom essence

Morels stuffed with chicken and tarragon mousse

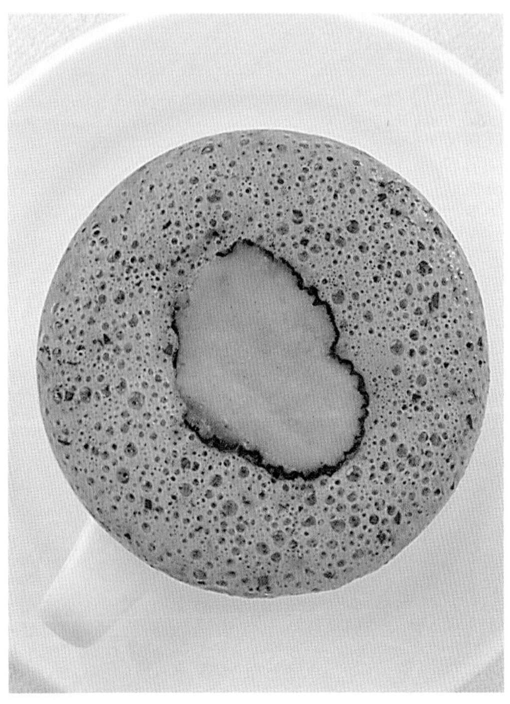

Cappuccino of mushroom

Morels stuffed with chicken and tarragon mousse

[serves 4]

On the rare occasion when you may find fresh morels, you will need a recipe that will do them justice. I have simplified a dish I serve at Vue de monde to enable you to reproduce it at home. Just make sure the morels are thoroughly washed.

*16 large fresh morels**
16 large thick asparagus spears, trimmed
1 bunch of tarragon

CHICKEN MOUSSE

200 g (6½ oz) chicken breast fillet
1 teaspoon salt
2 eggs
2 egg yolks
150 ml (5 fl oz) thickened cream
*20 g (¾ oz) goose fat**
*100 g (3½ oz) cultured butter**
4 shallots, finely chopped
2 cloves of garlic, crushed
100 ml (3½ fl oz) white wine
12 sprigs of chervil

Place the bowl, blade and lid of the food processor in the freezer • Using a sharp knife, trim the stems of the morels until a hollow opening is revealed. Wash the morels in cold water 4–5 times or until the water runs clear • Place the morels on a cake rack resting on a tray and set aside to dry for 30 minutes • Cut the asparagus spears into 5-cm (2-in) lengths • Blanch the tarragon in boiling salted water to preserve its intense green colour. Refresh in ice-cold water, squeeze out excess water in a tea towel and chop finely • To make the chicken mousse, chop the chicken breast into four. Remove the bowl, blade and lid of the food processor from the freezer. Add the chicken breast and salt and process, being careful to keep the bowl cold • Incorporate the eggs and egg yolks, one at a time, while the motor is running. Using a rubber spatula, scrape around the sides of the bowl • Add the cream, but do not overwork the mix. Transfer to a cold bowl and fold in the tarragon. Place in the refrigerator for 30 minutes • Spoon the minced (ground) chicken into a piping bag with a medium plain nozzle attached. Pipe into the hollow opening in the stem of each morel. This may be done a day in advance • Set a steamer basket over a saucepan of boiling water • Place the morels and asparagus in the steamer. Steam for 5 minutes or until the morels are cooked. If the morels are cooked, the mousse will start to squeeze out of the opening in the stem • Melt the goose fat and butter in a heavy-based saucepan, add the shallots and garlic and cook over medium heat for 3 minutes or until the butter turns brown • Deglaze with the white wine. Add the asparagus and morels and toss to combine. Season, garnish with the chervil and serve.

Cappuccino of Mushroom

[serves 10]

Do not be put off by the extravagant use of cream in this recipe. The soup is in fact light and fluffy and relies on the use of the cappuccino froth and whipped cream to transform the intensely reduced stock into a delicious winter soup.

2 cups milk
1 tablespoon olive oil
1 onion, finely diced
1 clove of garlic
50 g ($1\frac{3}{4}$ oz) wild mushrooms, finely chopped
Salt and freshly ground pepper
$\frac{1}{4}$ teaspoon finely chopped tarragon
600 ml (1 pt) mushroom stock (see page 109)
1 cup double cream
Juice of $\frac{1}{2}$ lemon
*10 slices black winter truffle**
2 teaspoons truffle oil, optional*

Heat the milk in a saucepan until almost boiling. Froth up using a hand blender. Rest for a few minutes to enable the froth to rise to the top • Heat the olive oil in a frying pan, add the onion, garlic and mushrooms, season with salt and pepper, and cook over medium heat for 6 minutes or until tender. Stir in the tarragon and transfer to warmed serving bowls • Put the mushroom stock in a saucepan, bring to the boil and cook until reduced by two-thirds • Whisk the cream to ribbon stage. To test for correct consistency, draw a figure 8 in the top of the cream, the figure 8 should hold momentarily. If the cream is over-whipped the figure 8 will not disappear; try thinning with 2 tablespoons of milk • Whisk the cream into the stock and bring to the boil. Remove from the heat and fold in the milk froth. Season with lemon juice, salt and pepper. Pour over the mushrooms • Top with a slice of truffle and drizzle over a dash of truffle oil. Serve with warmed sourdough bread.

Mushroom and truffle broth baked in puff pastry

[serves 4]

This recipe started out as a way to use accumulated leftover truffles. It's easy to put together and can be stored in the freezer.

*2 tablespoons goose fat**
1 onion, thinly sliced
2 cloves of garlic, crushed
300 ml (10 fl oz) mushroom stock (see page 109)
300 ml (10 fl oz) double chicken stock (see page 381)
*1 tablespoon truffle paste**
Salt and freshly ground pepper
*2 teaspoons white truffle oil**
250 g (8 oz) puff pastry (see page 54)
1 egg, lightly beaten
*100 ml ($3\frac{1}{2}$ fl oz) egg wash**

Heat the goose fat in a heavy-based saucepan, add the onion and garlic and caramelise over medium heat for 10 minutes or until golden brown • In a medium saucepan, bring the mushroom stock and chicken stock to the boil. Stir in the truffle paste and season with salt, pepper and a little truffle oil • Divide the caramelised onion between four soup bowls or large coffee cups. Pour in the soup, so that each bowl is three-quarters full. Transfer the bowls to the refrigerator for 30 minutes • Lightly flour a clean work surface and roll out the puff pastry until 6 mm ($\frac{1}{4}$ in) thick. Cut out four round discs, one and half times the diameter of the bowls being used • Brush the egg over each pastry disc. Place a disc, egg washed-side down, on the top of each bowl. The egg wash acts as an adhesive. Firmly press the pastry around the side of the bowl. Gently egg wash the top • Preheat the oven to 180°C (350°F) • Using a lattice cutter, cut the remaining puff pastry into lattice. Place the lattice over the top of the egg washed pastry. Trim any overhanging pastry. For those of you without a lattice cutter, place the egg washed bowl in the fridge for 30 minutes to dry out. Using a blunt knife, carefully create a crisscross pattern in the pastry • Place the pastry-covered bowls in the oven and bake for 15 minutes or until the pastry is golden. Serve.

DUCK EGG OMELETTES FILLED WITH ASPARAGUS PURÉE AND SLIPPERY JACK MUSHROOMS

[serves 4]

THE SLIPPERY JACK (or *pine bolete*) is only available during the autumn months. It has a glutinous coating that is washed off under cold running water. I like its mild subtle flavour and firm texture. The European pied bleu or the cultivated Swiss brown are good substitutes.

1 bunch of asparagus
1½ tablespoons olive oil
1 onion, finely diced
1 cup baby spinach
Salt and freshly ground pepper
100 ml (3½ fl oz) chicken stock (see page 378)
*200 g (6½ oz) slippery jacks**
*1 tablespoon goose fat**
1 clove of garlic, crushed
1 shallot, finely chopped
1 tablespoon finely chopped curly-leaf parsley
Juice of ½ lemon
1 tablespoon butter
6 duck eggs, lightly beaten*

Snap the asparagus spears, discarding the woody ends, and slice as thinly as possible • Heat the olive oil in a heavy-based saucepan, add the onion and cook over high heat for 8 minutes, stirring constantly with a wooden spoon. Do not allow the onion to colour. Add the asparagus and cook for 10 minutes or until tender. Add the spinach and season with salt and pepper • Bring the chicken stock to the boil in a small saucepan • Transfer the sautéed onion, asparagus and spinach to a food processor and blend until smooth. You may need to add 2–3 tablespoons of chicken stock to help the asparagus purée smoothly. Taste and season • Wash the slippery jacks several times under cold running water and pat dry • Heat the goose fat in a heavy-based frying pan, add the mushrooms and cook over high heat for 2–3 minutes, stirring constantly. Add the garlic and shallot and cook for 30 seconds. Add the parsley, season with salt, pepper and a squeeze of lemon juice • Divide equally among warmed serving plates • Gently warm the asparagus purée in a saucepan • To make the omelettes, melt 1 teaspoon of the butter in a non-stick frying pan over medium heat, add a quarter of the beaten duck eggs and cook for 2 minutes, stirring constantly with a wooden spoon, to prevent the omelette colouring • When the egg begins to set, use the wooden spoon to shape the omelette into a round. Remove from the heat and allow the residual heat to finish the cooking process. The omelette should be still soft and slightly runny on top. Season with a little salt • Spoon a quarter of the hot asparagus purée into the centre of the omelette • Tip the pan on an angle and, with the help of the wooden spoon, fold the omelette into a cigar shape. Tip onto a warmed serving plate and cover with aluminium (aluminum) foil to keep warm • Repeat three more times • Serve with a seasonal salad and pommes sauté (see page 103).

Roast veal fillet with garlic, sage and pine mushroom sauce

[serves 4]

Australia's best source of veal is in Western Australia. 'White Rocks' is a farm 160 kilometres (100 miles) south of Perth. It has been a farm for over 100 years and has been in the Partridge family since it was established in 1887.

Leaves of ½ bunch of sage
8 cloves of garlic
Salt and freshly ground pepper
1 kg (2 lb) veal fillet, trimmed of sinew and fat
*8 thin slices of flat pancetta**
16 cups water
4 large silver beet (Swiss chard) leaves

SAUCE

100 ml (3½ fl oz) double cream
1½ tablespoons olive oil

Preheat the oven to 200°C (400°F) • Blanch the sage in boiling salted water, refresh in iced water and squeeze out excess water • Place the garlic cloves in a saucepan of salted water, bring to the boil and blanch for 1 minute. Repeat four times. Peel, the garlic skin will easily slide away after blanching • Combine the sage and garlic in a bowl and season with salt and pepper, trying not to break up the garlic • Place the veal fillet on a chopping board. Take a clean sharpening steel and insert the steel horizontally through sections of the veal to form divots in the meat. Try to imagine the portion size of each slice of veal and make 2–3 divots in each slice • Push the sage and garlic

2 cloves of garlic, crushed

2 shallots, finely diced

100 g ($3\frac{1}{2}$ oz) fresh pine mushrooms, finely chopped

200 ml (7 fl oz) mushroom stock (see page 109)

Juice of ½ lemon

4 pommes beaucaire (see page 103)

⅓ bunch of watercress

into each divot. Tie with butcher's twine. Season well with salt and pepper • Wrap the pancetta slices around the fillet • Combine the water and salt in a large saucepan and bring to the boil • Separate the silver beet leaves from the stem. Cook the leaves in the boiling salted water for 2 minutes. Refresh in iced water. After 4 minutes remove and pat dry • Wrap the silver beet around the pancetta and veal. Tie with butcher's twine at 3-cm ($1\frac{1}{4}$-in) intervals. Season with salt and pepper • Place the veal in a steamer (a homemade steamer is easy to assemble from a fish kettle or a Chinese steamer basket) over a saucepan of boiling water, cover, and steam for 10 minutes. Turn, cover, and steam for a further 5 minutes • Wrap the veal in plastic wrap and rest for 10 minutes in a warm place • For the sauce, whip the cream to ribbon stage. To test if it has been whipped to the correct consistency, take a spoon and create a figure 8 in the top of the cream, the figure should hold momentarily. If the cream is over-whipped add 2 tablespoons of milk • Heat the olive oil in a heavy-based saucepan, add the garlic and shallots and cook over medium heat for 3 minutes or until the shallots are soft and transparent. Add the mushrooms and continue to cook for 3 minutes • Add the mushroom stock, increase heat to high and bring to the boil. Reduce by half. Whisk in the cream, and season with salt, pepper and lemon juice • Remove the butcher's twine from the veal and slice into eight. Place a pommes beaucaire on each warmed serving plate and top with two slices of veal. Drizzle the sauce over and around the veal. Garnish with the watercress and serve.

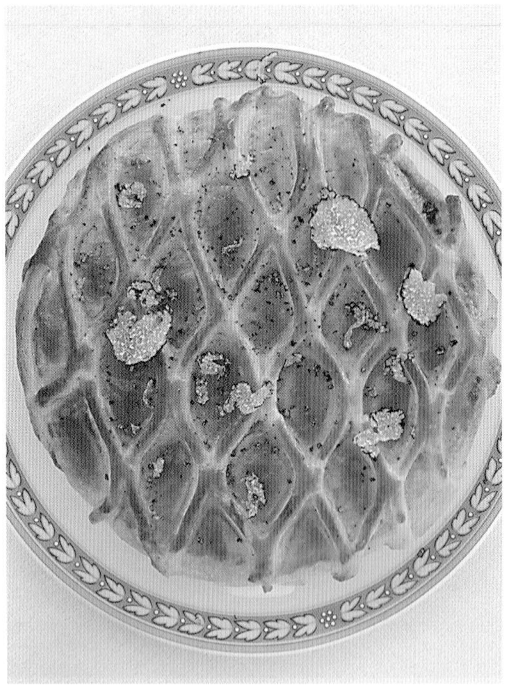

Mushroom and truffle broth baked in puff pastry

Duck egg omelettes filled with asparagus purée and slippery jack mushrooms

Roast veal fillet with garlic, sage and pine mushroom sauce

John Dory fillets with spinach and wild mushroom fricasee

JOHN DORY FILLETS WITH SPINACH AND WILD MUSHROOM FRICASSEE

[serves 4]

JOHN DORY IS the finest quality white-fleshed, line-caught fish available. Roasted, steamed or grilled on the bone is the best way to appreciate it.

*5 g (1/4 oz) dried morels**

2 tablespoons olive oil

100 g (3 1/2 oz) button mushrooms, quartered

50 g (1 3/4 oz) frozen cèpes, roughly chopped

50 g (1 3/4 oz) Swiss brown mushrooms, quartered

*2 tablespoons goose fat**

1 onion, finely chopped

2 cloves of garlic, crushed

3 cups baby spinach

Salt and freshly ground pepper

Juice of 1/2 lemon

80 g (2 3/4 oz) double cream

200 ml (7 fl oz) mushroom stock (see page 109)

2 x 600 g (1 1/4 lb) John Dory fillets, skinned

1/2 tablespoon finely chopped flat-leaf parsley

*1 tablespoon cultured butter**

1 cup watercress

Soak the morels in hot water for 10 minutes • Heat the olive oil in a heavy-based frying pan, add the mushrooms and cook on high heat for 3 minutes or until tender. Place in a colander to drain • In the same pan, reduce the heat to medium and melt the goose fat. Add the onion and garlic and cook for 2 minutes or until tender • Return the mushrooms to the pan and cook until warmed through. Toss through the spinach. Season with salt and pepper and a squeeze of lemon juice • Divide the mushroom fricassee among four warmed serving plates • Whip the cream to ribbon stage. To test the correct consistency, draw a figure 8 in the top of the cream, the figure should hold momentarily. If the cream is over-whipped the 8 will not disappear; try thinning it with 2 tablespoons of milk • Place the mushroom stock in a small heavy-based saucepan and cook over high heat until reduced by half • Place a heavy-based frying pan on high heat, bring to smoking point, and add the seasoned John Dory fillets. Cook for 2 minutes or until crispy and golden. Turn and cook for a further minute. Add the parsley, a squeeze of lemon juice and the butter, and cook for 2–3 minutes or until the butter browns. Transfer to the serving plates and place on the mushrooms • Whisk the cream into the mushroom stock over medium heat; this will take 30 seconds, season and spoon over the John Dory. Garnish with the watercress and serve.

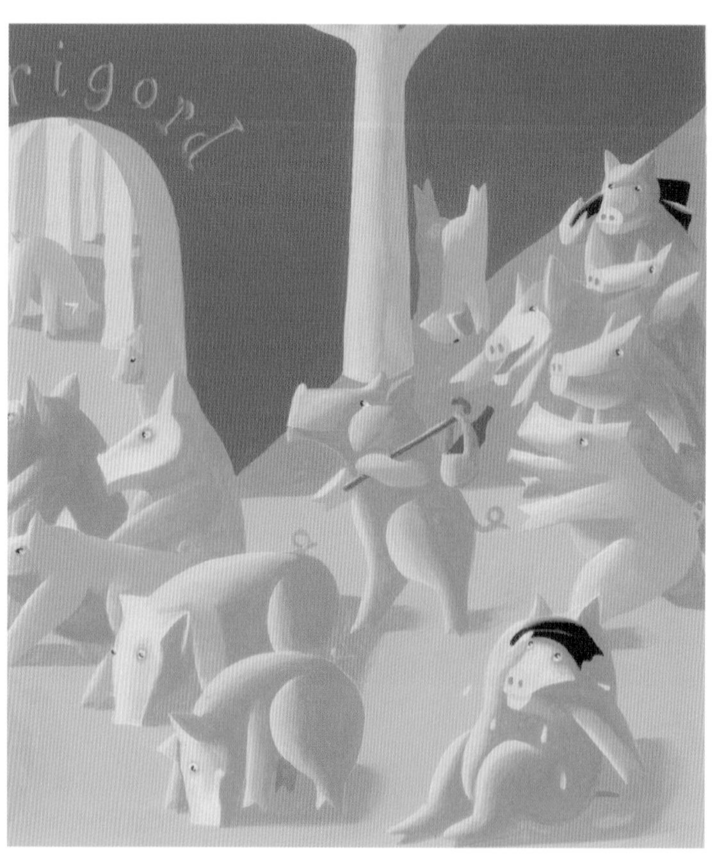
rigord

The Truffle

Truffles are becoming increasingly rare and as a result are reaching astronomical prices. White truffles from Alba, Italy, are twice as expensive as most other white truffles at around $US3000 per 500 g (1 lb). They are at their best from October to late December. Black truffles from Perigord, in south-west France, are priced at a measly $US1800 per 500 g (1 lb) and are available from November to late March. Don't even consider trying a truffle until the New Year.

The truffle family is a subterranean fungus that lives in symbiosis with certain trees, such as the hazelnut, walnut and oak. Truffles first appear in the Northern Hemisphere in April, pale, small and approximately the size of a pinhead. In mid-summer they become red, and humidity causes them to sprout. From mid-November, truffles begin to acquire their characteristic smell reminiscent of musk and laurel. They reach their full ripeness and aroma at the end of December.

In the past pigs acted as truffle hunters; however, dogs have begun to take over: they are harder to train, but easier to handle. The truffle is located, then carefully dug out, scrubbed with a nailbrush, wrapped in damp cloth and stored in an airtight jar for up to one week. They should never be stored in rice, as so many do, it will dry them out.

When eating truffles, remember to keep it simple. The aroma is, to be fair, not comparable with most other ingredients, thus your experience may be spoilt by the use of other overshadowing flavours. Eggs and steamed delicate fish — such as barramundi, turbot, sea bass or cod — green vegetables, rice, pasta, potato, chicken and pheasant are all suitable. Use light sauces, jus or vinaigrettes based on hazelnut or walnut oils and sherry vinegar.

Truffle oil may be used to enhance the flavour of truffles, sauces and mayonnaises. When purchasing, keep in mind that a small bottle will go a long way and that white truffle oil is far superior. I have been asked on many occasions what would be my ten essential items in the pantry; well, white truffle oil would be in there, no doubt. It is a wonderful substitute for the out of season truffle.

White truffles are much more fragrant than the black variety. Found from Alba in the north to Umbria, 100 kilometres (60 miles) north of Rome, locals call the white truffle 'diamante bianco' (white diamond). It is most notably eaten raw by finely slicing over pasta, rice, cheese and white meats. I use it as the final touch to many simple ingredients, such as duck eggs, roasted chicken, steamed whiting or grated zucchini (courgette) tossed in olive oil and seasoned with salt and pepper. It is indispensable in cheese fondues and an absolute must on porcini or cèpe mushroom salads.

Alba is situated on the banks of the Tanaro River. At the centre of Alba, in the old town, is Via Vittorio Emmanuelle. Off-limits to traffic, the street is full of people strolling along past cafés, bars and shops full of cakes and sweets, pasta, meat and cheese, wine, stylish clothing, leather goods, and, of course, during late-autumn and early winter, truffles. Halfway down the street is the entry into the Mercato del Tartufi, the principal truffle market of Italy. At the centre of the market are truffle hunters, along with their slick middlemen and private security, surrounded by tables of truffles of all sizes set out for inspection and sale. You'll see men in expensive tailor-made suits, standing, sniffing and debating on the truffle in question. God, I love Europe!

Black truffle risotto

[serves 10]

This dish is best described as simplicity transformed into perfection. Truffle paste makes a satisfactory substitute for the fresh product. Two tablespoons of authentic truffle paste will suffice as a replacement. Be aware of cheap truffle paste substitutes, most are noticeable by the inclusion of a large amount of mushroom on the ingredients list.

400 ml (13 fl oz) mushroom stock (see page 109)
1 cup chicken stock (see page 378)
1½ tablespoons extra virgin olive oil
1 onion, finely diced
200 g (6½ oz) Arborio rice
100 ml (3½ fl oz) dry white wine
50 g (1¾ oz) black truffle, shaved
50 g (1¾ oz) Grana Padano Parmesan cheese
*50 g (1¾ oz) cultured butter**
Salt and freshly ground pepper
1 cup watercress

Heat the mushroom stock in a heavy-based saucepan over low heat • Heat the chicken stock in a small heavy-based saucepan over low heat • Heat the olive oil in a heavy-based saucepan, add the onion and cook over medium heat for 4 minutes or until softened. Add the rice and cook, stirring, until each grain is coated with oil. Deglaze with the white wine and cook until evaporated • Add the stocks and truffle shavings. Cook until all the stock has been absorbed, stirring constantly to prevent the rice from sticking. If the risotto appears too dry; add a little extra chicken stock to create a looser consistency • Remove from the heat and stir in the Parmesan, butter and salt and pepper • Spoon onto warmed serving plates and garnish with a few sprigs of watercress.

Preserved black truffles

[makes 500 g (1 lb)]

A HIGH-YIELDING SEASON will provide more truffles than can possibly be used. The easiest way to overcome this is also the oldest: the Romans preserved their truffles in a kind of verjuice. My method ensures that this intense jelly can be used in a variety of ways — whisked into sauces and mayonnaises and incorporated into terrines. The preserved truffles have all the characteristics of fresh ones and can be used in any way seen fit.

*2 cups ruby port**
*2 cups Madeira**
100 g (3½ oz) fresh black truffles
4 cups veal stock (see page 294)

Heat the port and Madeira in a heavy-based saucepan, add the truffles and cook over medium heat until reduced by half • Add the veal stock and simmer for 30 minutes or until reduced by half • Pour into hot sterilised jars straight from the dishwasher and cover. Leave for one month before use, and store in the refrigerator after opening. The jelly will last for 1 week after opening.

Black truffle risotto

Preserved black truffles

Scrambled duck eggs with white truffle and asparagus custard

White truffle and haricot blanc soup

White truffle risotto

White truffle ice cream

Scrambled duck eggs with white truffle and asparagus custard

[serves 6]

THE VELVETY SILKY texture of duck eggs is not apparent in hen's eggs. There is a large component of complexity in the method of the following recipe, do not be deterred.

*50 g ($1^{3}/_{4}$ oz) white truffle**
*6 duck eggs**
$2^{1}/_{2}$ tablespoons olive oil
1 onion, finely diced
1 clove of garlic, crushed
200 g ($6^{1}/_{2}$ oz) asparagus, thinly sliced
$^{1}/_{3}$ cup double cream
*1 teaspoon white truffle oil**
Salt and freshly ground pepper

Place the white truffle in a basket with the duck eggs. Let the truffle aroma infuse into the eggs for 48 hours • Heat $1^{1}/_{2}$ tablespoons of the olive oil in a heavy-based saucepan, add the onion and garlic and cook over medium heat until transparent. Add the asparagus, increase heat to high and cook for 8 minutes • Transfer to a food processor and purée • Place the purée in an airtight container in the refrigerator for 30 minutes • Preheat the oven to 180°C (350°F) • Using a small serrated knife, carefully slice off the top quarter of each egg, bearing in mind that duck eggs have a softer shell than hen's eggs • Combine five of the eggs in a mixing bowl and gently whisk until blended, the less agitation and air incorporated into the eggs the smoother the final custard will be • Combine the asparagus purée with the remaining egg and the cream and whisk to form a custard. Season with the truffle oil, salt and pepper • Place the eggshells into an egg carton with the open end facing up. Fill each eggshell half full with the asparagus custard • Place the carton containing the eggshells into a baking tray. Add boiling water to just above the height of the carton. The carton will not collapse, so do not be concerned. Cover with aluminium (aluminum) foil and bake in the oven for 20 minutes • Heat the remaining olive oil in a heavy-based saucepan over medium heat, add the beaten duck eggs, and scramble, keeping the eggs fairly runny. Remove from the heat and continue to stir with a wooden spoon. Grate over some fresh white truffle and season with salt and pepper • Spoon the scrambled egg into each eggshell on top of the custard. Add at least 5–6 thin slices of truffle on top of each egg • Serve each egg in an eggcup or on rock salt.

White truffle and haricot blanc soup

[serves 4]

Please do not season the haricot blanc during the cooking process, a reaction will take place, making the husk hard to purée and digest.

500 g (1 lb) dried haricot blanc
4 cups water
2 sprigs of thyme
1 bay leaf
20 black peppercorns
$2\frac{1}{2}$ tablespoons olive oil
1 onion, thinly sliced
1 stick of celery, thinly sliced
1 leek, thinly sliced
3 cloves of garlic, crushed
4 cups chicken stock (see page 378)
*2 teaspoons white truffle oil**
Salt and freshly ground pepper
30 g (1 oz) white truffle, shaved*

Soak the haricot blanc in the water for at least 6 hours • To make the bouquet garni, wrap the thyme, bay leaf and peppercorns tightly in some cheesecloth • Heat the olive oil in a heavy-based saucepan, add the onion, celery, leek, garlic and bouquet garni and cook over medium heat for 5 minutes or until soft • Drain the haricot blanc and add to the vegetables. Immediately add the stock and simmer for 40 minutes or until the haricot blanc are cooked • Remove the bouquet garni, and 3 tablespoons of the cooked haricot blanc for garnishing the soup. Blend the soup in a food processor until smooth. Flavour with the truffle oil and season with the salt and pepper • To serve, place a few of the reserved cooked haricot blanc in the bottom of each bowl. Froth the soup with a hand blender, pour into the bowls and garnish with a generous amount of shaved white truffle.

White truffle risotto

[serves 6]

Food and wine matching will mean a lot more after serving this risotto with an Australian barbera from Victoria's picturesque King Valley, such as a Dalzotto 2002 Barbera or a '98 Pizzini Nebbiolo.

ACID BUTTER

1/3 cup Champagne vinegar
150 ml (5 fl oz) dry white wine
1 medium onion, sliced
1 teaspoon fresh thyme leaves
1 bay leaf
1 kg (2 lb) cultured butter, chopped into small dice*

RISOTTO

450 ml (15 fl oz) chicken stock (see page 378)
1/4 cup mushroom stock (see page 109)
2 1/2 tablespoons olive oil
1 medium onion, finely diced
250 g (8 oz) Arborio rice
350 ml (12 fl oz) dry white wine
60 g (2 oz) Grana Padano Parmesan cheese, grated
50 g (1 3/4 oz) white truffle, grated*
Salt and freshly ground pepper
*2 teaspoons white truffle oil**
Juice of 1/2 lemon

To make the acid butter, combine the vinegar and white wine with the sliced onion, thyme and bay leaf and reduce to 2/3 cup. Gradually add the butter, whisking constantly for 3–4 minutes or until the sauce is thick and smooth. Pass through a fine sieve. Cover and place in the refrigerator to set • Heat the chicken stock in a small heavy-based saucepan over low heat • Heat the mushroom stock in a small heavy-based saucepan over a low heat • To make the risotto, heat the olive oil in a heavy-based saucepan, add the onion and cook over medium heat for 4 minutes or until softened • Add the rice and cook, stirring, until each grain is coated with oil • Deglaze with the white wine and cook until the liquid has evaporated • Stir in two-thirds of the warm chicken stock and cook, stirring occasionally, for 5 minutes or until the liquid is absorbed • Add the mushroom stock to the risotto and simmer, stirring, over a gentle heat until all the stock is absorbed. If the risotto appears a little firm add the remaining chicken stock to loosen the texture • Stir in 90 g (3 oz) of the acid butter per spoonful of rice. Add 1 1/2 tablespoons of the Parmesan and 1 1/2 tablespoons of the truffle and stir well. Season with salt, pepper, truffle oil and a squeeze of lemon juice • Spoon the risotto into warmed serving dishes. Liberally and generously sprinkle more truffle oil over the risotto. Serve immediately. The remaining Parmesan can be passed around at the table.

White Truffle ice cream

[makes 4 cups]

This is neither a joke, nor a dish for the true truffle diehards, but it is a wonderful and unique way to experience truffles. I recommend serving the dish as a finale to a meal that has showcased white truffles (it's a great way to use up any leftovers). Serve with poached pears, salted white chocolate caramel and a glass of Sauternes.

400 ml (14 fl oz) milk
60 g (2 oz) glucose
100 g ($3\frac{1}{2}$ oz) Arborio rice
2 cups crème anglaise (see page 379)
*1 teaspoon white truffle oil**
*2 tablespoons grated white truffle**

Combine the milk, glucose and rice in a heavy-based saucepan and gently simmer, stirring occasionally, for 20 minutes • Transfer to a container, cover, and place in the refrigerator until cool • Combine the rice and the crème anglaise • Stir in the truffle oil and half of the grated truffle. Transfer to an ice-cream churner. (If an ice-cream churner is not available, place the ice cream in an airtight container and freeze for 4 hours, stirring every hour with a wooden spoon.) • Place in the freezer for 2–3 hours or until firm. Serve, garnished with slices of truffle, if desired.

The Market Garden

AUSTRALIA OVER THE YEARS has built an international reputation on its agricultural resources and rightly so! However, complacency has now set in and I and other young members of the industry must convince our suppliers to keep being innovative, committed to providing the best and to look to the future. Profit-driven suppliers are only living for today and flood the market with second-rate produce that has over the last decade destroyed our reputation as being leaders in quality fruit and vegetables. Wake up greengrocers of Australia!

This chapter is not devoted to vegetarians, in fact, the recipes are more a celebration of the seasons, when each particular vegetable is at its best and deserves the honour of being the star performer.

Chervil, chives, tarragon, sage, fenugreek, watercress, rosemary, wild thyme, lime leaves, fresh turmeric, ginger, nasturtium flowers, vanilla beans, dandelion leaves, lavender, marjoram and flat-leaf parsley all play a vital support role in my repertoire at Vue de monde. Without the research and persistence of my team many

of these products would be near impossible to purchase on a regular basis. If any of the following recipes contain ingredients that you cannot find at your local greengrocer, log into the support website: myvue.com.au for possible answers to such frustrating questions as alternative ingredients and possibly even in some instances replacement dishes or recipes. A big thanks must go to some of my suppliers in Melbourne for their tireless effort in putting up with my consistent demands for better produce week in week out.

Peas are my favourite vegetable, buying fresh ones can be a real exercise. I advise growing them yourself, even a pot on your balcony will produce the ideal fresh humble pea. If peas at the market are fresh, they will appear bright green and unwrinkled and will smell very herbaceous. Remove one from the pod before you buy, the sweetness will be apparent. Escoffier preaches in all his writing that peas should be shelled no more than 12 hours after purchasing. The flavour changes in the pod, dramatically for the worse, the longer they go unshelled.

Second to peas would have to be asparagus. I'm sad in some ways that it has become an all-year vegetable. From the age of twelve I can remember the first batch of asparagus coming into the house in mid-October, mid-spring. The versatility of asparagus as a main ingredient is such a pleasure when the pressure of menu planning demands coming up with original ideas. Asparagus goes with just about any ingredient, from smoked salmon, eggs and caviar to lamb sweetbreads and all types of shellfish. Certain wine connoisseurs I have come across throughout my career are negative about placing asparagus on a menu with wines matched. I don't understand their philosophy as I find the subtle taste of fresh asparagus with its contrasting texture easy to pair with wine. Get over it, I say!

Promise me something: after reading this you will never buy canned artichokes again. After all, fresh artichokes are available for seven months of the year. When buying artichokes remember that they are a flower: the outside petals should be tightly closed, bright green or purple and firm to touch. The middle hairy heart or the choke is difficult to remove. The best way to do so is to dig it out with a teaspoon. The outer leaves can be cooked in many ways. The base and stem of baby artichokes can be eaten raw when thinly sliced, tossed in a salad and dressed with vinaigrette. Look out for Sole Murat in brasseries. It is a delectable dish of sole goujons, baby potatoes and roasted artichoke.

Vegetable stock

[makes 8 cups]

THIS LIGHTLY FLAVOURED liquid base is essential to any cook or chef serious about their vegetables — partly because the chicken stock used in this book can be replaced with this.

2 onions, roughly chopped
2 sticks of celery, roughly chopped
1 bulb of fennel, roughly chopped
1 medium leek, roughly chopped
1 zucchini (courgette), roughly chopped
1 small celeriac, roughly chopped
1 head of garlic, chopped in half
10 fennel seeds
5 star anise, crushed
10 peppercorns
3 bay leaves
1½ cups white wine
8 cups water
5 sprigs of thyme
5 sprigs of coriander (cilantro)

Combine the vegetables, spices, white wine and water in a heavy-based stockpot and bring to the boil over high heat. Reduce heat to low and simmer for 30 minutes • Remove from the stove, add the thyme and coriander and infuse for 30 minutes • Strain through a fine chinois* and use as required. The stock freezes well for several months.

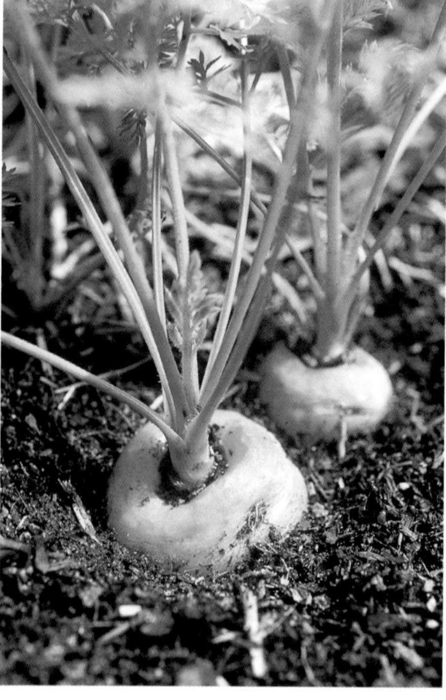

Vegetable emulsion

[makes enough for 12 serves]

A good way to present all classically boiled or steamed vegetables is to glaze them with this vegetable emulsion. Simply keep the warmed emulsion to one side, then at the last minute toss the cooked vegetables in a small amount. For carrots and turnips include two tablespoons of reduced orange juice in the emulsion.

100 ml (3½ fl oz) chicken stock (see page 378)
1 clove of garlic, crushed
100 g (3½ oz) butter, chopped into small dice
Sea salt and freshly ground pepper

In a small heavy-based saucepan, combine the chicken stock and garlic. Cook over a high heat until reduced by two-thirds • Whisk in the butter and season with salt and pepper. Reserve until needed.

Petits pois à la française

[serves 6 as side portions]

Try serving peas à la Française paired with confit of Atlantic salmon accompanied by a tangy béarnaise sauce.

2 tablespoons olive oil
2 onions, diced
500 g (1 lb) shelled peas
*200 g (6½ oz) bacon lardons**
2 cloves of garlic, crushed
1 iceberg lettuce, finely shredded
75 g (2½ oz) butter
Juice of ½ lemon
Salt and freshly ground pepper

Heat the olive oil in a heavy-based saucepan, add the onion and sauté over medium heat, until transparent • Add the peas, bacon lardons and garlic, and sauté for 2 minutes • Add the lettuce and sauté for 2 minutes • Add the butter and cook for 3 minutes or until the butter starts to emulsify with the pan juices. Occasionally stir with a wooden spoon. Season with a squeeze of lemon juice and salt and pepper • Serve immediately in a large bowl.

Pea purée with sea urchin and quail eggs

[serves 6]

I USE THIS RECIPE to surprise people; the pea component of this dish acts as an invitation to be experimental and try the sea urchin hidden by the delectable quail eggs.

PEA PURÉE

500 g (1 lb) fresh peas
1 tablespoon olive oil
1 onion, diced
2 cloves of garlic, crushed
½ cup baby spinach
100 ml (3½ fl oz) chicken stock (see page 378)

6 fresh sea urchins
6 quail eggs
Salt and freshly ground pepper

Preheat the oven to 180°C (350°F) • To make the pea purée, blanch the peas in boiling salted water for 4–5 minutes or until cooked. Refresh in iced water and drain thoroughly • Heat the olive oil in a heavy-based saucepan, add the onion and garlic and cook over medium heat for 4 minutes or until transparent. Add the spinach and peas and cook for 3–4 minutes or until the spinach has wilted • Remove from the heat, add the stock, and blend until smooth • Place the purée on a tray and chill in the refrigerator to preserve the colour and speed up the cooling process • Wearing heavy rubber gloves, open the sea urchin shells carefully with a serrated knife or a sharp pair of scissors by removing the top to create a clean opening in the same way a boiled egg is opened. The top is easy to identify, it has a white opening or mouth. Place the sea urchin on its side, run the knife carefully around the inside of the shell. A substantial amount of liquid will run out. Do not be alarmed it is simply seawater. Alternatively a good fishmonger may be able to open the sea urchins for you • The sea urchin meat is a pale orange colour. Using a teaspoon, scoop everything but the orange roe out of the shell and discard. Repeat for all six shells • Place the shells onto a tray and rest in the refrigerator for 10 minutes • Spoon 1 tablespoon of the pea purée into each shell, making a well in the centre with the back of a teaspoon

• Crack a quail egg into each sea urchin shell directing the yolk into the well • Place the filled sea urchins on a baking tray and pour in enough boiling water to come halfway up the sides of the shells. Cover with aluminium (aluminum) foil and bake in the oven for 6–8 minutes. Season the top of each egg and serve immediately.

Petits pois bonne femme

[6 side serves]

'Whichever way they are to be cooked and served, peas should be very green, freshly gathered and shelled at the last minute. This is one of those vegetables that easily lose their quality if not cooked carefully. When prepared with care the flavour of peas is of incomparable delicacy but the slightest negligence will result in a vegetable of poor flavour and little value.' Escoffier, 1898.

*125 g (4 oz) smoked pork belly lardons**

*2 tablespoons goose fat**

12 pickling onions, peeled

*30 g (1 oz) cultured butter**

*Bouquet garni**

15 g (½ oz) plain (all-purpose) flour

400 ml (13 fl oz) chicken stock (see page 378)

650 g (1 lb 5 oz) freshly shelled peas

Place the pork belly lardons in a saucepan of cold water, bring to the boil, strain and refresh in iced water. This process needs to be included for two reasons: first, the water will draw any unwanted saltiness from the pork and secondly it will soften the pork and give it a more pleasing texture • Heat the goose fat in a heavy-based saucepan, add the onions and cook for 4 minutes or until soft and transparent • Add the pork belly, butter and bouquet garni and cook for 6–7 minutes • Stir in the flour to form a roux. Cook for a few moments to create a slightly nutty aroma. Stir in the chicken stock and bring to the boil • Add the peas and cook for 5 minutes or until the liquid is reduced by half, cover, and cook for a further 5 minutes or until the peas are tender. Serve.

Vegetable stock

Vegetable emulsion

Petits pois à la Française

Pea purée with sea urchin and quail eggs

Petits pois bonne femme

Pea soup with roasted scallops wrapped in pancetta

Velouté de champignons à l'Italienne

Onion purée

Pea soup with roasted scallops wrapped in pancetta

[serves 6]

This soup is perfect for a spring evening of light indulgence, paired with a glass of crisp New Zealand sauvignon blanc.

4 x 8 cm (3 in) veal bones with 500 g (1 lb) bone marrow
500 g (1 lb) fresh peas
2 tablespoons olive oil
1 onion, diced
2 cloves of garlic, crushed
$^1/_2$ cup baby spinach
2 cups chicken stock (see page 378)
18 slices of flat pancetta or prosciutto*, thinly sliced*
18 large scallops, cleaned
Juice of $^1/_2$ lemon
Salt and freshly ground pepper
100 ml ($3^1/_2$ fl oz) double cream

Ask your butcher to push out the marrow from the bones • Slice the bone marrow tubes into 1-cm ($^1/_3$-in) discs to make 18 discs. Soak the discs in iced water for at least 12 hours • Blanch the peas in salted water for 3 minutes or until cooked. Refresh in iced water and drain thoroughly • Heat 1 tablespoon of the olive oil in a heavy-based saucepan, add the onion and garlic, and cook over medium heat for 4 minutes or until transparent. Add the spinach and peas, and cook for 3–4 minutes or until the spinach has wilted • Remove from the heat, add the stock, and blend until smooth • Wrap 1 slice of pancetta around each scallop and secure with a toothpick • Heat the remaining 1 tablespoon of olive oil in a heavy-based frying pan, add the scallops in batches, and cook over medium heat for 1 minute each side. Don't crisp the pancetta • Place a slice of bone marrow on top of each scallop • Place under a hot grill (broiler) for 1 minute or until the marrow is translucent • Season the scallops with lemon juice, salt and pepper • Whip the cream to ribbon stage. To test for the correct consistency, draw a figure 8 in the top of the cream, the figure should hold momentarily. If the cream is overwhipped try thinning it with 2 tablespoons of milk • Add the cream to the soup, season, and bring to the boil and bubble for 2 minutes • Pour the soup into serving bowls; place the scallops in the centre of the soup and serve.

Velouté de champignons à l'Italienne

[serves 4]

A CLASSICALLY INSPIRED dish from the vegetable gardens of Catherine de Medici, the red tomatoes, green spinach, linguine and grated cheese represent the colours of the Italian flag.

The dish needs to be made in a short amount of time, to preserve the green colour. Have all your ingredients *mise en place* ready before you get going.

10 ripe Roma (plum) tomatoes
20 cups double chicken stock (see page 378)
50 g (1¾ oz) cultured butter, chopped into small dice*
2 shallots, finely chopped
2 cloves of garlic, crushed
200 g (6½ oz) baby spinach
Salt and freshly ground pepper
100 g (3½ oz) linguine
200 ml (7 fl oz) pouring (light) cream
1 cup béarnaise sauce (see page 385)
100 g (3½ oz) buffalo mozzarella, grated
80 g (2¾ oz) Grana Padano Parmesan cheese, grated

Score a cross in the top and base of each tomato. Plunge into boiling water for 1 minute. Peel, deseed and chop the tomatoes into 5-mm (¼-in) dice • Heat the stock to simmering point in a large heavy-based saucepan over medium heat • Melt the butter in a heavy-based saucepan over low heat, add the shallots, garlic and spinach and cook for 6 minutes. Season with salt and pepper. Add half of the stock and cook for 5–6 minutes. Purée until smooth • Cook the linguine in boiling salted water until *al dente*. Remove and refresh in iced water. Cut the linguine into 4-cm (1½-in) lengths • Place the tomato and linguine in warmed serving bowls • Add 100 ml (3½ fl oz) of the cream to the spinach soup and bring to the boil • To make the velouté, bring the remaining chicken stock to the boil, add the remaining cream and continue to boil over a medium heat for 2–3 minutes. Whisk in the béarnaise sauce and season with salt and pepper • Preheat the grill (broiler) to hot • Place alternate ladles of the spinach soup and the velouté in each bowl to create a marbled effect. Scatter the mozzarella and Parmesan on top. Place under the grill to melt the cheese. Serve with fresh crusty bread.

Onion purée

[makes 3 cups]

To avoid the relentless tears and appreciate the sweet velvety taste of cooked onions I have one tip: always peel onions that have been stored in the refrigerator.

I use this purée to accompany roast meats, particularly chicken, it also works as a soup, garnished with Gruyere cheese croutons and seasoned with a little sherry vinegar to counteract the sweetness of the onions.

2½ tablespoons olive oil
4 large brown onions, halved and finely sliced
1 bay leaf
2 sprigs of thyme
4 cloves of garlic, crushed
*20 g (¾ oz) cultured butter**
100 ml (3½ fl oz) white wine
350 ml (13 fl oz) chicken stock (see page 378)
Salt and freshly ground pepper

Heat the olive oil in a large heavy-based saucepan, add the onions, bay leaf and thyme, and cook over very low heat for 25 minutes or until the onions caramelise • Add the garlic and continue to cook slowly for 5 minutes. The onions should be golden and sweet to taste. Add the butter and increase the heat to medium • Deglaze with the white wine and cook until the wine has evaporated. Add the stock and simmer over medium heat for 20 minutes. Season with salt and pepper • Blend until smooth. At this stage, 1½ cups of stock can be added to form a soup, if desired. Serve immediately.

Confit of shallots

[serves 10 as a garnish]

SHALLOTS ARE A fantastic vegetable in their own right, served with roast meats and meaty sauces they combine to give a wonderful array of aromas and a subdued sweetness that complements well-structured red wines. This is a fun and simple way to enjoy the shallot. Serve the shallots in their skins with any roast.

1 head of garlic, cut in half
*50 g (1¾ oz) goose fat**
250 g (8 oz) butter
1 tablespoon fresh thyme leaves
50 g (1¾ oz) sea salt
20 evenly sized shallots
2 sprigs of rosemary
800 g (1lb 10 oz) rock salt

Preheat the oven to 140°C (275°F) • Make a pouch with four 30 x 30 cm (12 x 12 in) sheets of aluminium (aluminum) foil. Place the dull side of the foil on the outside and add the garlic, goose fat, butter, thyme, sea salt, shallots and rosemary. Fold all sides of the foil inwards and seal very tightly so that there are no holes • Place the rock salt on a baking tray. Place the foil pouch on the bed of salt and bake for 1½ hours or until the shallots are tender and soft. Do not open the bag until the very last stages of cooking as the shallots will not cook unless the bag is fully sealed • Remove the shallots, discard the other ingredients. Serve the shallots while still hot or store in an airtight container until required. To reheat, deep-fry the shallots at 180°C (350°F) for 2–3 minutes. Remove the roots from the shallot by pinching them away before serving. For best results use the day of making.

Artichokes à la barigoule

[serves 6]

THE TERM BARIGOULE is derived from the Provençal mushroom of the same name. Throughout the years, however, the mushrooms have come to be left out of the recipe. The basic preparation now combines white wine and butter with artichokes and chicken stock. This dish is wonderful as a meal in itself or as an accompaniment to such delights as roast chicken or sea bass.

2 tablespoons virgin olive oil

10 small globe artichokes, peeled, base and leaves trimmed (see page 159)

1 large brown onion, thinly sliced

3 cloves of garlic, thinly sliced

2 carrots, thinly sliced

3 sprigs of thyme

2 bay leaves

1 teaspoon sea salt

200 ml (7 fl oz) white wine

100 ml (3½ fl oz) freshly squeezed orange juice

2 cups chicken stock (see page 378)

*50 g (1¾ oz) cultured butter**

Heat the olive oil in a heavy-based saucepan over a medium heat until it begins to smoke. Add the artichokes, onion, garlic, carrots, thyme, bay leaves and a pinch of sea salt • Cook for 5 minutes, add the wine and orange juice and reduce by half. Add the chicken stock and butter and bring to the boil • Reduce the heat to low and simmer for 20 minutes or until the artichokes are cooked. Slide a small knife into the heart of an artichoke, if the knife slides in with little force or pressure applied, then the artichoke is cooked. Serve hot, or store in an airtight container for up to 4 days to allow the flavour to develop.

Zucchini salad

[serves 6]

SIMPLE, CLEAN AND adaptable, this zucchini (courgette) salad is delicious with tempura-battered prawns or semi-dried roasted tomatoes.

2 cloves of garlic, crushed
2 shallots, finely chopped
2½ tablespoons extra virgin olive oil
1 tablespoon grapeseed oil
1 tablespoon sherry vinegar
Juice of ½ lemon
1 tablespoon finely chopped tarragon
Salt and freshly ground pepper
5 small zucchini (courgettes), grated
*50 g (1¾ oz) pepper cress (peppergrass)**
2½ tablespoons crayfish oil (see page 252)

To make the salad dressing, combine the garlic, shallots, olive oil, grapeseed oil, sherry vinegar, lemon juice, tarragon, salt and pepper • Toss the zucchini and dressing together • Transfer to a serving platter, top with pepper cress, drizzle over crayfish oil and serve.

Zucchini tian

[serves 6]

THIS SIMPLE DISH will give great pleasure. Serve as an accompaniment to any meat or fish dish or as an entrée with a simple sauce.

20 confit tomato halves (see page 86), chopped into 1-cm (1/3-in) dice

200 ml (7 fl oz) extra virgin olive oil

4 cloves of garlic, crushed

1 tablespooon finely chopped oregano

1 tablespoon finely chopped thyme

5 small zucchini (courgettes)

2 teaspoons sea salt

Pinch of freshly ground pepper

Preheat the oven to 190°C (375°F) • Macerate the tomatoes in 3/4 cup of the olive oil, the garlic and herbs • Slice the zucchini thinly lengthwise so the slices will bend easily and break • Blanch the zucchini for 30 seconds in boiling salted water. Refresh in iced water and drain thoroughly • Line six dariole moulds with the zucchini ribbons, slightly overlapping to cover the base and overhang the rim • Spoon the chopped tomatoes into the zucchini-lined moulds until three-quarters full. Wrap the overhanging zucchini ribbons inward to form a covered parcel • Brush with the remaining olive oil, season and bake in the oven for 6–8 minutes. Serve while still hot.

Eggplant caviar

[serves 6]

EVERY APPRENTICE I have worked with has at some point asked me why we call this eggplant caviar. Well, before you ask the same question, I will tell you: the eggplant (aubergine) seeds are very similar (with the help of a few glasses of good plonk), when the flesh is cooked and processed, to caviar.

This recipe goes well with other provençal vegetables, such as capsicum (sweet pepper) and tomato. Serve with roasted red mullet, lamb fillets or as a pre-dinner nibble on a tapenade-spread garlic crouton.

3 large eggplants (aubergines), peeled
4 cloves of garlic, crushed
Juice of 2½ lemons
¾ cup extra virgin olive oil
5 sprigs of thyme
Salt and freshly ground pepper
10 basil leaves, shredded
2 tablespoons tomato fondue (see page 81)

Cut the eggplant into six wedges lengthwise. Place in a microwavable container. Add the garlic, juice of 2 lemons, 155 ml (5 fl oz) of the olive oil and the thyme and toss well. Season with salt and pepper. Cover tightly with plastic wrap and cook in the microwave on medium–low for 20–25 minutes • Rest, covered, for 30 minutes. The mixture will be soft and opaque and light green in colour • Place the eggplant mixture in a colander, discard the thyme, and allow to drain for 20 minutes to remove excess moisture. Finely chop. The eggplant may be stored in an airtight container in the refrigerator for 3–4 days • Heat the remaining olive oil in a large heavy-based saucepan, add the eggplant mixture and cook for 3–4 minutes or until heated through • Season with the salt, pepper and the remaining lemon juice • Fold through the basil and tomatoe fondue to give a marbled effect to the eggplant. Serve quenelles of eggplant caviar as a garnish to a main course or as a side dish.

Confit of shallots

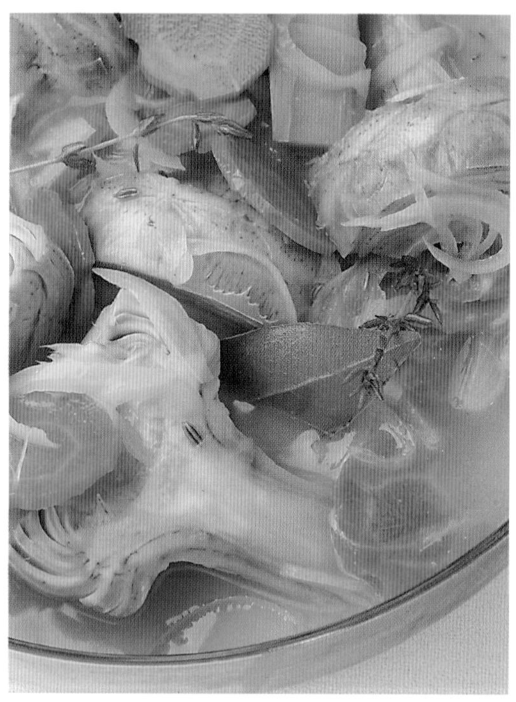

Artichokes à la barigoule

Zucchini salad

Zucchini tian

Eggplant caviar

Eggplant à la Espagnole

Chestnuts cooked in a bag

Chestnut soup

Eggplant à la Espagnole

[serves 6]

THIS IS ESCOFFIER'S recipe, which I first discovered in my 1913 edition of *Le Guide Culinaire* when researching the Three Emperors' Dinner menu. I now cook this particular dish at home, served with steamed fish it makes a great meal with little fuss.

10 finger eggplants (aubergines)
2 red capsicums (sweet peppers)
2½ tablespoons olive oil
2 onions, thinly sliced
3 cloves of garlic, crushed
4 sprigs of thyme
2 bay leaves
Salt and freshly ground pepper
*200 ml (7 fl oz) Madeira**
200 ml (7 fl oz) red wine
400 ml (13 fl oz) veal stock (see page 294)

Preheat the oven to 180°C (350°F) • Cut the eggplant in half, lengthways, cook on a char grill (bar marks crossed) and set aside • To roast the capsicum, place onto a char grill and cook until the skin is blackened. Transfer to a bowl, cover tightly with plastic wrap and allow to cool. Peel the capsicum and deseed by cutting in half lengthways, removing the green stem and scooping out the white part of the flesh and any seeds. Cut the capsicum into 1.5-cm (½-in) squares • Heat the olive oil in a heavy-based flameproof casserole dish, add the onions and cook over high heat, stirring constantly to prevent burning. Add the eggplant and capsicum and cook for 5 minutes • Stir in the garlic, thyme, bay leaves and season well • Deglaze with the Madeira and cook until reduced by half. Repeat with the red wine • Add the veal stock, bring to the boil, and cover • Transfer to the oven and bake for 1 hour • Serve on a warmed plate or as part of a main dish, such as roast beef fillet. There will be sufficient sauce in the eggplant not to warrant any extra sauce being made to complement the beef.

Six recipes for chestnuts

1. Cook 300 g (10 oz) peeled chestnuts in 600 ml (1 pt) chicken stock (see page 378) with 2 cloves of garlic, half a diced onion, 5 cloves, 2 sprigs of thyme and a bay leaf for about 5 minutes, then purée. Add a little more stock and serve as a soup or purée with chicken or game.

2. Stew 300 g (10 oz) peeled chestnuts by frying them in 1 tablespoon of olive oil, then adding 1 cup of white wine, 2 tablespoons of roughly chopped celery, 400 ml (13 fl oz) chicken stock (see page 378), 20 g (3/4 oz) butter and 2 teaspoons of caster (superfine) sugar. Cover the frying pan and braise for 45 minutes.

3. Braise 300 g (10 oz) peeled chestnuts in 2 cups of milk for 15 minutes. While still hot, roughly chop and add equal amounts of boiled cream and chocolate (see chocolate ganache on page 349). Allow the mixture to set, and then use a melon baller to make truffles. Roll in grated chocolate or cocoa.

4. Simmer 300 g (10 oz) peeled chestnuts in 2 cups of milk for 10 minutes. Strain, then fry the chestnuts in 2 tablespoons of peanut oil until golden brown. Dip in caramel (see page 331) and serve with coffee.

5. To preserve chestnuts, put 400 g (13 oz) of chestnuts in boiling water and cook for 45 minutes. Add 350 g (11 oz) of caster (superfine) sugar, 2 deseeded vanilla beans and 150 ml (1/4 pt) water. Simmer in a pan for 30 minutes, then place in sterilised jars. Use as required.

6. Combine 300 g (10 oz) chestnuts, 100 g (3 1/2 oz) brown sugar, 2 deseeded vanilla beans*, 6 roughly chopped dried apricots, 20 g (3/4 oz) sea salt, 2 tablespoons of cultured butter* and 1 cup of cognac. Wrap in four sheets of aluminium (aluminum) foil and bake in the oven at 140°C (275°F) for 1 hour. Serve with vanilla ice cream.

Chestnut soup

[serves 6]

Before cooking chestnuts, the shells must be pierced. Score both ends of the nut with a knife. Gently deep-fry at around 160°C (325°F) for 3–5 minutes, or microwave on high for 5–6 minutes, stirring several times, or roast in a frying pan for 5 minutes, then transfer to the oven at 180°C (250°F) for 40 minutes. Then, using a knife, peel back the outer husk and the chestnuts are ready for cooking.

After scoring the chestnuts, deep-fry for 5 minutes in fresh peanut oil. Don't stand near the fryer as the chestnuts may pop (explode). Peel while hot with a paring knife.

This soup is fantastic with some fresh prawns fried quickly in olive oil.

2½ tablespoons extra virgin olive oil
1 onion, diced
1 stick of celery, peeled and diced
2 cloves of garlic, crushed
4 sprigs of thyme
2 bay leaves
350 ml (12 fl oz) dry white wine
8 cups chicken stock (see page 378)
1 kg (2 lb) roasted chestnuts, peeled
Salt and freshly ground pepper

Heat the olive oil in a heavy-based saucepan, add the onion, celery, garlic, thyme and bay leaves and cook for 10 minutes or until soft and tender • Deglaze with the white wine and cook until evaporated • Add the chicken stock and chestnuts and simmer for 45 minutes • Purée until smooth • Return to the boil, season with salt and pepper and serve.

Cooking stock for artichokes

[serves 6]

THIS RECIPE IS A meal in itself. Add some flaked confit rabbit leg to the final product for exceptional results.

To prepare globe artichokes, snap the stems at the point where they bend, in the same way as you would with asparagus. Baby artichokes are sweet and tender enough to use the stem, but older and bigger artichokes develop a stringent bitterness in the stem. Peel away the tough outer leaves until you reach the base where the bulb and stem meet. Using a sharp knife, cut the base flat. Rub with half a lemon to prevent oxidising. Trim around the artichoke to form a cylinder, rub in more lemon juice. If the artichoke is to be cooked in a stock, the inside leaves will be edible. The artichoke must be consumed within the hour to prevent oxidisation. When cooked, cut the top off the artichoke, scoop out the hairy choke and discard.

100 ml (3½ fl oz) olive oil
1 onion, diced
4 cloves of garlic, crushed
3 sprigs of thyme
2 bay leaves
Pinch of cayenne pepper
1 cup white wine
1 large bulb of fennel, chopped
2 large carrots, chopped
8 cups water
Salt and freshly ground pepper
12 globe artichokes, trimmed

Preheat the oven to 180°C (350°F) • Heat the olive oil in a heavy-based flameproof casserole, add the onion and cook over medium heat for 5 minutes or until tender. Add the garlic, thyme, bay leaves and cayenne pepper • Deglaze with the white wine and reduce over high heat by two-thirds • Add the fennel, carrot and water. Season with salt and pepper • Bring to the boil and add the artichokes, cover with a paper cartouche* • Place in the oven for 30 minutes. Test the artichokes with a knife, they should be tender and succulent. If they are not quite cooked return to the oven and monitor closely until they pass the knife test.

Salad beaucaire

[serves 4]

THIS DISH WAS originally two dishes: salade Alexandra and fonds d'artichauts à la moële. I have joined the dishes to form a slightly new dish that Escoffier would approve of. I believe it is a good blend and will balance the meal nicely. Try a good chilled rosé with this style of food, nothing fancy just wholesome summer fun.

1 cooked beetroot, thinly sliced

1 cooked potato barrel (refer to pommes Anna on page 95), thinly sliced

FILLING

150 g (5 oz) button mushrooms

3 sticks of celery, julienned

1 celeriac weighing 250 g (8 oz), peeled and julienned

3 chicory, julienned

100 ml (3½ fl oz) French vinaigrette (see page 396)

200 g (6½ oz) cooked ham, julienned

2 Granny Smith apples, julienned

100 g (3½ oz) mayonnaise (see page 388)

1 tablespoon roughly chopped flat-leaf parsley

4 globe artichokes, cooked and choke removed (see page 159)

4 sprigs of chervil

Using a 3-cm (1¼-in) round cutter, shape the beetroot into round discs. Repeat this process with the potato • To julienne the mushrooms, remove the stems, slice across the cap to create round discs of different sizes and carefully cut these discs into thin strips • To make the filling, combine the celery, celeriac and chicory and macerate in the French vinaigrette for 10 minutes, then add the ham, apples and mushrooms • Mix with the mayonnaise and add the parsley. Arrange the artichokes on a serving platter and fill each with a spoonful of the filling, then garnish with the chervil. Surround with a border of alternating slices of beetroot and potato and serve.

Topinambour soup

[serves 6]

JERUSALEM ARTICHOKES ARE not an artichoke scientifically speaking, but the taste is not dissimilar. To save confusion I call them by the French word 'topinambour'. I particularly like to transform the tuberous bulbs into a silky smooth velouté or soup. Another simple idea is to treat the bulbs as you would baby potatoes, cooked and tossed in butter and herbs with a generous amount of seasoning.

*50 g ($1\frac{3}{4}$ oz) goose fat**

2 onions, finely diced

4 cloves of garlic, crushed

1 kg (2 lb) Jerusalem artichokes, peeled and thinly sliced

100 ml ($3\frac{1}{2}$ fl oz) Calvados

8 cups chicken stock (see page 378)

Juice of $\frac{1}{2}$ lemon

Salt and freshly ground pepper

Heat the goose fat in a heavy-based saucepan, add the onion and cook over medium heat for 5 minutes or until soft, tender and transparent. Add the garlic and Jerusalem artichokes and cook, stirring constantly, for 7–8 minutes or until the artichokes start to soften and break up • Deglaze with the Calvados and cook until evaporated • Pour in the chicken stock, bring to the boil, reduce heat and simmer for 30 minutes • Purée and season with the lemon juice and salt and pepper. Serve piping hot or well chilled.

Cooking stock for artichokes

Salad beaucaire

Topinambour soup

White asparagus and lamb sweetbread vol-au-vent

Vichyssoise of white asparagus

Consommé à la Française

Green asparagus wrapped in ham with béarnaise sauce

Watercress and hazelnut salad

White asparagus and lamb sweetbread vol-au-vent

[serves 6]

Flavours and textures abound with subtle delicacy in the way the buttery puff pastry complements the asparagus and the sweetbreads. Use this as a garnish for roast lamb with sensational results. If serving as an entrée try a viognier from the Rhone Valley, France, or a Hunter Valley, Australia, semillon.

12 spears of white asparagus, trimmed
*1 tablespoon garlic oil**
12 lamb sweetbreads, trimmed*
6 vol-au-vents (see page 396)
100 g (3½ oz) baby pine mushrooms or chanterelles
2 shallots, finely chopped
100 g (3½ oz) shelled broad beans
*20 g (¾ oz) cultured butter**
½ tablespoon finely chopped curly-leaf parsley
2 tablespoons veal stock (see page 294)
Juice of ½ lemon
Salt and freshly ground pepper

Preheat the oven to 180°C (350°F) • Blanch the asparagus in boiling salted water for 2 minutes or until tender. Refresh in iced water and cut into quarters lengthwise • Heat the garlic oil in a medium-sized saucepan, add the sweetbreads and cook for 10 minutes or until crispy and golden. Drain on paper towel. Strain and reserve the garlic oil • Warm the vol-au-vents in the oven for 3 minutes • Heat the reserved garlic oil in a frying pan, add the asparagus, mushrooms and shallots, sweetbreads and broad beans, and sauté for 2–3 minutes • Add the butter, parsley and veal stock , and toss all the ingredients together, taste and season with lemon juice, salt and pepper • Place a vol-au-vent in the centre of each serving plate. Carefully spoon the sautéed mixture into each vol-au-vent, arranging any remaining mixture on the plate. Drizzle the pan juices over and around each vol-au-vent and serve.

Vichyssoise of white asparagus

[serves 6]

THE CLASSICAL SOUP containing the key components of potato, any other vegetable and a touch of cream. Traditionally served chilled, I like it served warm with oysters.

2 large sebago potatoes, peeled and thinly sliced

2 cups milk

1½ tablespoons olive oil

500 g (1 lb) white asparagus, trimmed and thinly sliced

1 onion, diced

4 sprigs of thyme

2 bay leaves

2 cloves of garlic, crushed

4 cups chicken stock (see page 378)

100 ml (3½ fl oz) double cream

1 tablespoon finely chopped chives

*2 teaspoons white truffle oil**

Combine the potatoes and milk in a heavy-based saucepan. Bring to the boil, reduce heat and simmer for 20 minutes or until potatoes are soft. Drain • Heat the olive oil in a heavy-based saucepan, add the asparagus, onion, thyme, bay leaves and garlic, and cook over low heat, without colouring, for 8 minutes • Add the potatoes and chicken stock, bring to the boil, reduce heat and simmer for 20 minutes • Add the cream; briefly bring the soup to the boil and cook for 5 minutes. Purée until smooth. Pass through a fine sieve • Serve chilled or hot with the chives and a few drops of truffle oil.

Consommé à la Française

[serves 6]

This lovely classic dish can be easily made at home with good veal stock. The white asparagus is a lovely contrast to the meaty consommé.

8 cups light veal stock (see page 294)
200 g (6½ oz) chopped celery leaves
200 g (6½ oz) chopped green leek tops
2 carrots, chopped
3 tablespoons coarsely chopped flat-leaf parsley leaves and stem
2 medium tomatoes, chopped
350 g (11 oz) chicken breast fillets
10 egg whites
18 baby new potatoes
Sea salt
2 eggs
200 ml (7 fl oz) thickened cream
18 white asparagus tips

Preheat the oven to 190°C (375°F) • Pour the veal stock into a stockpot and warm over a very low heat • Combine the celery leaves, leek tops, carrots, parsley and tomatoes with 100 g (3½ oz) of the chicken in a food processor. Blitz until finely minced (ground). Add the egg whites and mix well. Add to the stock, whisking well to break up the egg whites and keep them fluid. Bring to the boil, stirring constantly, to prevent the egg whites from sticking and burning • Reduce heat to low and simmer, undisturbed, for 20 minutes. Strain into a large sieve lined with a double thickness of cheesecloth and set over a deep bowl. Allow the liquid to drip through without disturbing. Gently reheat the consommé to serve (never boil, as it will go cloudy). Add the asparagus tips and cook for 5 minutes • In salted water boil the potatoes until cooked but still firm to touch. Slice the potatoes in half. Scoop the flesh out to make a hollow in the centre • To make the chicken mousse, in a food processor, mince the remaining 250 g (8 oz) of the chicken with a pinch of salt. Add the eggs, pulse to combine, and add the cream. Do not overwork the cream. As soon as it is combined remove from the bowl and rest in the refrigerator for 15 minutes • Spoon the chicken mousse into the potatoes. Transfer the potatoes to a baking tray and bake in the oven for 10 minutes or until the mousse is firm to touch • Place six potato halves in each warmed serving bowl. Spoon over the consommé, top with three asparagus tips each and serve.

Green asparagus wrapped in ham with béarnaise sauce

[serves 6]

If you feel extravagant, add a little sautéed crab to the end dish. The smokiness of the ham will call for a heavier style wine, try something from my favourite producer Didier Dagueneau from Sancerre.

*18 very thin slices of prosciutto**
18 spears of asparagus, trimmed
2½ tablespoons olive oil
2 shallots, finely chopped
100 ml (3½ fl oz) red wine sauce (see page 296)
Salt and freshly ground pepper
200 ml (7 fl oz) béarnaise sauce (see page 385)
2 cups watercress

Wrap each slice of prosciutto around a stem of asparagus. If necessary, fix the prosciutto in place with a toothpick • Heat the olive oil in a large heavy-based saucepan, add the asparagus and sauté over a low heat until the prosciutto turns transparent, about 5 minutes. Add the shallots and cook until softened • Remove from the heat, stir in the red wine sauce and reserve • Season with salt and pepper • Place the béarnaise sauce in a squeezeable bottle • Arrange the asparagus in the centre of a serving plate. Squeeze over the béarnaise sauce and drizzle the pan juices over and around the asparagus. Garnish with a little watercress and serve.

Watercress and hazelnut salad

[serves 6]

Wash and prepare the salad as close as possible to serving time.

200 g (6½ oz) hazelnuts
6 cups watercress
5 shallots, finely chopped
Salt and freshly ground pepper
2 ½ tablespoons hazelnut vinaigrette (see page 396)

Preheat the oven to 180°C (350°F) • Roast the hazelnuts for 5–8 minutes or until the skin easily rubs off between the fingers. Peel and coarsely crush • Place the hazelnuts, watercress and shallots in a serving bowl, mix and season • Dress the salad with the vinaigrette. Season and serve immediately.

The Foie Gras

LEGEND HAS IT THAT the Egyptians using geese fed with figs produced the first foie gras. Then the Greeks and the Romans used foie gras in their banquets. The tradition followed through to Israel where it is still revered today, and served with anything and everything at very reasonable prices. Just bring your own bottle of Sauternes!

The first recorded foie gras produced since Roman times in Europe was in 1780 by a Mr Clause in the picturesque city of Strasbourg. Since then the tradition has been perpetuated throughout France for over two centuries. The foie gras was originally made with geese in Alsace then with ducks in the Gers region in south-west France.

You may be still wondering what foie gras is. Let me explain. Wild geese and ducks, before migrating, need to build up their reserves for their long journey, and overfeed for this purpose. In doing so their livers becomes oversized in storing nutrients needed during migration and the long harsh winter.

When farmed, to obtain a liver for foie gras, geese or ducks are fed two to five times per day for a period of up to three weeks. By then, their liver has increased in size to a weight of up to 1 kilogram (2 lb). The optimal weight is 600–800 g (1¼–1 lb 10 oz).

There are two types of foie gras: goose and duck. Goose has a delicate texture and flavour and is creamy pink in colour. It is slightly more expensive than duck because geese require more food and attention during the fattening process. Duck foie gras has a slightly stronger flavour and is yellow pink in colour.

This exotic product is best eaten in moderation and, where time allows, the preparation and consumption should never be rushed. To serve, use a sharp thin-bladed knife, which has been dipped in hot water to make cutting more accurate, and portion a lobe into 50-g (1¾-oz) pieces, slicing across the lobe from side to side. Roast each slice on a cast-iron griddle pan over medium heat for 2 minutes on each side and season well. Serve with a glass of Sauternes or a good sweet wine that has a balanced acid to sugar ratio. Some perfect partners with roasted foie gras are: toasted brioche; country-style sourdough; quince; roasted beef fillet; crayfish; caramelised citrus fruits or figs; shallots en papillote and watercress salad with hazelnut vinaigrette.

Brace yourself: expect to pay around $160 Australian, $US50 or 60 Euros for a duck lobe weighing approximately 500 g (1 lb) which would give you 8–9 serves. Goose liver can sometimes be slightly higher in price. Quality purveyors will stock several different grades of foie gras. Try the premium grade first and slice and roast it, and served with freshly toasted brioche. This will be a great introduction.

The Foie Gras

I have devised recipes that showcase foie gras at different times of the year. In the summer months, a terrine of foie gras, served cold, is an attractive dish on any menu. Another standing fact is the seasonality of foie gras. Summer months bring poorer quality lobes weighing a lot less. This makes foie gras terrine a more practical alternative because it can be made from preserved foie gras. In the winter months, at the height of foie gras season, it is best suited to being poached, steamed or roasted. Enjoy!

Terrine of foie gras, ox tongue and lentils du Puy

[makes 15–18 slices]

THE MOST IMPORTANT accompaniment to this dish is freshly toasted brioche. Keep the serving plate free of any other garnish — the artistic flare comes from the terrine itself. Be patient in the making of this terrine, if you rush the results will show.

LAYER ONE

1 kg (2 lb) pickled and smoked ox tongue

*1 kg (2 lb) goose fat**

*20 thin slices of flat pancetta**

LAYER TWO

300 g (10 oz) lentils du Puy, soaked in water for 24 hours*

1 carrot, chopped into large dice

1 stick of celery, chopped into large dice

1 onion, chopped into large dice

1 leek, chopped into large dice

3 cloves of garlic, crushed

100 g (3½ oz) bacon bone

*Bouquet garni**

8 cups chicken stock (see page 378)

400 ml (13 fl oz) veal stock (see page 294)

*200 ml (7 fl oz) Madeira**

6 sheets or 20 g (¾ oz) gelatin, soaked in water

150 ml (5 fl oz) hazelnut vinaigrette (see page 396)

Preheat the oven to 100°C (210°F) • To make layer one, place the ox tongue and goose fat in a deep baking tray, cover with aluminium (aluminum) foil, and confit in the oven for 3 hours • In a plastic wrap-lined 7 x 27-cm (2¾ x 11-in) terrine mould, place the slices of pancetta widthways and slightly overlapping to cover the base and overhang the rim • Remove the ox tongue from the goose fat and place on a cooling rack positioned over a tray. Refrigerate overnight • Cut the ox tongue into 2.5-cm (1-in) thick slices, squaring them up with a knife • Press the tongue firmly and evenly into the bottom of the terrine mould • To make layer two, combine the lentils, carrot, celery, onion, leek, garlic, bacon bone, bouquet garni and chicken stock in a large saucepan and simmer for 1 hour. The cooking liquid may need topping up with water from time to time so it doesn't boil dry • Allow to cool and remove all ingredients but the lentils • Bring the veal stock and Madeira to the boil and reduce by two-thirds. Add the softened gelatin and stir to dissolve. Remove from the heat and add the lentils, vinaigrette, shallots and tarragon and season well • Layer the lentils over the ox tongue to a thickness of 2.5 cm (1 in) • To make layer three, fill to the top of the mould with the foie gras. Press down, then fold over the pancetta to enclose the top of the terrine.

2 shallots, chopped
¼ tablespoon chopped tarragon
salt and freshly ground pepper

LAYER THREE

500 g (1 lb) lobe of pasteurised foie gras (demie cuic), sliced

Cover tightly with aluminium (aluminum) foil. Weight the top of the terrine with cans of food and refrigerate overnight • Turn out onto a platter and serve, sliced, with toasted brioche.

Grilled foie gras, caramelised apple, poached walnuts and grapes with Sauternes emulsion

[serves 8]

The classic combination of apple, Calvados and foie gras was suggested by a customer at Vue de monde with a very large Sauternes cellar. I was initially sceptical about being able to combine all the ingredients in a modern presentation. The eight-spice powder brings the whole dish together and solves that problem.

400 g (13 oz) seedless green grapes, peeled, if desired
100 ml (3½ fl oz) Sauternes
200 g (6½ oz) whole walnuts
2 cups milk
100 ml (3½ fl oz) walnut oil

EIGHT-SPICE POWDER

100 g (3½ oz) juniper berries
50 g (1¾ oz) whole cloves
200 g (6½ oz) star anise

Marinate the grapes in the wine • Combine the walnuts and milk in a small heavy-based saucepan. Bring to the boil, reduce heat and simmer for 2–3 minutes. Strain and discard the milk. Peel the walnuts, and discard the bitter-tasting skin, being careful not to break the nuts in half. Marinate the walnuts in the walnut oil for 24 hours. This can be done a few weeks in advance. The walnuts will keep this way for 6 months • To make the eight-spice powder, in a food processor, combine the juniper berries, cloves, star anise, peppercorns, cinnamon, sea salt, saffron and cardamom. Blend until you have a medium-coarse powder with a little texture in the mix. Place the mix into a non-stick frying pan

¼ cup white peppercorns

4 sticks of cinnamon

50 g (1¾ oz) sea salt

Pinch of saffron

50 g (1¾ oz) cardamom seeds

SAUTERNES SAUCE

1 cup Sauternes

300 g (10 oz) cultured butter, chopped into small dice*

500 g (1 lb) lobe duck foie gras

2 tablespoons sugar

2 Granny Smith apples, peeled, cored, halved and thinly sliced

*200 ml (7 fl oz) Calvados**

Sea salt and freshly ground pepper

and gently roast over medium head until fragrant. Store in an airtight container for up to 4 weeks • To make the Sauternes sauce, reduce 100 ml (3½ fl oz) of the Sauternes by two-thirds in a small saucepan • Add the remaining Sauternes and bring to the boil. Remove from the heat and gradually whisk in the butter. Cover with plastic wrap and set aside in a warm part of the kitchen.The sauce should be served at room termperature • To serve, slice the foie gras into eight equal portions using a knife that has been dipped in hot water • Heat a cast-iron griddle pan, add four slices of foie gras at a time and grill for 60 seconds or until golden on each side • Rest for 5 minutes in a warm place • Heat a non-stick frying pan, sprinkle in the sugar, and cook until it begins to melt and turn golden. Add the apple and two pinches of eight-spice powder and cook for 30 seconds • Deglaze with the Calvados • Fan the caramelised apple in the centre of each serving plate. To the left of the apple make a thin line from the top to the bottom of the plate with the eight-spice powder • Place the grapes and walnuts in the Sauternes sauce and warm through for 30 seconds • Rest the foie gras on top of the apples. Spoon over the sauce and arrange the grapes and walnuts around the foie gras. Season with salt and pepper and serve.

Twice-cooked duck leg with foie gras and orange sauce

[serves 6]

CONFIT DUCK LEG is the most divine full-flavoured joint of meat. Match this with the classic combination of duck foie gras and orange. The tart acid from the oranges balances the delicate fatty texture of the foie gras and the duck. If foie gras is unavailable, chicken livers sautéed very quickly with Grand Marnier over a high heat are a good substitute. Serve with a bowl of seasonal salad leaves dressed with hazelnut vinaigrette (see page 396) and crispy pommes sauté (see page 103).

6 duck legs

MARINADE

100 g (3½ oz) sea salt
4 star anise
5 sprigs of thyme
20 white peppercorns

*1 kg (2 lb) duck fat**
*2 tablespoons goose fat**
Sea salt and freshly ground pepper

ORANGE SAUCE

20 g (¾ oz) butter
2 shallots
2 cloves of garlic, crushed
2 bay leaves
5 sprigs of thyme
4 star anise
1 cup Grand Marnier

Combine the duck legs, sea salt, star anise, thyme and peppercorns in an airtight container and marinate for 24 hours in the refrigerator. Rinse in cold water to remove the marinade • Preheat the oven to 120°C (250°F) • Heat the duck fat in a large flameproof casserole dish, bring to the boil, add the duck legs, and cover with aluminium (aluminum) foil. Place in the oven for 3–4 hours • Test to see if the duck is cooked by picking up a leg with a slotted spoon. The delicate meat should immediately start to fall away from the bone. Carefully remove the duck legs from the fat. Place on a tray and refrigerate for 24 hours or until completely cold. Strain the fat, reserve in an airtight container in the refrigerator for up to 8 weeks. The fat is good for roasting vegetables • Once the duck legs have cooled, clean the bone by scraping with a sharp knife and trimming away any excess fat • Heat the goose fat in a non-stick frying pan. Season the confit duck legs with salt and pepper. Place the legs in the pan and gently fry on low to medium heat for 10 minutes or until golden • To prepare the orange sauce, melt the butter in a heavy-based saucepan, add the shallots, garlic, bay leaves, thyme

2 cups freshly squeezed orange juice
100 g ($3\frac{1}{2}$ oz) cultured butter, chopped into dice*

1 Savoy cabbage
*1 tablespoon goose fat**
*12 thin slices flat pancetta**
2 tablespoons julienned carrot
2 tablespoons julienned celeriac
5 onions, thinly sliced
1 tablespoon water
100 ml ($3\frac{1}{2}$ fl oz) double cream
6 x 60 g (2 oz) slices of foie gras
6 sprigs of rosemary
5 oranges
80 g ($2\frac{3}{4}$ oz) sugar
$2\frac{1}{2}$ tablespoons Grand Marnier
*50 g ($1\frac{3}{4}$ oz) confit orange zest**

and star anise and cook for 5 minutes or until the shallots are transparent • Add the Grand Marnier and reduce by two-thirds • Add the orange juice and reduce by half. Gradually add the diced cultured butter, whisking constantly, until the sauce thickens and has a lovely glistening shine. Strain through a fine sieve and season. Keep warm • Peel away eight cabbage leaves, discarding the bitter outer leaves and saving the heart for another use, such as coleslaw. Wash the leaves, remove and discard the central stalk. Chop the leaves into ribbons • Heat the goose fat in a large frying pan, add the pancetta slices, carrot, celeriac and onions and sauté for 2 minutes without colouring. Strain in a colander • In the same pan, sauté the cabbage for 1 minute. Add the water to create some steam. Return the carrot and pancetta mixture to the pan, add the cream and reduce for 5–6 minutes or until the cabbage is well coated with the cream • Place a spoonful of the cabbage in the centre of each warmed serving plate. Place a duck leg on top • Slice the foie gras into 3 x 3-cm ($1\frac{1}{4}$ x $1\frac{1}{4}$-in) cubes with a hot knife. Skewer three foie gras cubes onto each rosemary sprig • Heat a cast-iron griddle pan, add each foie gras skewer and grill for 2 minutes or until cooked and golden brown. Place on top of the duck leg • Peel and segment the oranges, using a sharp paring knife, making sure all the pith is removed • Heat a non-stick frying pan over medium heat, sprinkle in the sugar and cook for 2 minutes or until it begins to caramelise. Add the orange segments, toss and add the Grand Marnier • Place the orange segments on top of the foie gras and around the duck leg • Put the confit of orange zest on top of the foie gras. Spoon over the orange sauce, season and serve.

PAN-FRIED FOIE GRAS WITH APRICOTS AND TOBACCO SAUCE

[serves 4]

The distasteful aromas of tobacco are discarded in this controversial recipe in favour of the earthy sourness derived from first-grade quality pouch tobacco (never use tobacco from a rolled cigarette). The combination when paired with roasted apricots blends into a lingering moment of sweet and sour. Foie gras is the real winner with this dish as it has the earthy and subtle characteristics to partner the end result perfectly. The only tough question to answer is: what wine? I like the Muscats from the hills above Malaga on the Costa del Sol in Southern Spain.

1 thick slice of brioche, crusts removed
3 eggs
1 teaspoon ground cinnamon
1 tablespoon clarified butter (see page 381)
4 x 60 g (2 oz) slices of foie gras
4 apricots, halved
4 sprigs of thyme
2 tablespoons of peeled pistachio nuts
150 ml (5 fl oz) Sauternes
3 tablespoons of double cream
1 cup of maple syrup
2 teaspoons of freshly dried julienned tobacco leaves

Slice the brioche into four even squares • Place the eggs and cinnamon in a bowl and whisk to combine • Soak the brioche squares in the egg mixture for 1 minute • Melt the clarified butter in a heavy-based frying pan over medium heat. Add the brioche squares and fry on each side for 1 minute or until golden and crisp. Remove from the pan and drain on paper towel. Transfer to four warmed serving plates • Heat a non-stick frying pan over medium heat. Add the foie gras and pan-fry on each side for 1 minute or until caramelised and a lovely golden colour. Place a slice of foie gras on top of each brioche square • In the same pan add the apricots, thyme and pistachio nuts and cook for 1 minute. Add the Sauternes and cook for 1 minute to allow the Sauternes to impart its aromatic qualities • Remove the apricots, pistachios and thyme and arrange on each serving plate. Return the Sauternes to the stove and add the cream. Bring to the boil for 30 seconds, then spoon over and around the foie gras • Combine the maple syrup and tobacco in a saucepan and bring to the boil over low heat. Simmer for 2 minutes and spoon over the foie gras. Serve immediately.

Terrine of foie gras, ox tongue and lentils du Puy

Grilled foie gras, caramelised apple, poached walnuts and grapes with Sauternes emulsion

Twice-cooked duck leg with foie gras and orange sauce

Pan-fried foie gras with apricots and tobacco sauce

Parfait of chicken livers and foie gras

Foie gras baked in brioche

Baked crayfish with foie gras, sauce Nantua and braised winter vegetables

Hot quail paté

Parfait of chicken livers and foie gras

[makes 20 slices]

Excuse me, for including such a complicated recipe — it contradicts everything I said earlier about the simplicity of foie gras — but the work involved is worth the extra effort. You can match this dish with anything from Sauternes, or pinot gris to crisp Beaujolais. This recipe resembles the texture and appearance of parfait.

800 g (1lb 10 oz) chicken livers
Sea salt
80 g (2¾ oz) foie gras
*2 tablespoons saltpetre (sodium nitrate)**
*200 ml (7 fl oz) Madeira**
*200 ml (7 fl oz) ruby port**
3 shallots, thinly sliced
2 cloves of garlic, thinly sliced
*Bouquet garni**
250 g (8 oz) butter, melted
5 eggs
3 egg yolks

FOIE GRAS BUTTER
150 g (5 oz) butter, softened
*50 g (1¾ oz) foie gras fat**
*2 teaspoons white truffle oil**
3½ tablespoons olive oil

Preheat the oven to 120°C (250°F) • Purée the chicken livers and 1 tablespoon of sea salt in a food processor until thick. Pass through a fine sieve, pushing the mixture through with a ladle. Return the puréed liver to the food processor and blend with the foie gras and saltpetre • In a heavy-based medium-sized saucepan, combine the Madeira, port, shallots, garlic and bouquet garni and cook until reduced by two-thirds. Strain while still hot. Add to the puréed livers in the food processor and blend for 2 minutes • Slowly pour in the butter while the motor is running • Add the eggs and egg yolks with the motor running and process for 1 minute • Pour into a plastic wrap-lined 9 x 32-cm (3½ x 13-in) terrine mould, filling to the top • Cover the entire mould with plastic wrap, to act as a seal. If the mould has a lid, place it on top • Place the terrine mould on a baking tray and pour in boiling water to come halfway up the sides of the mould • Place in the oven for 45–60 minutes. To test if the mix is cooked, treat it like a crème caramel, if it wobbles while retaining its shape then it's ready. If there is any sign of liquid in the middle, give it another 20 minutes or so • Allow the terrine to cool, then transfer to the refrigerator for 2 weeks, allowing the flavour to develop • To make the foie gras butter, place the butter in the food processor and blend until pale. Add the foie gras fat, truffle oil and olive oil and process until fully amalgamated • Remove the plastic wrap from the terrine. Using a spatula, carefully remove the top 3-mm (1/8-in) dark dry layer on the parfait • Place a thin layer of the foie gras butter over the top. This will become the bottom of the unmoulded terrine. Place in the refrigerator to allow this layer to set • Remove the terrine from the refrigerator; dip the terrine mould in hot water to help unmould. Tip the mould face down onto a serving platter. Ease out the terrine from the mould. Break the suction by pulling on the plastic wrap. The terrine will gently slide out • Spread the foie gras butter over the top and sides of the exposed terrine. Do not spread it on the ends. Use a palette knife to smooth the surface. Cover gently with plastic wrap and place in the refrigerator for 30 minutes • Use a long thin knife dipped in hot water to slice the parfait. Carefully slide the parfait from the blade of the knife and place directly onto each serving plate. Serve with a slice of warm toasted brioche.

Foie gras baked in brioche

[serves 12]

One strong word of advice: try to complete this recipe as close to serving time as possible. Brioche turns stale and rapidly dries out in the refrigerator. This dish is best served with a late harvest Alsatian variety of wine, such as gewürztraminer.

*500 g (1 lb) bakers' flour**
*2 teaspoons gluten**
1 teaspoon salt
20 g (3/4 oz) fresh yeast
80 g (2 3/4 oz) sugar
2 tablespoons milk
6 eggs
400 g (13 oz) butter, softened and chopped into fine dice
1 x 600 g (1 1/4 lb) lobe of duck foie gras
2 1/2 tablespoons cognac
2 1/2 tablespoons sweet white wine
20 g (3/4 oz) sea salt
20 pink peppercorns, crushed*
200 ml (7 fl oz) Madeira jelly (see page 386)
1 shallot, finely chopped
100 g (3 1/2 oz) mâche (corn salad)
2 1/2 tablespoons walnut vinaigrette (see page 396)

Place the flour, gluten, salt, yeast and sugar in a large mixing bowl, add the milk and, using a mixer with a dough hook attached, mix until a dough forms • Add the eggs slowly, one at a time, beating well between each addition • Add the butter and mix until the dough just comes together • Cover with plastic wrap and rest for 12 hours in the refrigerator • Marinate the foie gras in the cognac, wine, sea salt and peppercorns for 12 hours in the fridge. Drain the foie gras • Preheat the oven to 200°C (400°F) • Knead the brioche dough for 1 minute and roll out on a floured work surface until 2.5 cm (1 in) thick. Place the foie gras in the centre and roll up into a neat tight parcel, trying to keep the shape of the foie gras when folding the brioche around. Place onto a greaseproof paper-lined baking tray • Bake for 25 minutes or until golden brown • Rest on a cake rack until cool. (Any foie gras fat in the baking tray can be kept in the freezer and used for foie gras butter.) Transfer to the refrigerator until cold • Warm the Madeira jelly in a saucepan on a very low heat • Make a small hole in the top of the brioche. Carefully pour in the jelly. Return to the refrigerator for 1 hour • Combine the shallot and mâche in a serving bowl. Add the walnut dressing and toss • Slice the brioche with a sharp serrated knife that has been dipped in hot water. Serve with the salad.

Baked crayfish with foie gras, sauce Nantua and braised winter vegetables

[serves 4]

THIS IS A VARIATION of the combination of foie gras and crayfish made famous by Antonne Careme in the eighteenth century.

2 x 650 g (1 lb 5 oz) live crayfish
20 baby carrots
1½ tablespoons olive oil
⅓ cup Calvados
*50 g (1¾ oz) cultured butter**
Juice of ½ orange
Salt and freshly ground pepper
300 ml (10 fl oz) Nantua sauce (see page 248)
100 ml (3½ fl oz) whipped cream
Juice of 1 lemon
½ bunch of tarragon, chopped
1 x 500 g (1 lb) lobe of duck foie gras
4 sprigs of chervil

Place the crayfish in the freezer for 30 minutes to anaesthetise them • Cook the crayfish in boiling salted water for 8 minutes • Peel and shape the carrots into 5 x 2-cm (2 x ¾-in) batons • Remove the heads of the crayfish, reserve the coral*, wrap in plastic wrap and place in the freezer. (The coral can be used in soups and mousses, such as the lobster mousse on page 251.) Cut the crayfish tails in half • Preheat the oven to 180°C (350°F) • Heat the olive oil in a flameproof casserole dish, add the crayfish tails flesh-side down and cook on high heat for 2 minutes or until browned. Turn, add the Calvados and flambé. Place in the oven for 3 minutes • Remove from the shell leaving the end of the tail attached • Cook the carrot in boiling salted water for 4 minutes. Toss in the butter, add a squeeze of orange juice and season with salt and pepper • Place the Nantua sauce in a saucepan and cook over medium heat until reduced by two-thirds. Add the cream and whisk until boiling. Season with the lemon juice, tarragon and salt and pepper. Remove from the heat • Place the carrot in the centre of four warmed serving plates • Slice the foie gras into 16 pieces using a knife dipped in hot water • Heat a cast-iron griddle pan and grill the slices of foie gras, in batches, for 2 minutes on each side or until golden • Place the crayfish tail and foie gras neatly on the bed of carrot. Spoon over the Nantua sauce and garnish with a sprig of chervil. Serve with a bowl of pommes Pont Neuf (see page 99).

Hot quail paté

[serves 4]

I CREATED THIS recipe from an old Larousse *Gastronomique*. This version is not as heavy as the original, which is considered old-fashioned. Match this with a glass of Sauternes, the acidic finish will cut through the underlying richness of the foie gras.

400 g (13 oz) puff pastry (see page 54)
4 x 160 g (5¼ oz) quails
Salt and freshly ground pepper
240 g (8 oz) foie gras
*100 g (3½ oz) pork fat**
*50 g (1¾ oz) goose fat**
*2 tablespoons black truffle paste**
300 g (10 oz) minced (ground) veal
2½ tablespoons cognac
3 eggs
*8 slices black truffle**
30 g (1 oz) clarified butter (see page 381)
200 ml (7 fl oz) Sauternes
100 g (3½ oz) cultured butter, cut into fine dice*
1 cup mixed salad leaves

Roll out the puff pastry until 6 mm (¼ in) thick. Rest on a flat tray in the refrigerator for 10 minutes or until the dough is firm • Ask your butcher to bone the quail. Starting at the backbone, make two incisions either side of the bone. Remove the breastbone and flatten out the bird. Remove the four bones associated with the breast and legs by pushing them out with your fingers. Season inside each bird with salt and pepper • Cut the foie gras into four with a knife dipped in hot water • Combine the pork fat, goose fat, truffle paste and veal in a food processor and season with salt and pepper. Blend until smooth. Add the cognac • Add one of the eggs, blend for 1 minute. Remove from the food processor • Place a tablespoonful of the veal mixture in the cavity of each quail. Add a slice of foie gras, a slice of truffle and another spoonful of the veal mixture. Fold the quail legs and wings inwards to resemble a ball and place another slice of truffle on top of each breast • To make the pithiviers*, cut the puff pastry into four squares 2.5 cm (1 in) bigger than each quail. Reserve the remaining pastry for the top. Place a quail in the centre of each pastry square. Lightly beat 1 of the remaining eggs and with it brush the pastry around the quail • Preheat the oven to 180°C (350°F) • Cut another four pastry squares slightly larger than the base. Place each pastry square over the quail and shape into a dome. Flour a pastry cutter that will fit over the dome quite tightly. Press the blunt side of the cutter firmly onto the pastry to help create a dome • Warm the clarified butter and whisk in the remaining egg. Brush over the pastry • Transfer the pithiviers to the oven and bake for 25 minutes or until golden. Set aside to rest for 10 minutes • Reduce the Sauternes by two-thirds and gradually whisk in the butter until thick, smooth and shiny. The sauce should easily coat the back of a spoon • Slice the pithiviers in half widthways and serve with a drizzle of the Sauternes sauce and a few mixed salad leaves.

The Scallop

THE SCALLOP IS A favourite ingredient in many well-known kitchens. Farming of this revered and expensive bivalve is an area yet to be fully explored in Australian waters. The bivalve mollusc, found on sandy or weedy seabeds, moves through the water with the unique technique of opening and closing its shell. Although the scallop is found in very large quantities, world harvest numbers of about one million tons are decreasing every year because of overfishing. The demand for scallop meat cannot be sustained without the rapid introduction of aquaculture in Australian waters. It may seem like a relatively new scientific venture to us, but it has a very long and rich history. The roots of aquaculture can be traced back to 3500 BC in China. Asia is still, by far, the leader in aquaculture production. In Australia and the United States, aquaculture is a small, yet diverse industry with huge potential for growth due to the increasing environmental issues we face with overfishing.

Dredged wild scallops, such as those from Japan, America and Scotland, rate badly for their quality because they are normally killed during the process and are full of sand. Scallops gathered by divers are the best option for the wild variety. Net-farmed Atlantic sea scallops from Newfoundland and bay scallops from Nova Scotia are good alternatives because they are grown on suspended racks and cause less harm to the environment than dredged wild scallops. They are available worldwide, snap frozen in 1-kilogram (2-pound) bags.

Scallops are known as coquilles Saint Jacques, 'shells of Saint James', in the French culinary world. Saint James was the brother of John, and one of the Twelve Apostles. Supposedly his intervention saved the life of a drowning knight, who emerged from the sea covered with scallop shells. Scallops were thus named in Saint James's honour, as was the dish, and the scallop shell became the symbol of the Order of Saint James. In medieval times pilgrimages were made to the coastal area of Galicia in north-western Spain to Santiago de Compostela and the shrine of Saint James, where he is supposedly buried. The pilgrims were served a scallop for reaching the shrine.

The unique complexity of its flesh means the scallop can be served roasted, steamed, braised or raw. My fishmonger occasionally supplies me with wild scallops from the Derwent River in Tasmania. These scallops have been left to their own devices and the result is fat, juicy four–five-year-old scallops that are incredibly large, sweet and delicate.

Shark Bay scallops are found wild and cultivated in Shark Bay and its surrounds in Western Australia. They are normally purchased frozen in the half shell without the roe. Coffin Bay scallops are a similar type of large white scallop. Occasionally they are found live in the closed shell. The scallops are mostly exported to Asia and are very rarely seen on tables in Australia.

Sea scallops grow in deep waters off the east coast of the United States. Bay scallops, also called Cape Cod scallops, grow in bays and harbours and are smaller. Calico scallops, grown in waters off Florida, are about the size of bay scallops, and are mechanically shucked and partially cooked. Scallops are also imported fresh from countries such as China and Peru. They are available shucked and, rarely, live in the shell. Their mild-flavoured orange roe is sometimes sold along with the scallop meat. To use the orange roe, carefully butterfly the scallop open, lay the roe on a greaseproof paper-lined tray, dry out in a warm part of the kitchen or place in a very low oven for 24 hours. Once the roe is completely dried, blend into a fine powder. Use the powdered roe to crumb scallops and prawns, then fry in olive oil. The flavour is an intense burst of the sea.

Quality fresh scallops are easy to recognise. They smell of the sea, not strong and fishy, and are ivory to light pink in colour. Pure white scallops may have been soaked in a solution to make them appear plumper. Brown or dull-looking scallops are just too old. Fresh live scallops in the shell are slightly opened, but will close when pinched.

To store scallops, unwrap, place in a bowl covered with a wet paper towel, and refrigerate, prepare, and eat the same day. To freeze, lay the scallops on a clean tray, double wrap with plastic wrap and leave for up to 2 months. To thaw, unwrap, place the scallops in a bowl, cover, and thaw overnight in the refrigerator. Scallops are easier to overcook than other shellfish; they become rubbery, dry and tasteless. When roasting use a very hot heavy-based frying pan and a generous amount of olive oil, seal both sides very quickly until golden.

Scallops wrapped in smoked salmon with blini and salmon roe

[serves 8]

SMOKED SALMON AND delicate white scallops are the perfect match for a lazy Sunday brunch with a glass of crisp white Burgundy.

100 g ($3\frac{1}{2}$ oz) hazelnuts
2 cups hazelnut oil
1 kg (2 lb) side of smoked salmon
24 extra large scallops
250 g (8 oz) fromage blanc, drained*
2 shallots, finely chopped
1 tablespoon finely chopped chives
1 tablespoon finely chopped curly-leaf parsley
$\frac{1}{3}$ cup double cream
Salt and freshly ground pepper
Juice of $\frac{1}{2}$ lemon
2 tablespoons olive oil
2 cups mixed salad leaves
100 ml ($3\frac{1}{2}$ fl oz) hazelnut vinaigrette (see page 396)
24 blini (see page 64)
50 g ($1\frac{3}{4}$ oz) mature salmon roe

Preheat the oven to 180°C (350°F) • Place the hazelnuts on a baking tray and roast in the oven for 5–10 minutes or until the skin starts to flake off. Place in a tea towel and rub off the skin • Place the hazelnuts in the hazelnut oil. Macerate for a minimum of 30 minutes. The nuts develop a more concentrated flavour in the oil and may be stored for up to 6 months • Slice the smoked salmon into 2-cm ($\frac{3}{4}$-in) strips long enough to cover the outside of a scallop • Wrap each scallop in a strip of smoked salmon. Use two strips if necessary. Secure with a toothpick • To make the fromage blanc mixture, place the fromage blanc in a mixing bowl, add the shallots, chives and parsley and mix well • Fold in the cream and season with salt, pepper and lemon juice. Place in the refrigerator for 20 minutes or until firm • Heat the olive oil in a heavy-based frying pan, add the scallops and cook for 2 minutes or until golden • Dress the salad leaves with half of the hazelnut vinaigrette • To serve, place three blini on each serving plate. Top with a small amount of the salad and three scallops. Using a teaspoon that has been dipped in hot water, form a quenelle with the fromage blanc mixture and place on top of each scallop. Finish by placing salmon roe on each quenelle. Drizzle over the remaining hazelnut vinaigrette and scatter five hazelnuts around each plate. Serve immediately.

Roast scallop, pork belly, pig's ear and truffle salad

[serves 6]

THIS IS VERY SIMILAR to the pig's ear and prawn dish that has become a signature at Vue de monde. The combination of the fat, salty and moist pork with the crispy pig's ear and the delicate harmoniously sweet scallops will send you and your fellow diners into raptures. When braising, season before and during the cooking process to ensure maximum flavour, colour and texture.

The textures and flavours in this dish will harmonise well with a light red wine.

150 ml (5 fl oz) olive oil
300 g (10 oz) pork belly
Salt and freshly ground pepper
1 carrot, peeled and chopped into 3
1 stick of celery, chopped into 3
1 onion
2 cloves of garlic
4 sprigs of thyme
1½ cups dry white wine
4 cups veal stock (see page 294)
2 x 100 g (3½ oz) pig's ears
50 g (1¾ oz) plain (all-purpose) flour
2 eggs
100 g (3½ oz) panko breadcrumbs*
12 large scallops
1 cup mixed salad leaves
200 g (6½ oz) truffle mayonnaise (see page 394)

Preheat the oven to 150°C (300°F) • Heat 2 tablespoons of the olive oil in a medium-sized frying pan, add the pork belly, salt and pepper, and cook for 5 minutes or until crisp and golden • Heat 1 tablespoon of the olive oil in a flameproof casserole dish, add the carrot, celery, onion, garlic and thyme, season with salt and pepper and cook for 8 minutes. Add the white wine and reduce until evaporated. Add the veal stock, bring to the boil, and allow to bubble for 5 minutes • Add the pig's ears and pork belly, cover with aluminium (aluminum) foil and place in the oven for 3 hours. Use a slotted spoon to remove the pig's ears. Transfer to a container, cover, and place in the refrigerator overnight • Continue to braise the pork belly for 40 minutes or until soft and jelly-like. Test to see if the pork belly is cooked by sliding a skewer into the centre of the meat. If there is no resistance, then it is ready. Place the pork belly into the fridge for 3–4 hours until it is firm enough to slice without crumbling or breaking up • Slice the braised pork belly and the pig's ears into 2.5-cm (1-in) cubes

6 garlic croutons (see page 383)
1 medium bulb of fennel, thinly sliced
2 shallots, finely chopped
Juice of ½ lemon
6 quail eggs
100 g (3½ oz) chlorophyll, optional*

• Place the flour in a shallow bowl • In a second bowl, lightly beat the eggs • Place the panko breadcrumbs in a third bowl • Dip the pig's ears in the flour to coat, then in the egg and lastly in the breadcrumbs • Heat 3½ tablespoons of the olive oil in a heavy-based frying pan, add the pork belly cubes and cook over medium heat for 6–7 minutes or until crispy. Season and set aside. In the same pan, add the scallops and pig's ears and gently fry in the fat from the pork belly for 2 minutes or until the scallops are golden • Dress the salad with 1 tablespoon of the truffle mayonnaise; add the garlic croutons, fennel and shallots. Season with salt, pepper and lemon juice • Wipe the frying pan clean with paper towel, heat the remaining olive oil and crack the quail eggs, well spaced, into the pan. Cook over very low heat for about 1 minute. The egg white starting to set will determine that the eggs are ready. Gently slide the eggs onto a chopping board. Use a 3-cm (1¼-in) round cutter to shape the eggs • Spread the remaining truffle mayonnaise inside a 9-cm (3½-in) metal ring placed in the centre of each serving plate. Remove the ring • Place the pork belly, left of centre, on the mayonnaise. Place two scallops next to the pork. Rest the pig's ear cubes on top of the scallops and pork, directly in the centre of the circle. Scatter over a pinch of salad, then position a quail egg on top • Place the chlorophyll, if using, around the outside of the truffle mayonnaise and serve.

Ceviche of scallops

[serves 8]

You will impress yourself as well as your friends by mastering this eye-opening dish, which isn't as complicated as it may first appear.

1 celeriac, julienned
1 Granny Smith apple, julienned
Salt and freshly ground pepper
Juice of 1 lemon
200 g (6½ oz) truffle mayonnaise (see page 394)
2 shallots, finely chopped
16 scallops
2½ tablespoons hazelnut vinaigrette (see page 396)
1 tablespoon finely chopped tarragon
1 tablespoon finely chopped curly-leaf parsley
½ tablespoon finely chopped chives
*1 tablespoon squid ink**
2 tablespoons salmon roe

Season the celeriac and apple with the salt and pepper and a little lemon juice. Set aside for 30 minutes • Place the celeriac and apple in a tea towel and squeeze out any moisture • Fold 100 g (3½ oz) of the truffle mayonnaise in with the celeriac and apple. Add half of the shallots and stir. Taste, season with salt, pepper and half the lemon juice • Slice each scallop into three and combine with the hazelnut vinaigrette, herbs, the remaining lemon juice and salt and pepper. Set aside to marinate for 10 minutes • Combine 1 tablespoon of the truffle mayonnaise with the squid ink. Fill a piping bag or a squeezeable sauce bottle with a very fine nozzle with the squid ink mayonnaise • Spread the remaining truffle mayonnaise inside a 10-cm (4-in) metal ring placed in the centre of each serving plate. Remove the ring • Place squid ink dots around the mayonnaise in a circular fashion • Pile the celeriac and apple inside an 8-cm (3-in) metal ring centred on the plate, press the mixture down firmly. Arrange the scallops on top. Place 1 teaspoon of salmon roe in the centre of each plate and serve.

Coquilles Saint Jacques voilées

[serves 6]

The name suggests this dish belongs in an old *Reader's Digest* collector's issue, but let me tell you now, what goes around comes around — and this dish is back! Simple, flavoursome and easy to prepare, scallops baked in puff pastry with dry vermouth is a great low maintenance social dish. Prepare the dish a day ahead, then relax and enjoy a drink with friends before serving. Try a buttery Chardonnay from the Margaret River in Western Australia or the Montrachet region of Burgundy.

350 g (11 oz) puff pastry (see page 54)
18 large scallops in their shells
Salt and freshly ground pepper
360 ml (12 fl oz) fish stock (see page 243)
1 clove of garlic, crushed
8 tarragon leaves
1 bulb of fennel, julienned
1 large carrot, julienned
2 sticks of celery, julienned
2 leeks, julienned
2 zucchini (courgettes), julienned
90 ml (3 fl oz) dry white wine
*90 ml (3 fl oz) dry vermouth (Noilly Prat)**
100 g (3½ oz) butter, cut into fine dice
Pinch of cayenne pepper
Juice of ½ lemon
2 tablespoons olive oil
1 cup baby spinach

Roll out the puff pastry on a lightly floured work surface to 6 mm (¼ in) thick. Rest on a flat tray in the refrigerator to firm. This will make the pastry easier to cut and shape over the scallop shell • Remove the scallops from the shell and separate the orange roe. Clean six of the shells with a nail brush in hot soapy water. Season the roe and pierce with the point of a knife to prevent the roe from curling up when hitting the hot pan • Place the fish stock in a heavy-based saucepan and bring to the boil. Add the garlic and 2 of the tarragon leaves, and continue to boil • Add the fennel and cook for 1 minute, then add the carrot. Cook for 1 minute, and then add the celery and leek. Bring to the boil and immediately remove all the vegetables and set aside to cool. While still warm, add the zucchini and mix. The residual heat will cook the zucchini • To make the butter sauce, reduce the fish stock used for poaching the vegetables by three-quarters. Add the white wine and vermouth and reduce by two-thirds • Gradually whisk in the butter, a quarter at a time, until the sauce is thick, smooth and shiny. Season with salt, cayenne and lemon juice and set to one side • Heat 1 tablespoon of the olive oil in a heavy-based frying pan, add the scallop roes and fry for 30 seconds •

6 sprigs of chervil
3 eggs

Lightly brush the scallop shells with a thin coating of olive oil. Line the shells with two or three spinach leaves • Place the vegetables in the centre of the cleaned shells, then add the sautéed roes. Arrange three scallops around the vegetables, top with a sprig of chervil and a tarragon leaf. Season with salt and pepper. Spoon over a generous amount of the butter sauce • Cut the puff pastry into six pieces 2.5 cm (1 in) larger than the scallop shells. Roll out into rough circles and rest in the refrigerator for 10 minutes • Preheat the oven to 180°C (350°F) • Whisk the eggs to form an egg wash • Place a circle of puff pastry over each shell and press down firmly around the edges to prevent the pastry separating from the shell during baking. Trim any extra pastry around the shell. Brush with the egg wash • Place on an aluminium (aluminum) foil-lined baking tray to prevent the scallops from tipping over and losing the cooking juices during baking. Bake for 10 minutes or until crispy and golden. Serve immediately.

Scallops wrapped in smoked salmon with blini and salmon roe

Roast scallop, pork belly, pig's ear and truffle salad

Ceviche of scallops

Coquilles Saint Jacques voilées

Scallop mousseline serving suggestion

Scallop mousseline

[makes 750 g (1½ lb)]

As an apprentice chef I regarded, and I certainly wasn't alone in thinking this way, scallop mousseline as my nemesis. It is simply puréed scallops lightened with cream and eggs. The main point to remember is that the ingredients and equipment used to make the mousseline need to be kept as cold as possible so that the scallops aren't cooked in the process — shellfish starts to change its form at 30°C (85°F) and over.

500 g (1 lb) scallop meat, cleaned
2 tablespoons salt
*2 teaspoons lobster roe**
1 egg
2 egg yolks
200 ml (7 fl oz) double cream

Place the bowl, blade and lid of the food processor in the freezer for 10 minutes • Blend the scallops and salt in the food processor until puréed • Add the lobster roe and purée • Add the egg and egg yolks, one by one, using a rubber spatula to scrape the sides of the bowl between each addition • Add the cream and process briefly. Do not overwork or the mousseline will split • Use as required or poach quenelles in simmering fish stock (see page 243) for 5 minutes or until firm. Also see poached trout royale on page 229 • The serving suggestion in the photograph on page 196 is simply cooked macarini pasta placed in a ring then filled with mousseline bound with chopped cooked mussels, steamed for 6 minutes and served with mussels and fish velouté (see page 244).

The Oyster

LET'S GET THE FACTS straight. We are dealing with a creature that pumps up to 40 litres (70 pints) of salt water an hour through its system and at the same time feeds on that ever-elusive microscopic animal called plankton. The oyster has the ability, using its 1 million or so gills, to determine different compounds, toxins and chemicals and expel them through its specially devised waste system. In this age of environmental damage to our ever decreasing wilderness both on land and at sea, the oyster deserves a medal.

To purchase oysters, you first of all have to know what varieties are available. The most common oyster found all over the world is the Pacific cup. The Pacific oyster mostly seen in the markets around the world is a hybrid breed originating from Japan. They are a tough, fast growing oyster that is easily cultivated. The other type of oyster is the flat oyster, which is harder to farm and better suited to colder waters. These are a rare find at a retail outlet. The native variety in Australia is called the Angasi, *Ostrea angasi*, named after the explorer, George French Angus. It is very

similar to the belon oyster, found at the mouth of the Belon River in Brittany, France.

If I were in Sydney right now I would choose a Sydney rock. If I were sipping on a cool, crisp glass of riesling in Auckland, it would be a New Zealand bluff. If I were taking a lunch break from fishing for an elusive brown trout in the Tamar Valley in Tasmania, it would be the Tamar mud. These are examples of wild oysters, true to where they are sourced and each different in flavour and mystery.

Wherever you are in the world, look for displayed oysters that are closed and presented flat. Fishmongers buy oysters two ways: directly from the source farm or at the morning markets where the oysters are placed into a large holding container. Oysters from all regions will be placed together — they are sorted by size, not region.The oyster normally suffers badly in this process. The chances are that the water inside the shell will drain out and the oyster will dehydrate and die.

Don't buy oysters with smooth polished shells; they have been tumbled in a large processor to remove the molluscs and silt off the shell, making them more appealing to supermarkets. This kills the oyster and removes the lovely juices inside.

Buying fresh, closed oysters directly from the source is incomparably better. I make sure all my oysters have a certificate and map lot number showing their origin and date of harvest. Many people are confused by the oyster's seasonality — to be honest, so am I. The easiest way to remember when oysters are at their best is by asking a meteorologist! It's all about the water temperature: when it heats up over 18°C (67°F), the oysters spawn, giving that milky, fat appearance with less juice in the shell and a much more subdued, creamy flavour.

The Oyster

Some avid gourmets may criticise meddling with such a beautiful product of nature that is at its best when plucked from the water, shucked, given a squeeze of fresh lemon or lime juice and guzzled immediately. My great friend Gavan Disney introduced me to the wonders of freshly cracked pepper and a squeeze of lime juice on top of an oyster. As an artist, chef and restaurateur I feel it is my duty to provide you with an oyster dish or two that might convince even an avid oyster hater to try their luck.

To present oysters, rest them on a bed of rock salt on a serving platter. For best results, place the rock salt in a food processor and blend for a good 5–10 minutes before carefully adding enough water to form a paste.

Another inexpensive and effective presentation is to ask your supplier for some fresh seaweed, wash and blanch the seaweed in boiling water for 30 seconds. It will turn a bright green. Rest the oysters on the seaweed when serving.

Oysters with smoked salmon and citrus jelly

[serves 10 as an entrée]

OYSTERS AND SMOKED SALMON evoke fond memories of my Irish heritage. I am tempted to tell you simply to butter some freshly sliced brown bread, place on the bread some slices of smoked salmon, top with two or three oysters and sprinkle with cracked pepper, but on a special occasion the following recipe makes a colourful and professional start to a glass of bubbles.

CITRUS JELLY

1 tablespoon olive oil
8 shallots, thinly sliced
2 cloves of garlic, thinly sliced
4 sprigs of thyme
4 sprigs of tarragon
1 bay leaf
*2 cups pastis (Pernod)**
Pinch of saffron
*2 cups dry vermouth (Noilly Prat)**
2 cups freshly squeezed orange juice
*12 cups fish stock (see page 243)**
10 egg whites
*12 leaves gelatin**

FROMAGE BLANC FILLING

*250 g (8 oz) fromage blanc**
2 shallots, finely chopped
2 tablespoons finely chopped curly-leaf parsley
2 tablespoons finely chopped chives

To make the citrus jelly, heat the olive oil in a heavy-based saucepan, add the shallots, garlic, thyme, tarragon and bay leaf, and cook for 6 minutes or until the shallots are soft and transparent • Add the pastis, saffron, vermouth and orange juice and reduce by two-thirds • Add the fish stock and bring to the boil. Reduce heat to low and simmer for 20 minutes • Whisk in the egg whites to clarify. (The protein in egg whites acts as a filter by trapping particles in the raft it forms as it cooks.) Strain through a sieve lined with a layer of cheesecloth • Add the gelatin and stir to dissolve. Ensure the jelly has cooled, but is not set before using • To make the fromage blanc filling, combine the fromage blanc, shallots, parsley and chives • Fold in the cream. Season with salt and pepper and lemon juice • Carefully remove the oysters from their shells, reserving the juice and oysters. Clean the oyster shells in hot soapy water, rinse and drain well • Line each shell with a slice of smoked salmon. Press your finger around the edge of each shell letting the sharp edges cut away the excess salmon • Place a small teaspoon of the fromage blanc filling in each lined shell and top with an oyster • Place the lemon, orange and lime zest in a saucepan of cold water and blanch for 2 minutes. Refresh in cold water to preserve the colour.

100 ml ($3\frac{1}{2}$ fl oz) double cream
Salt and freshly ground pepper
Juice of ½ lemon

30 oysters
1 kg (2 lb) side of sliced smoked salmon
Zest of 2 lemons
Zest of 2 oranges
Zest of 2 limes
10 sprigs of watercress

Place a few strands of each on top of the oysters • Blanch the watercress in boiling water for 5 seconds. Refresh in ice cold water and drain. Place a watercress leaf on each oyster • Place the filled oyster shells on egg cartons to balance. Transfer to the refrigerator for 20 minutes to chill • Spoon the citrus jelly into each shell until each oyster is covered. Refrigerate for 5 minutes, then add more citrus jelly so that the oysters are completely covered. Return to the refrigerator. The jelly will take 30 minutes to set before you can serve.

Tempura-battered oysters with crispy black pudding and quail eggs

[serves 6 as an entrée]

Crispy oysters are the best way to entice an oyster hater to have a go. I love the versatility they give when paired with other flavours, such as black pudding. Try the same recipe with pan-fried slices of chorizo sausage.

30 Pacific oysters

TEMPURA BATTER

200 g ($6\frac{1}{2}$ oz) plain (all-purpose) flour
200 g ($6\frac{1}{2}$ oz) cornflour (cornstarch)
2 teapoons baking powder
2 cups water

1 cup plain (all-purpose) flour, extra
8 cups peanut oil
Salt and freshly ground pepper
Juice of $\frac{1}{2}$ lemon
6 small black pudding sausages
$2\frac{1}{2}$ tablespoons olive oil
30 quail eggs
750 g ($1\frac{1}{2}$ lb) rock salt
1 cup mixed salad leaves
2 tablespoons watercress
2 shallots, chopped
1 bulb of fennel, thinly shaved
100 ml ($3\frac{1}{2}$ fl oz) French vinaigrette (see page 396)

Carefully open the oysters and remove from their shells. Clean the shells inside and out with hot soapy water. Rinse well and drain • To make the tempura batter, sift the flour, cornflour and baking powder into a mixing bowl, add the water and whisk until smooth and creamy • Place half of the extra flour in a shallow bowl. Pierce each oyster with a toothpick and dip into the flour and then into the batter • Heat the peanut oil to 180°C (350°F) in a deep-fryer, add the oysters, in batches, and fry until golden brown and crispy, about 2 minutes. Season with salt and lemon juice. Rest on paper towel until all have been cooked • Chop each black pudding sausage into five evenly sized slices and lightly dust in the remaining flour • Heat a heavy-based frying pan and fry the black pudding until crispy, about 3 minutes. Place on paper towel to drain • Heat the olive oil in a non-stick frying pan and gently fry the quail eggs, in batches, for 2 minutes • Place spoonfuls of rock salt in mounds on a serving plate. Press the oysters shells firmly into the salt • Combine the salad leaves, watercress, shallots and fennel. Drizzle over the vinaigrette and season with salt and pepper. Place a little salad in each oyster shell • Place a crispy oyster and a slice of black pudding neatly next to each other on top of the salad • To make the sauce bois boudran, combine the ketchup, mustard, shallots, Tabasco, Worcestershire, olive oil, sherry vinegar, chives and

SAUCE BOIS BOUDRAN

200 ml (7 fl oz) tomato ketchup
3 teaspoons Dijon mustard
1½ tablespoons finely chopped shallots
½ teaspoon Tabasco sauce
3 teaspoons Worcestershire sauce
300 ml (10 fl oz) olive oil
1 tablespoon sherry vinegar
2 teaspoons chopped chives
2 teaspoons chopped tarragon

tarragon in a bowl and stir • Spoon a small amount of sauce bois boudran over each oyster. Place a quail egg on top. Serve immediately. (I recommend five oysters per person as an entrée.)

OYSTERS WITH CUCUMBER RELISH AND CAVIAR

[serves 6 as an entrée]

THIS DISH IS A favourite of mine when entertaining at home. Quick and easy, its success relies on great quality oysters and the perfection of the caviar.

2 Lebanese cucumbers, peeled and cut into 5-mm (¼-in) dice
2 shallots, finely chopped
2½ tablespoons Champagne vinegar
2 tablespoons caster (superfine) sugar
2½ tablespoons dry white wine
2½ tablespoons extra virgin olive oil
Salt and freshly ground pepper
30 oysters
500 g (1 lb) rock salt
1 tablespoon finely chopped chives
50 g (1¾ oz) caviar

Combine the cucumber and shallots in a mixing bowl • Combine the vinegar, sugar and wine in a small heavy-based saucepan, bring to the boil and cook for 5 minutes. Pour over the cucumber and shallots • Add the olive oil and season with salt and pepper. Place in the refrigerator for 30 minutes or until cold • Carefully open the oysters and remove from their shells. Clean the shells inside and out in hot soapy water. Rinse well and drain • Place the shells onto mounds of rock salt on a serving plate • Add the chives to the cucumber relish • Spoon a small amount of cucumber relish into each oyster shell. Place an oyster on top, add a small amount of caviar and serve.

Oysters with smoked salmon and citrus jelly

Warmed oysters with linguine and Champagne velouté

Tempura-battered oysters with crispy black pudding and quail eggs

Oysters with cucumber relish and caviar

Crumbed oysters with brandade and bouillabaisse

Poached oysters with scrambled duck eggs

Wild oysters with lobster mousse and puff pastry

Chicken and oyster pie

WARMED OYSTERS WITH LINGUINE AND CHAMPAGNE VELOUTÉ

[makes 30]

FOR THIS DISH I recommend opening your own oysters so that you can utilise the sea-flavoured juices in the velouté. You may like to make the pasta the day before.

LINGUINE

15 egg yolks (size 55 g [1¾ oz] eggs)
*300 g (10 oz) Italian 00 flour**

30 freshly shucked oysters

CHAMPAGNE VELOUTÉ

1½ tablespoons olive oil
5 shallots, finely sliced
2 cloves of garlic
5 sprigs of thyme
1 bay leaf
200 ml (7 fl oz) dry white wine
2 cups fish stock (see page 243)
*200 ml (7 fl oz) oyster juice**
200 ml (7 fl oz) double cream
200 ml (7 fl oz) Champagne
Salt and freshly ground pepper
Juice of ½ lemon

1 tablespoon olive oil
1 cucumber, peeled, deseeded and julienned
100 g (3½ oz) mature salmon roe

Combine the eggs and flour in a food processor and work for 10 minutes or until a firm dough forms • Run the pasta through the thickest setting on a pasta machine dusted with flour to prevent the dough from sticking. Repeat until you reach the second last setting, attach the linguine cutter and roll through • Cook the linguine in a large saucepan of salted water for 3 minutes, then drain • Carefully open the oysters and remove from their shells. Strain and reserve the juice for the velouté. Clean the oyster shells inside and out with hot soapy water. Rinse well and drain • To make the Champagne velouté, heat the olive oil in a heavy-based saucepan, add the shallots, garlic, thyme and bay leaf and cook for 10 minutes or until the shallots are softened • Add the white wine and reduce by half • Add the fish stock, bring to the boil, add the oyster juice and cream, and return to the boil. Cook for 3 minutes • Strain through a fine sieve and place in a large heavy-based saucepan over medium heat. Bring to the boil and add the Champagne, taste and season with salt, pepper and lemon juice. Angle a hand blender slightly out of the pan to create froth • Preheat the oven to 180°C (350°F) • Warm the oyster shells in the oven for 1 minute or until hot. Transfer to a serving plate, resting each shell on a small mound of rock salt • Warm the linguine in the olive oil and season. Twirl a small amount around a roasting fork and slide into an oyster shell, being careful not to overfill the shells

The Oyster

• Warm the oysters over a low heat for 1 minute in a little of their own juice, don't boil them • Place an oyster on top of each linguine-filled shell • Spoon over the Champagne velouté • Crisscross four pieces of cucumber, and place a few pearls of roe on top of each oyster. Serve immediately.

Crumbed oysters with brandade and bouillabaisse

[serves 6 as an entrée]

THE SOFT TEXTURE of the brandade, the crispiness of the succulent oysters and the subtlety of the bouillabaisse makes this the sort of restaurant dish that is very easily replicated at home. Rosé Champagne is always going to be an attractive match with this arty starter.

30 oysters
100 g (3½ oz) plain (all-purpose) flour
4 eggs
300 g (10 oz) panko breadcrumbs*
8 cups peanut oil
Salt
Juice of ½ lemon
200 g (6½ oz) brandade (see page 230)
2½ tablespoons warm milk
200 g (6½ oz) pommes mousseline (see page 102)
*80 g (2¾ oz) cultured butter**
1 tablespoon finely chopped flat-leaf parsley
Freshly ground pepper
500 g (1 lb) rock salt
1 cup bouillabaisse (see page 258)
30 sprigs of chervil

Carefully open and remove the oysters from their shells. Strain and reserve the oyster juice. Clean the shells inside and out with hot soapy water. Rinse well and drain • Place the flour in a shallow bowl • In a second bowl, lightly beat the eggs • Place the panko breadcrumbs in a third bowl • Dip the oysters in the flour to coat, then in the egg and lastly in the breadcrumbs • Heat the peanut oil in a deep-fryer, add the oysters and deep-fry in batches of 10 for 3–4 minutes or until golden • Season with salt and half the lemon juice; drain on paper towel • Heat the brandade in a medium-sized saucepan over low heat, add the warm milk, then whisk in the pommes mousseline and the butter. If the brandade mix becomes too hot, remove from the heat and continue to whisk. Add the parsley • Taste and season with salt, pepper and the remaining lemon juice • Preheat the oven to 180°C (350°F) • Warm the shells in the oven for 1 minute. Place the shells on mounds of rock salt on a serving plate • Place a teaspoonful of the brandade mix in each shell and top with an oyster • Heat the bouillabaisse in a small saucepan and bring to the boil • Using a hand bender; froth the bouillabaisse to create a light foam. Spoon the foam over each oyster. Garnish with a sprig of chervil and serve.

Poached oysters with scrambled duck eggs

[serves 6 as an entrée]

THIS RECIPE IS GREAT as part of a special occasion, such as a Champagne breakfast on Christmas day. Eggs are always a great match with oysters because both are subtle in texture and flavour. Once again Champagne is undoubtedly the best match.

5 duck eggs
30 oysters
*2 tablespoons goose fat**
1 tablespoon finely chopped curly-leaf parsley
Pinch of salt
500 g (1 lb) rock salt
200 ml (7 fl oz) Champagne velouté (see page 208)

Break the duck eggs into a bowl and whisk until the eggs are fully incorporated • Carefully open and remove the oysters from their shells. Strain and reserve the juice for the Champagne velouté. Clean the shells inside and out with hot soapy water. Rinse well and drain • Heat the goose fat in a heavy-based saucepan over medium heat, add the eggs and, using a spatula, scrape the eggs from side to side to prevent them sticking to the bottom of the pan. The eggs will start to thicken and set after 2 minutes. Do not overcook. Remove from the heat and add the parsley and salt • Gently warm the oysters in a saucepan for 30 seconds • Preheat the oven to 180°C (350°F) • Warm the oyster shells in the oven for 1 minute • Place the shells on mounds of rock salt on a serving plate. Spoon in the scrambled eggs. Place an oyster on top • Warm the Champagne velouté in a small saucepan. Using a hand blender, create foam by angling the blender slightly out of the saucepan. Spoon the froth over each oyster and serve.

WILD OYSTERS WITH LOBSTER MOUSSE AND PUFF PASTRY

[serves 4 as an entrée]

WILD OYSTERS ARE THE result of spawning that farmed oysters go through when water temperatures rise. Readily available upon request from all reputable fishmongers who buy their oysters directly from the farms, they grow uncontrollably in and around the coves and sanctuaries where the farms are situated. Being twice the size of normal oysters, they are best suited to full-flavoured baking or crisp tempura-style dishes.

12 large oysters

*2 tablespoons dry vermouth (Noilly Prat)**

100 ml (3½ fl oz) fish stock (see page 243)

100 ml (3½ fl oz) mussel stock (see page 389)

100 g (3½ oz) cultured butter, cut into dice*

Juice of ½ Tahitian lime

½ tablespoon finely chopped chives

Salt

300 g (10 oz) lobster mousse (see page 251)

4 sheets of puff pastry (see page 54)

2 tablespoons warm clarified butter (see page 381)

2 egg yolks

500 g (1 lb) rock salt

Preheat the oven to 180°C (350°F) • Carefully open and remove the oysters from their shells. Strain and reserve the juice. Clean the shells inside and out with hot soapy water. Rinse well and drain • Heat the vermouth in a small saucepan. Bring to the boil for 30 seconds. Add the fish and mussel stocks and reduce by half. Add 2 tablespoons of the reserved oyster juice and gradually whisk in the butter until thick and smooth. Season with a squeeze of lime juice. Add the chives and season with salt. Cover and set to one side • Fill each oyster shell three-quarters full with the lobster mousse. Place an oyster on top • Roll out the puff pastry to a thickness of 6 mm (¼ in). Cover each shell with the puff pastry, pressing firmly around the edges • Whisk the clarified butter with the egg yolks to form the glaze. Brush the glaze gently over the pastry • Place in the oven and bake for 8 minutes or until golden. Place the oysters on mounds of rock salt on a serving plate and serve immediately.

Chicken and oyster pie

[makes 10 individual pies]

THE DELICATE FLAVOURS in this dish harmonise beautifully with the chicken and pastry. The key ingredient for me is the spring onion. The smaller the pie, the better.

FILLING

20 oysters
1 tablespoon olive oil
1 onion, finely chopped
5 spring onions (scallions), finely sliced
100 g ($3\frac{1}{2}$ oz) baby button mushrooms
2 cloves of garlic, chopped
2 tablespoons oyster sauce
1 cup cooked, chopped chicken
2 tablespoons water
50 g ($1\frac{3}{4}$ oz) cornflour (cornstarch)
$\frac{1}{4}$ teaspoon cayenne pepper
$\frac{1}{2}$ tablespoon chopped tarragon
Salt and freshly ground pepper
Juice of $\frac{1}{2}$ lemon

Short crust pastry (see page 74)

EGG WASH

3 eggs, lightly beaten
1 tablespoon water

To make the filling, heat the olive oil in a heavy-based saucepan, add the onion and cook until soft. Add the spring onions, mushrooms and garlic and cook for 3 minutes, stirring constantly • Add the oysters, oyster liquid, oyster sauce and chicken. Bring to the boil • Combine the water and cornflour and mix to form a paste. Gently whisk in with the filling until slightly thickened. Mix in the cayenne pepper, tarragon, salt and pepper and a squeeze of lemon juice • Cool in the refrigerator for 30 minutes. The mixture needs to be cold before being placed into the pastry • Roll out the short crust pastry to 5 mm ($\frac{1}{4}$ in) thick. Using a 9-cm ($3\frac{1}{2}$-in) round cutter, cut out twenty discs • Preheat the oven to 180°C (350°F) • Press the pastry discs into pie moulds 5 cm (2 in) in diameter and 3 cm ($1\frac{1}{4}$ in) deep. Spoon in a generous amount of filling; ensuring that each pie contains two oysters. Cover with the remaining discs of pastry and gently press to seal the edges • Rest the pies in the fridge for 20 minutes to let the pastry firm • Combine the eggs and the water and brush over the pastry • Place the pies in the oven and bake for 15–18 minutes or until golden. Remove from the oven, carefully unmould and serve.

The Caviar

GENGHIS KHAN (C. 1162–1227) is known — apart from his conquering exploits — as the man who travelled all day with chunks of meat between his horse and his saddlebags to tenderise them. In 1240 his grandson, Batu Khan, was honoured by a feast at a monastery on the banks of the River Volga. The menu included fish soup made from sterlet, a large roasted sturgeon, eel pâté and piroshki (pies) stuffed with finely chopped mushrooms, crystallised apples and caviar. He later declared his love for caviar and took over the Black and Caspian seas to ensure his supply!

Popular types of caviar include: **Beluga** which was the variety favoured by Pablo Picasso, who used to pay his favoured purveyor by sending a note wrapped in a signed original sketch. Beluga is found in the Caspian Sea and is the largest and most endangered sturgeon. Beluga caviar is considered to be the best because it has the largest grain and most delicate flavour, tasting somewhat like a velvety textured ocean. Its colour varies from light to dark grey. The caviar from the highly endangered

osetra sturgeon is the favourite of many, including the late Ian Fleming, author of the James Bond novels. Osetra caviar is medium-grained, a little smaller than Beluga, with a nut-like flavour. It varies in colour from golden-yellow to brown. Charles de Gaulle preferred **sevruga** caviar, which is the smallest in size and has the boldest flavour and creamiest texture. Sevruga caviar ranges in colour from light to dark grey.

I put it down to two parts snobbery and one part ignorance that people don't realise the fact that eggs are found in every species of fish, and most of them, when treated with a bit of know-how, are in fact delicious. I agree that there is the allure of the Caspian Sea, rich in history and culture, and its treasure, which attracts us all to that golden tin and the expense, but anyone who says that nowhere else in the world can produce the same quality in a farmed or semi-wild environment free of chemicals, pollution and stress on the fish is deluding themselves. Last time I looked in the newspapers Iran, Kazakhstan and Russia had a little bit more to worry about than cleaning up the Caspian Sea.

White sturgeon caviar is a beautiful, dark brown bead with a mild nutty flavour. It is very similar to the osetra from the Caspian Sea. Indigenous to the waters of the Pacific Coast of North America, the white sturgeon is one of the oldest creatures found on earth! Thankfully, white sturgeon are being farmed in northern California.

Salmon roe, also known as Ikura, is bright orange-red and is a gorgeous garnish and flavour enhancer. The chum salmon is specifically prized for its roe. The eggs are quite large, about the size of a small pea, making for a glorious burst of salmon flavour. Australia is one of the few countries producing mature salmon roe in the only fresh-water aquaculture farm in the world in the pristine waters off the Rubicon River, Yarra Valley, 75 kilometres (46 miles) north-east of Melbourne. Surprisingly, this style of caviar is the most popular with Russians because it has a distinctive strong flavour. It is known as Keta Russian Red.

Other types of roe that can easily be used as a substitute in the following recipes are from flying fish, paddlefish, hackleback and black bowfin. All are types of farmed fish roe available on the world market today. Ask your local purveyor for advice on the best way to obtain this wonderful delicacy.

Caviar in grains is preserved in tins and must be kept at 0–4°C (30–40°F). The shelf life is three months. Once opened, it is advisable to consume it within 24 hours. You can eat as much as you like, but a normal portion is around 50 grams (1³⁄4 ounces) per person. Blini (see page 64) or Melba toast (see page 54) are ideal to serve with caviar, as the texture and flavour do not interfere with its delicate nature. It is the custom to serve caviar with vodka, but it should not be forgotten that in rich families during the times of the Tsars this was thought to be the drink of the hoi polloi, and therefore preference was given to Champagne.

Traditional caviar service

[serves 4]

CAVIAR PAIRED WITH certain types of protein has the potential flavour characteristics to transform the subtleness of a dish into a stratospheric explosion of excitement, texture, colour and flavour. The traditional garnishes to complement caviar are finely chopped cornichons, finely chopped hard-boiled egg, finely sliced chives, and blini and sour cream or fromage blanc. With these recipes I intend to respect tradition, but at the same time build upon the knowledge learned in the kitchens of my mentors to create dishes that will transform the experience.

4 hard-boiled eggs
100 g (3½ oz) cornichons, finely diced*
2 shallots, finely chopped
1 tablespoon finely chopped chives
12 blini (see page 64)
*3 tablespoons fromage blanc**
80 g (2¾ oz) caviar
1 lemon, cut into wedges

Separate the yolk and white of the hard-boiled eggs, then finely chop each • Arrange the cornichons, eggs, shallots and chives on each serving plate • Evenly space three blini on the plate next to the garnishes. Quenelle* a teaspoonful of the fromage blanc on the blini. Using a traditional mother of pearl teaspoon place a quenelle of caviar next to the blini. Place a lemon wedge on the side and serve.

VENISON CARPACCIO WITH CAULIFLOWER AND CAVIAR

[serves 4]

CARPACCIO ORIGINATED FROM Harry's Bar in Venice, Italy, as a light first course, and was named in honour of a well-known fourteenth-century Venetian painter. The traditional version uses very thin slices of beef — I find venison is better suited. I have lightly seared the outside of the venison to make it easier to slice and to allow for the inclusion of cracked pepper. Rolling the venison in cracked pepper then roasting the surface releases the spicy fragrance of the pepper.

400 g (13 oz) venison fillet
20 g (3/4 oz) sea salt
1 tablespoon freshly cracked black pepper
2 1/2 tablespoons olive oil
200 g (6 1/2 oz) cauliflower purée (see page 395 for vegetable purée)
3 tablespoons extra virgin olive oil
1 clove of garlic, crushed
1 shallot, finely diced
1 tablespoon finely chopped chives
4 tablespoons sevruga caviar

Season the venison with the salt and black pepper • Heat the olive oil in a heavy-based frying pan, add the venison and quickly seal on each side over high heat until brown, about 3 minutes. Rest until cooled to room temperature • Warm the cauliflower purée in a saucepan. Transfer to a squeezeable sauce bottle and liberally squeeze the purée around each serving plate in a circular fashion • Gently heat the extra virgin olive oil and garlic in a saucepan for 10 minutes to allow the garlic to infuse into the oil. Transfer to a bottle and allow to cool to room temperature • Carefully slice the venison, drape the slices over the cauliflower purée. Sprinkle over the shallot and chives • Spoon over a generous amount of caviar and a drizzle of the garlic-infused olive oil and serve.

Traditional caviar service

Venison carpaccio with cauliflower and caviar

Poached snapper with smoked baby potatoes and caviar

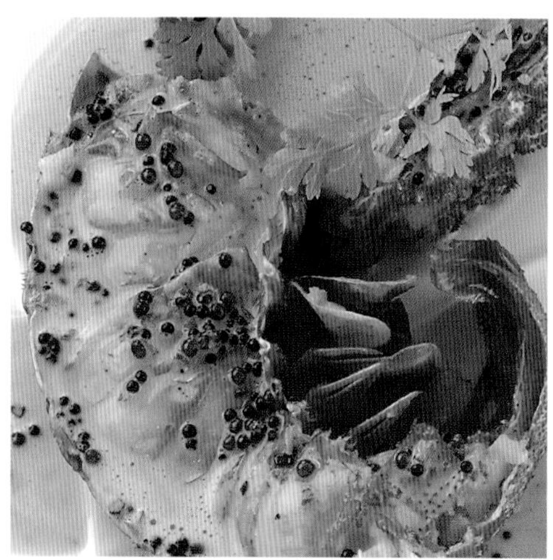

Crayfish with caviar butter sauce

Baby potatoes filled with pommes mousseline and caviar

Poached snapper with smoked baby potatoes and caviar

[serves 4]

Snapper is a fish that is rarely surpassed for its consistency in flavour and texture. When gently poached, snapper has a soft texture that is well suited to denser flavoured foods such as caviar. In keeping with the theme, smoked potatoes give the palate a sense of rustic satisfaction and are a neat way of making this dish a little more wholesome, yet intricate.

250 g (8 oz) kipfler potatoes
Sea salt
300 g (10 oz) woodchips for smoking
2½ tablespoons hazelnut vinaigrette (see page 396)
900 g (1¾ lb) snapper fillet
100 ml (3½ fl oz) olive oil
4 shallots, finely diced
2 cloves of garlic, crushed
2 sprigs of tarragon
*100 ml (3½ fl oz) pastis (Pernod)**
400 ml (13 fl oz) mussel stock (see page 389)
100 ml (3½ fl oz) double cream
3 tablespoons sevruga-style caviar
1 tablespoon finely chopped flat-leaf parsley

Parboil the potatoes in boiling salted water for 7 minutes. Drain and leave to cool. When the potatoes are comfortable enough to handle, carefully peel and slice into 6-mm (¼-in) discs • Line a wok or double boiler with aluminium (aluminum) foil. Heat the wok on medium, add the woodchips. They will start to smoke after 5–10 minutes. Place a cake rack over the smouldering woodchips, scatter the potatoes on the rack and season with a generous pinch of salt. Reduce the heat to low, cover and smoke for 20 minutes. (You may also like to experiment with this method on the barbecue.) Transfer the potatoes to a mixing bowl, dress with the hazelnut vinaigrette, cover with plastic wrap and set aside • Slice the snapper into four, leaving the skin on. Lightly rub with sea salt and 2 tablespoons of the olive oil • Heat 2½ tablespoons of the remaining olive oil in a heavy-based saucepan, add the shallots, garlic and tarragon and cook over medium heat for 4 minutes. Add the pastis and cook until reduced by two-thirds • Add the mussel stock and simmer, covered, for 3 minutes. Place the snapper fillets in the poaching liquid; reduce the heat to the lowest setting possible and poach for 7 minutes. Remove the fillets and strain the poaching liquid into a saucepan. Bring to the boil and add the cream. Return to the boil and cook for 3 minutes, remove from the heat • Place the poached fillets skin-side up in the centre of warmed serving plates. Peel off the skin and discard. Place a generous teaspoonful of caviar in the centre of each fillet and spread evenly over the top • Warm the potatoes in the remaining olive oil in a saucepan, season with salt and pepper and add the parsley. Scatter the potato discs around the fish • Froth the poaching liquid with a hand blender and spoon the froth over and around the snapper. Serve immediately.

Baby potatoes filled with pommes mousseline and caviar

[serves 10]

These delectable hors d'oeuvres are great when paired with a good glass of vintage Champagne. Watch the mood-swinging fun begin.

10 baby new potatoes
4 cups peanut oil
Sea salt
Pommes mousseline (see page 102)
1 tablespoon chopped tarragon
100 g (3½ oz) crème fraîche
2½ tablespoons beluga caviar

Parboil the potatoes in salted water for 7 minutes. Allow to cool • Preheat the peanut oil in a deep-fryer to 180°C (350°F) • Cut a small slice off the bottom of each potato to ensure it sits flat. Using a melon baller, scoop out the top of each potato to create a hollow centre • Place the potatoes in the deep-fryer and fry until crispy and golden. Remove, drain well on paper towel and season with salt. Transfer to a warmed serving dish • Place 2½ tablespoons of pommes mousseline in a saucepan, add the tarragon and cook over low heat for 3 minutes. Fold in the crème fraîche and half of the caviar. Season with salt, then carefully spoon into each potato. Top each potato with the remaining caviar and serve.

Crayfish with caviar butter sauce

[serves 2]

GRILLED CRAYFISH FLAMBÉ with vodka is a clean, simple, attractive way of highlighting the harmony between caviar and crustaceans. Match this dish with a slightly chilled red, such as a gamay, or a couple of shots of decent vodka straight from the freezer.

1 x 900 g (1 3/4 lb) crayfish
1 tablespoon olive oil
2 shallots, finely chopped
1 clove of garlic, crushed
100 ml (3 1/2 fl oz) vodka
100 ml (3 1/2 fl oz) chicken stock (see page 378)
100 g (3 1/2 oz) cultured butter, cut into fine dice*
Salt and freshly ground pepper
2 tablespoons finely chopped curly-leaf parsley
Juice of 1/2 lemon
3 tablespoons sevruga-style caviar
6 sprigs of chervil

Preheat a grill (broiler) to high • Cook the crayfish in boiling salted water for 8 minutes. Refresh in iced water for 6 minutes. Carefully cut in half lengthways with a serrated knife. Rinse the head and remove any impurities • Remove the tail meat and return it to the opposite shell, reversing the meat to show the beautiful red flesh • Heat the olive oil in an ovenproof frying pan, add the crayfish and cook for 3 minutes over medium-high heat. Add the shallots and garlic, and cook for 1 minute. Pour the vodka over, place under the grill and flambé, reducing the liquid by half • Place each crayfish half on warmed serving plates • Add the chicken stock to the pan juices and bring to the boil. Cook for 2–3 minutes on high heat or until reduced by half. Slowly whisk in the butter to form a butter sauce. Bring the sauce to the boil and cook for 1 minute • Blend the butter sauce with a hand blender until frothy and light. Season with salt and pepper and add the parsley and lemon juice. Fold in the caviar. Spoon the sauce over the crayfish. Garnish with the chervil and serve immediately.

The Freshwater Fish

FRESHWATER FISH FALL INTO two categories: the delicate, delicious and very versatile flowing fresh river fish, such as salmon, trout, and certain species of perch; and lake or dam fish, such as pike, carp, red fin, eel and the Australian Murray River cod. These fish have a certain muddy texture and taste to them and tend to respond best to smoking and more rustic styles of cooking with bigger robust flavours.

As an eating fish, barramundi, a member of the perch family, is second to none. The soft, moist, thick white flesh is superb, especially when freshly caught and more so if killed by the ike jime method — a spike in the brain! This sounds ghoulish but it assures instant death and stops the release of adrenalin into the bloodstream. It also delays the onset of rigor mortis, considered to lessen the shelf life of a fish.

Farmed barramundi is hard to pick out from wild; the only clue I can give is that the wild has a noticeable pink tinge to the flesh and longer fins that are less uniform in shape. When cooked, farmed barramundi has a soft-textured flesh that is best suited to roasting.

The name barramundi is native to Australia, but it is certainly not an indigenous fish — they are found across Asia and as far away as the Persian Gulf. They are also found in freshwater dams and rivers. The wild-caught variety is available only in season from February to September. Fish that feed in the mangroves and river systems have a cleaner taste than the rather more earthy-flavoured freshwater fish that are found in dams, creeks and slow flowing rivers. They are mostly caught in small nets but many in the industry seem to advertise line-caught fish on their menus. The fish is very difficult and feisty when lured, making it a highly prized catch among sporting fishermen. Found in the waters of Northern Australia from Queensland to the Northern Territory and Western Australia, they are protected from commercial fishermen during a period of fishing closure, timed to coincide with the breeding season.

The Atlantic salmon is a world traveller; an anadromous fish, a species that spawns in fresh water but spends much of its life at sea. The Atlantic salmon's range encompassed the North Atlantic Ocean and its freshwater tributaries, from Ungava Bay to Lake Ontario, to Connecticut in North America, and Russia's White Sea to Portugal on the European coast. However, many of these migratory avenues are now closed. Atlantic salmon can still be found in the rivers of Ireland, the United Kingdom, Canada, the Faroe Islands, Iceland, Norway, Sweden, Finland, Russia, France, Spain, Canada and the United States.

Marron (*Cherax tenuimanus*) are very large freshwater crayfish native to the rivers in the dense rainforest areas in south-west Western Australia. Marron have been known to reach weights in excess of 2 kilograms (4 pounds), but they are most commonly sold when they reach a size of 300 grams (10 ounces), which generally takes eighteen months to two years under ideal aquaculture conditions. The shell colour of marron can vary from brown to blue to black, depending on genetics and the environment, but will change to an attractive crimson red when roasted or poached. The meat to shell ratio for marron is very high at about 50 per cent, the claws also yield good meat. To prepare crayfish and marron, a simple bouillon is

needed, such as the vegetable bouillon on page 395. To calculate the correct time for cooking crustaceans allow 90 seconds per 100 grams (3½ ounces). For example a 400-gram (13-ounce) crayfish will take 4½ minutes to cook. I have always found the results are better cooking crustaceans beforehand rather than refreshing the meat, then reheating at a later stage. Crustaceans need resting time before serving in the same way as any other meat.

Marron flesh has a subtle sweet, nutty flavour with a fine grain and firm consistency and is a good red colour on the outside. The two best producers of marron are Pemberton in southern Western Australia and Kangaroo Island off South Australia. The sizes available range from 100 grams (3½ ounces) up to 400 grams (13 ounces). My opinion is, the bigger, the better and the more developed the flavour.

Smoked trout and salmon pâté

[serves 10]

THIS IS A VERY old recipe I first came across in a cookery school text when in my competition days as an apprentice. I have since altered it to suit the menu at Vue de monde, by adding less cream and eggs to lighten the end result. At Vue de monde the dish is complemented with pan-fried sardines and sauce verte.

*100 ml ($3\frac{1}{2}$ fl oz) dry vermouth (Noilly Prat)**

200 ml (7 fl oz) fish stock (see page 243)

620 g ($1\frac{1}{4}$ lb) smoked trout

300 g (10 oz) skinless salmon fillet

4 egg whites

300 ml (10 fl oz) double cream

Juice of 1 lemon

Salt and white pepper

400 ml (13 fl oz) double cream

400 g (13 oz) smoked perch or haddock fillet

Preheat the oven to 120°C (250°F) • Pour the vermouth into a small saucepan, bring to the boil and cook until reduced by half. Add the fish stock and continue to cook until reduced by two-thirds. Refrigerate until cold • Combine the smoked trout and salmon in a food processor and blend until fine • Add the reduction to the puréed fish, process well • Add the egg whites and blend until incorporated • Add the cream and purée briefly until just incorporated • Season with the lemon juice, salt and pepper • Place half of the pâté in a plastic wrap-lined 30 x 10-cm (12 x 4-in) terrine mould. Smooth the top and place the perch or haddock fillet in the centre of the terrine to create a second layer. Cover with the remaining pâté, smooth the top and wrap the terrine tightly in plastic wrap • Transfer to a baking tray, pour in enough boiling water to come halfway up the sides of the terrine mould and bake in the oven for $1\frac{1}{2}$ hours • Test the middle of the pâté with a temperature probe, which should read 45°C (113°F) when cooked. Alternatively, pierce the pâté with a thin-bladed utility knife, hold the knife in the centre of the terrine for 30 seconds, then test by cautiously placing the knife on the inside of the wrist, the knife should feel hot • When cool, place the pâté in the refrigerator for 12 hours to develop the flavour • Slice the pâté and serve with toasted soda bread (see page 50) and caviar.

Poached trout royale with sauce Normande

[serves 4]

I have always wanted to cook trout in the restaurant but was unable to think of a dish suited to my style — I eventually had the opportunity with this. It is a complex dish for someone to complete at home, but as your confidence increases as you progress through the book, you will find the dish worthwhile.

Think gewürztraminer for a suitable wine match.

4 x 400 g (13 oz) rainbow trout
*4 cups bouillon**
20 small crayfish tails
8 cups fish stock (see page 243)
200 g (6½ oz) lobster mousse (see page 251)
20 new potatoes, peeled
*125 g (4 oz) cultured butter**
Salt and freshly ground pepper

SAUCE NORMANDE

100 ml (3½ fl oz) olive oil
200 g (6½ oz) button mushrooms
Juice of ½ lemon
400 ml (13 fl oz) mussel velouté (see page 244)
100 ml (3½ fl oz) mushroom stock (see page 109)
200 ml (7 fl oz) béarnaise sauce (see page 385)
1 black truffle, sliced*

Scale, gut and trim the fins of the trout, leave the head on • In a large heavy-based saucepan, bring the bouillon to the boil. Add the crayfish tails and cook for 4 minutes. Refresh in iced water • Shell the crayfish. (Freeze the shells for other recipes, such as lobster bisque see page 249.) • Place the trout and the fish stock in a well-buttered fish poacher (the butter prevents the fish sticking). Bring to the boil over high heat, then reduce heat to low. Drop in small teaspoons of the lobster mousse and simmer for 8 minutes • Cook the potatoes in boiling salted water for 10 minutes or until soft, drain and then toss in the butter and season with salt. Keep warm • To prepare the sauce Normande, heat the olive oil in a heavy-based saucepan, add the mushrooms, salt, pepper and a squeeze of lemon juice and sauté for 4 minutes over medium heat • Combine the sautéed mushrooms, the mussel velouté and mushroom stock in a saucepan. Bring to the boil, remove from the heat and, using a hand blender, mix in the béarnaise sauce. Season with a little more lemon juice • Place each trout on an oval serving plate. Arrange three mushrooms, three quenelles of lobster mousse, five crayfish tails and four slices of truffle on top. Surround the trout with the potatoes. Spoon the sauce Normande over and around the dish.

Brandade

[serves 6]

THE FAMOUS *brandade de morue* of Provence is a pounded mixture of salted cod (though barramundi, Patagonian tooth fish and harpuka make good substitutes), olive oil, garlic, milk and cream. This flavourful purée is served with fresh crispy vegetable batons, garlic croutons or crusty bread and is often garnished with sliced black truffles. Other salted or smoked fish can also be used to make brandade, though I do prefer to cure my own. Good quality salted cod is hard to find outside France and Spain.

1 kg (2 lb) side of barramundi
250 g (8 oz) sea salt
90 g (3 oz) caster (superfine) sugar
2 pinches of saffron
4 cloves of garlic, thinly sliced
¼ bunch of thyme
10 juniper berries
1 lemon, sliced
10 fennel seeds
2 cups milk
2 cups fish stock (see page 243)
2 sprigs of thyme
1 bay leaf
1½ cups pommes mousseline (see page 102)
2 cloves of garlic, crushed
200 ml (7 fl oz) olive oil
Juice of ½ lemon

Marinate the barramundi in the salt, sugar, saffron, garlic, thyme, juniper berries, lemon and fennel seeds for 12 hours in the refrigerator, making sure you rub the marinade into the fish. Turn and marinate for another 12 hours. Rinse under cold water and pat dry with a tea towel • Slice the barramundi into six fillets • Combine the milk, stock, thyme and bay leaf in a heavy-based saucepan. Bring to a simmer, add the fish fillets and gently poach for 10 minutes • Drain and discard the poaching liquid. Place the fish in a food processor, add the pommes mousseline and garlic and blend until puréed. With the motor running, slowly drizzle in the olive oil and lemon juice until all the oil is absorbed • Use in salads, as a side dish or roll into small balls, dip in breadcrumbs and deep-fry.

GRILLED BARRAMUNDI AND ZUCCHINI FLOWERS STUFFED WITH BRANDADE

[serves 4]

THIS INTERPRETATION OF Provençal cooking is designed to be approachable and easily cooked at home. Barramundi can be replaced with sea bass.

2 cups vegetable oil
4 x 200 g (6½ oz) wild barramundi fillets
1½ tablespoons olive oil
Salt and freshly ground pepper
200 g (6½ oz) fresh peas
*30 g (1 oz) cultured butter**
400 g (13 oz) mussels
200 g (6½ oz) vongole
1 tablespoon finely chopped tarragon
4 zucchini (courgette) flowers
100 g (3½ oz) brandade (see page 230)
½ cup plain (all-purpose) flour
Tempura batter (see page 204)
Juice of ½ lemon
200 ml (7 fl oz) bouillabaisse (see page 258)
1 tablespoon crayfish oil (see page 252)

Heat the vegetable oil in a deep-fryer to 180°C (350°F) • Heat a cast-iron griddle pan over medium heat. Brush the barramundi with 1 tablespoon of the olive oil and season with salt and pepper. Fry gently on both sides for 3 minutes or until the fish is golden and white on the edges, and firm to touch. Rest for 3–4 minutes • Cook the peas in boiling salted water for 2 minutes • Combine the butter and the remaining olive oil in a saucepan, add the peas and toss to coat. Add the mussels and vongole and cook for 5 minutes or until the shells have opened. Season with salt and pepper. Add the tarragon and cook for a further 2 minutes. Remove the mussels and vongole from their shells • Prepare the zucchini flowers by rinsing under cold water. Remove and discard the stamens inside the flowers. Spoon the brandade into each flower until three-quarters full. Twist the top of each flower to seal • Place the flour in a shallow bowl. Lightly coat each flower with flour, then dip into the tempura batter. Place in the deep-fryer and fry for 3 minutes or until golden. Season with lemon juice and salt • Pour the bouillabaisse into a heavy-based saucepan, bring to the boil and reduce by two-thirds. Add the crayfish oil • Place the peas, mussels and vongole in the centre of each serving plate. Place the barramundi on top and a zucchini flower to the side. Drizzle the bouillabaisse on and around the plate and serve.

Smoked trout and salmon pâté

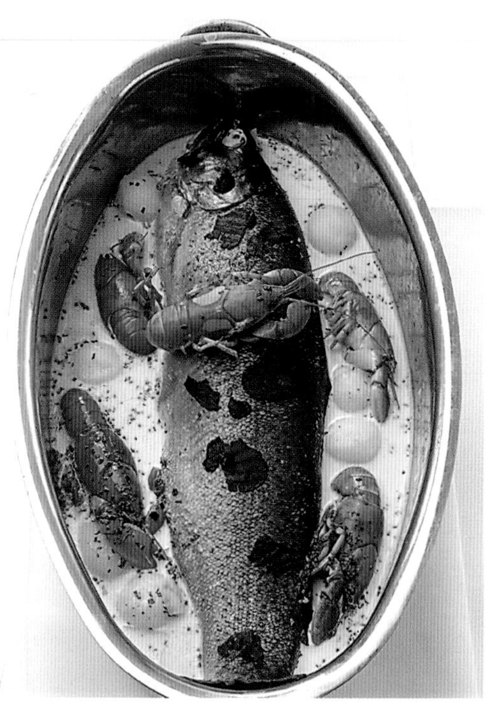

Poached trout royale with sauce normande

Brandade

Grilled barramundi and zucchini flowers stuffed with brandade

Smoked salmon paupiettes

Wild barramundi with vanilla sauce

Confit of salmon with osso bucco jus

Salmon tartare

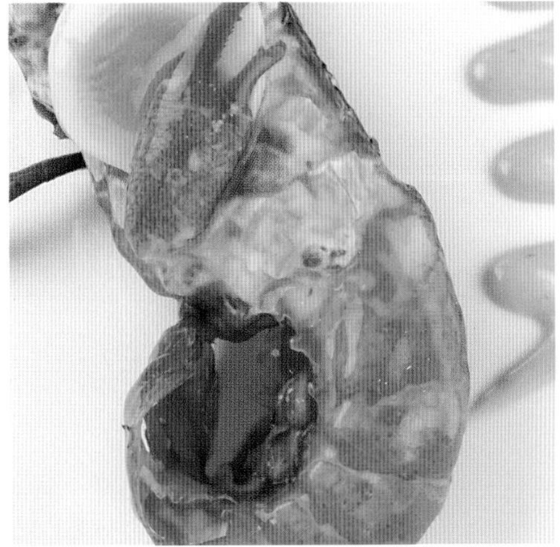
Marron á la parisienne

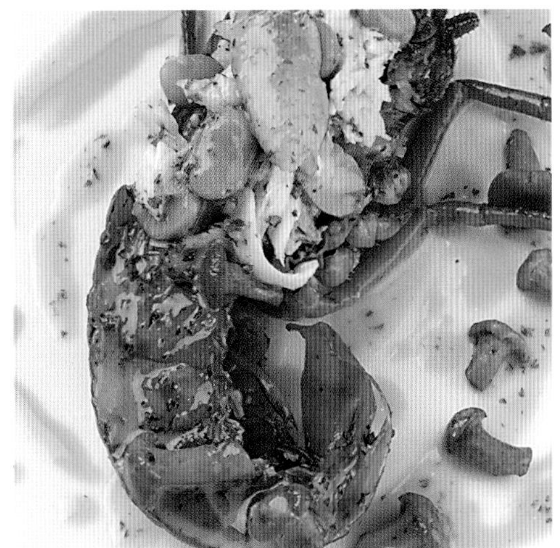
Grilled marron with Grand Marnier

Smoked salmon paupiettes

[serves 6]

I WAS INTRODUCED TO this recipe when working with Marco Pierre White. This is a great function dish because it is easy to prepare and even easier to serve. Toast a few slices of brioche, cut into small 2-centimetre (¾-inch) squares, cut a ready-made salmon paupiette into quarters, place a quarter on each square, spoon a little salmon roe on top and you have a complete canapé.

MOUSSE

250 g (8 oz) smoked salmon
1 cup thickened cream
Juice of 1 lemon
Salt and freshly ground pepper
2 cups double cream, whipped
½ tablespoon chopped tarragon

PAUPIETTES

12 slices Royal Tasmanian or Scottish smoked salmon

HAZELNUT VINAIGRETTE

200 ml (7 fl oz) hazelnut oil
200 ml (7 fl oz) peanut oil
100 ml (3½ fl oz) sherry vinegar

18 snails, freshly cooked or canned*
1 cup plain (all-purpose) flour
Yeast batter (see page 65)
4 cups olive oil
1½ cups mixed salad leaves

To make the mousse, place the food processor bowl in the freezer for 20 minutes. Purée the smoked salmon in the food processor until smooth. Don't let the friction of the blade warm the bowl as it will cook the smoked salmon and destroy the lovely smooth texture we are trying to achieve • Add the thickened cream and incorporate, being careful not to overmix, using the pulse action. Season with a little lemon juice, salt and pepper • Transfer to a cold mixing bowl • Fold in the whipped cream and tarragon. Check the seasoning and adjust accordingly • Rest the mousse in the refrigerator for 30 minutes to firm • To make the paupiettes, overlap two smoked salmon slices on a work surface. Place 1 large tablespoon of mousse in the centre of the slices. Fold up into a square parcel. Repeat until all of the salmon and the mousse have been used. These may be made a day ahead and stored in the refrigerator until needed • To make the hazelnut vinaigrette, whisk the hazelnut oil, peanut oil and sherry vinegar until thickened • Insert a toothpick in each snail • Place the flour in a shallow bowl. Coat each snail in the flour, then dip into the yeast batter • Heat the olive oil in a deep-fryer to 180°C (350°F). Add the snails, in batches, and cook for 3–4 minutes or until golden. Season with salt and lemon juice • Dress the salad leaves with 1 tablespoon of the vinaigrette • Place a paupiette in the centre of each serving plate. Add the snails to the salad, mix well, then arrange on top of each paupiette. Spoon the remaining vinaigrette over and around and serve while the snails are still crispy and hot.

Wild barramundi with vanilla sauce

[serves 4]

VANILLA SAUCE WITH barramundi is hard to imagine, but in fact it has graced European dinner tables since the early twentieth century. Alain Senderens, of Restaurant Lucas Carton in Paris, is most famous for this sauce that he pairs with crayfish.

4 x 250 g (8 oz) wild barramundi fillets

Salt and freshly ground pepper

VANILLA SAUCE

350 g (11 oz) cultured butter, cut into fine dice*

Juice of 2 lemons

2 vanilla beans, split lengthwise and seeds scraped*

12 baby leeks, chopped into 6-cm (2½-in) batons

2 tablespoons olive oil

2 shallots, finely chopped

150 g (5 oz) chanterelle mushrooms

1 clove of garlic, crushed

200 g (6½ oz) pea purée (see page 142)

Season the barramundi fillets with salt and pepper • To make the vanilla sauce, place 150 g (5 oz) of the butter in a small heavy-based saucepan and cook over high heat until lightly browned (beurre noisette) • Deglaze with the lemon juice, but be careful not to burn yourself, as this process creates spitting. Using a hand blender, whisk in the remaining butter until thick and smooth (beurre blanc). Add the vanilla seeds and set aside until room temperature is reached • In a heavy-based frying pan, gently cook the barramundi over medium heat for 3 minutes on each side or until golden brown. Rest the fish for 4–5 minutes in a warm place • Cook the leeks in boiling salted water for 2 minutes or until tender • Heat the olive oil in a heavy-based saucepan, add the leeks, shallots, mushrooms and garlic and sauté for 5 minutes. Season with salt and pepper • Warm the pea purée in a saucepan, then spoon into the centre of each serving plate. Place the barramundi on top. Arrange the leek and mushroom sauté on one side of each plate. Drizzle the vanilla sauce over and around, and serve.

Confit of salmon with osso bucco jus

[serves 6]

This is the best way I know to preserve the integrity of a much-overused fish. Serve with crispy potatoes and buttered beans. Such a delicately textured dish screams out for a ripe New World pinot noir.

OSSO BUCCO JUS

500 g (1 lb) osso bucco cutlets
½ cup plain (all-purpose) flour
½ cup olive oil
Salt and freshly ground pepper
2 onions, diced
1 head of garlic, cut in half
*Bouquet garni**
2 cups dry white wine
4 cups freshly squeezed orange juice
500 g (1 lb) crushed tomatoes
200 ml (7 fl oz) veal stock (see page 294)
2 cups chicken stock (see page 378)

*1 kg (2 lb) goose fat**
6 x 250 g (8 oz) Atlantic salmon fillets
2 x 8-cm (3-in) sticks of bone marrow
100 g (3½ oz) herbed breadcrumbs (see page 384)
4 tablespoons olive oil

GARNISH

1 large carrot, finely diced
1 celeriac, finely diced

Preheat the oven to 180°C (350°F) • Lightly dust the osso bucco cutlets with the flour. Heat 2 tablespoons of the olive oil in a large heavy-based flameproof casserole dish; add the cutlets and brown on all sides over medium heat. Season with salt and pepper. Remove and set aside • Heat another 2 tablespoons of olive oil in the casserole dish, add the onion, garlic and bouquet garni and cook over medium heat for 6 minutes or until the onion is soft and transparent • Add the wine and orange juice and cook until reduced by two-thirds. Add the tomatoes and simmer for 5 minutes. Add the veal stock and chicken stock, and bring to the boil. Add the cutlets, cover, and place in the oven for 2 hours. Strain over a large bowl and reserve the meat for other purposes • Pass the osso bucco jus through a coarse sieve, then through a fine sieve. Place the sauce in a heavy-based saucepan and reduce by one-third or until the sauce coats the back of a spoon • Reduce the oven to 160°C (325°F) • Carefully warm the goose fat in a saucepan on very low heat to a temperature of 60°C (140°F). Add the salmon for 10 minutes or until almost transparent in colour. Remove the salmon with a fish slice • Cut the bone marrow into 5-mm (¼-in) discs using a hot knife. Place three discs parallel on each piece of salmon. Sprinkle the herbed breadcrumbs over the bone marrow and place under a grill (broiler) for 30 seconds to glaze the bone marrow • To make the garnish, add the carrot, celeriac, onion and

1 onion, finely diced
2 zucchini (courgettes), finely diced

zucchini to the osso bucco jus and season • Pour the osso bucco jus onto each serving plate, virtually flooding the whole plate. Centre the salmon on each plate and serve.

Salmon tartare

[serves 6]

ORIGINALLY THE WORD TARTARE meant all dishes that were covered in breadcrumbs, grilled (broiled), then served with a highly seasoned sauce. Over time the name has become associated with meats that are served raw with such ingredients as capers and finely chopped onions. The recipe below is a summer dish that is best complemented with a glass of clean, unwooded chardonnay.

500 g (1 lb) Atlantic salmon fillets, finely diced
50 g (1¾ oz) extra small capers
80 g (2¾ oz) cornichons, finely diced*
1 tablespoon finely chopped flat-leaf parsley
1 tablespoon finely chopped chives
2 shallots, finely chopped
100 ml (3½ fl oz) hazelnut vinaigrette (see page 396)
Salt and freshly ground pepper
3 tablespoons olive oil
6 quail eggs
6 slices of stale sourdough bread
1 tablespoon clarified butter (see page 381)

Combine the salmon, capers, cornichons, parsley, chives, shallots and hazelnut vinaigrette in a mixing bowl and season well. Set aside for 20 minutes to allow the flavours to develop • Preheat the oven to 180°C (350°F) • Heat the olive oil in a non-stick frying pan, add the quail eggs, in batches, and gently fry for 2–3 minutes or until the egg white is set. If the pan becomes too hot, remove from the heat and continue to cook until the egg is white and has no bubbles • Slide the eggs onto a plate. Cut around each egg with a small round cutter 2.5 cm (1 in) in diameter • With the same cutter cut out six croutons from the bread. Place on a baking tray, brush each crouton with a little clarified butter and season with salt and pepper. Bake in the oven for 10 minutes or until golden brown. Place on a serving platter • Place the cutter on each crouton, press the salmon tartare mix into the cutter. Carefully remove the cutter, place an egg on top and season. Serve immediately.

Marron á la parisienne

[serves 6]

Here Western Australian freshwater marron is steamed and served on a Russian salad with boiled egg, accompanied by Mary Rose mayonnaise — fantastic!

3 x 350 g (11 oz) marron

RUSSIAN SALAD

1 carrot, diced

1 turnip, diced

1 large potato, diced

2 shallots, finely chopped

10 button mushrooms, diced

1 tablespoon olive oil

6 thick slices of pancetta, diced

*6 Ortiz anchovies**

1 tablespoon small capers, rinsed

2 tablespoons cornichons, finely diced*

2 eggs

100 ml (3½ fl oz) Mary Rose mayonnaise (see page 388)

Salt and freshly ground pepper

Juice of ½ lemon

200 ml (7 fl oz) citrus jelly (see page 202), at room temperature

6 lemon halves, wrapped in cheesecloth

Cook the marron in boiling salted water for 6 minutes. Refresh in iced water for 6 minutes. Carefully cut in half lengthwise using a serrated knife to ensure accuracy. Rinse the head and remove any impurities • Remove the tail meat and then return it to the opposite shell, reversing the meat to show the beautiful red flesh • Peel the claws by cracking the shell with the back of a knife and carefully prising away the flesh • To make the Russian salad, blanch the carrot, turnip and potato in boiling salted water for 4 minutes or until just cooked. Refresh in ice-cold water and drain. Transfer to a large mixing bowl. Add the shallots and mushrooms and stir to combine • Heat the olive oil in a heavy-based frying pan, add the pancetta and sauté for 5 minutes or until golden and crispy. Mix in with the vegetables • Crush the anchovies in a mortar and pestle. Add the anchovies, capers and cornichons to the vegetables • Place the eggs in a saucepan of cold water and bring to the boil. Cook for 10 minutes. Slice across each egg, picking out the six best slices • Mix the Russian salad with the Mary Rose mayonnaise. Season with salt, pepper and lemon juice. Place a large tablespoonful in the top half of each shell. Place a slice of egg and a claw on top. Glaze with the citrus jelly • Serve with extra Mary Rose mayonnaise and a cloth-wrapped lemon.

Grilled marron with Grand Marnier

[serves 2]

GRILLED MARRON FLAVOURED with Grand Marnier is a clean, simple and attractive way to highlight the sweet nutty flavours associated with grilling (broiling). I like to match this dish with a pinot noir and my favourite producer is Robert Chevillon of Nuits-Saint-Georges in Burgundy.

1 x 350 g (11 oz) marron
1 tablespoon olive oil
2 shallots, finely chopped
1 clove of garlic, crushed
100 ml (3½ fl oz) Grand Marnier
100 g (3½ oz) cultured butter, diced*
½ tablespoon finely chopped curly-leaf parsley
60 g (2 oz) white crabmeat
100 g (3½ oz) shelled broad beans
Salt
Juice of ½ lemon
6 sprigs of chervil

Heat a grill (broiler) to high • Cook the marron in boiling salted water for 6 minutes. Carefully cut in half lengthways using a serrated knife for greater accuracy. Rinse the head and remove any impurities • Remove the tail meat and return it to the opposite shell, reversing the meat to show the beautiful red flesh • Peel the claws by cracking the shell with the back of a knife and carefully prise away the flesh, remove the flesh and reserve • Heat the olive oil in an ovenproof frying pan, add the marron in the shell with flesh side up, shallots and garlic and cook over medium to high heat for 1 minute. Pour over the Grand Marnier • Place the pan under the grill, flambé and reduce by half • Whisk in the butter. Add the parsley, crabmeat and broad beans, season with salt and lemon juice and cook over high heat for 1½ minutes or until the sauce has thickened • Add the reserved claw meat to the pan and warm through • Place the crabmeat in the top part of each shell. Place a marron half on each warmed serving plate and drizzle the juices over and around. Garnish with a few sprigs of chervil and serve.

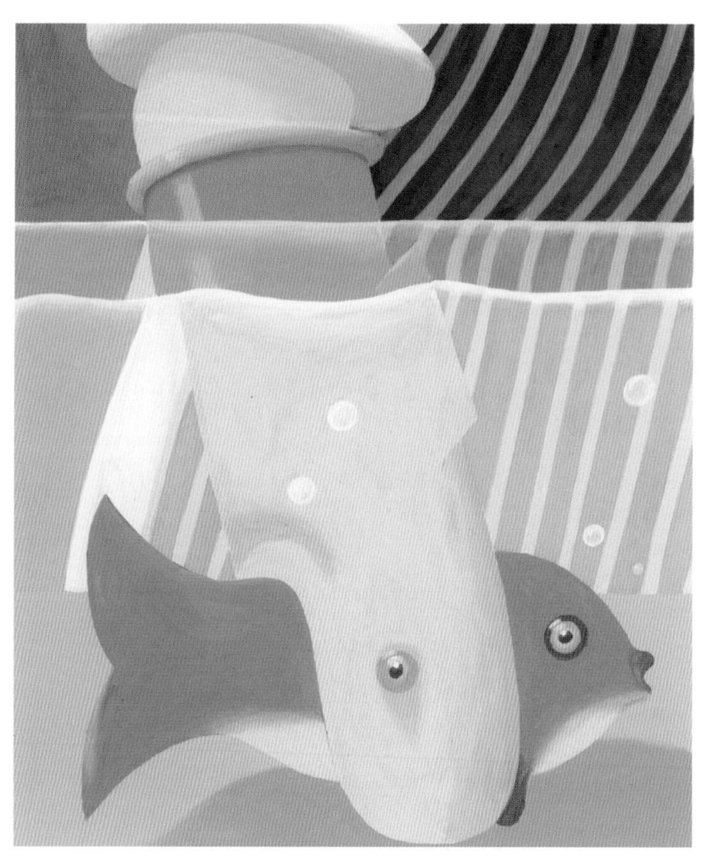

The Deep Sea

AUSTRALIA'S COASTLINE IS A treasure trove of exciting and undiscovered wild and exotic fish, shellfish and crustaceans. The north coast stretching from Broome in the west to the Gulf of Carpentaria in the North through the Coral Sea southwards to Cooktown and Mackay supplies such wonderful fish, including coral trout, red emperor, nannygai, job fish and parrotfish.

Lobsters, the king of crustaceans, contain sweet, succulent and delicate meat in their legs, claws and tail. Several varieties are sold on the commercial market, they are American, Canadian or Scottish lobsters. The finest American lobsters come from Maine; most of these slow-growing crustaceans are marketed at a weight of 500 grams (1 pound) to 1 kilogram (2 pounds). However, lobsters weighing 5 kilograms (10 pounds) or more are quite common in Asian restaurants and fishmongers. Surprisingly, their meat is no less tender than that of smaller specimens. Lobsters are sold live, fresh cooked, and frozen. In Australia we commonly see the Maine lobster in its frozen form because of the strict quarantine laws.

The Pacific or southern rock lobster, known as langouste in France and spiny rock lobster in England, are found in slightly warmer waters than their Atlantic cousins. The meat, all of which is in the tail and legs, is much coarser. Obtaining the meat from the legs can be an arduous task, so plan in advance. Rock lobsters lack the large claws of northern lobsters. The best season for these delicacies in Australia is from early October to March.

Live lobsters and crayfish are quite difficult to buy unless ordered, but if the rare occasion does confront you, look for active animals that move their legs when touched. A lively lobster will normally tuck or flap its tail under its body when lifted. Choose crustaceans that feel heavy for their size. Live crustaceans suffer great stress when moved from their natural environment, deteriorating within 36 hours. If they have come from a tank it doesn't make much difference as their food supply has been cut off. Pre-cooked lobster or crayfish should smell perfectly fresh, with no trace of ammonia. Be especially wary when buying cooked lobster tails, as dealers sometimes cook lobsters that are already dead, rather than killing them for cooking. Fresh-cooked seafood should not be displayed alongside raw fish or shellfish.

Cooking live lobster is a straightforward procedure: place the lobster in the freezer for 20 minutes, prepare a bouillon (see page 395), then boil the lobster, refresh to stabilise the meat and serve. Never serve lobster any other way than boiling, then refreshing because the meat can be very tough when served straight from the pan. The best way to eat lobster is warm or chilled. Lobster needs to be rested after cooking in the same way as meat.

Fish stock

[makes 12 cups]

No part of fish cookery is complete without the aid of a simple fish stock, whether it is to be used in citrus jelly (see page 202) or Champagne velouté (see page 208). Make the stock as clear as possible by controlling the heat, never allow it to boil, only simmer. The old-fashioned rule of cooking fish stock for only 20 minutes because any longer will allow the aroma of aluminium (aluminum) from the bones to overwhelm the flavour of the stock should be disregarded. I have often cooked my stock for 90 minutes, depending on the quantity and size of the bones and have never encountered this problem.

5 kg (10 lb) sole, whiting, turbot, brill and bass bones
12 cups water
1 onion, roughly chopped
2 sticks of celery, roughly chopped
2 leeks, roughly chopped
1 head of garlic, cut in half
2 bay leaves
2 lemons, sliced
6 sprigs of flat-leaf parsley

Rinse the fish bones under running water until the water is completely clear to ensure the stock will be clear and free of impurities. Place in a large heavy-based stockpot, add the water, and bring to the boil. Immediately reduce the heat to low, skimming any impurities that rise to the top with a ladle • Add the onion, celery, leek, garlic and bay leaves and simmer for 20 minutes • Remove from the heat, add the lemon and parsley and allow to infuse and settle for 20 minutes • Pass through a fine sieve trying not to disturb the sediment on the bottom of the pan. This sediment will turn the stock cloudy • Cool and use as required • It can be frozen for up to 3 months.

Fish velouté or mussel velouté

[makes 4 cups]

THIS IS THE SIMPLEST way to transform fish or mussel stock into a well-made sauce. I serve all my sauces in a frothy form. Simply use a hand blender to aerate the sauce, then carefully scoop the froth off the top and spoon over the desired subject.

2½ tablespoons olive oil
6 shallots, thinly sliced
6 cloves of garlic, thinly sliced
4 sprigs of thyme
2 bay leaves
*200 ml (7 fl oz) dry vermouth (Noilly Prat)**
200 ml (7 fl oz) dry white wine
4 cups fish stock (see page 243) or 4 cups mussel stock (see page 389)
300 ml (10 fl oz) double cream

Heat the olive oil in a heavy-based saucepan, add the shallots, garlic, thyme and bay leaves and cook over medium heat for 6 minutes or until shallots are softened • Add the vermouth and reduce by two-thirds. Add the white wine and reduce by two-thirds • Add the fish stock or mussel stock, bring to the boil and reduce by a quarter. Add the cream, bring to the boil. Immediately remove from the heat and strain. Use as required.

Lobster sauce

[serves 4]

TRADITIONALLY LOBSTER SAUCE is served over lobster or a lobster-based dish, but I love to serve this sauce with steamed whiting.

200 ml (7 fl oz) langoustine stock (see page 245)
*3 tablespoons semi-whipped cream**
Juice of ½ lemon
1 tablespoon sherry vinegar
Pinch of chopped tarragon
Salt and freshly ground pepper

Reduce the langoustine stock in a heavy-based saucepan over a high heat by three-quarters or until just starting to thicken and catch on the bottom of the pan • Add the cream, a squeeze of lemon juice, the sherry vinegar and tarragon and season with salt and pepper. Bring to the boil and cook for 1 minute. The sauce should be light and fluffy in appearance. Spoon over fish or lobster.

Langoustine stock

[makes 4 cups]

WHAT ARE LANGOUSTINES? you may ask. They are simply a type of prawn, very closely related to scampi or the Dublin Bay prawn. Great-quality langoustines are available from New Zealand waters and are usually found in 1 kg (2 lb) frozen packages; though expensive, their meat is sweet and delicate.

This stock works well with prawn shells. It is designed to be clarified into a consommé by adding seasoned egg whites when cold, slowly bringing to the boil while whisking constantly. This stock is my preferred base for any crustacean sauces.

½ cup olive oil
1 carrot, diced
1 stick of celery, diced
1 leek, diced
2 onions, diced
1 large bulb of fennel, diced
Cloves of 1 head of garlic, crushed
Juice of ½ lemon
Pinch of cayenne pepper
2 sprigs of tarragon
4 sprigs of thyme
1 bay leaf
2 kg (4 lb) langoustine, scampi or other crustacean shells
100 ml (3½ fl oz) cognac
1 cup dry white wine
7 tomatoes, squeezed and deseeded
3 tablespoons tomato paste
4 cups fish stock (see page 243)

Heat the olive oil in a large heavy-based saucepan, add the carrot, celery, leek, onion, fennel and garlic and cook over medium heat until soft and starting to colour. Add the lemon juice, cayenne pepper, tarragon, thyme and bay leaf • Increase the heat to high, add the langoustine or crustacean shells and cook for 10 minutes or until bright orange and fragrant • Add the cognac and flambé by igniting the cognac in the pan with a lighter or match. Do not be alarmed, the flame will burn out after 30–60 seconds. Reduce by two-thirds, add the white wine and reduce by half • Add the tomatoes and the tomato paste, cook for 3–4 minutes or until the tomato paste starts to catch on the bottom of the pan • Add the fish stock, bring to the boil, reduce heat to low and simmer for 40 minutes • Pass through a fine sieve. Return to the saucepan and reduce to the required consistency. This will depend on what you require the stock for, whether it is for a soup or sauce.

Shellfish vinaigrette

[makes 2 cups]

This, another derivitive of the langoustine stock, is a very useful and delicious dressing for crab or scallop salads and steamed fish. A simple and effective entrée is to marinate thinly sliced raw scallops in the vinaigrette for 10 minutes before serving.

2 cups langoustine stock (see page 245)
4 shallots, chopped
1 tablespoon cracked black peppercorns
2 tablespoons sherry vinegar
Salt
300 ml (10 fl oz) olive oil
1 tablespoon finely chopped chives
1 teaspoon finely chopped tarragon
1 teaspoon finely chopped rosemary
Juice of ½ lemon

In a large heavy-based saucepan, bring the langoustine stock to the boil and reduce by half. Cool to room temperature • Add the shallots, peppercorns and sherry vinegar. Season with a little salt • Whisk in the olive oil and stand for 1 hour • Add the chopped herbs and season with the lemon juice just before serving.

Fish stock

Fish velouté

Langoustine stock

Shellfish vinaigrette

Nantua sauce

Nantua sauce

[serves 10]

Escoffier made this sauce famous at the legendary Savoy Hotel. The sauce varies from lobster sauce by using chicken stock, mushrooms and truffles.

½ cup olive oil
1 carrot, diced
1 stick of celery, diced
1 onion, diced
1 cup diced fennel
1 leek, diced
5 cloves of garlic, crushed
Juice of 1 lemon
1 teaspoon cayenne pepper
6 tarragon stalks
1 sprig of thyme
1 bay leaf
2 kg (4 lb) crayfish shells
100 ml (3½ fl oz) cognac
1 cup dry white wine
7 tomatoes, squeezed and deseeded
3 tablespoons tomato paste
8 cups chicken stock (see page 378)
12 tiny button mushrooms
2 teaspoons sherry vinegar
4 cups pouring (light) cream

Heat the olive oil in a large heavy-based saucepan, add the carrot, celery, onion, fennel, leek and garlic and cook over medium heat until soft and starting to colour. Add the lemon juice, cayenne pepper, tarragon, thyme and bay leaf • Increase the heat to high, add the crayfish shells and cook for 15 minutes • Add the cognac and flambé by igniting the cognac in the pan with a lighter or match. Do not be alarmed, the flame will burn out after 30–60 seconds. Reduce until all the liquid has evaporated. Add the white wine and reduce by two-thirds • Add the tomatoes and tomato paste, cook for 5 minutes or until the tomato paste starts to catch on the bottom of the pan • Add the chicken stock, bring to the boil, reduce heat and simmer for 50 minutes • Pass through a fine sieve. Return to the saucepan and reduce until the sauce is thick enough to coat the back of a spoon. Add the mushrooms and cook for 3–4 minutes • Whisk in the sherry vinegar and cream. Bring to the boil for 1 minute and serve.

Lobster bisque

[serves 4]

I have included a few extra flavours that are in line with our modern tastes — star anise and cardamom — to give a lovely aromatic complexity to this soup. I have also added crème fraîche because it's lighter than cream and more intense. Serve with good crusty garlic bread and rouille (see page 259).

2 kg (4 lb) lobster shells, including legs
½ cup olive oil
1 carrot, diced
1 stick of celery, diced
1 leek, diced
2 onions, diced
1 large bulb of fennel, diced
Cloves of 1 head of garlic, crushed
2 sprigs of tarragon
4 star anise
7 cardamom pods, crushed
4 sprigs of thyme
1 bay leaf
300 ml (10 fl oz) cognac
*300 ml (10 fl oz) Calvados**
150 g (5 oz) tomato paste
*50 g (1¾ oz) lobster roe**
8 cups fish stock (see page 243)
Pinch of cayenne pepper
Juice of 1 lemon, strained
300 ml (10 fl oz) crème fraîche
½ cup finely chopped flat-leaf parsley

Place the lobster shells in a food processor and blitz, in batches, until a coarse mixture is formed. It is important to include the legs as the meat in the shells adds flavour • Heat the olive oil in a large heavy-based saucepan, add the carrot, celery, leek, onion, fennel and garlic and cook over medium heat until soft and starting to colour. Add the tarragon, star anise, cardamom, thyme and bay leaf • Increase the heat to high, add the processed shells and cook for 10 minutes or until the shells are bright orange and fragrant • Add the cognac and flambé by igniting the cognac in the pan with a lighter or match. Do not be alarmed, the flame will burn out after 30–60 seconds. Reduce until all the liquid has evaporated. Add the Calvados and repeat the process • Add the tomato paste and lobster roe, stir, and cook for 5 minutes • Add the fish stock and simmer for 2 hours • Pass through a fine sieve, return to the pan and cook over medium heat for 15 minutes or until the flavour is concentrated. Season with cayenne pepper and lemon juice • Whisk in the crème fraîche and parsley • Serve with sautéed fresh lobster or crayfish ravioli.

MARINIÈRE OF SPRING BAY MUSSELS

[serves 4]

I HAVE ADAPTED THIS recipe for you at home. It has the same flavours as the soup I ate at Marco's, but the method is simpler and the time involved a lot less. It is a dish that will make a great entrée or light main course. The key technique to take away with you is the cooking of the mussels: apply this method to all shellfish. Serve with some great sourdough and good butter.

200 ml (7 fl oz) olive oil
5 shallots, finely chopped
3 sprigs of thyme
2 cloves of garlic, finely sliced
2 kg (4 lb) large mussels, cleaned and debearded
2 cups dry white wine
200 g (6½ oz) linguine
1 onion, finely chopped
2 cloves of garlic, crushed
100 g (3½ oz) cultured butter, chopped into fine dice*
1 cup basil, shredded
Salt and freshly ground pepper

Heat 100 ml (3½ fl oz) of the olive oil in a heavy-based saucepan. Add the shallots, thyme and sliced garlic and cook over high heat for 4 minutes or until the shallots are transparent and soft. Add the mussels and white wine, cover, and cook for 5 minutes or until the shells have opened • Strain over a colander, reserving the juice of the mussels • Loosen the mussels in their shells • Bring a large saucepan of salted water to the boil, add the linguine and cook until *al dente*. Drain • Heat the remaining olive oil in a heavy-based saucepan, add the onion and crushed garlic and cook until transparent and tender, about 5 minutes • Pour in the strained mussel juice, and reduce by one-third. Whisk in the butter, bring to the boil, and cook for 3 minutes. Stir in the basil and mussels. Season with salt and pepper • Wind the linguine around a roasting fork and place in the centre of each serving bowl. Spoon over the marinière sauce and serve.

LOBSTER MOUSSE

[serves 10]

A MOUSSE IS A great way to carry the flavour of lobster, crayfish, yabbies or just about any crustacean you can think of. The light texture complements the immense burst of flavour. Wrap in a blanched Savoy cabbage leaf or use to fill a boned sea bass or whiting, the applications are endless and are only limited by your imagination. Play and enjoy!

350 ml (12 fl oz) lobster bisque (see page 249)
300 g (10 oz) John Dory or whiting fillets
Pinch of salt
*10 g (1/3 oz) lobster coral**
1 egg
1 egg yolk
200 ml (7 fl oz) pouring (light) cream
1 tablespoon chopped tarragon
Juice of 1/2 lemon

Place the bowl, blade and lid of the food processor in the freezer until cold. This step is essential to ensure the mousse is kept cold to prevent the fish cooking • Place the lobster bisque in a small heavy-based saucepan and cook over medium heat until reduced by two-thirds. Allow to cool • Mince the fish with the salt in the food processor. Add the lobster coral and continue to blend for 1 minute or until the roe is completely incorporated into the fish. At this stage the mousse should be very cold or there is a good chance it will split once the cream is added. Place the bowl and mixture in the freezer for 5 minutes, if necessary • With the motor running, pour in the cooled lobster bisque, incorporating well, then add the egg and egg yolk. Scrape the sides of the bowl with a rubber spatula. Add the cream and tarragon while the motor is running. Do not overwork the mousse once the cream has been incorporated • Pass through a fine sieve • Test the mousse by placing a teaspoonful in some plastic wrap. Shape and tie into a ball, then gently poach in a saucepan of simmering water for 5 minutes. Taste, if satisfied, use the mousse as required. If not, adjust the seasoning with salt and a little lemon juice.

CRAYFISH OIL

[makes 4 cups]

OIL HAS THE UNIQUE quality to enhance simple ingredients, for example, fresh crusty sourdough bread dipped into extra virgin olive oil or a simple salad of red mullet and endive drizzled with aromatic crayfish oil. This oil will store well in the fridge for up to 3 months.

1 kg (2 lb) crayfish or other crustacean shells

300 g (10 oz) tomato paste

1 onion, diced

1 stick of celery, diced

1 large carrot, diced

1 cup of fennel, diced

1 head of garlic, cut in half

*Bouquet garni**

1 star anise

6 cups extra virgin olive oil

Place the crayfish shells in the food procesor and blitz, in batches, until coarsely ground • Preheat the oven to 120°C (250°F) • Combine all of the ingredients in a large flameproof casserole dish. Bring to the boil, immediately reduce heat to low and simmer for 5 minutes • Cover and place in the oven for 4 hours • Strain through a fine sieve lined with cheesecloth • Refrigerate for 24 hours. The oil will coagulate and separate from any liquid remaining from the vegetables. This liquid is easy to extract • Use as required.

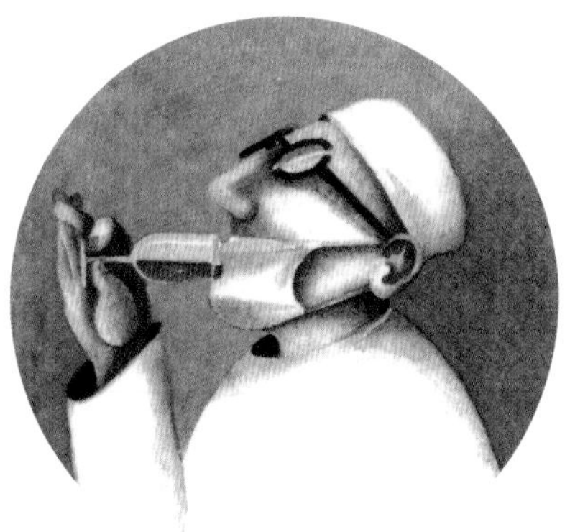

Sole monseigneur

[serves 4]

Vatel, a famous sixteenth-century chef, killed himself moments before he was about to serve a banquet for the king because the fish delivery had not turned up. Only minutes after his death the fish arrived! Once during a culinary display in Tours, France, a man approached Escoffier and asked 'What would you have done, sir, in Vatel's place?'. Escoffier answered, 'Surely, I would never have thrown myself on a sword for a question of tide. I would have replaced the fillets of sole with the flesh of young chickens, and not even the most exacting gourmet would have noticed the difference!'

2 x 200 g (6½ oz) chicken breast fillets
Pinch of salt
5 egg whites
4 thick slices of white bread, crusts removed
1 cup water
4 eggs, lightly beaten
200 g (6½ oz) fresh breadcrumbs
*100 g (3½ oz) Ortiz anchovies**
300 g (10 oz) cultured butter, chopped into dice, at room temperature*
Juice of 1 lemon
1 tablespoon finely chopped tarragon
1 tablespoon finely chopped flat-leaf parsley
1 tablespoon finely chopped chives
2 tablespoons clarified butter (see page 381)
*1 tablespoon cultured butter**

Combine the chicken breasts and salt in a food processor and blend until smooth. Add the egg whites and blend for 1 minute • Soak the bread in the water, squeeze out the excess water and add the bread to the chicken mixture. Blitz briefly • Transfer to a mixing bowl, cover, and refrigerate for 30 minutes • Place the cold chicken mixture onto a lightly floured work surface and mould into eight rectangular fillets 12 x 5 cm (5 x 2 in) • Dip each fillet in the egg and roll in the breadcrumbs. Rest in the refrigerator for 10 minutes or until firm • Crush the anchovies to a paste using a mortar and pestle. Add the butter and incorporate. Season with lemon juice and add the tarragon, parsley and chives. Store the anchovy butter in the fridge until required • Melt the clarified butter in a heavy-based frying pan over medium heat. Add the fillets, four at a time, and cook on each side for 2 minutes or until golden and crisp. Drain on paper towel. Place two fillets onto each warmed serving plate • Wipe out the pan with paper towel, add the butter and cook briefly until a nutty brown colour. Spoon over the fillets • Garnish with a small salad of herbs, finish with the anchovy butter and serve.

Lobster bisque

Marinière of spring bay mussels

Lobster mousse

Crayfish oil

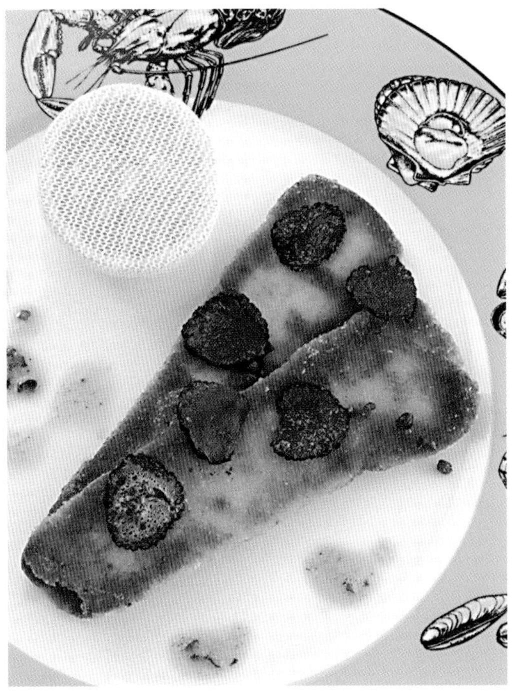

Sole monseigneur

Crab rillette

Filet de daurade et pommes de terre au crabe

Bouillabaisse serving suggestion

Crab rillette

[serves 8]

An invariable classic that is so French and so easy to produce at home you will wonder why there is such a thing as a chef. Well, almost. Serve with Melba toast or brioche.

*2 leaves titanium gelatin**
100 ml (3½ fl oz) cognac
100 ml (3½ fl oz) langoustine stock (see page 245)
2 cloves of garlic, crushed
1 tablespoon finely chopped tarragon
100 g (3½ oz) brown crabmeat
500 g (1 lb) white crabmeat
Juice of 1 lemon
1 tablespoon finely chopped curly-leaf parsley
Salt and freshly ground pepper
*350 ml (12 fl oz) semi-whipped cream**
8 slices smoked salmon
2 tablespoons salmon roe
1 continental cucumber
2 ruby grapefruit, peeled and segmented

Place eight non-stick dariole moulds on a tray • Soak the gelatin in cold water for 10 minutes. Squeeze out excess water • Pour the cognac into a heavy-based saucepan, flambé and reduce by half. Add the langoustine stock, garlic and tarragon and cook until reduced by half • Gently warm the brown crabmeat in a heavy-based saucepan, add the gelatin and simmer until reduced by a quarter. Transfer to a mixing bowl and fold in the white crabmeat • Add the lemon juice and parsley, season with salt and pepper and fold in the cream • Spoon into the dariole moulds and transfer to the refrigerator for 24 hours • To serve, dip the dariole moulds into boiling water for 10 seconds. Invert and unmould the rillettes into the centre of each serving plate • Cut the smoked salmon with a 4-cm (1½-in) round pastry cutter and place on top of rillette • Top with a teaspoon of salmon roe • Thinly slice the cucumber and arrange the slices in a fan around each rillette • Arrange the grapefruit segments on the plate. Serve with dressed seasonal salad leaves.

FILET DE DAURADE ET POMMES DE TERRE AU CRABE

[serves 4]

A GREAT ADDITION to your summer lunch repertoire. Always roast small fillets in a hot pan quickly and at the last minute and remember to season the fish well. An aged semillon will answer your thirst problems when consuming this dish.

TOMATO VINAIGRETTE

200 g (6½ oz) cherry tomatoes
100 ml (3½ fl oz) tomato ketchup
2½ tablespoons sherry vinegar
100 ml (3½ fl oz) extra virgin olive oil
Salt and freshly ground pepper
Juice of ½ lemon

250 g (8 oz) kipfler potatoes
2 shallots, finely chopped
100 g (3 ½ oz) blue swimmer crabmeat
½ tablespoon chopped flat-leaf parsley
100 ml (3½ fl oz) French vinaigrette (see page 396)
150 g (5 oz) broad beans
8 x 150 g (5 oz) baby snapper fillets
¼ cup plain (all-purpose) flour
2 tablespoons olive oil

GARNISH

1 cup frisée leaves
8 sprigs of chervil
4 stems of chives
4 sprigs of flat-leaf parsley

To make the tomato vinaigrette, purée the tomatoes in a food processor, add the ketchup, vinegar, olive oil, salt and pepper and a squeeze of lemon juice. Pass through a fine sieve to remove any skin and seeds. Set aside for 2 hours to allow the flavours to develop • Cook the potatoes in boiling salted water for 15 minutes or until very tender. Peel while the potatoes are still hot • Place the potatoes in a bowl with the shallots, crabmeat, parsley, ⅓ cup of French vinaigrette and salt and pepper, and break up with a fork until resembling badly mashed potato. Add the broad beans, cover, and keep warm • Season the snapper fillets with salt and pepper. Dust with a little of the flour • Heat the olive oil in a non-stick frying pan, add the snapper fillets and cook on medium heat for 2 minutes until the fish is golden and crisp, turn over and cook for 1 minute • To make the garnish combine the frisée leaves and chervil and dress with the remaining French vinaigrette • To serve, on each serving plate, place the potatoes in a 5-cm (2-in) round cutter and press down with a fork. Remove the cutter, pour the tomato vinaigrette around the potato to flood the plate. Place two fish fillets on top, arrange the frisée leaves and chevril on the plate and garnish with a chive stem and a sprig of parsley.

Bouillabaisse

[serves 8]

Most food historians believe that the original bouillabaisse (*bouï abaisso* in Provençal, meaning to boil and press) evolved in the town of Saint-Raphaël on the Calanque coast between Marseille and Toulon. Although called a soup, this is really a main dish, a meal in itself. Bouillabaisse was made from locally caught fish, usually those unsold at the daily market, with local shellfish added. Bouillabaisse was a fisherman's dish, and never contained any expensive ingredients, such as lobster, although the common small green crabs were often used. The soup has many regional variations and the colour can change from place to place because of the fish used.

10 x 80 g (2¾ oz) red mullet carcasses
500 g (1 lb) crab shells
500 g (1 lb) crayfish shells
1 carrot, diced
1 stick of celery, diced
2 onions, diced
1 bulb of fennel, diced
1 leek, diced
1 head of garlic, chopped in half
3 sprigs of thyme
2 bay leaves
Pinch of cayenne pepper
2 pinches of saffron
4 star anise
2 cups dry white wine
*150 ml (5 fl oz) pastis (Pernod)**
*150 ml (5 fl oz) dry vermouth (Noilly Prat)**

Remove the eyes from the mullet (they will impart a bitter flavour to the soup) • Combine the mullet, crab shells and crayfish shells with the vegetables, herbs, spices, wine, pastis, vermouth, tomatoes, tomato paste and 100 ml (3½ fl oz) of the olive oil in a large container. Cover and leave to marinate in the refrigerator for 48 hours. Strain and set aside • Heat the remaining olive oil in a heavy-based saucepan, add the fish bones, shells and vegetables and cook for 4–5 minutes or until the bones are golden. Season with salt and pepper • Add the reserved marinade and reduce over low heat until evaporated • Add the fish and mussel stock and simmer for 2 hours • Using a hand blender, roughly purée the soup. Do not be concerned about the bones and shells. Pass the soup through a coarse sieve, then through a fine sieve • Reheat and serve with rouille, garlic croutons and Gruyere cheese.

5 ripe Roma (plum) tomatoes
150 g (5 oz) tomato paste
1 cup olive oil
Salt and freshly ground pepper
8 cups fish stock (see page 243)
2 cups mussel stock (see page 389)
Rouille (see below)
Garlic croutons (see page 383)
1 cup finely grated Gruyere cheese

Rouille

[serves 12]

Rouille is the traditional mayonnaise accompaniment to bouillabaisse, roast fish, French fries and shellfish. It contains abundant amounts of chilli and garlic; a powerful and perilous sauce for many palates. Some chefs include tomato paste, or cooked egg yolks for colour, but I find this unnecessary because the saffron is assertive enough when given essential time to impart its staining power.

1 large sebago potato, peeled
4 cups bouillabaisse (see pages 258–259)
1 bird's eye chilli
Pinch of sea salt
2 cloves of garlic, crushed
Pinch of saffron
5 egg yolks
350 ml (12 fl oz) olive oil
Juice of 1/2 lemon

Cook the potato in the bouillabaisse for 20 minutes or until soft • Using a mortar and pestle, crush the chilli, salt, garlic and potato into a paste • Transfer to a bowl, beat in the saffron and egg yolks. Whisk in the olive oil in three stages, to stop the mixture splitting. Continue to whisk until it resembles a thick mayonnaise. Add the lemon juice and set aside for 2 hours before using.

Risotto au fruits de mer

[serves 6]

Plump Arborio rice is cooked in a shellfish stock of clams, mussels and blue swimmer crab and dressed with crayfish oil. The key is a good stock and in this case the bouillabaisse is the star.

ACID BUTTER

1/3 cup Champagne vinegar
150 ml (5 fl oz) dry white wine
1 medium onion, sliced
10 sprigs of thyme
1 bay leaf
400 g (13 oz) cultured butter, chopped into fine dice*

RISOTTO

4 cups bouillabaisse (see pages 258–259)
2 1/2 tablespoons olive oil
1 medium onion, finely diced
250 g (8 oz) Arborio rice
350 ml (12 fl oz) white wine
4 cups vegetable oil
6 baby squid, cleaned
18 mussels, cleaned
18 clams, cleaned
1/2 cup grated Grana Padano Parmesan cheese
Salt and freshly ground pepper
1 tablespoon chopped tarragon

To make the acid butter, combine the vinegar, white wine, onion, thyme and bay leaf and cook until reduced by four-fifths. Whisk in the butter until smooth and thick. Pass through a fine sieve into a storage container and transfer to the refrigerator for 1 hour to set. The butter will keep for up to 1 month. The butter can be incorporated into the risotto warm, but for the best textural results cold butter is preferred • To make the risotto, bring the bouillabaisse to the boil in a heavy-based saucepan, reduce heat to low and simmer • Heat the olive oil in a large heavy-based saucepan, add the onion and cook for 3 minutes or until soft and tender. Add the rice stirring until each grain is coated with oil • Deglaze with the white wine, stirring constantly to prevent the rice from sticking. Cook until all the wine is absorbed. • Add the hot bouillabaisse and cook over low heat for 10 minutes, stirring occasionally, until all the liquid is absorbed • Heat the vegetable oil in a deep-fryer until it reaches 200°C (400°F) • Prepare the squid by washing under cold running water and separating the tentacles from the tubes. Clean the inside of the tubes in cold running water, removing any impurities and cartilage. Cut the squid tubes into thin rings. Drain the squid well and pat dry • Deep-fry the squid rings and tentacles for 5–6 minutes or until golden and crispy • Place the mussels and clams in a steamer over a saucepan of simmering water. Cover and cook for 5 minutes or until the shells have opened • Fold 3 tablespoons of the acid butter and a good pinch of Parmesan into the risotto. Season with salt and pepper, and add the tarragon • Serve immediately by spooning the risotto into a 12-cm (5-in) ring in the centre of each serving plate. Remove the ring and arrange the mussels, clams and crispy squid around and over the risotto. Pass the remaining Parmesan at the table.

Risotto au fruits de mer

Steamed grouper with confit potatoes and onions

Á la florentine soufflé d'ecrevisses

Shrimp butter

Steamed grouper with confit potatoes and onions

[serves 4]

Grouper, another name for harpuka, is very meaty and dense, not dissimilar to Atlantic cod.

*400 g (13 oz) goose fat**

4 large sebago potatoes

2 large brown onions, thinly sliced

Salt and freshly ground pepper

4 x 200 g (6½ oz) wild grouper fillets, skinned

*400 g (13 oz) caul fat (crepinette)**

200 ml (7 fl oz) mussel velouté (see page 244)

200 ml (7 fl oz) red wine sauce (see page 296)

300 ml (10 fl oz) fish stock (see page 243)

12 baby leeks, diagonally sliced

Parsley purée (see pages 302–3)

Heat the goose fat in a small heavy-based saucepan to 80°C (175°F) over a very low heat • Slice the potato into discs 3 mm (⅛ in) thick. Cook the potato in the goose fat for 5 minutes, until just cooked. Drain and reserve the potatoes on paper towel • Repeat the process with the sliced onion. Cook for 10 minutes until tender and transparent. Drain well in a sieve, then rest on paper towel. (Reserve the goose fat for other uses). Season potatoes and onion with salt and pepper and cool in the refrigerator for 20 minutes. If they are cold there will be less chance of them breaking when being assembled in the dish • Place a layer of onion on top of each fish fillet. Layer the potatoes over the onions, overlapping them slightly to resemble scales. Wrap tightly in the caul, ready to steam • Place the fish in a steamer, cover, and cook for 8 minutes. Test to see if the fish is cooked by inserting a toothpick, if it slides in without resistance, it is ready • Warm the mussel velouté in a small saucepan • In a separate saucepan, heat the red wine sauce and fish stock and reduce by two-thirds. Season with salt and pepper • Cook the leeks in a saucepan of boiling salted water for 2 minutes • Place a teaspoon of parsley purée in the centre of each serving plate, and place the fish on top. Drape three leeks over the top of each fish parcel • Froth the mussel velouté with a hand blender and spoon only the froth over and around the fish. Drizzle the red wine sauce around the velouté and serve.

Á LA FLORENTINE SOUFFLÉ D'ECREVISSES

[serves 6]

CAREME, THE WORLD'S first celebrity chef, invented this souffle in the eighteenth century for his employer, Tallyrand. Tallyrand, a notable French statesman and connoisseur of good food, was considered to host the finest table in Europe.

Crayfish soufflé is as close to French cookery as you can get without being in France. This dish calls out for a wine of the same calibre, Chablis.

1/3 cup béchamel sauce (see page 373)
100 g (3 1/2 oz) Grana Padano Parmesan cheese, grated
8 eggs, separated
1 tablespoon ground nutmeg
Salt and freshly ground pepper
1 kg (2 lb) fresh yabbies
10 g (1/3 oz) butter, softened
2 black truffles, shaved*

Preheat the oven to 180°C (350°F) • Combine the béchamel, Parmesan, egg yolks, nutmeg and salt and pepper in a mixing bowl • Beat the egg whites with a little salt until soft peaks form. Fold into the béchamel mixture to form the soufflé base • Place the yabbies in the freezer for 10 minutes. Cook in boiling salted water for 5 minutes, then refresh in iced water for 5 minutes. Separate the heads and tails of the yabbies. Devein by hooking a toothpick under the black tube running along the back of the yabby. Reserve the heads and shells for another use, such as soup or stock • Butter six 1-cup capacity soufflé moulds. Place a tablespoonful of soufflé base in each mould. Add a whole yabby tail and a slice of truffle. Add another spoonful of soufflé base, then some yabby meat and another slice of truffle. Repeat the layering until each mould is full, finishing with a spoonful of soufflé base. Be careful not to have air pockets in the soufflé • Bake in the oven for 12 minutes or until the soufflé has risen 5 cm (2 in). Serve immediately.

Shrimp butter

[makes $2\frac{1}{2}$ cups]

Shrimp butter can be used to dress salads, tossed with cooked and peeled prawns (shrimp) and served as a pâté with crusty sourdough bread. It is also great for cooking fish.

1 kg (2 lb) crayfish and yabby shells
*400 g (13 oz) cultured butter**
4 cups iced water

Preheat the oven to 120°C (250°F) • Remove any remaining flesh and particles from inside and outside the shells • Dry the shells in the oven, then pound until fine using a mortar and pestle • Mix with the butter and melt, stirring frequently, in a double boiler over a saucepan of simmering water. Pour through a cheesecloth-lined sieve into a basin of ice-cold water. When the warm mixture meets the cold water it will solidify quite spectacularly. Place this solidified butter in a layer of cheesecloth and squeeze to remove the water. Transfer to an airtight container and store in the refrigerator for 1 month.

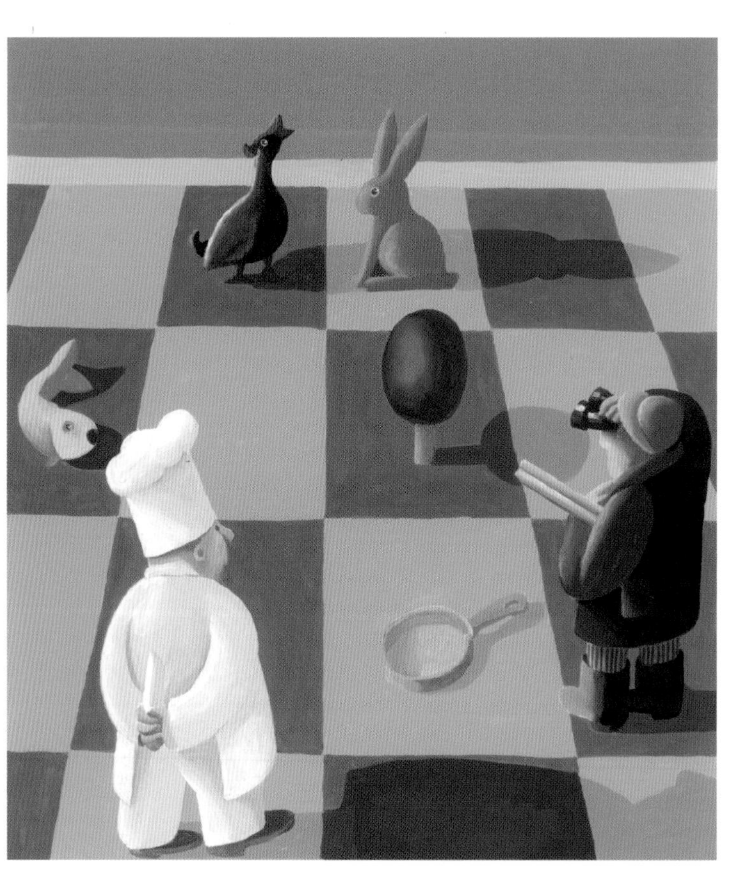

The Wilderness

ACCORDING TO ITS TRUE definition, game has somewhat lost its meaning in the past few years, especially in the New Worlds of Australasia and America. Game includes all animals and birds found in the wild that are hunted for human consumption. The types of game we consume have evolved dramatically with the improvement of our lifestyle. Game is no longer considered a hunted animal — these days 90 per cent of our game is farmed. Being an animal lover, I favour this practice. At the same time I love the mystique of the hunted and the hunter. There will always be a place for game at the table.

Australia is fortunate to be graced with a vast array of edible wild produce, ranging from everyday creatures, such as hare or rabbit, to exotic animals, such as crocodile and buffalo, Cape Barron geese, wild duck, boar, wood pigeon, kangaroo and emu. The meat from game is generally more intensely flavoured than meat from domesticated animals. Both types of meat are high in protein and minerals, but wild game is sometimes significantly lower in fat and cholesterol. In most states, wild game can be hunted only in season, normally mid-autumn to late-winter, depending on the species and its environment. Game cannot be sold commercially unless certified by a vet, but you don't have to be a hunter to sample it.

The most popular game animals are raised on carefully managed farms or reserves. Farmed game has been popularised by top restaurants with pheasant, partridge, quail and venison being favoured by consumers. Farm-raised game is more meaty and tender than wild game because the fat is marbled throughout the meat.

Game is traditionally noted for its tough texture, to counteract this, all game is hung in a cold environment for a certain period of time. Hanging anywhere from a few days to a few weeks traditionally ages it, which concentrates its flavour. The larger the game, the longer it will need to be hung. The general rule is all feathered game is to be hung by the neck and all furred game to be hung by the hind legs. Recommended storage temperature is 3–4°C (37–40°F). I find seven days is enough time for even the largest of furred game to hang.

The rules for other meats apply here. Store fresh game in the coldest part of the refrigerator, on a clean tray to prevent contamination with other food items and use within two days. Meat you buy from a reputable retailer will have been properly aged. Before cooking, trim away visible fat, which can impart a disagreeable flavour.

Too often in Australia we look overseas for our wine matches with game, when it is in fact in our own backyard that we make some of the world's most game-friendly wines. It is shiraz, of course, that provides the vehicle for this successful marriage. The spice in shiraz is the perfect foil for that rich meaty gamey character.

Australia is justly famous for its production of shiraz: the Barossa monsters, Coonawarra spice bombs and cool Victorian white pepper packets. At Vue de monde we tend to focus on premium cool climate shiraz as the better partner to game dishes. Castagna, and Giaconda from Beechworth are very popular as well as Berry's Bridge from the Pyrénées and Frankland Estate from Frankland River in Western Australia. That said there is still plenty of room for the traditional Aussie styles from the Barossa and Coonawarra although these do tend to benefit from a little age, which makes them harder to find.

It is the cooler styles with their inherent spice and pepper characters that add to the enjoyment of partridge and pheasant. The savoury characters of the wine help to season the dish and balance the rich meaty character of the bird. Venison needs wine with fuller flavour profiles, this is where the classic earthy traits of the rich red and purple fruit of the Barossa shiraz and the McLaren Vale shiraz make perfect partners.

Wild Hare is my favourite wild animal, it has a certain grace. Demand always outweighs supply because of its unique texture, flavour and versatility. Hare is not hung because it may spoil and its unique gamey flavour does not need to be enhanced.

Being able to buy hare at the market is a rare thing, but don't shy away from placing pressure on your butcher to search around. Three to four meals can be derived from one hare: the loins are great for roasting; the kidneys and livers are great for salads; the hind leg meat is great for braising; the front legs and trimmings are great for terrines, pâtés and mousses. Hare is the perfect partner for a classic Burgundy because its earthiness is backed up by aromatic fruits, which complement the sauces associated with hare dishes. Respect the raw product and have fun.

Assiette of wild hare

[serves 2]

THIS IS MY OWN interpretation of a classic Larousse dish, which highlights the synergy between mushrooms and hare. It is time consuming, but well worth it. Make it a Saturday night feature and go to the extra effort of serving with a big occasion pinot noir, may I even suggest a Grand Cru Burgundy.

500 g (1 lb) hare forequarter, including rib cage

Salt and freshly ground pepper

200 g (6½ oz) chicken mousse (see page 377)

*1 tablespoon black truffle paste**

*100 g (3½ oz) caul fat (crepinette)**

2 twice-cooked hare legs (see page 272)

200 g (6½ oz) pea purée (see page 142)

2 sheets puff pastry (see page 54)

1 egg, lightly beaten

3 tablespoons olive oil

2 hare kidneys, trimmed of sinew

100 g (3½ oz) broad beans, double shelled

3 tablespoons mushroom stock (see page 109)

1 frozen or fresh cèpe, chopped in half

*100 ml (3½ fl oz) semi-whipped cream**

2 pinches of dried cèpe powder (see page 376)

Ask your butcher to separate the saddle from the rib cage and remove the loins from the saddle. Chine (cut through the backbone vertically with the butt end blade of a knife to separate both sides of the saddle) the forequarter and scrape the rib bones from the inside. Peel away the skin around the rib bones starting from the top. Remove any sinew from the loin meat below the rib bones to create a rack roast. Bend the completed and Frenched racks into a circle. Pin together with a toothpick • Season the saddles with salt and pepper • Combine the chicken mousse with the truffle paste and spoon over the top of each loin • Wrap one layer of the caul around each loin. Place the loins in plastic wrap and roll up tightly to shape into sausages; expelling any air. Tie each end of the plastic wrap with a tight knot • Heat a large saucepan of water and poach the loins for 7 minutes. Rest in a warm place for 10 minutes • Remove the hare meat from the bone. Tear the meat into small pieces • Preheat the oven to 180°C (350°F) • To make the pithiviers*, combine the braised hare meat with the pea purée and salt and pepper. Place in the refrigerator for 20 minutes • Roll out the puff pastry on a floured work surface to a thickness of 6 mm (¼ in). Cut two 8-cm (3-in) squares for the base of each pithivier. Centre a 5-cm (2-in) round cutter on each pastry square, press the hare and pea mixture into each cutter. Remove

the cutter and place a layer of puff pastry over the top • Press a heavily floured 6-cm (2½-in) cutter over the two layers of puff pastry to shape into a dome. Do not pierce the pastry. Press around the edges to seal. Rest in the refrigerator for 10 minutes. Cut out to form a dome using an 8-cm (3-in) cutter. Brush with the beaten egg • Bake in the oven for 7 minutes or until golden • Heat ½ tablespoon of the olive oil in a large frying pan, add the kidneys and cook over high heat, stirring constantly, for 1 minute or until dark brown. Set aside to rest. In the same pan, brown the hare racks in ½ tablespoon of the olive oil. Season with salt and pepper • Transfer the racks to a baking tray and place in the oven for 2–3 minutes. Set aside to rest in a warm place • Cook the broad beans in boiling salted water for 2 minutes. Drain, toss in enough olive oil to glaze the beans, and season with salt and pepper • Reduce the mushroom stock by two-thirds or until thick and dark. Add the cèpe and warm through. Whisk in the cream and season with salt and pepper. Remove from the heat immediately • Place a pithivier at 3 o'clock on each serving plate • Slice the poached loin into three and place at 9 o'clock on each plate. Place the rack at the top of the plate. Spoon the mushroom sauce artfully around each plate; don't flood the plate, too much of this sauce will detract from the delicate hare flavour • Position the broad beans around the plate with a slice of poached cèpe. Sprinkle a little cèpe powder on the side of each plate and serve.

Twice-cooked hare leg

[serves 2]

THE BRAISED LEGS will keep well in the refrigerator for two or three days. Try a big Australian shiraz to pair with the wonderful rich flavours.

2 tablespoons olive oil
2 x 250 g (8 oz) hind hare legs
1½ tablespoons eight-spice powder (see page 382)
1 carrot, diced
1 stick of celery, diced
1 onion, diced
1 leek, diced
salt and freshly ground pepper
3 cups red wine
4 cups veal stock (see page 294)
*50 g (1¾ oz) goose fat**
1 tablespoon cultured butter, cut into fine dice*
1½ cups pommes mousseline (see page 102)

Preheat the oven to 160°C (325°F) • Heat 1 tablespoon of the olive oil in a heavy-based frying pan, add the hare legs and brown on all sides on medium heat. Add 3 teaspoons of the eight-spice powder and cook for 2 minutes or until fragrant • Heat the remaining olive oil in a large flameproof casserole, add the carrot, celery, onion and leek and cook for 6 minutes or until tender. Season with salt and pepper. Deglaze with the red wine and cook until the wine has evaporated. Add the veal stock and bring to the boil • Add the hare legs, cover, and place in the oven for 2 hours or until the meat falls away from the bone • Remove and cool in the refrigerator to allow them to set and to enable easy handling for the second cooking process • Strain the braising sauce through a fine sieve; you may have to repeat the process to achieve a fine clear sauce. Set to one side • Prepare the legs by trimming away any untidy pieces of meat, French the leg bone by scraping the top of the thighbone with a sharp knife until the bone appears • Heat the goose fat in a heavy-based frying pan, add the hare legs and cook on high heat for 3–4 minutes or until caramelised and golden. Season with the remaining eight-spice powder and salt and pepper • Heat the braising sauce and reduce for 3–4 minutes or until thick. Whisk in the butter and season with salt and pepper • Warm the pommes mousseline in a small saucepan • On each warmed serving plate, place a hare leg on some creamy pommes mousseline, then drizzle the braising sauce over the leg. Serve with hot crusty bread.

Hare pâté

[serves 10]

MAKE THIS TERRINE a week in advance. The flavour will only improve. There are no particular rules about the shape of this terrine, but I do recommend buying a good sturdy terrine mould. Match this terrine with a New World buttery-style chardonnay.

500 g (1 lb) hare meat, trimmed
4 eggs
*100 g (3½ oz) goose fat**
20 thin slices of bacon
2 cloves of garlic, crushed
1 brown onion, finely diced
100 ml (3½ fl oz) brandy
2 tablespoons finely chopped curly-leaf parsley
Salt and freshly ground pepper
200 g (6½ oz) foie gras, diced
1 loaf of sourdough bread (see page 52)
200 g (6½ oz) apple and pear chutney (see page 370)

Preheat the oven to 150°C (300°F) • Place the hare in a food processor and blend until smooth. Add the eggs and 80 g (2¾ oz) of the goose fat. Process for 2 minutes or until smooth • Line the sides of a plastic wrap-lined 2-litre (3½-pt) terrine mould with the bacon, slightly overlapping each slice and making sure the bacon overhangs the rim of the mould • Sprinkle the garlic over the bacon • Heat the remaining 1 tablespoon of goose fat in a frying pan, add the onion, and cook over medium heat for 3–4 minutes or until tender and transparent. Add the brandy and flambé by igniting the brandy in the pan with a lighter or match. Do not be alarmed, the flame will burn out after 30–60 seconds. Transfer to the food processor and blend • Add the parsley and pulse • Season with the salt and pepper, then pour into the terrine mould • Fold in the foie gras to create a marbled effect. Smooth the top • Cover the terrine with the overhanging bacon slices. Cover with plastic wrap, then a layer of aluminium (aluminum) foil. Transfer to a baking tray, add boiling water to come halfway up the sides of the terrine mould and place in the oven for 90 minutes • Test with a thermometer, the terrine should be above 65°C (150°F) in the centre. Refrigerate for a minimum of 2 days • Turn the terrine out onto a chilled tray, slice thinly, and serve with salad, toasted sourdough and apple and pear chutney.

Marinated pheasant with lime and coconut sauce

[serves 4]

Farmed pheasant can sometimes be lacking in gamey flavour. Use this to your advantage by marinating the subtle flesh in lime, fresh coconut, ginger and cumin, then glaze and roast and serve with couscous, roasted cashews and baby spring onions. The results are sensational. Quail can be substituted for pheasant.

The dish will suit a cooler climate shiraz.

1.4 kg (3 lb) pheasant
½ bunch of coriander (cilantro)

MARINADE

Roots from the coriander
150 ml (5 fl oz) light soy sauce
*100 ml (3½ fl oz) kecap manis**
Juice of 2 oranges
Juice of 4 limes
2 tablespoons Madras curry paste
1 tablespoon garam masala
1 bird's eye chilli, deseeded and finely chopped
20 g (¾ oz) fresh ginger, bruised
1 tablespoon ground cumin
Milk from 1 fresh coconut
100 ml (3½ fl oz) extra virgin olive oil
Salt and freshly ground pepper
3 tablespoons olive oil
2 shallots, finely diced

Wash the pheasant and pat dry. Remove the wishbone, keep the skin surrounding the neck • Wash the coriander thoroughly and chop the roots for the marinade. Reserve the leaves for garnishing • To make the marinade, in a large bowl, combine the coriander roots, soy sauce, kecap manis, orange juice, lime juice, curry paste, garam masala, chilli, ginger, cumin, coconut milk and extra virgin olive oil. Season with salt and pepper. Add the pheasant and marinate for at least 24 hours • Preheat the oven to 200°C (400°F) • Remove the pheasant from the marinade and transfer to a baking tray, add 1 tablespoon of the olive oil and, starting with the legs first, brown over medium heat for 2–3 minutes or until crispy and golden. Be careful not to burn the skin, the sugars from the marinade will caramelise very quickly • Place in the oven for 15 minutes. Baste with the pan juices and cook for a further 5 minutes. Remove from the pan and rest on a rack in a warm place for 20 minutes • Strain the marinade through a fine sieve • Heat 1 tablespoon of the remaining olive oil in a large heavy-based saucepan, add the shallots, carrot, celery, onion and leek and cook over medium heat for 5–6 minutes or until soft • Add the redcurrant jelly and reduce until it

1 carrot, diced
1 stick of celery, diced
1 onion, diced
1 leek, diced
200 g (6½ oz) redcurrant jelly
2 cups chicken stock (see page 378)
*80 g (2¾ oz) semi-whipped cream**
Juice of ½ lemon

COUSCOUS

700 ml (23½ fl oz) boiling water
200 g (6½ oz) instant couscous
100 g (3½ oz) preserved lemons, finely diced*
200 g (6½ oz) cultured butter, chopped into fine dice*

4 spring onions (scallions), cut into 3-cm (1¼-inch) batons
100 g (3½ oz) cashews, lightly roasted
2 Roma (plum) tomatoes, diced

starts to stick to the bottom of the pan • Add the marinade and the chicken stock, bring to the boil, reduce heat and simmer until reduced by half. Strain through a fine sieve. Return to the pan and reduce by two-thirds. Whisk in the cream, season with salt, pepper and lemon juice and bring to the boil, whisking constantly. Boil for 30 seconds, then remove from heat • To make the couscous, combine the boiling water and couscous in a large bowl. Cover with plastic wrap and rest in a warm place for 10 minutes • Stir in the preserved lemon, then fold in the butter, with a fork, incorporating until light and fluffy • Heat the remaining 1 tablespoon of olive oil in a heavy-based saucepan, add the spring onions and cook over low heat for 30 seconds. Add the cashews, gently warm for 1 minute then remove • To make the garnish, combine the tomatoes, spring onions, cashews and coriander leaves in a bowl. Season with salt and pepper • Place 2 tablespoons of warm couscous in the centre of each serving plate • Joint the pheasant, by removing the legs and thighs. Cut each thigh and leg into two, ensuring that each diner receives a piece of leg meat. Remove the breast meat and slice into four. Place the pheasant meat on top of the couscous. Pour over the sauce. Arrange the spring onion garnish over the dish and serve.

Assiette of wild hare

Hare pâté

Marinated pheasant with lime and coconut sauce

Duck galette

Roast quail with vanilla and white peach

Pheasant mousseline à l'anglaise

[serves 8 as an entrée]

This is an Escoffier classic. Try the dish paired with a crisp chenin blanc. Ask your local wine merchant for a Vouvray with a touch of residual sugar — the weight of the wine will complement the experience. This dish is based on a recipe created in 1895. By the way, pheasant meat can be replaced with chicken breast.

Pheasant mousse

400 g (13 oz) pheasant meat
Salt
3 egg whites
550 ml (18 fl oz) thickened cream

2 turnips, diced
2 carrots, diced
100 g (3½ oz) baby green beans, trimmed

Parsley sauce

1 tablespoon olive oil
1 clove of garlic, crushed
2 onions, diced
4 cups chicken stock (see page 378)
3 cups curly-leaf parsley
8 sprigs of flat-leaf parsley
Salt and freshly ground pepper

Preheat the oven to 110°C (225°F) • Place the bowl, blade and lid of the food processor in the freezer until chilled • To make the pheasant mousse, blend the pheasant with a pinch of salt in the food processor, add the egg whites and cream and continue to blend for 1 minute until smooth and the cream is fully incorporated. Pass through a sieve into a mixing bowl and rest in the refrigerator for 2 hours • Spoon the mixture into eight buttered dariole moulds, cover each with aluminium (aluminum) foil and transfer to a baking tray. Pour in enough boiling water to come halfway up the sides of the moulds and place in the oven for 40 minutes • Blanch all the vegetables separately in boiling salted water for 1–3 minutes. Test to see if they are cooked by eating one. Refresh in iced water • To make the parsley sauce, heat the olive oil in a large heavy-based saucepan, add the garlic and onion and cook for 2 minutes. Add the chicken stock and bring to the boil. Add the curly-leaf parsley and boil until cooked, 2–3 minutes. Purée with a hand blender, return to the pan, add the vegetables and cook over low heat until warmed through. Season with salt and pepper • To serve, unmould each mousse onto individual serving plates. Spoon over the parsley sauce and garnish with a sprig of flat-leaf parsley. Serve immediately.

Pot-roasted partridge with calvados and apple

[serves 2]

I'm trying to prove a point here. First, the Americans are not the only people who like a pot roast. Second, because of the delicate accompaniments and flavours, I have chosen a white wine for this dish. Unfortunately, the new world does not yet have a wine capable of successfully completing the job — to my mind Alsace is the only region in the world that does. A full-blooded pinot gris with a good amount of residual sugar will help cement your love for the art of food and wine matching.

750 g (1½ lb) partridge
1 black pudding sausage, sliced
1 tablespoon plain (all-purpose) flour
*50 g (1¾ oz) goose fat**
Salt and freshly ground pepper
1 carrot, diced
1 stick of celery, diced
1 tablespoon caster (superfine) sugar
1 Granny Smith apple, peeled, cored and sliced into 12 wedges
*100 ml (3½ fl oz) Calvados**
*4 slices of flat pancetta**
100 g (3½ oz) Sauternes sauce (see page 174)
100 g (3½ oz) cooked lentils du Puy (see page 386)*
2 pommes mille-feuille (see page 101)

Wash the partridge and pat dry • Preheat the oven to 190°C (375°F) • Lightly coat the black pudding in the flour • Heat the goose fat in a heavy-based flameproof casserole dish, add the partridge and cook on high heat for 2 minutes on each side or until golden. Season with salt and pepper. Add the black pudding, carrot and celery, season once more, and cook for 3–4 minutes or until the black pudding is crispy • Heat the caster sugar in a heavy-based frying pan over medium heat for 2–3 minutes or until the sugar turns to caramel. Add the apple and coat in the caramel. Deglaze with the Calvados and flambé by igniting the cognac in the pan with a lighter or match. Do not be alarmed, the flame will burn out after 30–60 seconds • Transfer the apple and pan juices to the partridge, cover, and place in the oven for 15 minutes. Rest for 20 minutes in a warm part of the kitchen • Heat a non-stick frying pan, add the pancetta and fry on low heat for 6 minutes or until crispy • Warm the Sauternes sauce in a saucepan over a very low heat • Warm the lentils du Puy in a saucepan • Joint the partridge by removing the legs, then the breasts • Make a bed of lentils in the centre of each plate. Place a leg and a breast on top of the lentils, drizzle over the Sauternes butter and scatter around the black sausage and vegetables • Carefully place the caramelised apple between the partridge and the lentils. Place a pommes mille-feuille at the top of each plate. Spoon over any remaining pan juices, garnish with two slices of pancetta and serve.

Supremes de volaille chimay

[serves 4]

This is a classical interpretation of chicken Kiev. Pheasant meat is preferred for its defined flavour. You can complete the preparation in advance, say up to 48 hours, as the butter imparts a lovely flavour into the meat. The nuttiness of the dish pairs well with aged wines particularly viognier.

*40 g (1⅓ oz) dried morels**
4 corn-fed partridge breast fillets
Salt and freshly ground pepper
1⅓ cups plain (all-purpose) flour
4 eggs
200 g (6½ oz) fresh breadcrumbs
100 g (3½ oz) clarified butter (see page 381)
*250 g (8 oz) cultured butter**
2 cloves of garlic, crushed
2 shallots, finely chopped
1 tablespoon finely chopped curly-leaf parsley
Juice of ½ lemon
12 sprigs of watercress

Soak the morels in boiling water for 15 minutes. Wash well after soaking to remove excess dirt • Flatten the partridge breasts with a mallet • Season the partridge breasts with salt and pepper • Place the flour in a shallow bowl • In a second bowl, lightly beat the eggs • Place the breadcrumbs in a third bowl • Dip each partridge breast in the flour to coat, then in the egg and lastly in the breadcrumbs • Heat the clarified butter in a large non-stick frying pan, add the crumbed breasts, in batches, and shallow fry on medium heat for 3–4 minutes or until golden brown on each side • Melt the butter in a frying pan, when it starts to foam and smell nutty, add the morels, garlic, shallots and salt and pepper and sauté on high heat for 3 minutes. Add the parsley and lemon juice and toss in the pan • Place a crumbed breast on each warmed serving plate. Coat with the morel butter sauce, garnish with the watercress and serve.

Twice-cooked hare leg

Pheasant mousseline à l'Anglaise

Pot-roasted partridge with Calvados and apple

Supremes de volaille chimay

Wild duck with cherries

Duck à l'orange

Venison with sautéed cabbage and chocolate and raspberry sauce

Quail pasties

Wild duck with cherries

[serves 2]

In Australia, wild duck, by law, may not be served at a restaurant. For some reason people can go and blow as many of these beautiful majestic creatures out of the sky as they want, but they may only be cooked and eaten at home. I obtain a few wild ducks each year and serve them to friends. With full respect for the wild flavour, I always pair wild duck with sweet and bitter ingredients. To complement the cherries in this dish, try a wine from Piedmont, Italy.

1.5 kg (3 lb) wild mallard duck
2 tablespoons sea salt
Pinch of eight-spice powder (see page 382)
8 sprigs of thyme
2 bay leaves
*500 g (1 lb) goose fat**
Salt and freshly ground pepper
*90 g (3 oz) cultured butter**
6 baby turnips, trimmed
2 cloves of garlic, crushed
150 ml (5 fl oz) water
200 ml (7 fl oz) red wine sauce (see page 296)
50 g (1¾ oz) Agra Montana cherries
10 pommes soufflées (see page 98)
1 cup watercress

Wash the duck and pat dry. To confit the duck legs, remove the legs from the duck and cover with the sea salt, eight-spice powder, 4 sprigs of the thyme and the bay leaves. Refrigerate for 24 hours • Wash the legs under cold running water and pat dry • Preheat the oven to 140°C (275°F) • Heat the goose fat in a heavy-based baking tray, add the duck legs and brown over medium heat for 5 minutes. Place in the oven for 90 minutes to confit. The meat should be starting to fall away from the bone • Drain and refrigerate the duck legs for a minium of 2–3 hours • Preheat the oven to 160°C (325°F) • Heat 2 tablespoons of the goose fat in an ovenproof frying pan, add the duck breasts on the bone and cook over medium heat until browned on all sides. Season with salt and pepper. Transfer to the oven for 8 minutes • Heat 80 g (2¾ oz) of the butter and 1 tablespoon of the goose fat in a heavy-based saucepan, add the turnips and sauté for 2 minutes. Season with salt and pepper, add the garlic and the remaining thyme and cook for 2–3 minutes or until the turnips are lightly coloured. Add the water and simmer for 4–5 minutes or until the turnips are cooked • Increase the oven to 180°C (350°F) • In a small saucepan, bring the red wine sauce to the boil, add the cherries and their juice and cook for

5 minutes. Season with a little salt and stir in the remaining butter • Place the duck legs in a baking tray and roast in the oven for 3–4 minutes or until the skin is crisp. Do not overcook, as the legs will dry out. Drain on paper towel and position on warmed serving plates • Remove the breast meat from the bone and slice each breast into three. Fan on top of the duck legs • Spoon the red wine sauce over and around the meat. Position the cherries on the meat. Place the crispy pommes soufflées in a circular pattern around the plate. Garnish with the watercress and serve.

Duck galette

[serves 6]

This dish will evolve every time you prepare it. I have kept the method as simple as possible. At Vue de monde I serve it on a specially designed plate, with a very intricate plate-up. I love to dress the dish during a high-pressured service, closing my mind to everything else around me and letting the creative instinct take over. I hope you draw the same inspiration. Match any good pinot noir with this dish and you won't be disappointed.

4 confit duck legs (see page 282)
2 sheets puff pastry, each 25 x 25 cm (10 x 10 in) (see page 54)
1/4 bunch of tarragon
*3 1/2 tablespoons goose fat**
2 shallots, finely chopped
2 1/2 tablespoons hazelnut vinaigrette (see page 396)
Salt and freshly ground pepper

Preheat the oven to 160°C (325°F) • Remove all the meat from the duck legs • Sandwich the two sheets of puff pastry between two sheets of greaseproof paper and two baking trays. Bake in the oven for 8–10 minutes or until golden and crispy • Blanch the tarragon in boiling water for 1 minute and refresh in iced water for 2 minutes. Strain, squeeze dry and finely chop. This will help preserve the colour and prevent the tarragon from bruising • To make the galette filling, mix the duck leg meat, 2 tablespoons of the goose fat, the shallots, tarragon,

100 g (3½ oz) plain (all-purpose) flour
4 eggs
100 g (3½ oz) panko breadcrumbs*
2 x 250 g (8 oz) magret duck breasts
100 ml (3½ fl oz) red wine sauce (see page 296)
100 g (3½ oz) pea purée (see page 142)
2 cups mixed salad leaves
Hazelnut vinaigrette (see page 396), extra

hazelnut vinaigrette and salt and pepper in a large bowl • Place the galette filling on one sheet of pastry and spread to a thickness of 1 cm (⅓ in) • Position the second sheet of pastry on top, press with a 2 kg (4 lb) weight, and place in the refrigerator until cold. This pressing process will make the galette firm enough to cut evenly • With a serrated bread knife, cut the galette into six rectangles 6 x 8 cm (2½ x 3 in) • Place the flour in a shallow bowl • In a second bowl, lightly beat the eggs • Place the breadcrumbs in a third bowl • Dip each slice of galette in the flour to coat, then in the egg and lastly in the breadcrumbs • Heat ½ tablespoon of the goose fat in a heavy-based frying pan, add the duck breasts and cook, skin-side down, on low heat for 10–12 minutes or until crispy. Turn the breasts over and cook for 5 minutes. Rest in a warm place for 10 minutes • Place the crumbed galettes in the same pan and gently fry over medium heat for 3–4 minutes on each side or until golden • Reduce the red wine sauce in a heavy-based saucepan by half, season with salt and pepper. Remove from the heat and add 1 tablespoon of the goose fat to form a jus gras. Do not stir the fat into the sauce • Warm the pea purée in a saucepan • Slice the duck breasts into six and place on the left side of warmed serving plates. Position the galette on the right of each plate. Dress the salad leaves with the extra hazelnut vinaigrette and place on top of each galette. Arrange two slices of the breast meat on each • Using two dessertspoons dipped in hot water, quenelle* the pea purée to the right of each galette. Spoon the red wine sauce over and around and serve.

Duck à l'orange

[serves 4]

A VERY POPULAR offering at any dinner party. The only question is what to drink — orange is hard to match with wine. A young and peppery shiraz will be a pleasurable accompaniment, but for a big night go for a good bottle of Pomerol.

2 confit duck legs (see page 282)
2 x 250 g (8 oz) magret duck breasts
*2½ tablespoons cultured butter**
2 shallots, finely chopped
1 clove of garlic, crushed
5 sprigs of thyme
4 star anise
2 bay leaves
100 ml (3½ fl oz) Grand Marnier
2 cups freshly squeezed orange juice
Salt and freshly ground pepper
*1 tablespoon goose fat**
8 thin slices of pancetta, sliced*
2 tablespoons julienned carrot
2 tablespoons julienned celeriac
1 small onion, sliced
Savoy cabbage
100 ml (3½ fl oz) double cream

PASTA DOUGH (TORTELLINI)

7½ egg yolks
125 g (4 oz) plain all-purpose flour, sifted

Remove the meat from the duck legs • In a heavy-based frying pan, cook the duck breasts skin-side down in their own fat over low to medium heat for 10–12 minutes or until crispy skinned, but still pink. Rest for 10 minutes • To make the orange sauce, melt ½ tablespoon of the butter in a heavy-based saucepan, add the shallots, garlic, thyme, star anise and bay leaves and cook for 2 minutes. Add the Grand Marnier and reduce by two-thirds. Add the orange juice and reduce by half. Whisk in 1 tablespoon of the butter to give a smooth, thick sauce. Strain through a fine sieve. Season with salt and pepper • Heat the goose fat in a large frying pan, add the pancetta, carrot, celeriac and onion and sauté for 2 minutes without colouring. Toss in the duck leg meat. Remove from the pan and set aside • In the same pan, warm the cabbage for 1 minute. Add 1 teaspoon of water to create steam to help cook the cabbage. Return the carrot and pancetta mixture to the pan, add the cream and reduce for 2 minutes or until the sauce resembles mayonnaise. Taste and season with salt and pepper • To make the pasta dough place the ingredients in a mixing bowl. Using a mixer with a dough hook attachment, mix on a low speed for 5–8 minutes or until the dough is elastic. Cover with plastic wrap and rest in the refrigerator for 1 hour • Roll out the pasta dough on a floured work surface to 3 mm (⅛ in) thick. Starting from one end and leaving an 8-cm (3-in) gap between each, place teaspoonfuls

200 g (6½ oz) chicken mousse *(see page 377)*

80 g (2¾ oz) foie gras, chopped into 1-cm (⅓-in) dice

of the chicken mousse on the sheet of pasta. Place a cube of foie gras in the centre of each dollop of mousse. Cut out 21 circles (one is for tasting before serving) with a 4-cm (1½-in) round cutter, and fold over pasta to form semicircles • Poach the tortellini in simmering salted water for 6 minutes. Toss through the remaining 1 tablespoon of butter, and season with salt and pepper • Centre the sautéed cabbage on each serving plate. Slice each duck breast into ten. Place five slices on top of the cabbage. Place five tortellini around the cabbage. Spoon the orange sauce over and around the meat. Serve.

Venison with sautéed cabbage and chocolate and raspberry sauce

[serves 6]

Marco Pierre White introduced me to this dish. Treat the cabbage as a warm salad, working quickly to prevent water retention spoiling the consistency. This dish requires a wine of some power, yet with a refined elegance to compete with the sauce, look for a French merlot or an American zinfandel.

1 kg (2 lb) venison loin, trimmed of fat and sinew
2 tablespoons cracked black pepper
*50 g ($1^3/_4$ oz) goose fat**

SAUTÉED CABBAGE
1 Savoy cabbage
1 brown onion, finely sliced
1 large carrot, julienned
1 celeriac, julienned
1 tablespoon water
100 ml ($3^1/_2$ fl oz) double cream
Salt and freshly ground pepper

200 ml (7 fl oz) red wine sauce (see page 296)
50 g ($1^3/_4$ oz) dark couverture chocolate, chopped into small pieces
$1^1/_2$ tablespoons raspberry vinegar
100 g ($3^1/_2$ oz) frozen raspberries
Pommes gaufrette (see page 105)

Slice the venison loin into six steaks and roll in the cracked pepper • Preheat the oven to 200°C (400°F) • Heat 1 tablespoon of the goose fat in an ovenproof frying pan and seal the steaks over high heat. Transfer to the oven for 4 minutes. Rest for 15 minutes • To make the sautéed cabbage, separate the leaves of the cabbage. Wash 12 bright green leaves. Remove the stalks and cut into 8-cm (3-in) ribbons • Heat the remaining goose fat in a heavy-based frying pan, add the onion and cook over high heat for 2–3 minutes. Add the carrot and celeriac and sauté for 30 seconds • Add the cabbage, sauté for 30 seconds or until the cabbage is wilted, and add the water to create some steam. Push the contents of the pan to one side, add the cream and reduce until the sauce is thick and smooth. Season with salt and pepper • Divide the cabbage into six and position in the centre of each serving plate • Decrease the oven to 180°C (350°F) • Bring the red wine sauce to the boil and whisk in the chocolate until melted and smooth. Add the raspberry vinegar, and season with a little salt. Add the raspberries and boil for 20 seconds • Slice the venison steaks in half and place on the cabbage • Heat the pommes gaufrette in the oven for 30 seconds and place on top of the venison. Spoon the red wine sauce around the venison and serve.

Roast quail with vanilla and white peach

[serves 4]

VANILLA IS A SPICE and if you think outside the square a little, you will be amazed what you can come up with. An Auslese riesling is an unusual match; Doctor Loosen is a big, reliable producer — look out for any 2001 vintage.

4 x 220 g (7 oz) quails
*20 g (¾ oz) dried orange zest**
*20 g (¾ oz) dried lime zest**
3 star anise, lightly crushed
4 sprigs of thyme
2 bay leaves
100 ml (3½ fl oz) orange juice
150 ml (5 fl oz) olive oil
Salt and freshly ground pepper

VANILLA BUTTER

*220 g (7 oz) cultured butter**
*4 vanilla beans**
Juice of 1 lemon

2 firm white peaches, halved and stones removed

4 pommes Anna (see page 95)

Wash the quails and pat dry • Combine the orange and lime zest, star anise, thyme, bay leaves, orange juice, olive oil, salt and pepper in a large container. Add the quails and marinate for 48 hours • To make the vanilla butter, place 200 g (6½ oz) of the butter in a food processor, and blend until pale. Split the vanilla beans lengthwise and scrape the seeds into the butter. Season with a little lemon juice • Preheat the oven to 180°C (350°F) • Place the quails in a baking tray and cook over high heat until golden. Transfer to the oven for 3 minutes. Rest the quails for 10 minutes • Joint the quails by removing the legs and breast meat. Keep warm • Melt the remaining 1 tablespoon of butter in a heavy-based saucepan, add the peaches and cook over moderate heat until soft. Season with salt and pepper. Peel the skin off the peaches • Place the vanilla butter in a heavy-based frying pan and brown over medium heat. Add the boned quails and peaches and briefly toss for 1 minute. Season with salt and pepper • Place a pommes Anna in the centre of each serving plate. Arrange a quail on top, then finish with a peach half. Drizzle the vanilla butter remaining in the pan on and around the quail. Serve.

Quail pasties

[serves 4]

THESE ARE THE FANCIEST pasties you will ever eat, let alone make! The taste is sensational! They were a popular item in Escoffier's time because they could be made in advance and stored without spoiling. The origin of pasties, as we all know, is Cornwall where miners would eat the contents of the pasty but discard the inedible pastry after it had served its purpose of protecting the contents.

Serve as a light starter or appetiser with a glass of beer!

4 x 220 g (7 oz) quails
Pheasant mousse (see page 277)
*½ cup bacon lardons**
100 g (3½ oz) glace de viande (see page 295)
*20 g (¾ oz) truffle paste**
Salt and freshly ground pepper
300 g (10 oz) short crust pastry (see page 74)
*4 slices of black truffle**
4 eggs, lightly beaten

Nicely ask your butcher to debone the quails and coarsely mince (grind) them for you • Preheat the oven to 200°C (400°F) • To make the forcemeat, place the minced (ground) quail, pheasant mousse, lardons, glace de viande, and truffle paste in a mixing bowl and combine, season well • Roll out the short crust pastry to 6 mm (¼ in) thick on a floured work surface. Cut the pastry into circles twice as large as the quails • Place 1 generous tablespoon of forcemeat on each circle of pastry and top with a slice of truffle. Moisten the edges of the pastry with a little water and fold over to form a semicircle; sealing the edges well. Brush with the egg and bake in the oven for 20 minutes or until golden • Serve the quail pasties on warmed serving plates.

The Pasture

I SUPPORT ENVIRONMENTALLY friendly, sustainable agriculture. As individuals we all benefit from a quality sustainable product, rather than buying from corporations who are only worried about satisfying demand. The traditional, diversified family farm has a fighting chance for survival if we are all prepared to pay for quality and savour what wonderful potential our country has to produce.

Animals should be raised under the most humane conditions on pasture in open air and sunshine, without the need for antibiotics or hormones. All producers should be encouraged to promote farm-raised stock and the particular region it comes from.

Wagyu beef is a breed of cattle native to Japan. Many people have heard the term 'kobe' beef before. I had, and I thought 'kobe' was the general word for Japanese beef. Well, it's not. Kobe is a small town within the Hyogo Prefecture of Japan where, yes, they do use wagyu cattle — to be precise, they use Tajima bloodline cattle, the purest breed of wagyu.

We have all heard stories about cattle being massaged for thirty days by a 120 kg (264-lb) sumo wrestler, with both on their twenty-fifth can of full strength beer when they fall asleep and only one wakes up! When the cow is of the correct maturity and weight, it is prepared and handled in a way that ensures the animal suffers little to no stress, making the beef as tender as possible. The labour and expertise involved is reflected in the price of wagyu meat, normally up to nine times the price of normal beef. Let me tell you this is all true, as my last few months of research have found. This breed of cattle can be brought up in small areas. The animal's feed is a close-kept secret, with every producer having different opinions on what the most suitable diet is. Most agree that fermented grain high in protein is a key element in producing the dense marbling required to sell the primary cuts of meat at huge prices. The flavour of the beef is like no other. Importantly, the fat in the wagyu beef is almost exclusively mono-unsaturated, with low cholesterol and important relevant nutrients to everyday well being, such as Oleic acid. Oleic acid is an anti oxidant, one of the important ingredients in a healthy diet.

The wagyu beef that is on the menu at Vue de monde is from cattle raised in Moondarra, Gippsland, Victoria, an area celebrated for its clean, green environment, and wonderful wine and food. The beef is also special because it has not been exposed to growth hormones, non-therapeutic antibiotics, animal protein feed or genetically modified feed.

The best cut of beef for use at home is the rump; the five muscles within the rump are easy to separate by following the line of sinew that separates them. The more dense muscles found right in the rump have the most marbling and are the most tender. Use all the trimmings for braising. The richness of the beef also ensures that portion sizes need to be kept to a minimum. I love to leave the diner teased and wanting more. The explosion of the dense but delicate flavour, paired with subtle complementing garnishes, such as bone marrow, roast shallots, braised turnips, pumpkin purée, broad beans and, of course, crispy potatoes, will implant memories of a food experience forever yearned for.

An increasing number of chefs and producers are finding that lambs grow extremely well on saltbush and consumer reaction is very positive. Enthusiasts like me preach that saltbush has an important place in the rehabilitation of saline areas in Australia. Unlike most plants, it has a capacity to take in high saline water and is very efficient in utilising this water. Saltbush produces three times as much dry matter per unit of water as other plants. The other huge upside to this is the attraction sheep have to this hardy vegetation which subtly flavours the meat. The meat seems to be denser and takes a few extra degrees in cooking.

Veal stock

[makes 20 cups]

Always remember that a good stock should be clear and contain no fat. Another sign of a well-made stock is the firm gelatinous appearance when cold. To achieve this, always use veal bones with a high marrow content, such as shins and knuckles. Any heavy red wine will suffice. Never use expensive (nor the really cheap) wine in cooking — what a waste!

5 kg (10 lb) veal knuckle bones
2 cups olive oil
1 head of garlic, cut in half
¼ bunch of thyme
10 white peppercorns
1 large carrot, roughly chopped
2 brown onions, roughly chopped
1 stick of celery, roughly chopped
500 g (1 lb) tomato paste
6 cups red wine

Preheat the oven to 200°C (400°F) • Heat a baking tray in the oven for 10 minutes, add the veal bones and ½ cup of the olive oil and place in the oven for 40 minutes or until dark brown and caramelised • Heat the remaining olive oil in a heavy-based frying pan, add the garlic, thyme, peppercorns, carrot, onion and celery and cook for 15 minutes or until coloured and soft • Add the tomato paste and cook, stirring constantly, until a deep brown colour. This is the most crucial stage of the stock, use plenty of oil to prevent the tomato paste from burning • Add the red wine and reduce until evaporated • Place the veal bones into a large stockpot and cover with cold water. Bring to the boil and skim off any impurities, this is called despumé. Add the vegetable and wine reduction. Bring to the boil and proceed to skim off the red fat that rises to the top, this is called degrassé. Simmer the stock on very low heat for 24 hours, continuously topping up with water to prevent the liquid level falling below the bones • Carefully strain the stock through a coarse sieve, then a fine sieve. Return to the stove and reduce by half, skimming any impurities that rise to the surface. Strain once more and store in the refrigerator or freezer until required.

Glace de viande

[makes 10 cups]

GLACE DE VIANDE is the French term for meat glaze, and is made by reducing meat juices to a thick syrup. I use the traditional method of combining pan juices and small amounts of glace de viande to enhance sauces. Freeze the recipe in small amounts ready for use.

*3 cups Madeira**
20 cups veal stock (see page 294)
3 kg (6½ lb) veal bones

Bring the Madeira to the boil in a large saucepan and reduce by half • Add the veal stock, bring to the boil and add the veal bones; skimming any impurities that rise to the surface. Boil rapidly until reduced by half • Pass through a fine sieve. Use as required.

Red wine sauce

[makes 2 cups]

I HATE THE FACT that now and again people see my sauce recipes and complain that they would not be able to produce them because the ingredients are too expensive. I have included this recipe to prove them wrong. A good sauce should be the artist's final stroke to the dish. Just as a painter would sign his name to his work, a good chef will take the time and thought to complement the dish with an appropriate sauce.

6 cups heavy red wine
*350 ml (12 fl oz) ruby port**
4 shallots, thinly sliced
4 cloves of garlic, thinly sliced
5 sprigs of thyme
3 star anise
10 white peppercorns
300 ml (10 fl oz) glace de viande (see page 295)
100 g (3½ oz) cultured butter, chopped into fine dice*
Salt and freshly ground pepper

Combine the red wine and port in a large saucepan and bring to the boil • Add the shallots, garlic, thyme, star anise and peppercorns. Return to the boil and rapidly reduce by half • Add the glace de viande and bring to the boil. Boil rapidly for 10–15 minutes or until reduced by one-third • Pass the still hot sauce through a fine sieve • Let the sauce settle for 10 minutes, then pass through a cheesecloth-lined sieve 3–4 times until there are no impurities • Bring the sauce to the boil in a heavy-based saucepan. Whisk in the butter, salt and pepper and continue to boil, whisking constantly. Test the sauce by spooning some onto a plate; it should be glossy and smooth, not runny. Sauce the finished dish immediately.

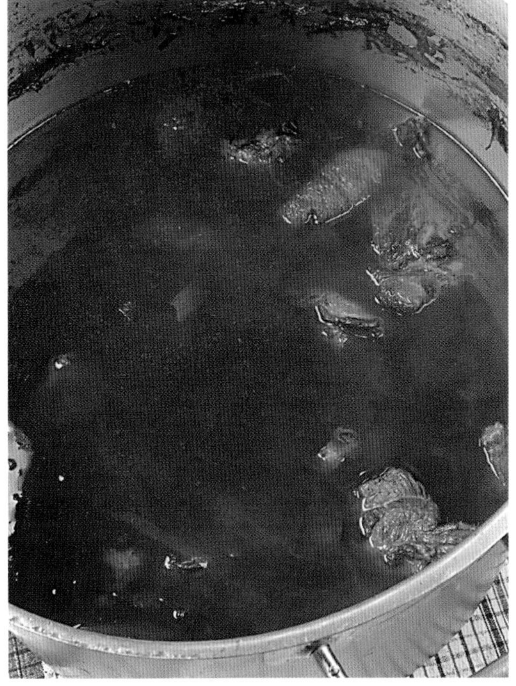

Veal stock

Glace de viande

Red wine sauce

Madeira sauce

Madeira Sauce

[makes 2 cups]

A GREAT COMPLEMENT to any roast meat, the sweetness in this sauce makes it more suited to meats such as pork and venison.

10 shallots, peeled
500 g (1 lb) chicken winglets, roughly chopped
200 g (6½ oz) redcurrant jelly
200 ml (7 fl oz) sherry vinegar
300 ml (10 fl oz) brandy
400 ml (13 fl oz) dry red wine
*700 ml (24 fl oz) Madeira**
4 cups chicken stock (see page 378)
300 ml (10 fl oz) glace de viande (see page 295)

Cook the shallots and chicken in a heavy-based saucepan over medium heat for 10 minutes or until golden. Add the redcurrant jelly and cook, stirring constantly, for 5 minutes or until caramelised • Deglaze with the sherry vinegar and reduce until evaporated. Add the brandy and flambé by igniting the brandy in the pan with a lighter or match. Do not be alarmed, the flame will burn out after 30–60 seconds • Add the red wine and reduce by two-thirds, then add the Madeira and reduce by half • Add the chicken stock; simmer over low to medium heat until reduced by half. Incorporate the glace de viande. Pass through a coarse sieve, then through a fine sieve. Return to the pan, bring to the boil, then for extra body and shine pass through a cheesecloth-lined sieve several times until completely clear. Use immediately.

Jus Gras

[makes 2 cups]

You're thinking what I used to think — jus gras is just a fancy name for something complicated and not worth the effort. Let me assure you that this recipe will become the household signature sauce to be poured over roast loin of pork, drizzled over chicken salads, and combined with béarnaise sauce to make rump steaks come alive. The terminology is simple, jus means the juices of the meat and gras means the fat of the meat. I use the following recipe for all roasts and even certain fish dishes.

1 kg (2 lb) chicken thighs
2 tablespoons olive oil
*3 cups Madeira**
2 cups veal stock (see page 294)

Preheat the oven to 180°C (350°F) • Heat a baking tray in the oven for 10 minutes. Place the chicken thighs skin-side down in the tray, add the olive oil and roast in the oven for 30 minutes • Remove the chicken, leaving any sticky residue in the tray. Drain the chicken fat and reserve • Reheat the baking tray over medium heat, stirring occasionally, being careful not to burn any residue. Deglaze with the Madeira, stirring and scraping until reduced by half. Add the veal stock, bring to the boil and taste. At this stage if the taste is too strong, add a little water and pass through a fine sieve • To complete the sauce, warm the chicken fat in a saucepan and add to the sauce at the last moment. Do not stir the fat into the sauce, traditionally, the desired effect is a warm split vinaigrette.

Miniature Beef Pies

[makes 20]

GREAT FOR A PRE-DINNER bite or as part of a main dish, the humble meat pie is an Australian icon. Different sized pie dishes can be used but, the smaller the mould, the more intricate and attractive the pies will be at your next cocktail party. Serve with a hazelnut and watercress salad and a glass of good Australian shiraz.

BRAISED BEEF

*100 g (3½ oz) goose fat**
1 stick of celery, finely diced
1 large carrot, finely diced
1 onion, finely diced
Salt and freshly ground pepper
2 cups shiraz
1 cup port
6 cups veal stock (see page 294)
2 kg (4 lb) wagyu silverside, finely diced
*Bouquet garni**

Pâte sel (short crust pastry) (see page 74)
1 egg, lightly beaten

Preheat the oven to 150°C (300°F) • To make the braised beef filling, heat the goose fat in a large flameproof casserole dish, add the celery, carrot and onion and cook for 4–5 minutes or until soft and transparent. Season with salt and pepper. Add the shiraz and port and reduce by half. Add the veal stock and reduce by one-third. Add the beef and bouquet garni, cover with aluminium (aluminum) foil and a lid, and place in the oven for 3 hours. Cool, then rest in the refrigerator for 24 hours. Discard the bouquet garni • Roll out the pâte sel on a lightly floured work surface to 5 mm (¼ in) thick. Cut out twenty 8-cm (3-in) discs of dough to line 4-cm (1½-in) pie tins, then twenty 4-cm (1½-in) discs for the top • Place the larger discs in the bottom of the pie tins; pack in the filling well over the top to create a dome shape • Top with two layers of pastry. For the first layer, place the smaller discs of pastry over the filling, press around the rim to seal and trim the edges with a knife. Brush with the beaten egg. For the second layer, cut the pastry into thin 5-mm (¼-in) strips and arrange in a lattice pattern over the first layer, brushing on a little water to ensure the pastry sticks • Rest the pies in the refrigerator for a few hours for the pastry to firm up • Preheat the oven to 180°C (350°F) • Brush each pie with the beaten egg and bake in the oven for 25 minutes or until golden. Serve.

Beef tartare with quail eggs

[makes 15 canapés]

THE FOLLOWING RECIPE is an all time classic incorporating the delightful freshness and taste of raw beef complemented by the sharpness of pickles and capers. The diversion from the classic recipe starts with the use of mayonnaise instead of raw egg yolk, which you could still add if you prefer.

The recipe acts as a great light lunch by enlarging the process, adding a few lightly dressed salads leaves and replacing the quail eggs with a hen's egg, either poached or lightly fried.

500 g (1 lb) premium beef
50 g (1¾ oz) extra small capers
*80 g (2¾ oz) finely diced cornichons**
1 tablespoon finely chopped flat-leaf parsley
1 shallot, finely chopped
100 ml (3½ fl oz) tomato ketchup
1 tablespoon Worcestershire sauce
5 drops of Tabasco sauce
2½ tablespoons mayonnaise
1½ tablespoons Dijon mustard
Salt and freshly ground pepper
1 tablespoon olive oil
15 quail eggs
5 slices of stale sourdough bread
1 tablespoon clarified butter (see page 381)

Finely dice the beef with a sharp knife; don't mince, the texture of the beef should be noticeable • Combine the beef, capers, cornichons, parsley, shallot, ketchup, Worcestershire sauce, Tabasco, mayonnaise and mustard in a large bowl and season well. Rest for 20 minutes to allow the flavours to develop • Heat the olive oil in a non-stick frying pan, add the quail eggs, in batches, and fry over low heat for 2–3 minutes. The process is very quick, don't overcook them! • Slide the eggs onto a plate and cut out with a 2.5-cm (1-in) round cutter • Preheat the oven to 180°C (350°F) • Using the 2.5-cm (1-in) cutter, cut out 15 croutons from the bread slices. Transfer to a baking tray, brush each crouton with the clarified butter and season with salt and pepper • Bake in the oven for 10 minutes or until golden brown • Arrange the croutons on a serving platter. Position the cutter over each crouton and push the tartare mix into the mould. Place an egg on top and season. Serve immediately.

Beef with crispy snails and anchovy butter

[serves 4]

Beef, snails and butter are as old as French cuisine itself, in fact, older! This particular combination owes its discovery to Seville and the Spanish art of tapas. The presentation is unique as it depended on the imagination of the bar owner and its clientele. This dish came about because of my yearning for someone to cook such a meal for me. A good Yarra Valley cabernet from Yeringberg or Yering Station will have your guests in raptures.

620 g (1¼ lb) wagyu porterhouse
1 tablespoon olive oil
200 g (6½ oz) braised beef (see page 300)
*200 g (6½ oz) caul fat (crepinette)**

ANCHOVY BUTTER

500 g (1 lb) butter, softened
1 clove of garlic, crushed
50 g (1¾ oz) small capers
25 g (1 oz) Ortiz anchovies, crushed*
2 tablespoons shredded basil
1 teaspoon Dijon mustard
Juice of 1 lemon

CRISPY SNAILS

*12 snails**
2 cloves of garlic, crushed
1 cup vegetable oil
Tempura batter (see page 204)
Salt and freshly ground pepper

Preheat the oven to 180°C (350°F) • Trim the beef of sinew and shiny membrane. Tie with butcher's twine at 5-cm (2-in) intervals, to ensure even cooking while roasting • Heat the olive oil in a cast-iron frying pan over high heat until it gives off a haze. Quickly brown the steak on all sides. Transfer to the oven and roast for 10–12 minutes. Rest in a warm place for 15 minutes • To make the beef balls, mould the braised meat into balls the size of walnuts, wrap in the caul, then place in plastic wrap and tie into neat balls • To make the anchovy butter, blitz the butter in a food processor until pale. Add the garlic, capers, anchovies, basil, mustard and half the lemon juice and process to combine • To make the crispy snails, marinate the snails in the garlic for 30 minutes • Preheat the vegetable oil to 180°C (350°F) in a deep-fryer • Place the tempura batter in a bowl • Preheat the oven to 150°C (300°F) • Spear each snail with a toothpick, dip in the tempura batter, then deep-fry for 2 minutes or until golden. Season with salt, pepper and the rest of the lemon juice. Keep warm in the oven • Place the parsley in boiling salted water, boil on high for 2–3 minutes or until soft. Test by pressing between two fingers, the parsley should break up when rubbed.

PARSLEY PURÉE

2 tablespoons finely chopped curly-leaf parsley

*100 g (3½ oz) cultured butter**

2 shallots, finely diced

1 cup double cream

4 pommes mille-feuille (see page 101)

*4 slices ventrèche bacon**

Refresh in iced water. Drain and squeeze dry • To make the parsley purée, melt the butter in a heavy-based frying pan, add the shallots and cook for 2–3 minutes or until soft and transparent. Add the cream, bring to the boil and reduce, stirring constantly, until thick and smooth. Beat in the parsley, salt and pepper • Cook the beef balls in a saucepan of boiling water for 10 minutes. Unwrap • Heat the anchovy butter in a saucepan over low heat until foaming • Warm the pommes mille-feuille in the oven for 5 minutes • Bake the slices of ventrèche bacon between 2 flat baking trays until crisp • To serve, place the parsley purée in the centre of each serving plate. Position the warmed pommes mille-feuille next to the purée. Slice the steak into four. Place a slice on top of the parsley purée. Scatter the crispy snails on top of each steak. Top with a slice of ventrèche bacon. Pour the foaming anchovy butter over each steak. Serve.

Beef tartare with quail eggs

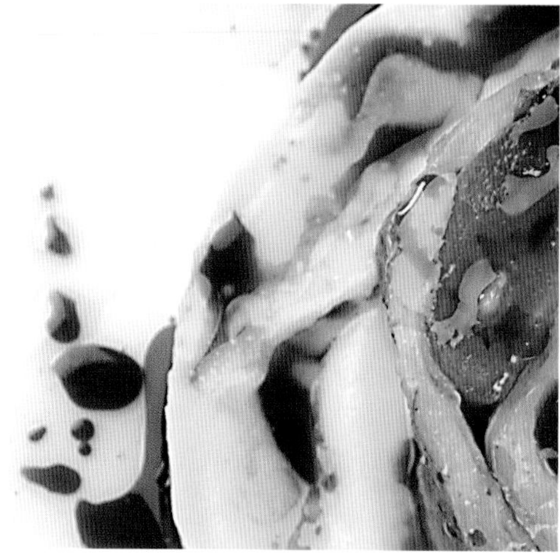
Jus gras

Miniature beef pies

Beef with crispy snails and anchovy butter

Filet de bœuf et pommes mille-feuille au jus gras

The extravagant burger

Filet de bœuf et pommes mille-feuille au jus gras

[serves 4]

ROASTED WAGYU BEEF topped with a shallot and bone marrow crust is an idea I first learned at The Restaurant at Hyde Park. Match this beauty with a tightly crafted Oregon pinot noir.

*2 x 8-cm (3-in) sticks of bone marrow**
1½ tablespoons olive oil
4 x 200 g (6½ oz) eye fillet steaks 5 cm (2 in) thick
Salt and freshly ground pepper
⅓ cup clarified butter (see page 381)
8 banana shallots, thinly sliced
4 pommes Anna (see page 95)
200 ml (7 fl oz) red wine sauce (see page 296)
200 ml (7 fl oz) béarnaise sauce (see page 385)

Soak the bone marrow in cold water for 24 hours to remove any impurities • Preheat the oven to 190°C (375°F) • Heat the olive oil to smoking point in a large heavy-based frying pan, add the steak and cook over high heat for 3–4 minutes. Turn and season with salt and pepper and cook for 2–3 minutes. Rest in a warm place for 10 minutes • Melt the clarified butter in a frying pan, add the shallots and fry for 3–4 minutes or until just golden. Do not allow the shallots to crisp as they will continue to cook after they have been removed from the heat. Season with salt • Cut each bone marrow into eight round discs • Pile the shallots on top of each steak, then cover the shallots with four bone marrow discs. Place all four steaks on a plate, cover with an inverted plate and place in the oven for 5 minutes • Heat the pommes Anna in the oven for 1 minute or until warm • Heat the red wine sauce in a saucepan • Cut each steak in half. Place the pommes Anna in the centre of each serving plate. Arrange the steak on top of the pommes Anna. Carefully spoon the red wine sauce around the potato. Serve with a little béarnaise sauce at the table.

The extravagant burger

[serves 4]

The word burger is synonymous with quick, cheap dining, but this recipe challenges that perception. Just pack as many extravagant ingredients as possible between two grilled sesame seed buns.

I recommend a glass of 1990 Penfolds Grange Hermitage Shiraz from South Australia.

BEEF PATTIES

300 g (10 oz) minced (ground) wagyu beef

*1 tablespoon goose fat**

1 tablespoon finely chopped shallots

½ tablespoon finely chopped curly-leaf parsley

Salt and freshly ground pepper

2 tablespoons olive oil

*4 thin slices of pancetta**

4 quail eggs

4 x 30 g (1 oz) slices of foie gras

4 confit tomatoes (see page 86)

4 white dinner rolls (see page 53)

*1 tablespoon cultured butter**

2 tablespoons watercress

*4 cornichons, fantailed**

4 tablespoons bois boudran sauce (see page 205)

1 x 40 g (1⅓ oz) black truffle, shaved

12 pommes Pont Neuf (see page 99)

To make the beef patties, combine the beef, goose fat, shallots, parsley, salt and pepper in a mixing bowl. Roll the beef mixture into 5-cm (2-in) balls and flatten the balls into 2.5-cm (1-in) thick patties. Place in the fridge for 10 minutes • Heat 1 tablespoon of the olive oil in a heavy-based frying pan over high heat, add the beef patties and pancetta and cook for 1 minute or until the pancetta is transparent. Remove the pancetta. Continue to cook the burgers for 2–3 minutes. Set aside to rest • Heat the remaining olive oil in a non-stick frying pan, add the quail eggs and fry over low heat for 2–3 minutes. Don't overcook them! Slide onto a plate and cut around each egg with a 2.5-cm (1-in) round cutter • Fry the foie gras in a heavy-based frying pan over medium heat for 2 minutes or until golden on each side. In the same pan, heat the tomatoes for 1 minute or until warm • Cut each bun in half and toast under a hot grill (broiler) for 1–2 minutes or until golden. Spread with the butter • To assemble the burgers, on the bottom half of each bun arrange 3–4 watercress leaves and top with a confit tomato. Place a pattie on the tomato, a slice of foie gras on the pattie and a quail egg on top. Add a cornichon, a drizzle of the sauce bois boudran and a generous shaving of truffle. Garnish with 2–3 pommes Pont Neuf and serve immediately.

Selle de pré-salé aux laities

[serves 6]

Pré-salé is lamb that is reared close to the Atlantic Ocean and feeds on salty grasses. In the Clare Valley in South Australia they feed lambs on saltbush, which imparts a similar flavour to the salt grasses of France. A hogget is a sheep that has 2–4 adult teeth and has not been shorn.

2 kg (4 lb) saddle of saltbush hogget
Salt and freshly ground pepper
8 cups red wine sauce (see page 296)
*500 g (1 lb) goose fat**
2 shallots, diced
2 cos lettuces
2½ tablespoons eight-spice powder (see page 382)

Preheat the oven to 120°C (250°F) • Ask your butcher to bone the saddle leaving the belly attached. Reserve all trimmings and bones • Place the trimmings and bones in a baking tray and transfer to the oven for 20 minutes or until golden brown • Season the back fat from the saddle with salt and pepper. Line a baking tray with greaseproof paper. Place the back fat on the tray, cover with more greaseproof paper and another baking tray. Bake in the oven for 30 minutes or until crisp • Increase the oven temperature to 180°C (350°F) • Trim the lamb loin of sinew and fat. Tie with butcher's twine to form a circular shape • Place the red wine sauce in a large saucepan, add the trimmings and bones and simmer for 1 hour. Strain and reduce by half • Heat ⅓ cup of the goose fat in a large flameproof casserole dish, add the shallots and cook for 2–3 minutes or until soft and transparent. Add the lettuce leaves and sauté until limp, about 1½ minutes. Add the red wine sauce and the lamb loin, cover, and place in the oven for 7 minutes. Rest for 5 minutes. Slice the loin into six steaks, then halve those • Strain the liquid into a saucepan and reduce until the sauce coats the back of a spoon • To serve, place a small portion of the braised lettuce on each serving plate. Place two slices of the loin on top and flood the plate with the red wine sauce. Garnish with the crispy back fat and sprinkle over the eight-spice powder.

Spicy lamb samosas

[makes 40 canapés]

THIS RECIPE IS ALSO ideal as a light lunch or snack. Simply cut the strips of dough larger and add more filling. I don't normally serve any dipping sauce with these samosas, but if you wish, try them with a lemon-flavoured mayonnaise. If you are a vegetarian, double the amount of lentils and vegetables used. Samosas freeze well and can be deep-fried from frozen.

SPICY LAMB FILLING

1 tablespoon olive oil
1 medium carrot, finely diced
3 sticks of celery, finely diced
1 onion, finely diced
2 cloves of garlic, crushed
1 kg (2 lb) minced (ground) lamb
1 tablespoon Madras curry paste
100 g (3½ oz) tomato paste
2 tablespoons redcurrant jelly
1½ cups coconut milk
250 g (8 oz) cooked lentils (see page 386)

Samosa dough (see page 64)
Vegetable oil for deep frying
Salt

Heat the olive oil in a heavy-based saucepan, add the carrot, celery, onion, garlic and lamb and cook over medium heat for 30 minutes or until the meat is starting to catch on the bottom of the pan • Add the curry paste, tomato paste, redcurrant jelly, coconut milk and lentils, stir and simmer for 20 minutes. This can be done a few days in advance to allow the flavours to develop • Remove from the pan and place on a flat tray to cool rapidly in the refrigerator • Roll out the dough on a lightly floured work surface to 5 mm (¼ in) thick. Cut the dough into 3 x 15-cm (1¼ x 6-in) strips. Place a generous teaspoonful of the filling at the top of each strip, shape and fold into triangles • Heat the vegetable oil to 180°C (350°F). Add the samosas, in batches, and deep-fry for 3–4 minutes or until golden • Season with a little salt and rest on paper towel before serving.

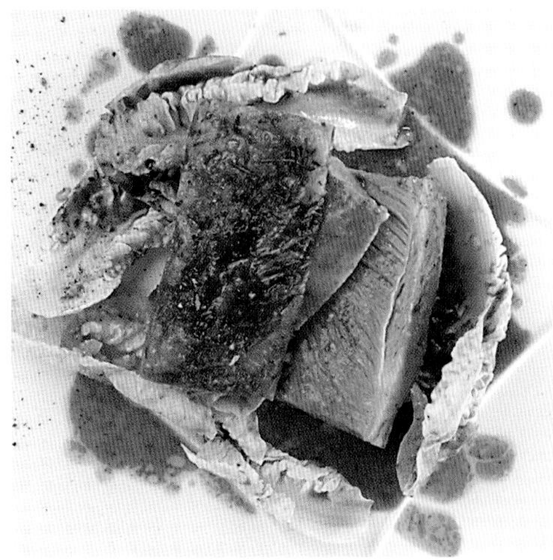

Selle de pré-salé aux laities

Spicy lamb samosas

Stuffed spring lamb with jus gras

Poached hogget in soy sauce

Poached lamb with basil mousse and ratatouille

Lamb provençal

Stuffed spring lamb with jus gras

[serves 8]

Another party favourite for the summer months, serve with rich buttery pommes mousseline and plenty of sauce. When looking for a suitable wine, go for an upmarket barbecue wine, such as the Jacob's Creek Reserve Shiraz. This wine is no slouch and it has enough finesse to match the Provençal-type flavours of the lamb filling.

2.5 kg (5 lb) saddle of lamb, boned with the belly still attached

200 g (6½ oz) black olive tapenade (see page 375)

Salt and freshly ground pepper

10 confit tomatoes (see page 86)

20 large basil leaves

*500 g (1 lb) caul fat (crepinette)**

100 ml (3½ fl oz) olive oil

8 serves of pommes mousseline (see page 102)

200 ml (7 fl oz) jus gras (see page 299)

Ask your butcher to prepare the saddle by cutting the flaps to 10 cm (4 in) on each side and flattening them with a meat mallet • Preheat the oven to 180°C (350°F) • Use a palette knife to spread the olive paste around the inside flaps of the lamb • Season the meat with a generous amount of salt and pepper, then scatter over the tomatoes and basil leaves • Roll up the meat lengthwise. Wrap in 3–4 layers of caul. Tie with butcher's twine at intervals of 4 cm (1½ in). Season with salt and pepper • Heat the olive oil in a heavy-based frying pan over high heat, add the lamb and brown quickly on all sides. Place on a cake rack resting in a baking tray and roast in the oven for 18–20 minutes. Rest for at least 20 minutes • Warm the pommes mousseline in a saucepan over low heat • Warm the jus gras in a separate saucepan over low heat • Place a large tablespoonful of potato in the centre of each serving plate • Slice the lamb into eight. Place on the pommes mousseline. Spoon the jus gras over and around the lamb and serve.

Poached hogget in soy sauce

[serves 2]

This is a fresh, light and healthy approach to a Mediterranean-inspired dish that is served with a very light sauce. Wine matching is difficult here because of the acidity in the sauce. Try a glass of crisp gamay.

300 g (10 oz) lamb loin
100 ml (3½ fl oz) light soy sauce
1 cup chicken stock (see page 378)
1 shallot, halved and sliced
1 clove of garlic, halved and sliced
2 sprigs of thyme
2 zucchini (courgette) flowers stuffed with asparagus mousse (see page 371)
100 g (3½ oz) cauliflower purée (see page 395 for vegetable purée)
2 pommes Anna (see page 95)
2½ tablespoons sauce vierge (see page 392)
6 basil leaves, shredded
*2 tablespoons tomato paysanne**

Trim the lamb of sinew and fat and slice in half • To make the poaching liquid, in a heavy-based saucepan, combine the soy sauce, chicken stock, shallot, garlic and thyme and simmer for 3–4 minutes • Place the lamb in the stock and poach for 3 minutes, then turn and poach for another 3 minutes. Remove from the stock and rest in a warm place for 6 minutes. Slice the lamb lengthwise into five strips • Place the zucchini flowers in a steamer and cook for 2 minutes or until tender • Warm the cauliflower purée in a small saucepan • Preheat the oven to 180°C (350°F) • Warm the crispy pommes Anna in the oven for 1 minute • Warm the sauce vierge in a small saucepan • To serve, place a generous spoonful of cauliflower purée in the centre of each serving plate and position the pommes Anna on top. Fan the lamb over the pommes Anna, then place a zucchini flower on top. Add the basil and tomato and spoon the sauce vierge over and around the lamb. Serve.

Poached lamb with basil mousse and ratatouille

[serves 6]

The visual impact of this dish on diners at Vue de monde has always been one of pleasure and excitement. The combination of ingredients depicts our evolving need for healthier Mediterranean flavours. Grenache has a lovely soft approachable taste with a good balance of soft fruit and acids to make a reputable partner for this dish.

2 x 300 g (10 oz) lamb loins
2 bunches of basil
250 g (8 oz) chicken breast fillet
1 tablespoon salt
1 egg
100 ml ($3\frac{1}{2}$ fl oz) double cream
*200 g ($6\frac{1}{2}$ oz) caul fat (crepinette)**
1 red capsicum (sweet pepper)
1 yellow capsicum (sweet pepper)
1 cup olive oil
1 zucchini (courgette)
1 eggplant (aubergine)
100 ml ($3\frac{1}{2}$ fl oz) jus gras (see page 299)
4 sprigs of sage
100 g ($3\frac{1}{2}$ oz) pumpkin purée (see page 395 for vegetable purée)
*12 Ligurian or Niçoise olives**

Place the bowl, lid and blade of the food processor in the freezer until chilled • Trim the lamb of sinew and fat and slice into three • Pick, wash and cook the basil in boiling salted water for 3–4 minutes. To test if the basil is cooked, rub a leaf between two fingers. If ready, the leaf will easily break up. Refresh the leaves, then drain and purée in a food processor. Refrigerate in a covered container until cold • Combine the chicken breast, basil purée and salt in the food processor and blitz until fine. Add the egg and blend until just incorporated. Add the cream and blend until smooth. Transfer to an airtight container and rest in the refrigerator for 20 minutes to firm up • Preheat the oven to 250°C (500°F) • Place a large spoonful of chicken mousse onto each slice of lamb. Wrap each loin in a layer of caul fat to form a cylindrical shape. Then wrap in plastic wrap and tie tightly at each end • Place the lamb parcels in a large saucepan of simmering water and poach for 7–8 minutes. Rest in a warm place for at least 10 minutes • Place the red and yellow capsicums on a baking tray, sprinkle over 1 tablespoon of the olive oil and a little salt and place in the oven for 12 minutes or until the skin is blackened and blistered. Transfer to a bowl, cover with plastic wrap and leave to cool for 10 minutes. Peel and deseed the capsicum • Peel the zucchini and eggplant and cut the skin into 2-cm (3/4-in) squares. Repeat for the capsicum • Heat 1 tablespoon of the olive oil in a heavy-based saucepan, add the capsicum, zucchini and eggplant and sauté over low heat until the vegetables are tender. Season with salt and pepper • Warm the jus gras in a small saucepan over low heat • Heat the remaining olive oil in a large saucepan and deep-fry the sage for 2 minutes or until crispy and the oil stops fizzing • To serve, place the vegetables on each serving plate in a checkerboard fashion. Cut the lamb in half and place on the opposite side of the vegetables. Drizzle the jus gras around the plate in a circular fashion, add a quenelle of pumpkin purée and garnish with the olives and sage. Serve.

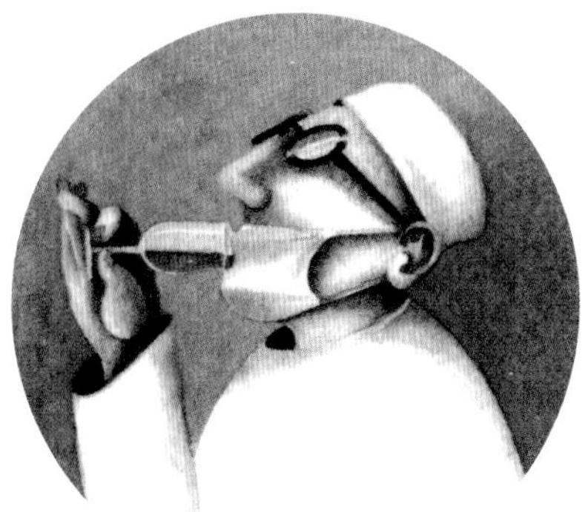

Lamb provençal

[serves 4]

FOND MEMORIES OF MY time in southern France are brought to mind with the classic Provençal flavours of cumin, tomato, black olives and lamb. Wine matching is a hard task in this instance because of the tomato's acidity, look to Italy for inspiration: a light and fragrant earthy wine, such as a dolcetto, will balance well with this dish.

500g (1 lb) lamb loin, trimmed of sinew and fat

200 g (6½ oz) herbed breadcrumbs (see page 384)

1 large leek

PROVENÇAL SAUCE

3 tablespoons olive oil

1 onion, diced

2 cloves of garlic, diced

1 stick of celery, diced

1 red capsicum (sweet pepper), diced

1 zucchini (courgette), diced

1 small eggplant (aubergine), diced

50 g (1¾ oz) ground cumin

Salt and freshly ground pepper

6 cups hot chicken stock (see page 378)

250 g (8 oz) canned tomatoes, roughly chopped

*20 g (¾ oz) cultured butter**

Slice the lamb into four pieces. Place the lamb in a bowl and coat completely with the breadcrumbs. Set aside • Top and tail the leek, reserving only the white part, and trim to 15 cm (6 in) in length. Split the leek lengthwise and wash well under cold water. Peel away the separate layers of the leek to form thick ribbons • Blanch the leek ribbons in boiling salted water for 1 minute or until just tender. Remove and refresh in iced water. Drain and pat dry • Place one slice of lamb at one end of a leek ribbon and roll up to form a sausage-like shape • Tightly cover the rolled lamb in plastic wrap and tie at each end to create a sausage shape • Poach the lamb in simmering water for 7 minutes. The water temperature should be 90°C (195°F). Remove and rest in a warm place for 7 minutes. Remove the plastic wrap and slice each leek and lamb sausage in half • To make the Provençal sauce, heat the olive oil in a heavy-based frying pan, add the onion and garlic and cook for 5 minutes or until soft and transparent • Add the celery, capsicum, zucchini and eggplant and sweat for 5 minutes or until tender • Add the cumin, season with salt and pepper and cook for 10 minutes or until the cumin is fragrant and starts to catch on the bottom of the pan • Add the chicken stock and tomatoes and cook over medium

GARNISH

1½ tablespoons olive oil

2 small Lebanese eggplants (aubergines), cut in half lengthwise

4 baby yellow squash

125g (4 oz) spicy lamb filling (see page 308)

4 confit tomatoes (see page 86)

4 bulbs of baby fennel, trimmed to 6 cm (2½ in) in length and thinly sliced

2 tablespoons black olive tapenade (see page 375)

heat for 25 minutes or until the tomatoes start to break up. Blend with a hand blender until smooth • Push the sauce through a fine sieve with the back of a ladle. Repeat the process if the sauce is still lumpy • Reheat the sauce in a heavy-based saucepan and whisk in the butter (this will add a nice shine to the sauce). Season with salt and pepper • Preheat the oven to 180°C (350°F) • To make the garnish, heat 1 tablespoon of the olive oil in a baking tray, add the Lebanese eggplant and roast in the oven for 3 minutes or until soft. Drain well and season with salt and pepper • Remove the tops from the baby squash and hollow them out. Blanch the squash in boiling water for 1 minute. Refresh in iced water. Fill each squash with the spicy lamb filling and bake in a moderate oven for 5 minutes or until heated right through • Place half an eggplant in the centre of each serving plate. Next to this place a confit tomato and a baby squash. Arrange each halved leek and lamb sausage on top of the eggplant and rest a slice of baby fennel to one side of the lamb. Pour the sauce around the vegetables leaving some of the plate exposed. Drizzle ½ tablespoon of tapenade over and around each dish and serve.

The Dessert

DESSERT MEANS TO FINISH a meal with a dish, usually sweet, but it can also mean to finish with fruit or cheese. The word comes from the French *disservir* which means to clear the table.

I believe the biggest challenge for a chef is to transform simplicity into perfection — and ice cream, of all the desserts, should be applauded for fulfilling this role. Ice cream may be overlooked as being boring and too simple, but for the true gourmet, the fascination lies in how the frozen formula of sugar and fat transforms flavours, from puréed fruits to Tahitian vanilla beans, into heavenly bliss.

Sorbets are traditionally served between main courses of a French banquet. The sorbet is more delicate in texture and lighter than ice cream, which enables the chef to introduce a vast range of flavours. The basic components are sugar syrup, fruit purée or flavouring and an Italian meringue incorporated at the last moment for added texture. Sorbets should not be icy, but rather smooth and on the verge of melting once removed from the freezer.

That most famous of French desserts, the light fluffy cylindrical formation known as a soufflé strikes fear into many domestic cooks' hearts. Yet a soufflé is merely a combination of a base flavour and meringue, baked and immediately taken from the oven to the table, and served with ice cream or coulis.

There are two types of soufflé. The first, which is the easiest is the egg white soufflé. It consists of a heavy French meringue and a thick, flavoured jam. That's it! The best examples are raspberry, or any berry for that matter, and lemon or lime. To ensure the success of an egg white soufflé, add a little more sugar than normal to the egg white at soft peak stage. The traditional recipe calls for Italian meringue instead of the French version. Italian meringue consists of softball caramel (water and sugar carefully boiled to a temperature of 121°C [250°F]) combined with egg whites beaten to soft peaks. The caramel is slowly beaten into the egg whites until they are at room temperature and have established firm peaks, then a few tablespoons of a fruit jam (the quantity will depend on the taste and the depth of colour desired) are folded in. The mixture is placed in chilled ramekin moulds that have been lined with a collar of greaseproof paper to enable the meringue to come over the top of the ramekin to resemble a cold soufflé.

The second type of soufflé is the crème pâtissière soufflé; a simple French meringue is flavoured with a thick cream custard combined with any flavouring imaginable and is then baked in a buttered ramekin mould in a moderate oven. See page 334 for this basic soufflé recipe.

Tarte aux pommes à la tatin

[serves 6]

Thierry Busset is the owner and master of this caramelised apple tart with caramel sauce and homemade vanilla ice cream. I am privileged to have learned how to make it from him. Enjoy!

200 g (6½ oz) puff pastry (see page 54)
4 Golden Delicious apples
15 g (½ oz) caster (superfine) sugar
5 g (¼ oz) butter
*1½ tablespoons Calvados**
Vanilla ice cream (see page 327)
100 ml (3½ fl oz) caramel Calvados sauce (see page 376)

Preheat the oven to 190°C (375°F) • Roll out the pastry on a lightly floured work surface to 5 mm (¼ in) thick. Using a 12-cm (5-in) round cutter, cut out six discs. Place the pastry discs on a greaseproof paper-lined tray. Crimp the edges with your fingertips pressing firmly. Prick each disc with the tines of a fork to prevent the pastry from rising. Transfer to the refrigerator • Cut the ends off each apple, then peel. Cut three cheeks off each apple avoiding the core. Slice each apple cheek as thinly as possible. Fan these slices on each puff pastry disc until only a small hole remains in the centre. Fill the hole with a 2.5-cm (1-in) disc of apple • Sprinkle the sugar onto each tart, place a dot of the butter on top and cook in the oven for 20 minutes or until the apple is coloured. Add a splash of Calvados to each tart, then carefully flip over using a fish slice. Cook for 5 minutes or until the base is golden • Remove from the oven and place a tray weighed down with a saucepan on top of the tarts for 15 minutes. This will give the tarts a wow effect visually • Reheat the tarts in the oven for 5 minutes or until crisp and hot • Serve hot with vanilla ice cream and caramel Calvados sauce.

Roasted apple ravioli with star anise and white pepper

[serves 6]

RAVIOLI AS A DESSERT sounds a bit weird, but trust me, it is lovely in winter. Serve with a glass of crisp, sweet chenin blanc to complement the slight spiciness.

6 small Granny Smith apples

*50 g ($1\frac{3}{4}$ oz) cultured butter**

6 star anise

1 tablespoon coarsely crushed white peppercorns

200 g ($6\frac{1}{2}$ oz) salted peanuts, roughly crushed

100 ml ($3\frac{1}{2}$ fl oz) caramel Calvados sauce (see page 376)

Ravioli dough (see page 392)

APPLE GARNISH

2 tablespoons caster (superfine) sugar

Pinch of eight-spice powder (see page 382)

2 apples, peeled, cored and cut into 18 wedges

6 tablespoons praline ice cream (see pages 327–8)

Cut the tops and bottoms off the apples. Cut each apple into six wedges • Melt the butter in a heavy-based saucepan, add the apples, star anise, pepper and peanuts and cook over medium heat for 2 to 3 minutes or until nicely coloured. Add the Calvados caramel sauce, toss thoroughly and cook for 2 minutes. Remove the star anise and reserve. Transfer the apple mixture to a food processor and purée until smooth • Place the mixture on a tray to cool • Run the ravioli dough through the thickest setting on your pasta machine. Repeat running the dough through the settings until you reach the lowest setting • Place the dough onto a lightly floured work surface. Cut twelve 8-cm (3-in) discs from the dough • Spoon 1 tablespoonful of the puréed apple into the centre of six of the discs. Dab the six remaining discs with a wet pastry brush and place on top of the filled discs. Press around the edges to seal and trim the ravioli with a fluted cutter • To make the apple garnish, in a heavy-based saucepan combine the sugar and eight-spice powder and cook over medium heat until caramelised and a light golden colour. Add the apple and toss in the pan for 2–3 minutes or until cooked • Gently poach the ravioli in a large saucepan of simmering water for 5 minutes, stirring occasionally. Drain on paper towel • Fan three slices of caramelised apple on each serving plate. Arrange the ravioli next to the apple, garnish with praline ice cream and serve.

APPLE CRÈME BRÛLÉE WITH POIRE WILLIAM SORBET

[serves 4]

CRÈME BRÛLÉE IS A simple and clean way to finish a satisfying meal, however, the technique often scares enthusiastic cooks, so crème brûlée is very rarely seen in the home. If I can do it I think you might just be able to manage it as well.

300 ml (10 fl oz) double cream
200 ml (7 fl oz) milk
100 g (3½ oz) caster (superfine) sugar
8 egg yolks
2 vanilla beans, split lengthwise and seeds scraped*
2 Granny Smith apples, peeled, cored and diced
*1 tablespoon Calvados**
500 g (1 lb) poached pears (see page 390)
200 g (6½ oz) sugar syrup (see page 393)
*2 tablespoons eau de vie poire William**
100 g (3½ oz) soft brown sugar

Preheat the oven to 100°C (210°F) • To make the custard, mix the cream, milk, caster sugar, egg yolks and vanilla seeds in a bowl until just incorporated, do not overwork • Place the apple in a heavy-based saucepan and cook for 3–4 minutes or until soft. Deglaze with the Calvados. Remove from the heat and allow to cool. Line the base of four 1-cup capacity ramekin moulds or coffee cups with the apple • Pour the custard into each mould. Transfer the moulds to a baking tray. Pour boiling water in the tray to come halfway up the sides of the moulds. Bake in the oven for 35 minutes or until set to a light custard. Allow to rest for at least 30 minutes before serving • To make the sorbet purée the poached pears and the sugar syrup in a food processor until smooth. Add the eau de vie to taste and stir to combine. Pour into an ice-cream maker and churn following the manufacturer's instructions • Sprinkle the brown sugar over each mould and using a blowtorch or preheated grill (broiler), glaze the top of each brûlée until the sugar turns dark brown • Place each caramelised brûlée on a serving plate, top with a scoop of sorbet and serve.

Tarte aux pommes à la tatin

Roasted apple ravioli with star anise and white pepper

Apple crème brûlée with poire William sorbet

Apple and prune croustillant

Apple and prune croustillant

[serves 4]

THERE IS NOTHING MORE satisfying than placing a spoonful of aromatic crispy pastry topped with soft prunes and apple into your mouth. I like to perceive this as a dessert for non-dessert lovers. Oh and by the way, the English translation of croustillant is simply light and crispy.

*50 g (1¾ oz) cultured butter**

2 Golden Delicious apples, peeled and chopped into 1-cm (⅓-in) dice

300 g (10 oz) prunes soaked in Armagnac (see page 328), finely chopped

2 pinches of eight-spice powder (see page 382)

50 g (1¾ oz) flaked almonds

*100 ml (3½ fl oz) Sauternes**

*4 sheets of Tunisian Brique pastry**

100 ml (3½ fl oz) sugar syrup (see page 393)

Prune and Armagnac ice cream (see page 327–8)

Melt the butter in a heavy-based saucepan over low heat, add the apple and cook for 3–4 minutes or until soft. Add the prunes, eight-spice powder and almonds and stir well, cook for 2–3 minutes. Deglaze the pan with the Sauternes and cook for 5 minutes • Strain, reserving the juices • Place the pastry on a lightly floured work surface. Using a pastry brush, apply a liberal amount of sugar syrup on each sheet. Press each sheet into 8-cm (3-in) non-stick pommes Anna moulds. Place a generous amount of the apple and prune mixture in each pastry case. Fold over the pastry and secure the top with a toothpick. Place in the refrigerator for 20 minutes • Preheat the oven to 170°C (335°F) • Place the pastries in the oven and bake for 10 minutes or until golden • Unmould and place in the centre of a large warmed serving plate. Place a spoonful of prune and Armagnac ice cream on one side of each plate. Drizzle the reserved juices over and around the pastry and serve.

Sorbet au clicquot rosé

[makes 4 cups]

I LOVE THE VELVETY texture of the apple and the delicate dryness of the Champagne. It is a wonderful palate cleanser between courses, or a wonderful finish to a meal simply served with raspberries and a glass of rosé Champagne.

3 Granny Smith apples
Juice of 2 lemons

ORANGE SUGAR SYRUP
Juice of 1 orange
200 g (6½ oz) sugar
700 ml (23½ fl oz) water

250 g (8 oz) Italian meringue (see page 334)
4 cups Veuve Clicquot rosé Champagne
4 tablespoons raspberries

Wash and core the apples. Roughly cut into five or six pieces, squeeze over the lemon juice and place on a tray in the freezer for 2–3 hours, to preserve the bright green colour of the apples • Transfer to a food processor and blend until puréed • To make the orange sugar syrup, which is the base of the sorbet, combine the orange juice, sugar and water in a saucepan and bring to the boil. Continue to boil for 3–4 minutes over medium heat. If you have a saccharometer, measure the sugar and continue to boil until the reading has reached a sugar content of 22 Baumes. To serve it needs to be at 15 Baumes • Combine the sugar syrup and apple purée. Place in an ice-cream churner and follow the manufacturer's instructions. When the sorbet is smooth and completely frozen, add the meringue and 3 cups of the Champagne. Place in the freezer for 30 minutes before serving • To serve, place a scoop of sorbet in each coupe or martini glass, sprinkle over a tablespoonful of raspberries and ¼ cup of rosé Champagne, preferably the one you are going to drink with the dessert.

Calvados Crème Caramel

[makes 6]

I CANNOT GO PAST including a crème caramel in my dessert repertoire. With this particular dessert, apple purée or poached apples make the perfect accompaniment.

30 g (1 oz) currants
*200 ml (7 fl oz) Calvados**
4 eggs
2 egg yolks
80 g (2¾ oz) caster (superfine) sugar
2 cups milk

CARAMEL

300 g (10 oz) sugar
100 ml (3½ fl oz) water

Macerate the currants in the Calvados for 24 hours • Combine the eggs, egg yolks and caster sugar in a mixing bowl. Do not overbeat as it will create air bubbles in the caramel • Warm the milk in a saucepan and pour over the egg mixture, whisking constantly • Strain the Calvados from the currants and incorporate into the custard. Pass through a fine sieve and set aside • To make the caramel, combine the sugar and 2½ tablespoons of the water in a heavy-based saucepan and cook over medium heat for 3–4 minutes or until a light golden colour. Test with a sugar thermometer, the temperature should be between 128–132°C (262–270°F). Very carefully stir in the remaining 2½ tablespoons of water and boil for 2 minutes • Preheat the oven to 100°C (210°F) • Place a teaspoonful of the caramel in the bottom of six dariole moulds and set aside for 20 minutes to set • Pour the custard over the caramel until the dariole moulds are three-quarters full • Place a teaspoonful of the currants in each mould • Place the moulds in a baking tray. Pour boiling water in the tray to come halfway up the sides of each dariole mould. Bake in the oven for 45 minutes • Place in the refrigerator for 30 minutes or until ready to serve • To unmould, place each dariole mould in warm water, then gently invert onto a small serving plate. The crème caramels are best served within 24 hours.

The ice cream palette

Vanilla ice cream

[makes 4 cups]

THE EXECUTION IS simple, the perfume of vanilla is distracting, the texture is seductive and the only compromising decision to be made is what to serve it with. I prefer to simply pour over some sweetened fruit poached in Sauternes for the seductiveness to work its magic. If trimoline is a foreign word to your local quality purveyor then replace it with glucose.

2 vanilla beans, split lengthwise*
2 cups milk
2 cups thickened cream
*100 g (3½ oz) trimoline**
9 egg yolks
200 g (6½ oz) sugar

With the back of a knife scrape the seeds from the vanilla beans into a medium heavy-based saucepan. Add the vanilla beans, milk, cream and trimoline and simmer for 1 minute • In a mixing bowl, whisk the egg yolks and sugar until pale and thick • Pour a quarter of the milk mixture into the egg yolk mixture and stir to combine. Pour this mixture into the milk mixture and stir well • Place the saucepan over low heat and, using a wooden spoon, stir constantly until the mixture thickens slightly and coats the back of the spoon • Strain the crème anglaise through a fine sieve into a bowl over an ice bath. Set aside, stirring ocassionally, for 20 minutes or until cold • Place the crème anglaise in an ice-cream churner and, following manufacturer's instructions, churn until frozen and smooth. Let the ice cream set firm in the freezer for 1 hour before serving.

ICECREAM VARIATIONS

USE THE VANILLA ICE CREAM recipe as the base for the following flavours:

Glace au chocolat Add 50 g (8 oz) of chopped dark or white couverture chocolate at the end of the cooking process.

Pistachio At the first stage of boiling the milk and cream, add 200 g (6½ oz) of good quality pistachio paste.

Prune and Armagnac Place 1 kg (2 lb) of pitted good-quality Aegean prunes in a sterilised jar, pour over enough Armagnac to cover the prunes. Seal the jar and keep in a cool place for 2 weeks before using. Purée 200 g (6½ oz) of the macerated prunes in a food processor. Add the purée to 600 ml (1 pt) of the crème anglaise base.

Glace au café de Paris A classic recipe traditionally served with a sprig of mint in a coupe glass. Add 300 ml (10 fl oz) of espresso coffee during the last stages of cooling the crème anglaise base.

Praline ice cream Add 100 g (3½ oz) of crushed praline (see page 391) at the churning stage.

Fruit-flavoured ice cream Simply add 500 g (1 lb) of the desired fruit purée at the churning stage of the process. Raspberry, strawberry, banana, apricot, passionfruit and mango are highly recommended.

Lavender-scented ice cream Add 1½ teaspoons of dried lavender flowers, crushed to a fine powder, to the sugar in the basic vanilla ice cream recipe two days before proceeding. Garnish with fresh lavender flowers. If fresh lavender is not available, replace with 3–4 drops of lavender oil.

Peanut butter ice cream Add 4 tablespoons of unsalted smooth peanut butter to 600 ml (1 pt) of crème anglaise. Serve with chocolate sauce.

Liquorice ice cream Combine 100 g (3½ oz) of liquorice sticks, melted in a double boiler over a saucepan of simmering water, with ½ cup of double cream. Stir until the liquorice has dissolved, then strain through a fine chinois* into 600 ml (1 pt) of crème anglaise base.

For all the recipes above place in an ice-cream churner and follow manufacturer's instructions.

Calvados crème caramel

Sorbet au clicquot rosé

Various ice cream flavours

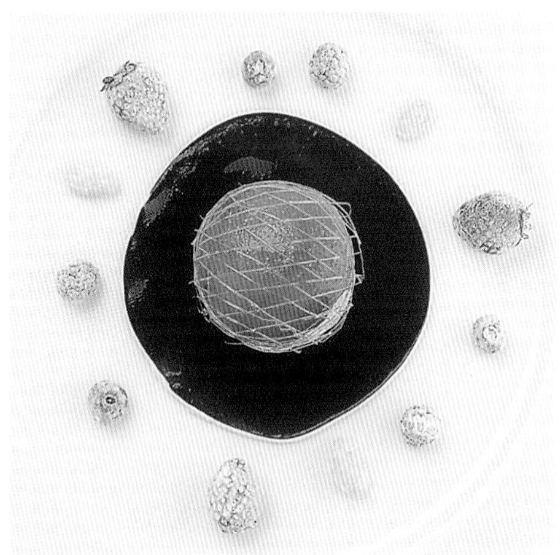
Pêche Melba

Biscuit glace savoy

Bombe Alaska showing Italian meringue

Syrup 30

[makes 5 cups]

Simple syrup is used in every day patisserie and 30°C (86°F) Baume is the standard measure for an all round syrup that can be used for everything, including to moisten sponges or biscuits and forming the base of sauces and glazes. Baume refers to the measurement of the density of sugar to liquid in syrups with the use of a saccharometer. This is a light to medium sugar syrup that is recommended for making sorbets and glazes.

750 g (1½ lb) sugar
650 ml (22 fl oz) water
90 g (3 oz) glucose

Combine all of the ingredients in a heavy-based saucepan and bring to the boil for 3–4 minutes. Measure with a saccharometer for an accurate recipe, it should read 30°C (86°F) Baume. Strain and store at room temperature in a clean airtight container for up to 1 month.

Sorbet

All sorbet recipes require 2 cups of syrup 30 (see above) and 100 g (3½ oz) of Italian meringue (see page 334) and should be churned in an ice-cream machine according to manufacturer's instructions.

Lemon and Lime Combine 300 ml (10 fl oz) of lemon juice and 200 ml (7 fl oz) of lime juice with the finely grated zest of 3 limes.

Spearmint Add 2 cups of milk infused with ¼ cup spearmint tea.

Raspberry Add 620 g (1¼ lb) of raspberry purée and the juice of ½ lemon.

Watermelon Mash 800 g (1⅔ lb) of watermelon including the seeds and then hang in cheesecloth over a bowl to collect the juice. Add the juice to the syrup and meringue.

Chocolate Add 150 g (5 oz) Dutch cocoa powder dissolved in 300 ml (10 fl oz) of milk.

Pear and Black Pepper Add 400 g (13 oz) puréed pears and 1 teaspoon of freshly cracked black pepper.

Granita If an ice-cream churner is inaccessible, a granita is a viable option. Use the sorbet recipe, but place the mixture onto a tray to set in the freezer. Scrape the mixture with a fork 3–4 times until the desired snow effect has been achieved.

Pêche melba

[serves 6]

Escoffier presented Dame Nellie Melba with a dessert of peaches on a bed of vanilla ice cream, covered with a lace of spun sugar, placed in a silver bowl nestled between the wings of a beautiful swan sculpted out of a large block of ice. The effect was stunning, and Madame Melba was delighted with the creation. The original name of the dish is Pêches au Cygne.

The Montreuil peach, for example, is perfect for this dessert.

3 perfectly ripe peaches

1½ tablespoons caster (superfine) sugar

RASPBERRY COULIS

250 g (8 oz) fresh raspberries, crushed

150 g (5 oz) icing (confectioners') sugar

SUGAR CAGE CARAMEL *(optional)*

1 cup sugar

30 g (1 oz) glucose

¼ cup water

6 x 8-cm (3-in) discs of jaconde sponge (see page 352)

40 g (1⅓ oz) white compound chocolate, melted

Vanilla ice cream (see page 327)

20 sugared almonds

18 raspberries

Blanch the peaches for 2 seconds in boiling water, remove immediately with a slotted spoon, and place in iced water for a few seconds. Peel, cut in half and remove the stone. Place peach halves flat-side down and sprinkle 1 teaspoon of caster sugar over each. Refrigerate • To make the raspberry coulis, mix the raspberries with the icing sugar. Place in a heavy-based saucepan and simmer over medium heat for 10 minutes. Transfer to a food processor and blend until smooth. Pass through a fine chinois* to remove the seeds. Cool in the refrigerator until required • To make the caramel, combine the sugar, glucose and water in a heavy-based saucepan and bring to the boil. Continue to boil over medium heat for 3–4 minutes or until the syrup reaches a soft ball caramel temperature of 121°C (250°F). Use a sugar thermometer to test the temperature • Cool the caramel for 2 minutes. Dip a fork into the caramel and pull it out to create a long drip. Drape the caramel over a clean ladle roughly the size of the peach halves, continually winding back and forward to construct a caramel cage. The caramel will set instantly and will be easy to slide off the ladle once it has cooled. Repeat until you have six sugar cages • Place a sponge disc in the centre of a serving

18 strawberries

18 blueberries

18 redcurrants

plate. Pipe a 15-cm (6-in) circle of white chocolate around the sponge disc. Fill inside this circle with the raspberry coulis. Place 1 scoop of vanilla ice cream on top of the sponge. Place a peach half on top of the ice cream. Place a sugar cage on top of each peach. Garnish with the sugared almonds and berries and serve.

Biscuit glace savoy

[serves 12]

Escoffier had a certain love for ice cream and its variety of adaptations. I used the following recipe for a gala dinner that was filmed for a TV special. I needed something visually appealing as well as a guarantee to bring smiles to the diners' faces. Mango ice cream is always a sure-fire winner.

250 g (8 oz) melted Valrhona chocolate (66 per cent Manjari), chopped

1 x 250 g (8 oz) tin sweet chestnut purée

4 cups mango purée (Boiron brand)

12 egg yolks

2 cups caster (superfine) sugar

250 g (8 oz) Italian meringue (see page 334)

4 cups whipped thickened cream

2 tablespoons brandy

1 sheet jaconde sponge (see page 352)

Melt the chocolate in the top of a double boiler over a saucepan of simmering water • Place the chestnut purée in a mixing bowl • Pour the mango purée into a second mixing bowl • Place the egg yolks and sugar in a double boiler and whisk over a saucepan of simmering water until the mixture becomes thick and pale. Remove from the heat and continue whisking until the mixture is cold • Combine one-third of the egg yolk mixture with the chestnut purée. Fold in one-third of the Italian meringue and the whipped cream • Combine one-third of the egg yolk mixture with the mango purée. Fold in one-third of the meringue and the whipped cream • Incorporate the remaining egg yolk mixture and the chocolate and fold in the remaining meringue and whipped cream • Sprinkle the brandy over the sponge • Line a 12 x 22-cm (5 x 9-in) mould with plastic wrap. Cut the sponge to fit the

GARNISH

16 whole roasted and peeled chestnuts

Sugar cage caramel (see page 331), warmed

2 cups chocolate glaze (see page 353)

12 tuiles (see page 340)

4 rockmelons, chopped into dice

4 honeydew melons, chopped into dice

4 Seville oranges, peeled and segmented

250 g (8 oz) strawberries

two longer sides and base and cover with the sponge • Pour in the chestnut cream, making sure that the mixture comes one-third of the way up the sides of the mould. Place the mould in the freezer for 30 minutes • Place another layer of sponge over the first layer. Pour in the mango cream and place in the freezer for 30 minutes • Place a layer of sponge over the second layer. Pour in the chocolate and cover with more jaconde sponge. Leave in the freezer for 6 hours or until set • To serve, slice into 2.5-cm (1-in) thick slices using a sharp knife dipped in hot water. Place each slice in the centre of a chilled serving plate • Insert a toothpick in each chestnut and dip in the warmed caramel. Hold the chestnut upside down until it sets • Warm the chocolate glaze and drizzle decoratively over and around the savoy slices • Place a tuile to one side of the savoy. Arrange the rockmelon, honeydew melon, orange segments and strawberries in each tuile and serve immediately.

Soufflés

Basic soufflé

[serves 6]

DON'T BE FRIGHTENED of making a souffle. This basic recipe is simply a French meringue with a crème pâtissière (a custard) added to it. Simple.

2 tablespoons soft butter

4 tablespoons caster sugar

10 egg whites

1 teaspoon lemon juice

3 tablespoons crème pâtissière (see page 335)

Desired flavouring (see soufflé variations page 339)

1 tablespoon icing (confectioners') sugar

Brush the butter inside six 1-cup capacity soufflé moulds stroking upwards in the same direction the soufflé will rise. Lightly dust the moulds with two tablespoons of the caster sugar then tip the moulds upside down and lightly tap to free them of any excess sugar. Place the moulds onto a baking tray 8 cm (3 in) apart • Preheat the oven to 160°C and disengage the fan • To make the French meringue, place the egg whites in a mixing bowl and whisk on high until soft peaks form, add the remaining caster sugar and the lemon juice and continue to whisk on high until shiny stiff peaks form • Place the crème pâtissière in another mixing bowl, fold in a quarter of the meringue and mix well. Incorporate the remaining meringue folding carefully • Spoon the mixture into each ramekin until full. Using a palette knife, smooth the top of each soufflé to ensure it is level with the top of the ramekin • Place in the oven for 6–8 minutes or until the soufflé has risen 2.5–4 cm (1–1½ in) above the mould and is golden on top. Dust with icing sugar and serve immediately.

Crème pâtissière

[makes 4 cups]

Make your own custard for use in sponges, pastry fillings and, my favourite, soufflé bases. Simply add different flavourings such as homemade jams, cocoa powder or alcohol to form the basis of great soufflés.

600 ml (1 pt) milk

1 vanilla bean, split lengthwise and seeds scraped*

6 egg yolks

1/2 cup sugar

2 tablespoons cornflour (cornstarch)

2 tablespoons plain (all-purpose) flour

Combine the milk, vanilla bean and seeds in a heavy-based saucepan and bring to the boil • Beat the egg yolks and sugar in a mixing bowl until pale and thick • Sift in the cornflour and flour and stir to combine • Pour one-third of the boiling milk over the egg-yolk mixture and whisk until smooth. Pour back into the remaining milk. Over low heat, continually whisk the custard until it starts to thicken and coats the back of a spoon. Remove from the heat as soon as it boils • Transfer the custard to a mixing bowl and beat on high speed until thick and smooth. Store in the refrigerator covered with plastic wrap for up to 3 days • The custard can be used for soufflé bases by simply adding the correct amount of desired flavouring then carefully folding in the meringue.

Italian meringue

[makes 10 serves]

Italian meringue was created by pastry chefs as a garnish for cakes and pastries. Try folding the meringue into sorbets and iced soufflés, piping it onto tarts and flans and as garnishing for bombe Alaskas.

⅓ cup water
300 g (10 oz) caster (superfine) sugar
30 g (1 oz) glucose
6 egg whites

Combine the water, sugar and glucose in a heavy-based saucepan and bring to the boil. Insert a sugar thermometer and continue to boil until the temperature reaches 121°C (250°F) • Beat the egg whites until soft peaks form. Slowly pour in the sugar syrup while continuing to beat. Once all the syrup has been added, increase speed to high and whisk until the meringue is smooth and glossy and at room temperature. Use immediately • To make a bombe Alaska, scoop a ball of ice cream onto a smaller round disc of jaconde sponge. Place the meringue into a piping bag and pipe stiff peaks over the entire ice-cream. Place under a grill to brown the tips. Alternatively bring to the boil ⅓ tablespoon of flavoured alcohol, ignite and while flaming pour over the bombe. Serve with fresh fruit or a fruit coulis.

Demoulded pistachio soufflé with a soft chocolate centre

[serves 6]

'The only thing that will make a soufflé fall is if it knows you are afraid of it,' James Beard said. I remember the day the six Michelin inspectors popped in for a lazy Sunday lunch at L'Ortolan. Everything was going well until the pastry chef tried to serve a collapsed version of the following soufflé. Burton Race spotted it and hit the roof. They ended up waiting 40 minutes for dessert and with that wait went our chances.

A sweet Spanish muscat from the Malaga region is delicious with this.

CHOCOLATE GANACHE

100 ml (3½ fl oz) double cream

250 g (8 oz) dark couverture chocolate (35% cocoa solids), roughly chopped

100 g (3½ oz) butter, softened

50 g (1¾ oz) finely grated dark couverture chocolate

CRÈME PÂTISSIÈRE

4 cups milk

1 vanilla bean, split lengthwise and seeds scraped*

*120 g (4 oz) pistachio paste**

100 g (3½ oz) sugar

10 eggs, separated

2 tablespoons plain (all-purpose) flour

2 tablespoons cornflour (cornstarch)

10 egg whites

150 g (5 oz) caster (superfine) sugar

300 ml (10 fl oz) crème anglaise (see page 379)

To make the chocolate ganache, bring the cream to the boil in a heavy-based saucepan, pour over the chopped chocolate and stir to combine. Pour into a shallow tray and transfer to the freezer for 90 minutes or until frozen. Cut into 2.5-cm (1-in) squares and return to the freezer • Grease six 1-cup capacity aluminium dariole moulds with the butter, then coat in the grated chocolate. Refrigerate until needed • To make the crème pâtissière, combine the milk, vanilla bean and seeds in a saucepan and bring to the boil. Remove the vanilla bean. Whisk in the pistachio paste. Incorporate the sugar, egg yolks, flour and cornflour in a mixing bowl and whisk for 2–3 minutes. Combine the milk mixture with the egg yolk mixture, whisking vigorously for 5 minutes or until thick and smooth. Continue to beat until the mixture has cooled. This prevents the custard forming lumps • Preheat the oven to 180°C (350°F) • To make the meringue, beat the egg whites until soft peaks form, add the caster sugar and continue to beat until shiny stiff peaks form • Place 6 tablespoons of the crème pâtissière in a mixing bowl, fold in a quarter of the meringue, mixing well. Incorporate the remaining meringue. Spoon the mixture into the aluminium dariole moulds until about three-quarters full. Place a cube of frozen chocolate ganache in the centre of each mould and cover with a little more mixture • Place in the oven for 6–8 minutes or until the soufflé has risen • Warm the crème anglaise to just simmering, then froth using a hand blender • Position each soufflé over a warmed serving bowl, invert into the centre of the bowl, unmould and pour the frothy crème anglaise around. Serve.

SOUFFLÉ VARIATIONS

Chocolate Half a tablespoon of Dutch cocoa powder per serve whisked into the crème pâtissière at the initial stage of the milk being boiled will give a rich velvety soufflé. Never add solid chocolate to a soufflé, it will burn and taste bitter. Quality cocoa powder is hard to find. Go for the 33 per cent fat content, which will melt in your fingers when picked up. The Dutch brands are normally the most consistent. I also recommend adding a dollop of chocolate ganache in the base of each ramekin. Keep away from port, sweet PX sherries and Australian muscats and think more along the lines of heavier style Sauternes that will not overwhelm the soufflé's delicate soft texture.

Calvados One and a half tablespoons of Calvados whisked into the crème pâtissière at the final stage will give a lovely dimension to the soufflé. Extra distinction can be added with the help of some diced and sautéed apple in the base of the ramekin. Try adding a fine crumble mix to the sides of the ramekin instead of caster (superfine) sugar. The crumble mix is 2 tablespoons of butter; 2 tablespoons of flour and 2 tablespoons of sugar. Place in a food processor and blitz for 2 minutes or until it forms a simple dough. Flatten the dough to 2.5 cm (1 in) thick, place onto a greaseproof paper-lined baking tray and bake at 180°C (350°F) for 10 minutes or until golden and crisp. The Italian sparkling dessert wine Moscato d'Asti contrasts delicately with the Calvados.

Grand Marnier A good splash of Grand Marnier and a generous teaspoon of grated orange zest per soufflé. Pair this dish with a glass of aged Grand Marnier or an Orange and Flora Muscat from Brown Brothers in the King Valley, Australia.

Blueberry Add 30 g (1 oz) of blueberry coulis, jam or compote to the crème pâtissière. Ensure the coulis or compote has been thickened with an agent such as cornflour (cornstarch). Best served with a creamy white glace au chocolat ice cream (see page 327–8) and a botrytis pinot gris.

Honey and Ginger Combine 3 tablespoons of crème pâtissière, 1 tablespoon of honey and 1 pinch of ground ginger. A more professional approach to this recipe is to add 50 g (1¾ oz) of sliced ginger to the first step when making the crème pâtissière base. Allow the ginger to infuse in the milk as it comes to the boil, and then remove it before adding the eggs and flour. Garnish the soufflé with glacé ginger before serving with peanut butter ice cream (see page 327–8) to produce a very controversial match. Serve with De Bortoli Noble One or a good viscous well-balanced botrytis semillon.

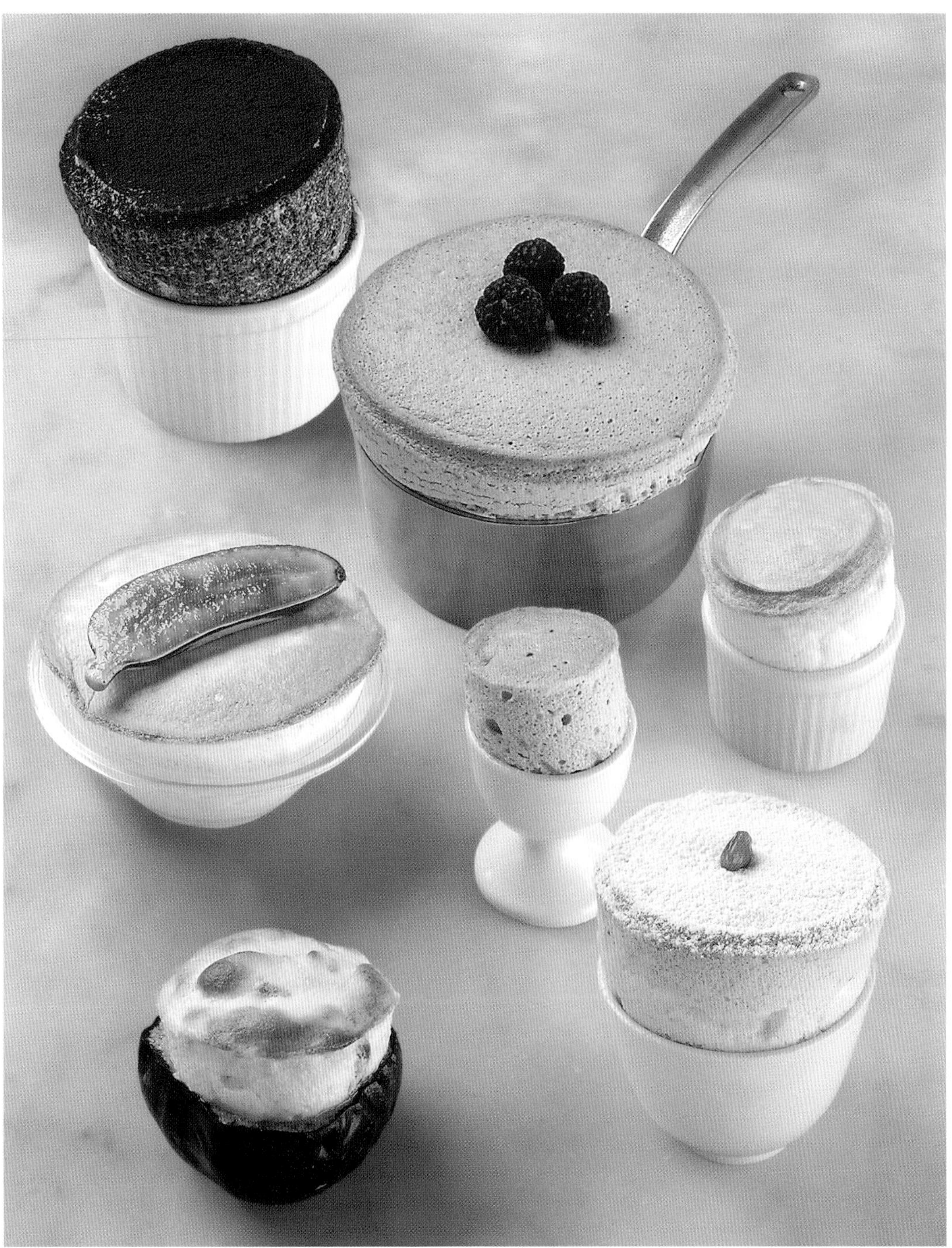

A selection of soufflés

My Vue

Petits four or mignardises

What do miniature teacakes, bon bons, macaroons, tuiles, chocolate-dipped fruits and sables have in common? They are all petits fours (meaning small ovens in French). The name is said to have originated from the ovens they were baked in. Once the large cakes were baked, the small cakes were placed in the ovens as they were cooling down. Mignardises means sweet delicacies. Very little is written directly on the subject, however, in *Le Guide Culinaire* a number of simple desserts were sized down to form a colourful and skilful array. In the following petits fours recipes I have followed the principles of Escoffier's writings and philosophies.

Tuiles

[makes 50]

Use this as a base recipe to create flavoured tuiles. My favourite is finely chopped almonds with orange zest or lemon zest and poppy seed.

6 egg whites
225 g (7 oz) plain (all-purpose) flour
$1^1/_3$ cups icing (confectioners') sugar
250 g (8 oz) butter, melted

Whisk the egg whites, flour and sugar in a mixing bowl to form a paste. Incorporate the butter, then rest in the refrigerator for 1 hour • Preheat the oven to 180°C (350°F) • Place dessertspoonfuls of the mixture on a greaseproof paper-lined baking tray. Flatten with the back of the spoon and bake in the oven for 5 minutes or until golden • Remove from the oven and immediately shape over a rolling pin to form a curl. Store in an airtight container in a dry place for up to 2 days. Serve with coffee.

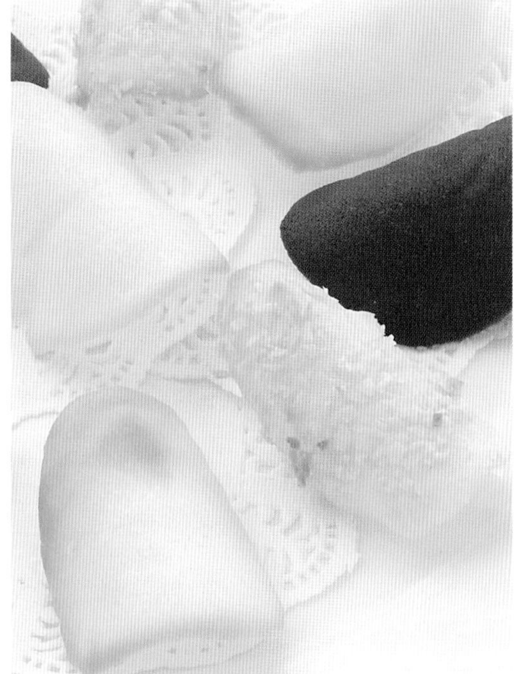

Tuiles

Macaroons

Madeleines

Macaroons

[makes 30 small teacakes]

THESE SMALL ROUNDS are best described as crunchy on the outside and delectably soft inside. Almonds and a well-made French meringue are the key ingredients; however, feel free to add different flavours, such as pistachio paste, raspberry coulis, coffee, finely ground hazelnut praline or Dutch cocoa powder. Always ensure that the butter cream is the same flavour as the macaroon to create one simple burst of flavour.

225 g (7 oz) icing (confectioners') sugar
120 g (4 oz) ground almonds
4 egg whites
45 g (1½ oz) caster (superfine) sugar

BUTTER CREAM

*300 g (10 oz) cultured butter**
100 g (3½ oz) icing (confectioners') sugar
1 vanilla bean, split lengthwise and seeds scraped*

Preheat the oven to 120°C (250°F) • Combine the icing sugar and ground almonds in a mixing bowl • Beat the egg whites until stiff peaks form, then add the sugar, a little at a time, to form a meringue • Mix half of the meringue into the almond mixture. Once fully incorporated, fold in the remaining meringue • Place teaspoonfuls of the mixture 4 cm (1½ in) apart on a greaseproof paper-lined baking tray. Flatten slightly with the back of the spoon. Set aside for 5 minutes in a dry part of the kitchen. This will help to create a lovely shine. Spray 2–3 tablespoons of water over the baking tray to help create some steam while baking • Bake in the oven for 20 minutes. Allow to cool on the tray • To make the butter cream, beat the butter, sugar and vanilla seeds in a mixing bowl until pale • Sandwich the macaroons together with the butter cream. Serve with coffee.

Madeleines

[makes 30 small teacakes]

Legend has it that this recipe was developed by a peasant girl named Madeleine who lived outside the castle of Commercy in a small village in Lorraine. The ruler at the time, Stanislaw Leszcynski, was so taken by the cakes he made them a part of the royal repertoire. Other flavours to consider are honey, hazelnut, maple syrup, orange, chocolate, macerated currants or pistachio.

*100 g (3½ oz) cultured butter**
125 g (4 oz) caster (superfine) sugar
3 eggs
1 cup plain (all-purpose) flour
1 teaspoon baking powder
Zest and juice of ½ lemon
1 vanilla bean, split lengthwise and seeds scraped*
Pinch of salt

Cream the butter and sugar in a mixing bowl until pale • Add the eggs and beat until combined. If the mixture curdles, don't be alarmed. Sift in the flour and baking powder and beat on low speed • Mix in the lemon zest and juice, vanilla seeds and salt. Cover and place in the refrigerator until cold • Preheat the oven to 180°C (350°F) • Brush Madeleine moulds with butter and dust with flour. Place a teaspoonful of mixture in each mould • Place in the oven and bake for 5–6 minutes or until golden. Remove from the moulds by carefully tapping the underside. Serve immediately with a cup of espresso.

CHOCOLATE
FACTORY

The Chocolate

DESSERT, TO MANY, WOULD be unimaginable without chocolate. Chocolate — the 'fruit of the gods' — comes in forms that taste so bitter it makes the hair on the back of your neck stand up or so sweet you will need to marry a dentist.

All chocolate starts with a liquor, the ground nib of the cocoa bean. The process of sourcing and roasting the bean, then finely grinding it into a coarse (nibbed) mixture is called conching. This takes place by putting the powder into a large, slowly churning vat. The fat turns to liquid and forms a smooth flowing paste known as pure chocolate or 100 per cent pure bitter. Different percentages of sugar and cocoa butter or fat are added to chocolate to give a variation of sweetness and stability. On good quality chocolate there is a percentage indicating the degree of bitterness. For example, 70 per cent means that 30 per cent of the chocolate is a mixture of cocoa butter and sugar. Chocolates available in supermarkets are much sweeter and less rich in chocolate than premium-quality, imported chocolate. By law, these companies are required to include a minimum of 10 per cent chocolate liquor in their product (who knows what the rest is!). Only a selected few producers, with nothing to hide and everything to be proud of, have listed precisely the ingredients included in their chocolate. Valrhona is one of these producers; the undisputed leader in the industry. Cacao Barry is another producer to look out for. At a recent tasting I was very impressed with some of their Single Estate chocolates.

Couverture is the French word used for chocolate with no additives and a higher proportion of cocoa fat, lowering the melting point. All chocolate with 40 per cent or more cocoa has this classification. This means it needs to be tempered before use. Tempering is the technique used to ensure a beautiful, shiny, crisp chocolate without any colour variation.

To temper chocolate: Melt the chocolate in the top of a double boiler over a saucepan of simmering water. Stir the chocolate until it reaches 60°C (140°F). Use a sugar thermometer to test.

Pour three-quarters of this mix onto a flat bench that is super clean. Marble is the best as it absorbs heat quickly and is a consistent temperature even throughout summer. With a plastic or stainless steel scraper work the mix around on the surface to bring the temperature down. This will enable the fat particles in the chocolate to crystallise evenly throughout the chocolate instead of settling to the bottom or on the top of the chocolate. (This is what the white particles often found in old chocolate are associated with.)

Return to the heat and stir with a wooden spoon until the chocolate melts and reaches 32°C (90°F). The chocolate is now ready for use. Any time you use the chocolate again after it has set, bring it up to 32°C (90°F).

Chocolate tart robuchon

[serves 8]

My good friend and mentor Thierry Busset passed this recipe on to me via another good friend and chef, Robert Reid, who worked for the legendary Joel Robuchon at his Michelin three-star Le Jamin in Paris. This recipe does not require glazing with chocolate ganache after baking — the baking process is so delicate the tart is left with a mirror finish. Best served simply with chocolate shavings and whipped cream and a fortified muscat from the Rutherglen region in Victoria, Australia.

Using an inferior chocolate will compromise the creaminess and richness of this tart.

500 g (1 lb) dark couverture chocolate, roughly chopped

200 ml (7 fl oz) milk

300 ml (10 fl oz) double cream

3 eggs, lightly beaten

1 x 25-cm (10-in) short crust pastry shell, baked blind (see page 74)

Preheat the oven to 250°C (500°F) • Melt the chocolate in the top of a double boiler over a saucepan of simmering water • Combine the milk and cream in a saucepan, bring to the boil and pour over the eggs. Strain through a fine sieve into the melted chocolate. Lightly combine with a wooden spoon until smooth, thick and shiny • Pour into the pastry shell. Turn off the oven, place the tart in the oven and leave for 30 minutes or until the chocolate is set like custard • Place on a cake rack and allow to cool to room temperature. Serve immediately with crème chantilly (see page 380) or vanilla ice cream (see page 327).

Chocolate crème

[makes about 4 cups]

Used as a filling for the chocolate sponge, you will find this chocolate crème a very handy addition to your repertoire. This recipe also makes a very suitable base for chocolate soufflés.

2 cups milk

4 egg yolks

½ cup sugar

20 g (¾ oz) cornflour (cornstarch)

⅓ cup plain (all-purpose) flour

250 g (8 oz) dark couverture chocolate, roughly chopped

Pour the milk into a saucepan and bring to the boil over medium heat • Beat the egg yolks and sugar in a mixing bowl until pale and thick. Sift in the cornflour and flour and mix to combine. Add one-third of the boiling milk, whisking until the mixture is smooth. Pour into the milk remaining in the saucepan and cook over low heat, continually whisking, until the custard starts to thicken. When the custard comes to the boil, remove from the heat and stir in the chocolate • Transfer the custard to a mixing bowl and beat on high speed for 10 minutes or until the mixture is at room temperature and is thick and shiny. Store, covered with plastic wrap, in the refrigerator for up to 3 days.

Chocolate sponge

[makes 2 cakes]

A variation of the classic Genoese sponge, I find this recipe very useful as the foundation for chocolate cakes and petits fours.

10 egg whites
100 g (3½ oz) caster (superfine) sugar
90 g (3 oz) Dutch cocoa powder
100 g (3½ oz) icing (confectioners') sugar
25 g (1 oz) cornflour (cornstarch)
6 egg yolks
1½ tablespoons cold water

Preheat the oven to 170°C (335°F) • Beat the egg whites in a mixing bowl until soft peaks form. Add the caster sugar and whisk until firm peaks form • Sift the cocoa powder, icing sugar and cornflour into a mixing bowl. Add the egg yolks and beat until thick and smooth. Fold in the water. Gently fold into the meringue • Pour into two buttered and greaseproof paper-lined 20-cm (8-in) square cake tins. Bake in the oven for 20 minutes. Test readiness by inserting a skewer in the centre of the cake, if it comes away clean the cake is cooked. Turn out onto a cake rack and allow to cool. The sponge responds well to freezing for up to 3 months in an airtight container.

Chocolate ganache

[makes 40 small chocolates]

Ganache is a French term referring to a smooth mixture of chocolate and double cream. To make a more liquid ganache for cakes and mousses, increase the ratio of cream to chocolate and when barely warm pour over the cake or mousse. If cooled to room temperature it becomes a filling or frosting. Refrigerated ganache can be moulded into balls for use in handmade chocolates. Certain nuts, dried fruits, and alcohol, such as Grand Marnier and brandy, can be added for extra flavour and contrast.

200 g (6½ oz) dark couverture chocolate, roughly chopped
200 g (6½ oz) double cream

Melt the chocolate in the top of a double boiler over a saucepan of simmering water. Stir occasionally • Remove from the heat and fold in the cream. Use as required.

Pistachio soufflé with a soft chocolate centre

Warm chocolate biscuit pudding

Chocolate crème used as a filling in a sponge

Chocolate tart robuchon

Chocolate sponge

Chocolate ganache

Classic opera cake

Chocolate truffle mousse

Classic opera cake

[serves 8]

RICH CHOCOLATE AND COFFEE cake slices, known as Opera, are artfully produced by the hundreds by patisserie chefs from Morocco to New York. This cake from Monaco was a favourite with opera singers and their entourages. It was developed by the famous pâtissier Gaston Lenôtre. In a true opera cake, you should never be able to see the layers of jaconde sponge — the coffee syrup should disguise it; so don't be afraid to drench the cake.

JACONDE SPONGE

8 large eggs, separated, at room temperature

4 large egg yolks, at room temperature

450 g (14 oz) sugar

Pinch of salt

280 g (9 oz) plain (all-purpose) flour, sifted

150 ml (5 fl oz) melted butter

COFFEE BUTTER CREAM

5 eggs

400 g (13 oz) sugar

1/3 cup water

550 g (1 1/4 lb) cultured butter, softened*

1 teaspoon vanilla extract

1 tablespoon strong espresso coffee

Preheat the oven to 180°C (350°F). Arrange two baking racks near the centre of the oven • Lightly butter the bottom and sides of three 25 x 37.5-cm (10 x 15-in) non-stick cake tins. Dust inside with flour and tap out the excess • To make the jaconde sponge, beat the 12 egg yolks and sugar at medium speed until just combined. Increase the speed to high and beat until pale and thick • In another mixing bowl, beat the egg whites and salt on low speed until foamy. Gradually increase the speed to high, beating until soft peaks form when the whisk is lifted. Fold the egg whites into the egg yolk mixture in three batches, alternating with the flour. Beat well after each addition • Pour the melted butter into a medium-sized mixing bowl. Stir a large scoop of the batter into the butter until combined • Gently fold the butter mixture into the batter • Pour the batter into the prepared tins, dividing it evenly. Use a spatula to smooth the top • Place one cake tin on the upper rack and two on the lower rack. Bake for 10–12 minutes or until the edges pull away from the sides of the tin and the top springs back when lightly touched. The cake on the upper rack may be done before the cakes on the lower rack — monitor carefully • Invert each cake onto a cake rack, and allow to

COFFEE SYRUP

150 ml (5 fl oz) espresso coffee

200 g (6½ oz) caster (superfine) sugar

CHOCOLATE GLAZE

1 kg (2 lb) bittersweet couverture chocolate, finely chopped

450 ml (14 fl oz) double cream

½ cup sugar

100 g (3½ oz) glucose

300 ml (10 fl oz) water

6 leaves gelatin, softened in water*

400 g (13 oz) chocolate ganache (see page 349)

cool completely • To make the coffee butter cream, beat the eggs in a mixing bowl on medium speed for 10–12 minutes or until pale and thick • Combine the sugar and water in a medium saucepan. Bring to the boil over medium to high heat, stirring constantly to dissolve the sugar. Insert a sugar thermometer and cook until the syrup reaches 117°C (243°F) • With the mixer running on medium speed, pour the hot sugar syrup down the side of the bowl into the eggs. Avoid pouring the hot syrup onto the whisk as it will splatter. Increase the speed to medium-high and continue beating until the eggs have doubled in volume, about 7 minutes • Beat in the butter, 1 tablespoon at a time. Increase the speed to high and continue beating until shiny and smooth, about 2 minutes. If the butter cream should separate while you are adding the butter, stop beating and heat 2 tablespoons of double cream in a small saucepan. Whisk the hot cream into the butter to bring it together, and then continue adding the butter • Add the vanilla extract and coffee and beat until incorporated • The coffee butter cream may be used immediately or placed in an airtight container and refrigerated. Bring to room temperature and beat with a whisk until smooth before using • To make the coffee syrup, combine the coffee and sugar in a mixing bowl and stir to dissolve • To make the chocolate glaze, place the chocolate in a mixing bowl. Combine the cream and sugar in a heavy-based saucepan and bring to the boil. Remove from the heat immediately and pour over the chocolate. Stir to combine • Combine the glucose and water in a heavy-based saucepan and boil for 3–4 minutes to form a sugar syrup. Add the gelatin, stirring well • Incorporate the melted chocolate with the sugar syrup, mixing well with a wooden spoon. Allow to rest for

20 minutes before transferring to the refrigerator for 20 minutes. The chocolate glaze may be stored in 2-cup portions in the freezer for up to 3 months and is great for glazing the top of mousses, sponges or biscuits • To assemble the cake, place one of the sponge layers on a serving plate. Brush generously with the coffee syrup • Spread the chocolate ganache in a thin even layer over the sponge. Place a second sponge layer over the ganache. Brush generously with coffee syrup. Spread half of the coffee butter cream in a thin layer over the sponge • Place the third sponge layer, right-side up, over the coffee butter cream. Brush generously with the coffee syrup. Spread the remaining coffee butter cream onto the top of the sponge in a thin even layer. Freeze for 20 minutes • Heat the chocolate glaze until just warm in the top of a double boiler over a saucepan of simmering water. Remove the cake from the freezer and pour over the warm ganache, smoothing the top • Using a long serrated knife, trim about 6 mm (1/4 in) off the sides of the cake, so that you can see the layers. Cut the cake into 8 x 1.5-cm (3 x 1 1/2-in) rectangles and serve.

Chocolate truffle mousse

[serves 6]

I OWE MY TIME in the kitchens of Albert Roux for the confidence to produce this recipe. Don't take this recipe as gospel: the objective is to make a bombe, then add flavour with the help of whipped cream. It is all about timing and feel for the technique. Don't be disheartened if this takes a few attempts, have fun and give the experiments to friends as jazzed up chocolate mousse. The biggest problem you will face is if the chocolate is too cold when adding it to the bombe; it will go lumpy before your eyes.

100 ml (3½ fl oz) crème anglaise (see page 379)
100 g (3½ oz) caster (superfine) sugar
2½ tablespoons water
4 egg yolks
500 g (1 lb) dark couverture chocolate
600 ml (1 pt) thickened cream
1 layer of jaconde sponge (see page 352)
200 g (6½ oz) chocolate glaze (see page 353)
100 g (3½ oz) white couverture chocolate
Spearmint sorbet (see page 330)
Raspberry coulis (see page 331)

Pour the crème anglaise into a large ice-cube tray and freeze • To make the bombe, combine the sugar and water in a saucepan and bring to the boil. Insert a sugar thermometer and cook until the syrup reaches 121°C (249°F). Beat the egg yolks in a mixing bowl until pale and creamy. With the motor running, pour the hot sugar syrup carefully down the side of the bowl into the egg yolks. Continue to beat until the mixture is thick and glossy • Melt the chocolate in the top of a double boiler over a saucepan of simmering water • Whip the cream to ribbon stage (lift the beaters, the cream should fall back into the bowl in a ribbon-like stream) • Place six greased 1-cup capacity dariole moulds on a tray. Trim the sponge to fit inside the moulds. Line each mould with a layer of sponge • Incorporate the cream and the bombe in two batches using a rubber spatula. When three-quarters is incorporated fold in the chocolate. The mousse will start to set quite quickly. Spoon the mousse into the moulds. Unmould a frozen cube of crème anglaise and place in the centre of each mousse. Spoon in more mousse to fill the mould and smooth with a warm knife. Place in the freezer for 90 minutes or until set • Unmould each mousse by dipping the mould in boiling water and inverting onto a clean tray. Transfer to a cake rack, ready for glazing • Warm the chocolate glaze in the top of a double boiler over a saucepan of simmering water and pour over each mousse. Return to the freezer for 90 minutes. The mousses may be stored in the freezer for several weeks • To serve, remove the mousses from the freezer and transfer to the refrigerator to allow the anglaise to melt, about 2 hours. To create a checkerboard effect, finish each square with 1-cm ($^{1}/_{3}$ in) white chocolate squares made simply by spreading tempered white chocolate over a plastic sheet. Place in the refrigerator until set, then using a small paring knife cut individual squares and peel off the plastic. Serve with spearmint sorbet and garnish with dots of raspberry coulis.

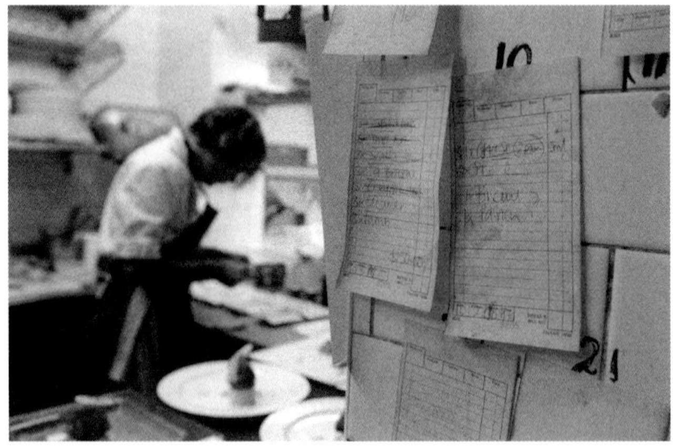

Warm chocolate biscuit pudding

[serves 6]

I HAVE TO DEDICATE this dessert to the legendary Michel Bras. A very good friend described this to me on returning from France where he had what he said was the meal of his life at Michel Bras's three-star restaurant in the Aubrac region. I have since become an avid follower of his cuisine and only recently made my own pilgrimage to this amazing hotel and restaurant. I was not disappointed.

CHOCOLATE GANACHE

½ cup double cream

125 g (4 oz) dark couverture chocolate, roughly chopped

2½ tablespoons clarified butter (see page 381)

100 g (3½ oz) Dutch cocoa powder

110 g (3¾ oz) dark couverture chocolate, finely chopped

50 g (1¾ oz) butter

2 tablespoons almond meal

2 eggs, separated

90 g (3 oz) sugar

2 tablespoons icing (confectioners') sugar

Pistachio ice cream (see pages 327–8)

To make the chocolate ganache, bring the cream to the boil in a small saucepan and pour over the roughly chopped chocolate. Stir well with a wooden spoon and pour into a shallow 12 x 20-cm (5 x 8-in) tray. Transfer to the freezer for 2 hours and allow to set before cutting into 3-cm (1¼ in) discs using a metal cutter. Return to the freezer • Cut six strips of greaseproof paper 15 x 8 cm (6 x 3 in). Brush with the clarified butter, then dust with cocoa powder. Curl the dusted strips into six 8 x 5 cm (3 x 2 in) metal rings and place on a greaseproof paper-lined baking tray • Melt the finely chopped chocolate and butter in the top of a double boiler over a saucepan of simmering water. Fold in the almond meal. Stir in the egg yolks • Beat the egg whites until soft peaks form, then add the sugar, a little at a time, beating until stiff and shiny to form a French meringue • Fold the meringue into the melted chocolate mixture • Spoon the mousse into the metal rings, pushing a ganache disc into the centre of each. Top with more mousse to cover the ganache disc. Transfer to the freezer for 3 hours or until solid • Preheat the oven to 200°C (400°F) • Place the frozen mousses in the oven for 13 minutes. Remove and rest for 1 minute. Carefully unmould using a knife and dust the tops with icing sugar. Serve with pistachio ice cream.

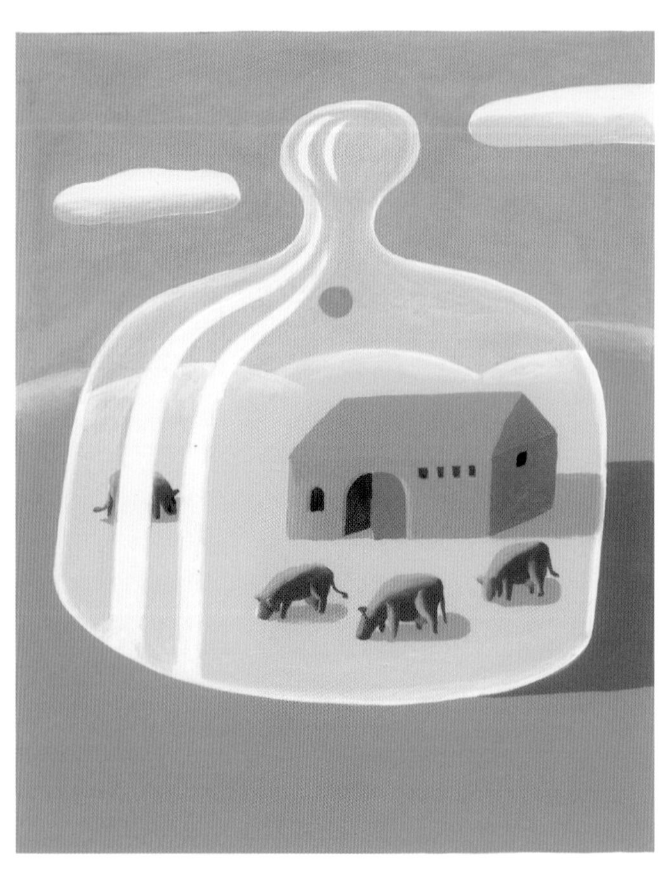

The Cheese

Menu planning with cheese can be the most important factor that decides the success of your cheese board. Remember: cheeses are seasonal. The flavour and texture of certain cheeses will vary from season to season. Always balance the cheese board with a variety of local and imported cheeses. Celebrate the fact that humans have developed a product that can travel the world and still arrive in prime condition at your table.

Ripeness is of huge importance to flavour development in cheese. Two factors to keep in mind are time and temperature. Cheese arrives at your table after possibly many months, sometimes years, of maturation in prime atmospheric conditions with controlled humidity. Only a professional can ensure success; so ask your local fromager about their commitment to this process — most modern cheesemakers don't have the time or space to mature their own product fully. Many of the cheeses you buy as a consumer are below standard because they haven't had time to ripen. If you buy them and they are unripe, leave them to mature in the refrigerator. Never buy cheese that is wrapped in plastic, as it can't breath and therefore will never ripen. Correct serving temperature is easier to control. Make sure you serve the cheese at the ideal temperature of 12–15°C (55–59°F). This will vary from variety to variety, so ask when purchasing.

There are six main cheese styles. Always remember that fewer varieties bring a more consistent result. One goat's, a sheep's milk cheese, at least one French and definitely a soft white or washed rind are essential to a well-balanced cheese plate. Always serve fresh bread, try to avoid acidic fruit, such as berries and citrus, and keep away from fancy cheese biscuits with strong flavours. Dried muscatels are always a healthy addition to a cheese plate.

Fresh curd cheese consists of curds, cottage cheese and non-processed spreads. This is the initial stage of the cheese making maturity and most cheeses will be only a few weeks old. I recommend cooking with this style of cheese because of its subtle flavour and versatile texture.

Soft rind or white cheeses have a fuzzy *penicillium candidum* coating. Brie is a classic example of this style of cheese; soft creamy and subtle in flavour. Try to look for handmade and well-matured versions, they are easy to spot as the white rind is a dark or off white and the cheese is quite rustic in appearance.

Natural-rind cheeses are a popular style with goat's cheese producers. They are normally blue-grey moulded, wrinkly and quite small in appearance. Fruity in flavour, this intensifies to a rich nutty flavour as the cheese matures. Good examples of this cheese are Crottin de Chavignol, Saint-Marcellin and Selles-sur-Cher.

Washed-rind cheeses were invented by the Trappist monks to enhance their meagre diet during fast days. These high-moisture moulded curd cheeses, which are matured in humid rooms, promote the growth of 'cat fur' style moulds. To discourage this, the newly formed cheese is rubbed or dunked into baths of salty water, wine or alcoholic solution. This produces a rather robust 'stinky' cheese that is orange in colour with quite a sticky texture. Spicy in flavour and subtle in texture, these cheeses are banned on French public transport because of their pungent

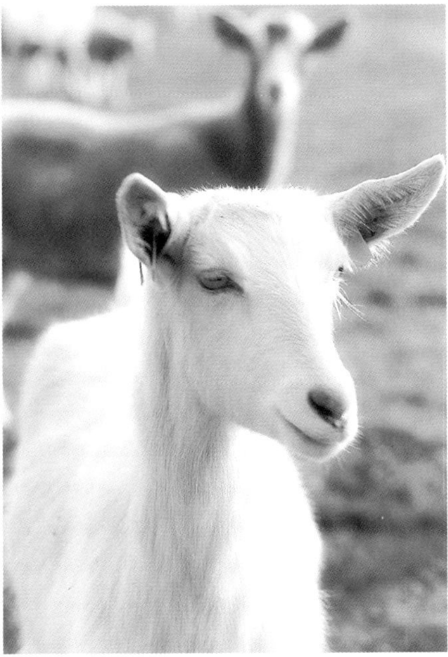

piquant smell. Good examples are found all around the world but the most famous are Epoisses, Herve and Munster.

Semi-soft cheeses are produced by cutting the curd to release some of the whey before they are placed in moulds. They are then lightly pressed to create a soft mature cheese that is firm enough to be used in various cooking processes, such as for grating in quiches and soufflés. I call most of these 'supermarket cheeses'. To prevent a hard rind forming and extra moisture loss through maturation on the supermarket shelves, most are wrapped in plastic. Better examples are Raclette, Edam and Fontina.

Hard cooked cheeses are produced by the curd being cut very finely, then heated to lose as much of the whey as possible to ensure a firm cheese while maturing with no influence of mould. The process varies greatly from cheese to cheese. Hard cheeses are user friendly, but must be stored properly as they are prone to absorbing other refrigerator flavours. Make sure to properly cover the cut surface of the cheese with foil or plastic wrap. The easiest of all cheeses to match with wine:

white or red wine is suited to the subtle texture and nutty salty flavours usually associated with this style. Good examples from all parts of the world are plentiful, such as cheddar, Manchego, Cantal, Gruyere and Parmigiano Reggiano.

Blue cheeses are neither pressed nor cooked. The curd is normally crumbled, then drained and moulded, turned every day, and after a few weeks unmoulded and rubbed with salt. The blue mould is a strain of penicillin that is added to the milk before the rennet. The cheese will not turn blue unless it is exposed to air to breathe. This is achieved by piercing the cheese with rods. Always store blue cheese wrapped in aluminium (aluminum) foil. Good examples are Stilton, Roquefort, Gorgonzola, Gippsland blue and Danish blue.

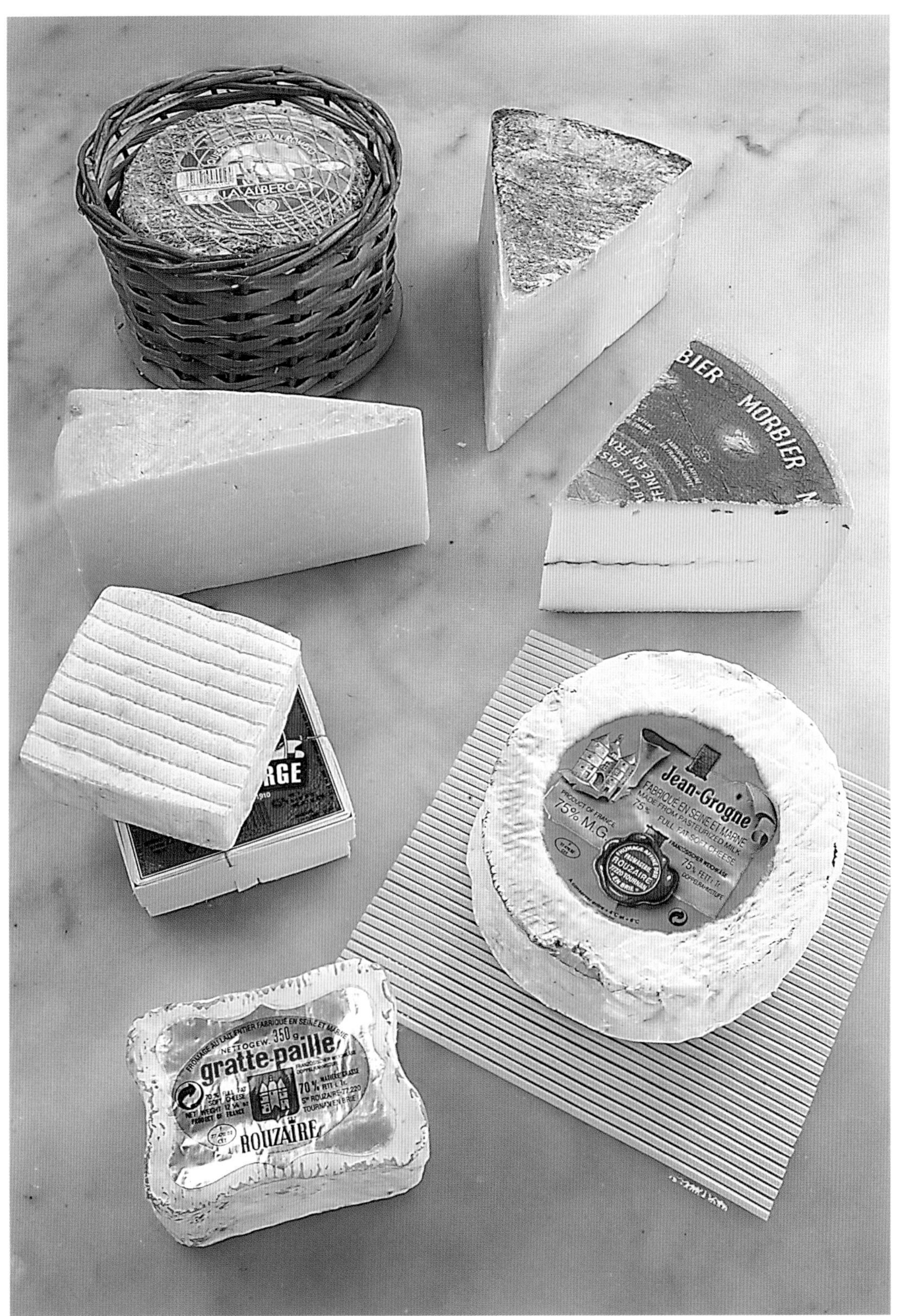

A selection of cheeses

Twice-cooked cheese soufflé

[serves 8]

An absolute must for any cheese aficionado and for anyone who has the time to impress. This is an easy and affordable recipe in which the bulk of the preparation can be done well in advance. The grated cheese to sprinkle over the top of the cooked soufflés can be leftover cheese from a previous occasion, try to use a hard cheese. My wine recommendation is a controversial one: Jacob's Creek Riesling; in fact, any reputable New World fresh, young, zesty riesling will suffice.

10 tablespoons coarsely grated Gruyere cheese

10 tablespoons béchamel sauce (see page 373)

10 egg yolks

10 egg whites

Pinch of salt

50 g (1¾ oz) butter

50 g (1¾ oz) plain (all-purpose) flour

400 ml (13 fl oz) double cream

100 g (3½ oz) finely grated Gruyere cheese

Salt and freshly ground pepper

100 g (3½ oz) silverbeet (Swiss chard), chopped into batons

1 tablespoon olive oil

50 g (1¾ oz) smoked ham, chopped into batons

Preheat the oven to 170°C (335°F) • Place eight ovenproof 1-cup capacity dariole moulds in the refrigerator • Whisk the coarsely grated Gruyere, béchamel sauce and egg yolks in a mixing bowl • Beat the egg whites until soft peaks form, add the salt and continue to beat until stiff peaks form. Gently fold the egg whites into the béchamel mixture • Butter and flour the moulds, remembering to brush upwards in the direction the soufflé will rise. Spoon in the soufflé mixture to fill each mould • Place in the oven and bake for 8 minutes • Unmould the soufflés onto a greased baking tray, and cover with plastic wrap. This can be done a day in advance • Preheat the oven to 180°C (350°F) • Pour 2½ tablespoons of cream over each soufflé, sprinkle over the finely grated Gruyere, then season with salt and pepper • Place in the oven and bake for 10 minutes or until they have risen to their original state • Blanch the silverbeet in boiling salted water for 2 minutes or until cooked • Heat the olive oil in a heavy-based frying pan, add the ham and silverbeet and sauté for 1 minute over medium heat • Transfer the soufflés from the baking tray to serving plates using a fish slice. Position in the centre of each plate and garnish with the silverbeet and ham. Serve immediately.

Goat's cheese wrapped in puff pastry

Twice-cooked cheese soufflé

Goat's cheese fromage blanc

Goat's cheese fromage blanc

[serves 6]

THIS IS THE IDEAL recipe to have on hand for the big night when your confidence is high, the right sort of crowd are coming for dinner and you are out to impress. This dish is best described as delicate and pretty, and is for guests who are not big cheese fans. I recommend a glass of botrytis semillon or Sauternes to lick through the fattiness and acidity of this dish. The sweetness of the wine will complement the prunes.

200 g (6½ oz) fresh goat's curd
1 cup pouring (light) cream
2 shallots, chopped
1 tablespoon finely chopped flat-leaf parsley
½ tablespoon finely chopped chives
Juice of 1 lemon
Salt and freshly ground pepper
6 slices of purchased fruit bread
2 tablespoons extra virgin olive oil
12 pitted prunes, soaked in Armagnac (see page 328)

Place the goat's curd in a bowl, fold in the cream, shallots, parsley, chives, lemon juice, salt and pepper. To prevent the mixture from splitting ensure all the ingredients are cold • Toast the bread until it is crispy. Brush with the olive oil and place a piece of toast on each serving plate. Using two tablespoons that have been dipped in hot water, quenelle the fromage blanc onto each slice of toast • Serve with two prunes and drizzle a little of the prune and Armagnac juice over and around each plate.

Goat's cheese wrapped in puff pastry

[serves 4]

To be completely honest I am not a goat's cheese lover, but when it is served warm or hot, the cheese becomes luscious and delicate — and I see it in a different light.

4 x 80 g (2¾ oz) goat's cheese
400 g (13 oz) puff pastry (see page 54)
2 eggs
2½ tablespoons water
100 g (3½ oz) chanterelle mushrooms
1 tablespoon olive oil
Salt and freshly ground pepper
16 peeled walnuts (see page 391)
1½ cups mixed salad leaves and herbs
2 shallots, finely chopped
8 garlic croutons (see page 383)
3 tablespoons hazelnut vinaigrette (see page 396)

Preheat the oven to 180°C (350°F) • Remove the bitter rind from the goat's cheese with a sharp knife • Roll out the puff pastry to 3 mm (⅛ in) thick. Rest in the refrigerator for 30 minutes to make the puff pastry easier to cut • Wrap each cheese in the pastry, folding and trimming around the cheese to ensure the parcels are fully sealed and to prevent the melted cheese leaking during baking • In a shallow bowl, lightly beat the eggs with the water. Brush the top of each goat's cheese parcel with the egg wash • Place in the oven and bake for 15 minutes or until golden • Wipe, scrape and trim the chanterelles • Heat the olive oil in a heavy-based frying pan, add the chanterelles and sauté for 2 minutes over medium heat. Season with salt and pepper, remove from the heat and add the walnuts • Combine the salad leaves, shallots and croutons in a mixing bowl, dress lightly with the hazelnut vinaigrette and season with salt and pepper • Place each goat's cheese parcel in the centre of a serving plate. Scatter the salad around each parcel, drizzle over a little more dressing, and place the chanterelles and walnuts on each plate. Serve.

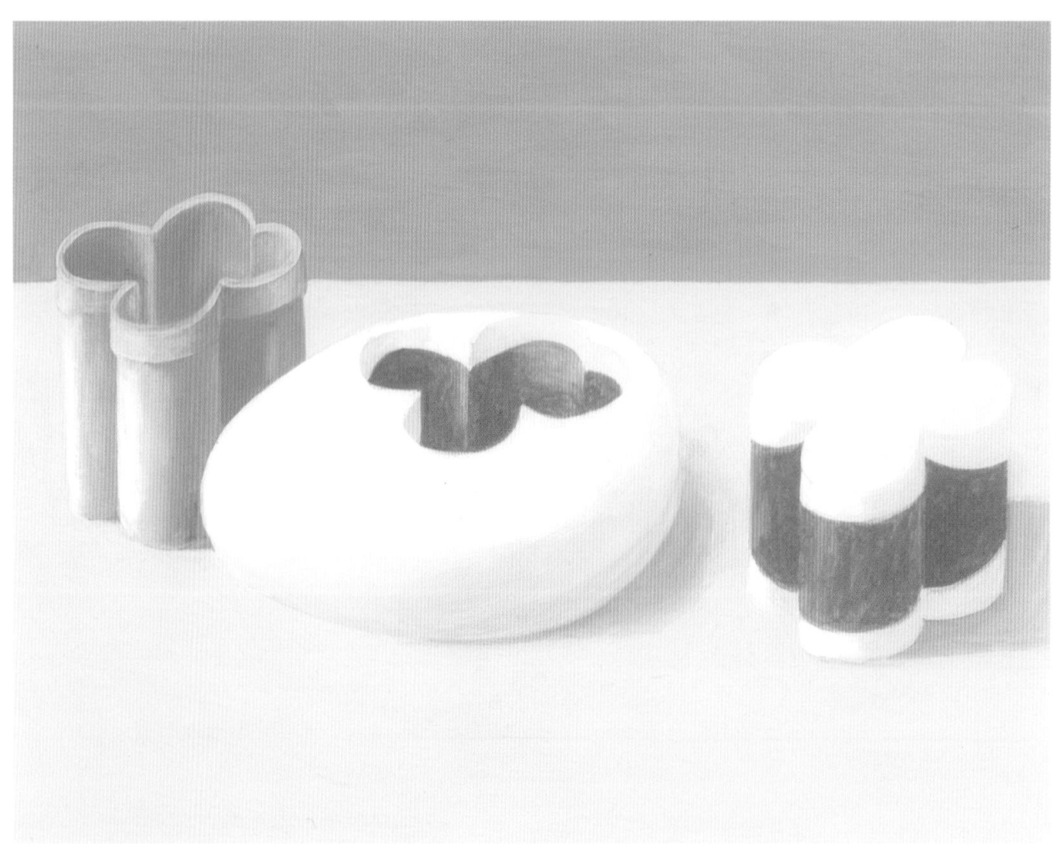

Foundation Recipes

Apple and pear chutney

[makes about 3 cups]

THIS SLIGHTLY SPICY chutney is one of those indispensable recipes that I continue to find uses for. It has a good three-month shelf life and my favourite pairings with this chutney are foie gras, game terrines and good washed-rind cheeses.

200 g (6½ oz) grated Granny Smith apples

½ tablespoon salt

2 onions, chopped

Juice and zest of 2 oranges

300 g (10 oz) caster (superfine) sugar

2 tablespoons ground cinnamon

2 tablespoons ground nutmeg

½ teaspoon cayenne pepper

20 g (¾ oz) freshly grated ginger

2 cups dry white wine

Pinch of saffron

250 g (8 oz) chopped tomatoes

500 g (1 lb) chopped William pears

100 g (3½ oz) sultanas

Combine the apples, salt, onions, orange juice and zest, sugar, cinnamon, nutmeg, cayenne pepper, ginger, wine and saffron in a large heavy-based saucepan. Bring to the boil, reduce heat and simmer for 1 hour • Add the tomatoes, pears and sultanas, bring to the boil, stir well and remove from the heat. Allow to cool, pour into sterilised jars straight from the dishwasher and keep in the refrigerator for a minimum of 2 weeks before using.

Asparagus mousse

[makes 6 portions]

An ideal recipe for when zucchini (courgette) flowers pop up at the market. There is no better way to celebrate this occasion than to fill the flowers with asparagus mousse and steam them for 3–4 minutes. When you have mastered the art of deboning a baby snapper, fill with this colourful and tasty mousse.

1 tablespoon olive oil
1 onion, finely diced
1 clove of garlic, crushed
2 leeks, thinly sliced
5 bunches asparagus, finely chopped
2 cups baby spinach

Heat the olive oil in a heavy-based saucepan, add the onion and garlic and cook for 5 minutes or until soft • Add the leek and cook for 2–3 minutes or until soft and tender. Add the asparagus and cook for 4–5 minutes. Add the spinach and cook for 2 minutes or until wilted • Blitz in the food processor until puréed. Transfer to the refrigerator for 25 minutes.

Basil purée

[serves 6]

USE THIS PURÉE in dressings and as a flavouring.

$1\frac{1}{2}$ tablespoons salt
Leaves of 1 bunch of basil

Blanch the basil in boiling salted water for 3 minutes or until the basil starts to break up when rubbed between two fingers. Refresh in iced water for 3–4 minutes then strain • Transfer the basil to a food processor and blend until smooth • Reserve in the fridge until required.

Béchamel sauce

[makes 2 cups]

IN FRANCE, IT IS one of the four basic sauces called *meres* or 'mother sauces' from which all other sauces derive. It is also known as white sauce. It is a smooth, white sauce made from a roux of flour, boiled milk and butter. It is usually served with white meat, eggs and vegetables.

Marquis Louis de Béchamel (1603–1703), a seventeenth-century financier who held the honorary post of chief steward to King Louis XIV's (1643–1715) household, is said to have invented béchamel sauce when trying to come up with a new way of serving and eating dried cod. There are no historical records to verify that he was a gourmet, a cook, or the inventor of béchamel sauce. The seventeenth-century Duke of Escars is credited with stating: 'That fellow Béchamel has all the luck! I was serving breast of chicken a la crème more than 20 years before he was born, but I have never had the chance of giving my name to even the most modest sauce.'

2 cups milk
1 onion studded with 5 cloves
1 bay leaf
2 sprigs of thyme
50 g (1¾ oz) butter
50 g (1¾ oz) plain (all-purpose) flour
Pinch of cayenne pepper

Heat the milk with the onion, bay leaf and thyme in a heavy-based saucepan and bring to the boil. Continue to boil for 3–4 minutes. Leave to infuse for 20 minutes, then strain • Melt the butter in a heavy-based saucepan, add the flour and cayenne pepper and cook on low heat, gently stirring with a wooden spoon, until the flour and butter come together. Cook briefly until the aromatic nuttiness of the flour is apparent. Quickly whisk in the boiling milk until smooth and shiny. Remove from the heat and continue to whisk for 1–2 minutes. Place in an airtight container and refrigerate until required. The sauce will keep for 3–4 days.

Beurre blanc

[makes 3 cups]

A sauce I just had to include because it is classic and forthright in its purpose of harmonising the perfect piece of cooked fish or chicken without interupting the flavour or texture.

2½ tablespoons olive oil
5 shallots, finely sliced
2 cloves of garlic, finely sliced
2 sprigs of thyme
1 bay leaf
10 white peppercorns
*150 ml (5 fl oz) vermouth (Noilly Prat)**
150 ml (5 fl oz) dry white wine
150 ml (5 fl oz) Champagne vinegar
2 cups chicken stock (see page 378)
250 g (8 oz) cultured butter, chopped into dice*
½ tablespoon double cream
Juice of ½ lemon

Heat the olive oil in a heavy-based saucepan, add the shallots, garlic, thyme, bay leaf and white peppercorns and cook for 5 minutes or until soft • Add the vermouth, white wine and vinegar and reduce until evaporated • Add the stock and reduce by half • Slowly whisk in the butter, being careful not to split the sauce. If the sauce splits add a ladleful of warm chicken stock and bring to the boil for 1 minute • Whisk in the cream and pass through a fine sieve. Season with lemon juice. Reserve in a warm part of the kitchen until required.

Black olive tapenade

[makes 2 cups]

Many versions exist, but capers and anchovies are essential to this recipe: they transport it to a different dimension with their tangy and salty aromas. For the simplest of ideas, brush some sourdough with extra virgin olive oil, grill (broil) until golden and crisp, top with a spoonful of tapenade and garnish with a slice of tomato.

*300 g (10 oz) pitted Ligurian or Niçoise olives**
*8 Ortiz anchovies**
2 cloves of garlic
Juice of ½ lemon
Salt and freshly ground pepper
100 ml (3½ fl oz) extra virgin olive oil

Combine the olives, anchovies and garlic in a food processor and blitz to form a smooth paste. Season with lemon juice, salt and pepper • Store in the refrigerator with a layer of olive oil over the contents to protect the tapenade from losing its flavour and drying out.

Caramel calvados sauce

[makes 2 cups]

THE SIMPLICITY OF ADDING Calvados to the caramel gives a lift to the sauce. This caramel Calvados sauce is wonderful with apple dishes, such as roasted apples with vanilla ice cream or apple crumble.

½ cup caster (superfine) sugar
200 ml (7 fl oz) double cream
*2½ tablespoons Calvados**

Melt the sugar in a heavy-based saucepan over low heat for 3–4 minutes or until golden brown • Stir in the cream and reduce for 4–5 minutes until thickened. Add the Calvados and bring to the boil. Remove and store in an airtight container in the refrigerator for up to 2 weeks. Serve hot.

Cèpe powder

10 g (⅓ oz) dried cèpes
Pinch of salt and white pepper

Place the dried cèpes in a warm, dry place for approximately 24 hours to ensure they are completely dry and brittle • Grind the dried cèpes to a fine powder with the salt and pepper in a pestle and mortar or a spice grinder • Store in an airtight container for up to 1 month. Use as required.

Chicken jus

[makes 4 cups]

The word jus simply describes the essence of this recipe: the concentrated flavours of roast chicken bottled in a sauce. I like to serve the sauce with steamed meat and fish, or as a dressing for a warm chicken salad.

2 kg (4½ lb) chicken wings, chopped
*100 g (3½ oz) goose fat**
1 tablespoon olive oil
5 shallots
5 sprigs of thyme
1 bay leaf
10 white peppercorns
2 cloves of garlic, crushed
8 cups chicken stock (see page 378)

Preheat the oven to 180°C (350°F) • Place the chicken wings and goose fat in a baking tray and roast in the oven for 20 minutes or until golden brown • Heat the olive oil in a large saucepan, add the shallots, thyme, bay leaf, peppercorns and garlic and cook for 5 minutes or until the shallots are soft and tender. Add the chicken wings, goose fat and chicken stock and gently simmer over low heat for 1 hour. Pass through a fine sieve, then serve or store in an airtight container in the fridge for 1 week or the freezer for 1 month.

Chicken mousse

[serves 6]

620 g (1¼ lb) chicken breast fillets
1 teaspoon salt
3 eggs
4 egg yolks
1 cup double cream

Place the lid, bowl and blade of the food processor in the freezer for 20 minutes • To make the chicken mousse, blitz the chicken and salt in the food processor • Add the eggs and egg yolks, one at a time, pulsing between each addition • Add the cream and pulse to incorporate • Rest the mousse in the fridge for 30 minutes to set. Use as required.

Chicken stock

[makes 20 cups]

CHICKEN WINGS MAKE A far better quality stock than ordinary carcases. The expense is always justified in terms of the end product. The yield derived from the wings is double that of carcases. The end stock should be clear, gelatinous and free of fat.

I think it is a good idea to make a large quantity of stock and to freeze it in 4-cup batches.

5 kg (11 lb) chicken wings
40 cups cold water
2 large carrots, roughly chopped
2 large leeks, roughly chopped
4 large onions, roughly chopped
4 sticks of celery, roughly chopped
1 head of garlic, peeled
1 bunch of thyme
2 bay leaves
10 white peppercorns

Place the chicken wings in a large stockpot and cover with the water. Bring to the boil, skimming any impurities that rise to the surface. Reduce the heat to low and simmer for 5 minutes, constantly skimming • Add the carrot, leek, onion, celery, garlic, thyme, bay leaves and peppercorns. Continue to skim the surface on a constant basis removing any oil or fat. Simmer for 7–8 hours. Do not replenish with water, as this will dilute the flavour and texture of the stock. Strain and refrigerate until needed.

Crème anglaise

[makes 4 cups]

There are two types of custard: baked and cooked. This is the cooked or pouring custard that can be served warm or cold over cakes and ice creams. It may even be made into ice cream. Any amount of flavouring can be added to create colour and textural contrast. I go by the French name for this recipe, as it sounds more delicious than just custard!

2 cups milk
2 vanilla beans, split lengthwise and seeds scraped*
200 ml (7 fl oz) double cream
8 egg yolks
1 cup caster (superfine) sugar

Combine the milk, vanilla seeds and cream in a heavy-based saucepan and bring to the boil • Beat the egg yolks and sugar in a mixing bowl until pale and creamy • Gently incorporate the egg mixture with the milk mixture and return to the stove, stirring constantly with a wooden spoon, for 3–6 minutes or until the mixture coats the back of the spoon • Strain through a fine sieve into a bowl over an ice bath. Stir occasionally until cool, then store in an airtight container for up to 4 days. Serve with hot desserts such as apple pie or chocolate fondant.

Crème chantilly

[serves 6]

A very basic recipe for the adornment of heavy rich desserts, or use to decorate cakes and biscuits. Ensure all ingredients and tools are cold to prevent the cream from splitting.

2 cups double cream
½ cup sugar
1 tablespoon Cointreau

Combine all of the ingredients in a food processor and blitz for 1–2 minutes or until soft peaks have formed. Use immediately. The cream will keep in the refrigerator for 24 hours.

Clarification of sauces

[makes 8 cups]

Jellies and consommés are two of those great professional cooking wonders that mere mortals never seem to be able to achieve. Well, the secret is no more, follow the procedure below and you will see how easy it is to make lovely clear soup or bouillabaisse.

1 bulb of fennel
1 onion
1 stick of celery
1 carrot
9 egg whites

Blitz the fennel, onion, celery and carrot in the food processor • Add the egg whites. Whisk the egg white mixture into a sauce or stock that needs clarifying and continue whisking until a raft forms on the surface • Simmer for 20–40 minutes depending on the clarity required. Do not allow to boil • Pass through a cheesecloth-lined sieve while the stock is still hot and use immediately.

Clarified butter

CLARIFYING BUTTER IS the process of removing the milk solids that burn at high temperatures. Clarified butter has a much higher smoking point than most oils. To finish with the amount of clarified butter you need, start with about 33 per cent more unsalted butter than the amount required. For example, if you want 6 tablespoons of clarified butter, start with 8 tablespoons of butter. Chop the butter into tablespoon-sized chunks and melt in a heavy-based saucepan over medium heat; do not stir. Continue to cook for 20 minutes or until the solids drop to the bottom of the pan and begin to turn brown. When the bubbling subsides, strain the butter through a fine sieve. Clarified butter will keep for months in an airtight container in the refrigerator.

Double chicken stock

[makes 4 cups]

THIS STOCK CAN EASILY be turned into a sauce by reducing it until the right consistency is achieved, or a tasty soup, simply by adding vegetables and seasoning.

2½ tablespoons olive oil
1 kg (2¼ lb) chicken wings
6 cups chicken stock (see page 378)
3 shallots, thinly sliced
3 cloves garlic, thinly sliced
4 sprigs of thyme
2 bay leaves
10 white peppercorns

Preheat the oven to 180°C (350°F) • Place the olive oil in a shallow baking pan, add the chicken wings and roast in the oven for 20 minutes or until golden • Drain the fat from the pan and discard • Combine the wings with the remaining ingredients in a heavy-based stockpot. Bring to the boil over high heat, then reduce heat to low and simmer for about 2 hours • Strain through a coarse sieve, then through a fine sieve. Store in an airtight container in the refrigerator for up to 5 days, or freeze for 1 month.

Eight-spice powder

[makes 130 g (4 oz)]

20 g (2/3 oz) juniper berries
30 g (1 oz) whole star anise
15 g (1/2 oz) white peppercorns
15 g (1/2 oz) cinnamon quills
15 g (1/2 oz) cloves
1 pinch saffron threads
25 g (3/4 oz) salt
10 g (1/3 oz) cardamom pods

Grind all the spices to a fine powder in a spice grinder • Toast the spices in a large pan over a medium heat. Allow to cool • Store in an airtight container and use as required.

Frangipane or almond cream

[makes 2 cups]

One of the earliest known baking recipes still in constant demand by the modern connoisseur is sweet pastry. Dating back to the late sixteenth century the frangipane tart was simply a baked almond and pistachio custard. The recipe has evolved to now include only almond. Clafouti is a derivative of this classic and is simply frangipane filled with marinated cherries baked and served hot with crème anglaise.

100 g (3½ oz) butter, softened
100 g (3½ oz) sugar
100 g (3½ oz) ground almonds, sifted
¼ cup plain (all-purpose) flour, sifted
2 eggs
5 drops of vanilla extract
100 ml (3½ fl oz) crème pâtissière (see page 335)

Cream the butter and sugar until pale • Gradually add the ground almonds and flour to the butter and sugar, mixing well • Add the eggs and beat well • Add the vanilla and crème pâtissière and stir to combine. Place in an airtight container and refrigerate for 30 minutes or until firm. Use as required. The frangipane may be refrigerated for up to 14 days and is also suitable for freezing once cooked in tartlets, clafoutis, etc.

Gaille espice marinade

[makes enough marinade for 6–8 birds]

THE NAME MAY BE confusing, but it is that way for a reason. The translation is spicy quail marinade and that is what I originally used the marinade for under the direction of mentor John Burton Race. I now use the recipe to marinate everything from mutton to chicken and pork. I also use this as a marinade for farmed pheasants to compensate for the lack of gamey flavour.

Juice of 8 oranges
Juice of 8 limes
2 cups coconut milk
3 tablespoons soft brown sugar
2 tablespoons Madras curry paste
2 tablespoons Malay curry powder
2 tablespoons freshly grated ginger
2 bird's eye chillies, crushed
2 sprigs of coriander (cilantro)
100 ml (3½ fl oz) sweet soy sauce
*100 ml (3½ fl oz) kecap manis**
200 ml (7 fl oz) olive oil

Combine all ingredients and allow 24 hours to marinate.

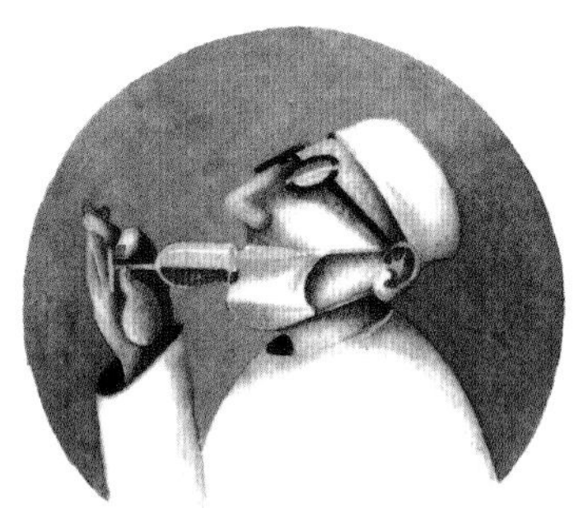

Garlic croutons

5 thick slices of sourdough bread
2½ tablespoons extra virgin olive oil
1 clove of garlic, peeled

Remove crusts from the bread and chop into 1 cm (⅓ in) cubes. Toss the bread cubes in the extra virgin olive oil and bake for 10 minutes or until golden. Remove and rub with garlic. Store in an airtight container for up to 3 days.

Herbed breadcrumbs

[makes 300 g (10 oz)]

The ideas and uses for these breadcrumbs will become quite apparent after making and tasting the fresh, aromatic ingredients. Use to enhance simple meats, such as chicken or grilled fish. After sprinkling on the chosen product, simply grill for 60 seconds to release the flavours.

1 bunch of curly-leaf parsley, chopped
1 tablespoon chopped tarragon
½ tablespoon thyme leaves
250 g (8 oz) dried breadcrumbs
2 cloves of garlic, crushed
Salt and freshly ground pepper
1½ tablespoons extra virgin olive oil

Blitz the herbs, breadcrumbs and garlic in a food processor. Season with salt and pepper and add a little of the olive oil. Use for coating roasted meats, sprinkling on steamed fish, in stuffings and farces. The herbed breadcrumbs can be stored in the refrigerator for 2–3 weeks.

HOLLANDAISE/BÉARNAISE SAUCE

[makes 1 cup]

HOLLANDAISE IS A BUTTERY rich sauce that has many uses and many derivatives. Béarnaise sauce, a variation of hollandaise sauce, was invented in Paris in the nineteenth century by chef Jules Colette at the restaurant Le Pavillon Henri IV. It was named Béarnaise in Henri's honour, as he was born in Béarn, a region in the Pyrénées mountains in south-west France. It is said that every chef at the restaurant tried to claim the recipe as his own.

Other derivatives of hollandaise sauce include: sauce aux capres (add drained capers); maltaise (add blood oranges); mousseline or chantilly (add whipped cream); and moutarde (with Dijon mustard).

6 egg yolks
2½ tablespoons dry white wine
2½ tablespoons white wine vinegar
Salt and freshly ground pepper
200 ml (7 fl oz) warm clarified butter (see page 381)
Juice of ½ lemon

Combine the egg yolks, white wine, vinegar and salt and pepper in a large mixing bowl • Whisk over a saucepan of simmering water for 3 minutes or until thick. Remove from the heat and continue to whisk for 1 minute to prevent lumps. If lumps do occur, strain the sauce through cheesecloth to remove them • Return to the heat and slowly whisk in the butter. If the mixture is too thick, thin with a little warm water. Continue whisking until all the butter has been used. If the sauce splits, add a ladleful of cold water and continue to whisk. Season with a little lemon juice. Keep at room temperature for no more than 3 hours. The sauce must be served at room temperature • To make béarnaise sauce, simply replace the white wine vinegar with tarragon vinegar and add chopped tarragon to the finished sauce.

Lentils de Puy

[serves 8]

200 g ($6\frac{1}{2}$ oz) de Puy lentils
*1 bouquet garni**
$\frac{1}{4}$ carrot, roughly diced
$\frac{1}{4}$ leek, roughly diced
$\frac{1}{4}$ onion, roughly diced
4 cloves of garlic, roughly chopped
*1 x 50 g ($1\frac{3}{4}$ oz) piece of ventrèche bacon**
Chicken stock to cover (see page 378)

Place all the ingredients in a medium-sized heavy-based saucepan. • Cover with chicken stock and bring to a simmer. Cook until tender, adding more stock if necessary • When the lentils are cooked through, strain off the liquid and discard. Remove the vegetables, the ventrèche and the bouquet garni and discard • Allow to cool and reheat as required.

Madeira jelly

[Makes 12 cups]

Madeira jelly is a wonderful accompaniment to terrines and charcuterie platters when set with gelatin. It can also be served hot as a soup with ravioli or braised baby vegetables. Serve with a glass of Madeira.

STOCK
2 x 500 g (1 lb) veal shins
2 onions, cut in half
*3 cups Madeira**
*3 cups ruby port**
3 large carrots, diced
1 head of celery, diced
2 leeks, diced
1 kg (2 lb) boiling chicken
2 kg (4 lb) ox tail

Ask your butcher to split the veal shins in half lengthwise to expose the marrow • Place the onions in a heavy-based frying pan over medium heat and cook for 25 minutes or until blackened and burnt looking • Combine the Madeira and port in a heavy-based saucepan, bring to the boil and reduce by half • Reserve a quarter of the vegetables for the clarification • Combine all of the stock ingredients in a large stockpot. Over high heat bring to the boil, skimming the surface to remove any impurities. Reduce heat to low and simmer for 3–4 hours, constantly skimming • Taste, if satisfied, strain through a coarse

12 cups chicken stock (see page 378)
1 head of garlic, peeled
1 bunch of thyme
10 white peppercorns
20 cups water
100 g (3½ oz) tomato paste
100 ml (3½ fl oz) light soy sauce

CLARIFICATION

8 egg whites
*1 bouquet garni**
Salt and freshly ground pepper

*15 leaves of titanium gelatin**
4 cups water

sieve, then repeat through a fine sieve • If the stock is cloudy, combine the reserved vegetables with the egg whites, bouquet garni and salt and pepper in a mixing bowl. Clarify by whisking into the stock over low heat. Continue to whisk to prevent the stock from catching and burning on the bottom of the pan. When the stock has reached 80°C (176°F), the egg white will form a raft on the surface, this will catch and filter out the impurities and transform the stock to a clear colour. Continue to cook for 30 minutes. Strain through a cheesecloth-lined sieve • Soak the gelatin leaves in cold water for 10 minutes. Remove and squeeze out the excess water • Bring 2 cups of the stock to the boil in a heavy-based saucepan. Remove from the heat and add the gelatin. Rest for a few minutes, then stir until completely dissolved. Stir this liquid into the remaining stock. Transfer to an airtight container and place in the refrigerator for 2 hours. Remember, the longer it is left in the refrigerator the harder it will set • To use the jelly once it has set, warm in a heavy-based saucepan over low heat. Do not allow to boil. Pour the jelly onto a cold plate or into a mould and place in the refrigerator for 20 minutes to set. Remove and dice the jelly and place around the edge of a terrine, parfait or rillette.

Mayonnaise

[makes 2 cups]

WELL, EVERYONE KNOWS what it is and most people eat it, but how many people know how to make it? Have a go and increase your confidence and repertoire.

3 egg yolks
1 tablespoon Dijon mustard
2½ tablespoons sherry vinegar
Salt and freshly ground pepper
300 ml (10 fl oz) sunflower oil
100 ml (3½ fl oz) extra virgin olive oil
1 tablespoon warm water
Juice of ½ lemon

Combine the egg yolks, mustard, vinegar, and salt and pepper in a food processor • While the motor is running, slowly pour in a little of the vegetable oil. Continue adding the oil very slowly until half has been incorporated. Drizzle in the remaining oil in a thin stream until incorporated. Add a little warm water if the mayonnaise gets too thick • Season with a squeeze of lemon juice.

MAYONNAISE VARIATIONS

Aioli The French word for garlic is ail. Sometimes called the butter of Provence, aioli, a common ingredient in Provençal food, is believed to have originated there because the landscape is not suited to cows; more to sheep, goats and olive trees. Aioli is a garlic-flavoured mayonnaise that is served as a sauce for a variety of garnishes and main courses. To make aioli, crush 8 cloves of garlic with ½ teaspoon of sea salt using a mortar and pestle. Incorporate with the mayonnaise recipe above.

Green mayonnaise To make a 'green mayonnaise' with a lovely herbaceous flavour and distinctive green colouring, combine two parts mayonnaise with one part chlorophyll. To make 2 tablespoons of chlorophyll blend the leaves from 1 bunch of curly-leaf parsley with 200 ml (7 fl oz) of cold water for 5 to 7 minutes or until the water has turned bright green. Strain through a fine sieve reserving the liquid only. Gently warm the liquid in a saucepan over medium heat, stirring occasionally. When the liquid reaches approximately 70–80°C (158–176°F) (just before it boils, but ensuring that it does not boil), the water will separate from the chlorophyll creating a 'split' liquid. Remove from the heat and immediately strain through a fine muslin cloth reserving the green purée left in the cloth. Discard the liquid. Chill the chlorophyll purée and use as required.

Mary Rose sauce [serves 4] To 300 ml (10 fl oz) mayonnaise add 100 ml (3½ fl oz) tomato ketchup, Tabasco, salt and pepper to taste. Whisk together until incorporated.

Mornay sauce

[makes 3–4 cups]

THIS RECIPE CAN BE glazed under a grill (broiler) or by blowtorch to achieve a lovely golden colour.

2 cups béchamel sauce (see page 373)
200 ml (7 fl oz) fish stock (see page 243)
100 g ($3\frac{1}{2}$ oz) grated Gruyere cheese
200 ml (7 fl oz) hollandaise sauce (see page 385)
Juice of $\frac{1}{2}$ lemon

Warm the béchamel sauce over low heat and whisk in the fish stock and cheese. Remove from the heat • Whisk in the hollandaise and season with lemon juice. Serve with grilled fish or prawns.

Mussel stock

[makes 450 ml ($14\frac{1}{2}$ fl oz)]

AN EXCELLENT SUBSTITUTE FOR fish stock in many sauce and soup recipes.

3 shallots, peeled and thinly sliced
5 sprigs of thyme
3 cloves of garlic, peeled and thinly sliced
50 ml ($1\frac{3}{4}$ fl oz) olive oil
2 kg ($4\frac{1}{2}$ lb) mussels, washed and debearded under cold running water
$1\frac{1}{2}$ cups white wine

In a heavy-based large saucepan sweat the shallots, thyme and garlic in the olive oil over a high heat for 2 minutes or until transparent • Add the mussels and continually stir for 30 seconds. Deglaze with the white wine. Cover the pot with a lid and cook for a further 5 minutes or until the mussels have opened. Remove from the heat and remove the mussels (they can be used for another purpose) • Strain the liquid through a fine sieve and use as required.

Percierge

[makes 200 g (6½ oz)]

2 tablespoons finely chopped curly-leaf parsley

1 teaspoon fresh thyme leaves

2 cloves of garlic

2½ tablespoons olive oil

500 g (1 lb) dried breadcrumbs

Place all of the ingredients in a food processor and pulse until the mixture is fine • Store in an airtight container in the refrigerator for 2–3 weeks.

Poached Pears

[makes 8]

Poached pears is one of those classic recipes that everyone thinks they know how to do, but don't be complacent — it is easy to overcook the pears. Check them regularly after 15 minutes in 5-minute intervals by inserting a thin knife or skewer. If the pears are cooked, the utensil should slide in with ease. Serve hot or cold with vanilla ice cream.

8 William pears, peeled

2 sticks of cinnamon

1 vanilla bean, split lengthwise and seeds scraped*

200 g (6½ oz) sugar

600 ml (1 pt) water or Sauternes or ½ and ½

Juice of 1 lemon

If a pear purée is required, remove the core and stem from each pear • Place all of the ingredients in a large heavy-based saucepan. Bring to the boil over high heat, reduce the heat to low and simmer. Add a cartouche* to the top of the pears, to ensure they are not exposed to air, cover and poach for 25 minutes or until soft • Leave to cool in the poaching liquid, then refrigerate for up to 5 days.

Peeled walnuts

SIMMER 250 G (8 OZ) OF walnut halves in 2 cups of milk and 200 ml (7 fl oz) of water for 2 minutes in a heavy-based saucepan. Remove from the heat and, one at a time, using the pointy end of a knife, carefully peel the skin off each walnut without breaking it. Walnuts are best peeled when hot, if the liquid containing the walnuts cools simply return to the stove. Store the walnuts, covered with walnut oil, in an airtight jar.

Praline

[makes 500 g (1 lb)]

THE CHEF OF THE Duke of Plessis-Pralin accidentally spilt boiling melted sugar on ground almonds. Delighted by this, the Duke gave his name to its preparation and discovery. The praline was born: shelled nuts covered in caramel and ground together. Praline can be used as a decoration for cakes and desserts.

*500 g (1 lb) trimoline**
400 g (13 oz) slivered almonds

Bring the trimoline to the boil in a heavy-based saucepan and cook for 6–8 minutes or until a medium coloured caramel starts to form. Test the temperature is 160°C (325°F) with a sugar thermometer. Remove from the heat, stir in the almonds • Pour the mixture onto a non-stick 20 x 30-cm (8 x 12-in) baking tray and spread out thinly. Set aside to cool • When the caramel is cool, roughly crush with a rolling pin • Place in a food processor and blitz until fine. Pass through a coarse sieve. Store in an airtight container in a dark, dry place. Use any remaining coarse caramel left from sieving in ice cream • Sift a layer onto a non-stick baking tray. Bake for 4–5 minutes at 180°C (350°F) until golden. Cut into squares while still warm and soft enough to cut without breaking.

Ravioli dough (eggless)

[serves 6]

25 g (1 oz) pork fat
150 g (5 oz) plain (all-purpose) flour
55 ml (2 fl oz) water
Pinch of salt

Place all ingredients in the bowl of a mixer and using the dough hook attachment, mix on low speed until the dough comes together. Cover with plastic wrap and rest in the refrigerator for 15 minutes • Use as directed in the recipe.

Sauce vierge

[serves 4]

This is an incredibly versatile sauce. I am always finding new and interesting ways to use it, such as over grilled fish or as in the brandade recipe on page 230.

10 coriander seeds
400 ml (13 fl oz) extra virgin olive oil
Juice of 1 orange, strained
Juice of 1 grapefruit, strained
Juice of 1 lemon, strained
Juice of 1 lime, strained
2 Roma (plum) tomatoes
4 basil leaves, finely shredded

Toast the coriander seeds in a heavy-based frying pan over medium heat for 2 minutes or until fragrant. Remove from the heat and add the olive oil. Infuse for 30 minutes, then strain • Whisk together the orange, grapefruit, lemon and lime juice and the infused olive oil • Scald the tomatoes in boiling water for 1 minute, peel and cut into quarters then into 2-cm (¾-in) squares • Gently warm the dressing in a saucepan over low heat and add the tomatoes and basil. Serve when required.

Snails marinated

Because fresh snails are hard to obtain, the canned variety will suffice here.

1 tin cooked snails (approximately 8 dozen snails)

1 teaspoon garlic purée (minced garlic with a couple of drops of olive oil)

1 tablespoon fresh parsley or tarragon, chopped

Salt and pepper to taste

1 tablespoon shallots, finely chopped

2 tablespoons olive oil

Combine all of the ingredients in a bowl, pour the marinade over the snails and marinate for 24 hours.

Sugar syrup

[makes 3 cups]

Recommended for savarins, poaching fruit, and adjusting sweetness in coulis and sauces.

500 g (1 lb) caster (superfine) sugar

3 cups water

Combine the sugar and water in a heavy-based saucepan and bring to the boil. Strain and reserve.

Truffle mayonnaise

[makes 3 cups]

A DERIVATIVE OF THE classic mayonnaise, the traditional way of enhancing this recipe was to add the jelly of cooked truffles from the previous season. This recipe was used when the truffle season was coming to an end. Replace the jelly with red wine sauce and truffle oil and you have an exact replica. Use in salads, as a dip or simply spread over some grilled sourdough bread.

8 egg yolks
Juice of 1 lemon
2½ tablespoons truffle jelly or red wine sauce (see page 296)
Salt and freshly ground pepper
2½ tablespoons sherry vinegar
2 cups peanut oil
2½ tablespoons white truffle oil

Combine the egg yolks, lemon juice, red wine sauce, salt and pepper and vinegar in a food processor and blitz for 1 minute until smooth and incorporated • While the motor is running, slowly pour in a little of the peanut oil. Continue adding the oil very slowly until half has been incorporated. Drizzle in the remaining peanut oil and the truffle oil in a thin stream until incorporated. Add a little warm water if the mayonnaise gets too thick.

Vegetable bouillon

[makes 600 ml (20 fl oz)]

600 ml (1 pt) water
1 onion, finely chopped
1 stick of celery, finely chopped
1 carrot, finely chopped
1 small leek, washed and finely chopped
½ bulb of fennel, finely chopped
1 clove of garlic, finely chopped
1 tablespoon olive oil
2 sprigs of tarragon, chopped
1 bunch of chervil, chopped
1 teaspoon freshly ground white pepper

In a medium saucepan, sweat all the vegetables in the olive oil for 2 minutes without colouring. • Cover with the water, add the tarragon and chervil, bring to the boil and simmer for 5 minutes. Season with the white pepper • Strain through a fine strainer and allow to cool • Use as required or freeze for up to 3 months.

Vegetable purée

[serves 8]

2 shallots, finely chopped
1 clove of garlic, finely chopped
*2 tablespoons goose fat**
200 g (6½ oz) vegetable (cauliflower, pumpkin, etc.), finely chopped
100 ml (3½ fl oz) chicken stock (see page 378)
Salt and pepper

Sweat the shallots and garlic in the goose fat until transparent in a medium-sized heavy-based saucepan • Add the chopped vegetable and sweat for a further 5 minutes • Add the chicken stock and cover the pot with a lid. Cook until tender on a low heat • Remove from the pot and purée in a blender/food processor until smooth • Season with salt and pepper to taste.

Vinaigrette, hazelnut and French

Two easy-to-make vinaigrettes that enhance any simple salad. You can also substitute walnut oil for hazelnut oil.

HAZELNUT VINAIGRETTE
[makes 4 cups]

350 ml (11¾ fl oz) peanut oil

350 ml (11¾ fl oz) hazelnut oil

150 ml (5 fl oz) sherry vinegar

Juice of 1 lemon

1 clove of garlic, crushed

Whisk all the ingredients together and place in an airtight bottle. Use as required. Store in the fridge for 1–2 months, or at room temperature if the dressing is to be used within 2 weeks.

FRENCH VINAIGRETTE
[makes 1 cup]

1 tablespoon Dijon mustard

1 clove of garlic, crushed

50 ml (1¾ fl oz) Champagne vinegar

200 ml (7 fl oz) olive oil

1 tablespoon curley-leaf parsley, chopped

Vol-au-vent

[makes 1]

100 g (3½ oz) puff pastry *(see page 54)*

1 egg yolk, lightly whisked with a fork

Roll out the puff pastry to a 6 mm (¼ in) thick, 6 cm (2½ in) wide, 20 cm (8 in) long rectangle piece. Leave to rest in the fridge of 30 minutes • Remove from the fridge and cut out two 5 x 5 cm (2 x 2 in) squares of pastry • Using a fork 'dock' one of the squares of pastry (prick it lightly several times to create small surface indents in the pastry). With the remaining square carefully cut out a 3 x 3-cm (1¼ x 1¼-in) square from the centre leaving a 5-cm (2-in) square frame of pastry. Reserve the square and the frame • Using a pastry brush, egg wash the docked square, place the reserved frame on the docked square. Place the square with the frame and the 3-cm (1¼-in) square in the fridge and rest for 10 minutes • To cook, egg wash the 3-cm (1¼-in) square and place both squares on a baking tray lined with greaseproof paper. Bake in a preheated oven at 200°C (400°F) for approximately 7 minutes or until golden brown and the frame has puffed up to form sides on the 5-cm (2-in) square, forming a small box. Remove from the oven and fill with filling, the 3-cm (1¼-in) square can be used as a lid if required.

White chocolate caramel crisp

[makes 8 decorative pieces]

I FEEL COMPELLED TO include this recipe as it is my favourite decorative garnish for simple desserts, such as the white truffle ice cream on page 135.

*155 g (5 oz) fondant**
60 g (2 oz) glucose
100 g (3½ oz) white couverture chocolate, roughly chopped

Combine the fondant and glucose in a heavy-based saucepan and bring to the boil. Insert a sugar thermometer and continue to boil for 6–7 minutes or until the temperature reaches 160°C (325°F). Remove from the heat, add the white chocolate and stir, using a wooden spoon, until smooth • Pour the mixture onto a lightly oiled 20 x 30-cm (8 x 12-in) baking tray and spread out thinly. Set aside to cool • When the caramel is cool, roughly crush with a rolling pin • Transfer to a food processor and blitz until fine. Store in an airtight container in a dark dry place • Preheat the oven to 180°C (350°F) • Sift the caramel powder onto a non-stick baking tray and smooth to form a thin layer. Bake for 4–5 minutes or until golden. Slice into squares while still warm and soft enough to cut without breaking.

Glossary

bakers' flour A strong slightly coarse flour that is able to absorb more liquid. Examples include Italian 00, kamut and spelt flour. Bread or strong flour has a high protein content and good gluten strength.

batons Small sticks approximately 1 x 5 cm ($^1/_3$ x 2 in) in size. Used throughout the book when referring to vegetable garnishing.

beignet 1 French square-shaped doughnut, minus the hole, lavishly sprinkled with sugar. 2 Food dipped in batter and deep-fried.

black pudding A sausage consisting of congealed pig's blood, fat and a binding ingredient.

blind baking A method of preparing a pastry case before adding a moist filling to prevent the bottom becoming soggy and undercooked. The pastry shell is baked with a lining of baking paper and is weighted down with dried beans before it is filled.

blini Russian pancakes traditionally made from buckwheat flour and served with caviar.

bone marrow Found in all bones with a varying degree of quantity. Veal bones are the best for quantity and quality. The soft, fatty centre is used in sauces as a garnish and is normally served in the bone.

bouillon A spiced aromatic liquor or stock used mainly for cooking fish and shellfish. Wine and vinegar may sometimes be added to the court bouillon, which is usually prepared in advance and allowed to cool. The recipe consists of 4 cups of water, bouquet garni, 1 sliced orange, 1 sliced lemon, 1 sliced grapefruit, 5 star anise and 4 cups of white wine.

bouquet garni A small bunch of herbs, classically 2 bay leaves, 3–5 parsley stalks, 3 sprigs of thyme, 10 peppercorns, wrapped in a leek leaf, cheesecloth or a piece of celery and tied with string; ideal for flavouring soups, stews and stocks during cooking. A bouquet garni is removed before serving.

brandade The French version of the Spanish bacalao consisting of salted cod and potato bound, then fried or steamed.

brioche A slightly sweet yeast bread rich in butter and eggs. The traditional shape has a fluted bottom and a topknot and is made in a special mould. Good as a sweet bread or served with cheese or pâté.

brunoise To dice a vegetable or fruit into a uniform size measuring 3 x 3 mm (1/8 x 1/8 in).

Calvados A dry spirit made from distilled cider in Normandy, northern France.

capers The pickled buds of a shrub native to the Mediterranean. Capers are usually packed in brine but can also be preserved in salt. They should be rinsed before use to remove excess salt. Their pungent flavour adds piquancy to many sauces. They can be used as a garnish for meat and vegetables and in tapenade.

cartouche A device made from silicon or greaseproof paper to fit over a stew, braise or confit to prevent exposure to air.

caul fat or crepinette The lacy fatty membrane encasing the internal organs of an animal, pork caul is often used for wrapping faggots, lamb and joints of meats. It helps preserve moisture during roasting.

caviar Sturgeon roe (eggs); lightly salted. The lighter the colour, the better the quality and the more expensive. True caviar is the salted and matured roe of the huge sturgeon fish, the most famous is from the Caspian Sea and is processed in Russia and Iran. Beluga is the most expensive variety, followed by osetra and sevruga.

cèpe A type of wild mushroom similar to porcini.

chinois A very fine strainer.

chlorophyll To extract the green from vegetables, such as spinach and parsley, for use in colouring and flavouring dressing and sauces.

choux pastry A very light, double-cooked pastry usually used for sweets, such as cakes and buns.

confit To slowly cook an item in fat. Examples are duck leg cooked in duck fat or pumpkin cooked in olive oil.

confit orange zest The pith-free skin of an orange that has been cooked slowly in sugar syrup for up to 12 hours. It is used in desserts and savoury dishes, such as duck à l'orange.

cooking apples Golden delicious or Granny Smith are best to cook with because of their high acidity and smooth texture.

consommé Clear soup, served hot or chilled.

coral The roe of a lobster or crab, which becomes pink when cooked.

cornichons Pickled baby gherkins, stronger in flavour and normally more expensive than small gherkins.

court bouillon See bouillon.

crayfish oil Oil, normally olive oil, infused with the essence of crayfish shells.

crème anglaise This is the French term for custard cream, made with sugar, egg yolks and milk flavoured with vanilla.

croutons Small cubes or slices of bread that have been fried, drained, cooled and rubbed with a clove of garlic. As they cool, they develop a crispy texture. They are used as a garnish in soups and salads.

crustacean oil Similar to crayfish oil but made with a mixture of shellfish. Recipes can sometimes contain only freshwater crustaceans, which is helpful for people with allergies.

cultured butter Butter made with no preservatives. Bacteria is added to preserve and stabilise the butter. The results are a more creamy and smooth-textured butter.

deglaze To heat wine, stock or other liquid with the cooking juices and sediment left in the pan after roasting or sautéing in order to make a sauce or gravy.

devein To remove the gritty intestinal vein from green prawns and langoustines. Remove the head, peel off the shell and make a shallow cut lengthwise along the back of the prawn. Pull out the intestinal vein in one long strip and discard. Rinse the prawn.

double boiler An instrument for cooking without using direct heat, it usually consists of two saucepans that fit together, one on top of the other. The bottom one is filled with water and the top one with the mixture to be cooked. May be stainless steel, aluminium (aluminum), or glass. Also known as a bain-marie: a metal bath half-filled with water to protect the ingredients (for example, chocolate) from burning.

duck eggs Used a lot in French cookery for their larger yolks and creamier consistency. Harder to find and more expensive than hen's eggs.

duck fat The fat derived from duck carcases. It is available in tins from speciality stores or is easily made by rendering duck skins slowly over low heat for 1–2 hours, then straining.

duxelles A thick pâté of chopped mushrooms cooked with onion and thyme. It is used as a stuffing or garnish and in the preparation of various dishes called *à la duxelles*. Traditionally used in beef Wellington.

eau de vie poire William An 80–90 per cent proof clear fruit alcohol made from William pears. Framboise (raspberry) is another popular type of eau de vie.

egg wash Beaten egg mixed with water and a little salt, used for glazing pastry or bread. There are two types used in the book. Egg yolks without any water are used to decorate pithiviers.

eight-spice powder A speciality developed by me containing eight spices ranging from pepper to saffron, used in a versatile range of recipes ranging from roast duck to spiced apple ravioli.

emulsify To combine fats, such as butter or oil, with vinegar or citrus juices to make a smooth and even blend using an emulsifier, such as an egg yolk, to bind the ingredients and prevent them from separating.

fish slice A thin flat kitchen utensil used to slide fish from a pan. It can be used when transferring ingredients from the pan to the plate.

flambé To add alcohol to a pan so that the food in the pan can absorb the alcohol. To do this the alcohol must be evaporated, this is done by heating the alcohol in the pan, then igniting it with a naked flame. The flame will burn out in a number of seconds.

foie gras fat Literally French for 'fat liver'. The remnants of rich yellow, low melting point waste product from the foie gras can be used for cooking vegetables and potatoes.

fondant A creamy white substance created by kneading cooked sugar syrup. Used as a filling for chocolates, or a frosting for cakes, petits fours or pastries. Also flavoured and made into individual sweets.

four-point veal rack The loin of veal with four bones from the rib cage still attached to the loin. The meat retains moisture more efficiently when roasted on the bone.

fromage blanc A French cheese made from pasteurised cow's milk to which a lactic bacteria culture has been added. This thickens the cream and gives it a distinctive sharp flavour. It is the first stage of the cheese-making process. It is a great way to accompany certain soups and pastries.

frisée leaves The yellow heart of a curly endive lettuce.

garlic oil Combine 12–14 cloves of garlic, 2 cups of olive oil and 1 teaspoon of sea salt and purée until completely smooth. Place in the refrigerator for 24 hours and the garlic will sink to the bottom. Use for cooking fish and vegetables. This is a very aromatic oil.

glace de viande Reduced double veal stock, used to enhance other sauces.

gluten A protein in flour which, when mixed with water, gives the dough elasticity and strength.

goose fat Similar in flavour to duck fat but a little more subtle. Best to buy rendered in tins and jars. Duck or roast chicken fat is a good substitute.

groundnut Also known as peanut. This edible seed is a member of the pea family, not a true nut. The pods mature underground and contain 2–4 seeds. Groundnuts can be roasted, salted and eaten whole or used in cooked dishes. Peanut or groundnut oil is widely used in cooking and margarine manufacture.

hare forequarter The front section of a hare including the front legs, ribcage and loins.

herb oil A herbaceous oil made from olive oil blended with various herbs, such as basil, tarragon, parsley, hyssop, thyme and sage. The oil is blended, set aside to infuse with herbs for 24 hours then passed through a fine sieve.

improver Used in the production of bread baking to help stabilise the dough.

Italian 00 flour A coarsely milled variety of flour that is commonly used in pasta making and is recommended for baking. It is available at all good providores. A good substitute is 50 per cent plain flour, 50 per cent semolina.

kecap manis Similar to soy sauce but sweeter, this extremely rich, dark, thick sauce is used in marinades or as a condiment in Indonesian cooking. The sweetness comes from palm sugar, other flavourings include garlic and star anise.

lardons Small, chunky strips of fat bacon or pork fat (smoked or unsmoked) used to flavour dishes, such as quiches or salads, or they can be sweated with onions as a base for soup.

lentils du Puy A green flat legume about the size of a split pea used for soups, stews and garnishes. The charcoal taste is derived from its origin in south-west France where the rich minerally soil imparts characteristics found nowhere else in the world.

Ligurian olives A type of olive that is small and concentrated in flavour. In Australia a similar variety is being marketed as the wild olive with varying degrees of success. In France it is known as the Niçoise olive.

lobster roe (coral) The meat of the lobster found in the head is the roe. It can easily be identified by its dark blue colour. Place in seafood mousses and soups for enhanced flavour and colour.

Madeira Madeira is a fortified wine that comes from the island of the same name. Drunk as an apéritif and increasingly being matched with particular dishes such as chilled soups, it is also used in cooking. It is similar to a dry sherry and can be bought as fortified Malmsey in some stores.

Madeira jelly A meat-based clear soup flavoured with Madeira and set with gelatin. Commonly served with terrines.

magret A portion of meat from the breast of the duck, usually the mallard or Barbary. Always presented with skin attached and crispy.

marinate To steep fish, meat or vegetables in a flavoured liquid (the marinade) usually containing oil, wine or lemon juice, herbs and spices, in order to tenderise and add flavour.

mille-feuille A pastry made of thin layers of puff pastry, whipped cream and jam or some other filling, such as fresh fruit. Mille-feuilles are usually small rectangular pastries, but can also be made as large gâteaux. Literally means 'a thousand leaves' mille-feuille is also commonly used throughout the French cooking world for a dish that is layered.

mirepoix A mixture of diced vegetables, usually onion, leek, carrot and celery, that are sautéed in butter to form a base for many sauces, soups and stews.

mise en place Literally 'put in place' in French. Refers to preparations for cooking, including setting out bowls, pots and pans, and measuring, washing, peeling, chopping and mincing ingredients.

mixed spice A mixture of whole spices used for pickling and in soups and stews.

morels A highly prized wild fungus that grows in dry, sandy areas and has a sponge-like cap. It is important to wash them well to get rid of any grit. They are often used dried and are excellent in all mushroom dishes and as additions to stews and casseroles.

mouli A hand-held kitchen utensil that enables the user to blend, purée and grate.

Niçoise olives Refer to Ligurian olives.

Ortiz anchovies An exceptional Spanish brand of processed anchovy.

osso bucco cutlets A cut of veal from the shank that is high in bone marrow and flavour. Requires an extensive amount of time to cook and tenderise properly.

oyster juice The juice from a freshly opened oyster. A valuable commodity to the professional cook for use in flavouring veloutés, sauces, jellies and dressings.

palette knife A flat stainless steel kitchen utensil in various sizes. Indispensable in the kitchen, it can be used to pick up items from trays and for spreading cakes and batters evenly before baking.

pancetta Cured belly pork used in Italian cookery. It is sold in rectangular or sausagelike rolls in thin slices or thicker cubes. Its flavour is salty and sweet with a hint of aniseed. Fry in its own juices or fry in oil and then use to flavour the rest of the dish. It can be grilled until crisp and then crumbled over pasta, rice, salads and soups. If unavailable, use thinly sliced, unsmoked, streaky bacon rashers.

panko breadcrumbs Flaky white Japanese-style breadcrumbs that are able to absorb a lot of oil without becoming greasy.

pastis A traditional aniseed-flavoured French apéritif, it has a strong association with Provençal cookery. Pernod and Ricard are the best-known brands.

papillote (en) The term *en papillote* is used to describe a dish cooked in a parcel to protect the food from the high heat of the oven and seal in the aroma and flavour. The dish is usually served in the parcel to be unwrapped by the diner. Greaseproof paper is the preferred wrapping material.

pepper cress A hybrid of rocket, these small cress shoots are used in salads as an accompaniment to terrines. Rocket is a useful substitute.

pink peppercorns Unripe berries obtained from Madagascan pepper trees, pink peppercorns are stronger and more aromatic in flavour than white or black.

pistachio paste The green colour makes it very popular for creams and ice creams. In confectionery it is associated with nougat.

pithivier A round puff pastry dome that can be sweet or savoury.

pork fat Rendered and clarified pork fat or lard is a fine white fat which is used less these days because of its high animal-fat content. It is used for slow cooking, deep-frying and making pastry.

preserved lemons Popular in Moroccan dishes, these are lemons that have been preserved in salt for approximately 30 days. Available at all good providores. Grated lemon zest can be a useful substitute.

prosciutto The Italian word for ham, prosciutto crudo is the raw form (which has been cured and is ready to eat) and prosciutto cotto is cooked. Prosciutto or Parma ham, as it is also known, is sold in very thin slices.

puff pastry A very light pastry made in layers that expand when cooked, leaving large air pockets inside. Used for sweet or savoury dishes.

quenelle A light, delicate dumpling made of seasoned minced or ground fish, meat or vegetables bound with eggs. However throughout this book it is referring to the shape of a classical quenelle which is made by moulding the particular item between 2 teaspoons, dessertspoons or tablespoons which have been dipped into boiling water.

quince When fully ripe, the quince has a wonderful perfume. It belongs to the apple family and is much the same shape as an apple, but with a yellow furry skin. Quince should not be eaten raw because it is very hard and bitter. It makes excellent preserves, especially marmalade.

ruby port Is the Portuguese-style of vintage port. Tawny port is a good substitute.

saltpetre Also known as sodium nitrate, saltpetre is used to flavour, colour and preserve terrines and confits. Sea salt is a good substitute.

sea salt Pure salt flakes extracted from seawater by a process of evaporation. Sea salt has a wonderful flavour that cannot be replaced. Be wary of chemically extracted salt as it can dramatically affect the way certain vegetables and seafoods cook.

seaweed A type of plant found in various forms, normally available in Japanese or specialty shops in a processed and dried form. Agar agar is a product developed from seaweed that has thickening and setting agents able to withstand heat and is widely being experimented with in French cookery.

semi-whipped cream Cream that is whipped until soft peaks are just formed.

shuck To open an oyster shell with a small, thick-bladed knife.

slippery jacks Also known as the pine bolete and poor man's cèpe, they have a dark brown cap with a yellow stem. When washed a gelatinous coat forms over the cap. They are found in spring and autumn in pine plantations. Use in risottos and omelettes.

snails Land-dwelling creatures of several sizes and varieties, only two types are widely used in French cookery: the Burgundy snail and the petit gris. The Burgundy snail is occasionally farmed in Australia. Snails are among the oldest known foods to humans, the Romans were the first to cultivate them for food.

sourdough bread A form of bread using naturally fermented yeasts to give rise to the bread and at the same time impart a particular flavour. Famous bakeries have different recipes for their ferments that are never revealed, such as the legendary Poilâne in Paris. Ferments can be made from anything that contains natural yeast, such as bananas or grapes.

tarragon Blanching tarragon has three benefits: it preserves the colour; prevents bruising when chopping and removes the harsh aniseed flavour that is sometimes associated with tarragon. It is one of the hardest herbs to find on a regular basis, the main reason is its vulnerabilty: it is destroyed during frost, extreme heat and consistent rain. When a large amount is spotted at the market, I always buy the lot and preserve it. After blanching, the tarragon can be portioned into small amounts, wrapped in plastic wrap and frozen. Defrost and chop as required.

titanium gelatin The premium grade gelatin normally weighing 3 g (1/8 oz) per sheet. It is more expensive, but less is used. Gelatin is normally packaged in three grades, regular bronze, gold or titanium.

tomato paysanne Scald tomatoes in boiling water for 1 minute, peel and cut into quarters then into 2-cm (¾-in) squares.

trimoline An inverted sugar (sugar that has been treated so that it will not crystallise and form sugary lumps) that is used in confectionary and ice cream. Glucose is a suitable replacement.

truffles A very strong tasting underground fungus that is expensive to buy. They are generally picked in the wild and are often found by specially trained pigs or dogs. Truffles are rounded, of variable size and shape and come in a range of colours. Truffle also refers to a chocolate and cream confectionery often flavoured with rum.

truffle oil Normally made by infusing white truffles in oil. Good oil is expensive, but a little goes a long way. Beware of imitations. Black truffle oil is a waste of time and money.

truffle paste Puréed truffles processed with truffle oil and mushroom duxelles. The Italian brands are always the best. Good for adding to butter sauces and risottos.

Tunisian Brique pastry A form of wheat pastry similar to spring roll paper but larger and less expensive. It can be found in good Middle Eastern grocery stores. Use in the preparation of spring roll-type dishes and sweet pastries.

vanilla bean To obtain the seeds from the bean, using a sharp paring knife, split the vanilla bean lengthwise down the centre and with the back of the knife scrape out the seeds.

vanilla sugar Sugar that has been infused with vanilla beans for a minimum of 1 month. Normally and most practically the beans have been scraped of their seeds, which have been used in another process.

ventrèche Similar to pancetta but is unsmoked and covered in ground pepper and other spices.It is often cut in thin strips and is used as a crispy garnish on fish or meat. It is a specialty from the Basque region in Spain.

vermouth An aromatic alcoholic drink originating from Turin and derived from the infamous absinthe, it is extremely useful for flavouring braises, sauces and jellies with its herby aromas. Once opened, a bottle will oxidise within 3 weeks, but for cooking purposes it will last indefinitely.

walnut oil The nutty flavoured oil extracted from the walnut. Use for cooking or drizzling on greens, pasta and vegetables. When mixed with sherry vinegar it becomes an aromatic way to enhance and flavour cold meats and salads. Hazelnut oil or dressing can be a useful substitute.

wild mushrooms Any mushroom that is found in the wild and is not cultivated. Good substitutes are farmed Paris or Swiss brown mushrooms, wood ear fungus and porcini.

Conversion Chart

Liquid ingredients

1 teaspoon	5 ml	1/4 fl oz
1 tablespoon	20 ml	3/4 fl oz
1/4 cup	60 ml	2 fl oz
1/3 cup	80 ml	2 3/4 fl oz
1/2 cup	125 ml	4 fl oz
2/3 cup	165 ml	5 1/2 fl oz
3/4 cup	185 ml	6 fl oz
1 cup	250 ml	8 fl oz
1 1/2 cups	375 ml	12 fl oz
2 cups	500 ml	16 fl oz
4 cups	1 litre	1 3/4 pints

Oven temperatures

120°C = 250°F
140°C = 275°F = gas mark 1
150°C = 300°F = gas mark 2
160°C = 325°F = gas mark 3
170°C = 335°F
180°C = 350°F = gas mark 4
190°C = 375°F = gas mark 5
200°C = 400°F = gas mark 6
220°C = 425°F = gas mark 7
230°C = 450°F = gas mark 8
240°C = 475°F = gas mark 9
250°C = 500°F = gas mark 10

Conversion Chart

Dry ingredients	
15 g	1/2 oz
30 g	1 oz
45 g	1 1/2 oz
60 g	2 oz
90 g	3 oz
100 g	3 1/2 oz
125 g	4 oz
150 g	5 oz
200 g	6 1/2 oz
250 g	8 oz
300 g	10 oz
350 g	11 oz
375 g	12 oz
500 g	1 lb
600 g	1 1/4 lb
750 g	1 1/2 lb
900 g	1 3/4 lb
1 kg	2 lb
1.5 kg	3 lb
2 kg	4 lb
2.5 kg	5 lb

US butter	
1 tablespoon	15 g
1/4 cup	60 g
1/3 cup	90 g
1/2 cup	125 g
1 cup	250 g

Acid butter
mushroom risotto 113–114, *117*
risotto au fruits de mer 260–261, *262*
white truffle risotto *131*, 134
Aioli 388
Almond gazpacho sorbet and crispy anchovies with tomato tarts 86–87
Anchovies
beef with crispy snails and anchovy butter 302–303, *304*
black olive tapenade 375
sticks *69,* 73
tomato tarts with almond gazpacho sorbet and crispy 86–87
Apple and pear chutney 370
hare pâté, served with 273, *276*
Apples
caramelised, grilled fois gras, poached walnuts and grapes with Sauternes emulsion 173–174, *178*
crème brûlée with poire William sorbet 321, *322*
partridge with Calvados and 278–279, *280*
pear chutney 370
prune croustillant *322*, 323
ravioli with star anise and white pepper 320, *321*
sorbet au clicquot rosé 324, *329*
tarte aux pommes à la tatin 319, *322*
Apricots and tobacco sauce with fois gras 177, *178*
Artichokes à la barigoule 150, *154*
Artichokes, cooking stock for 159, *162*
Asparagus
consommé à la Française *163*, 166
purée, duck egg omelettes filled with slippery jack mushrooms and 121–122, *124*
green, wrapped in ham with béarnaise sauce, *163*, 167
vichyssoise of white *163*, 165
white, and lamb sweetbread vol-au-vent, 162, 164
white truffle and asparagus custard with scrambled duck eggs *131*, 132–133
Asparagus mousse 371
hogget in soy sauce *309*, 311
Avocado, tomato stuffed with crab and 82, *84*

Barramundi
brandade 230, *232*
vanilla sauce with *233*, 235
zucchini flowers stuffed with brandade, and 231, *232*
Basil mousse and ratatouille with poached lamb *309*, 312–313
Basil purée 372
Béarnaise sauce 385
filet de bœuf et pommes mille-feuille au jus gras *304*, 305
green asparagus wrapped in ham with *163*, 167
trout royale with sauce Normande 229, *232*
velouté de champignons a l'Italienne *145*, 147

Index

Béchamel sauce 373
à la florentine soufflé d'ecrevisses *262*, 264
cheese soufflé, twice-cooked 364, *365*
mornay sauce 389
Beef
crispy snails and anchovy butter with 302–303, *304*
extravagant burger *304*, 306
filet de bœuf et pommes mille-feuille au jus gras *304*, 305
miniature pies 300, *304*
tartare with quail eggs *301*, 304
Beignets (yeast batter), deep fried 65, *68*
Beurre blanc 374
Biscuits, sable, *32*, 36
Bois Boudran sauce 205
extravagant burger *304*, 306
tempura-battered oysters with crispy black pudding and quail eggs 204–205, *206*
Black truffles *see* Truffles
Black pudding
partridge with Calvados and apples 278–279, *280*
tempura-battered oysters with quail eggs and crispy 204–205, *206*
Blini *63*, 64
scallops wrapped in smoked salmon with salmon roe and 190, *196*
traditional caviar service 218, *220*
Bouillabaisse *255*, 258–259
barramundi and zucchini flowers stuffed with brandade 231, *232*
oysters with brandade and *207*, 210
risotto au fruits de mer 260–261, *262*
rouille 259
Bourguignonne, rabbit stew à la 4–5, *32*
Brandade 230, *232*
barramundi and zucchini flowers stuffed with 231, *232*
oysters with bouillabaisse and *207*, 210
Breadcrumbs, herbed 384
confit of salmon with osso bucco jus *233*, 236–237
lamb provençal *309*, 314–315
Breads
brioche *see* Brioche
brown dinner rolls 51, *56*
melba toast 54, *57*
soda 50, *56*
sourdough *see* Sourdough bread
white dinner rolls 53, *56*
zopf dinner rolls, miniature *57*, 59
Brioche *57*, 58–59
foie gras baked in *179*, 182
Butter
acid *see* Acid butter
anchovy and crispy snails with beef 302–303, *304*
clarified 381
fois gras, and parfait of chicken livers *179*, 180–181
shrimp *262*, 265
vanilla 288

Cabbage and chocolate and raspberry sauce with venison *281*, 287
Cakes *see also* Chocolate, Desserts
jaconde sponge *see* Jaconde sponge
macaroons *341*, 342
madeleines *341*, 343
opera cake, classic *351*, 352–354
rum babas 60–61, *63*
tuiles 340, *341*
Calvados
caramel sauce *see* Caramel Calvados sauce
crème caramel 325, *329*
partridge with apple and 278–279, *280*
Cauliflower purée
hogget in soy sauce *309*, 311
venison carpaccio with cauliflower and caviar 219, *220*
Caramel Calvados sauce 376
apple ravioli with star anise and white pepper 320, *321*
tarte aux pommes à la tatin 319, *322*
Caramel, sugar cage
pêche Melba *329*, 331–332

Caviar
baby potatoes filled with pommes mousseline and *220*, 222
butter sauce with crayfish *220*, 223
oysters with cucumber relish and 205, *206*
snapper with smoked baby potatoes and *220*, 221–222
traditional service 218, *220*
venison carpaccio with cauliflower and 219, *220*
Caviar, eggplant *see* Eggplant caviar
Cèpe powder 376
assiette of wild hare 270–271, *276*
mushroom sauce 110, *116*
Champagne velouté, 208
poached oysters with scrambled duck eggs *207*, 211
warmed oysters with linguine and *206*, 208–209
Cheese *see also* Goat's cheese, Parmesan
soufflé, twice-cooked 364, *365*
velouté de champignons a l'Italienne *145*, 147
Cherries with wild duck *281*, 282–283
Chestnuts
braised 157
combined with vanilla beans and dried apricots 157
cooked 157
cooked in bag *155*
preserved 157
simmered 157
soup *155*, 158
stewed 157
Chicken
consommé à la Française *163*, 166
double chicken stock 381
jus 377
jus Gras 299, *304*
morels stuffed with tarragon mousse and *117*, 118–119
oyster pie *207*, 213
parfait of chicken livers and foie gras *179*, 180–181
sole monseigneur 253, *255*
stock 378
Chicken mousse 377
assiette of wild hare 270–271, *276*
duck à l'orange *281*, 285–286
morels stuffed with chicken and tarragon *117*, 118–119
Chocolate
biscuit pudding *350*, 357
crème 348, *350*
croissants *68,* 70
demoulded pistachio soufflé with a soft chocolate centre 336–337, *350*
ganache *see* Chocolate ganache
glace au chocolat 328
glaze 353
opera cake, classic *351*, 352–354
raspberry sauce and sautéed cabbage with venison *281*, 287
sponge 349, *351*
tart robuchon 347, *350*
truffle mousse *351*, 355–56
white chocolate caramel crisp 397
Chocolate ganache 349, *351*
chocolate biscuit pudding *350*, 357
demoulded pistachio soufflé with a soft chocolate centre 336–337, *350*
Chutney, apple and pear 370
Citrus jelly 202
marron á la parisienne *233*, 238
oysters with smoked salmon and 202–203, *206*
Clams, risotto au fruits de mer 260–261, *262*
Clarification of sauces 380
Coffee butter cream *352*
opera cake, classic *351*, 352–354
Confits
potato *97*, 99
potatoes and onions with steamed grouper *262*, 263
salmon with osso bucco jus *233*, 236–237
shallots 149, *154*
tomatoes *see* Tomatoes, confit
Consommé *see* Soups
Couscous 275

Index

Crab
bouillabaisse *255*, 258–259
filet de daurade et pommes de terre au crabe *255*, 257
marron with Grand Marnier *233*, 239
rillette *255*, 256
tomato stuffed with avocado and 82, *84*
Crayfish *see also* Yabbies
baked, with foie gras, sauce Nantua and braised winter vegetables *179*, 183
bouillabaisse *255*, 258–259
caviar butter sauce with *220*, 223
Nantua sauce *247*, 248
oil *see* Crayfish oil
shrimp butter *262*, 265
trout royale with sauce Normande 229, *232*
Crayfish oil 252, *254*
barramundi and zucchini flowers stuffed with brandade 231, *232*
zucchini salad 151, *154*
Crème anglaise 379
chocolate truffle mousse *351*, 355–56
Crème brûlée, apple, with poire William sorbet 321, *322*
Crème chantilly 380
Crème caramel, Calvados 325, *329*
Crème pâtissière 335
basic soufflé 334
Danish pastries *69*, 71–72
demoulded pistachio soufflé with a soft chocolate centre 336–337, *350*
frangipane or almond cream 382
Crêpes 61, *63*
suzettes 7, *32*
Croissants 66–67, *68*
chocolate *68*, 70
Croutons, garlic 383
goat's cheese wrapped in puff pastry *365*, 367
Cucumber relish and caviar with oysters 205, *206*

Danish pastries *69*, 71–72
Desserts *see also* Cakes, Chocolate, Ice cream, Pastries, Sorbets, Soufflées, Tarts
apple and prune croustillant *322*, 323
apple crème brûlée with poire William sorbet 321, *322*
apple ravioli with star anise and white pepper 320, *321*
beignets (yeast batter), deep fried 65, *68*
biscuit glace savoy *329*, 332–333
Calvados crème caramel 325, *329*
crème pâtissière *see* Crème pâtissière
meringue, Italian *see* Meringue, Italian
pears, poached 390
pêche Melba *329*, 331–332
rum babas 60–61, *63*
Doughs
beignets (yeast batter), deep fried 65, *68*
pasta 114
pizza *69*, 72–73
ravioli 392
samosa 64, *68*
Duck
à l'orange *281*, 285–286
consommé XXX
egg omelettes filled with asparagus purée and slippery jack mushrooms 121–122, *124*
galette *276*, 283–284
scrambled eggs with poached oysters *207*, 211
scrambled eggs with white truffle and asparagus custard *131*, 132–133
twice-cooked duck leg with foie gras and orange sauce 175–176, *178*
wild, with cherries *281*, 282–283

Eggplant à la Espagnole, *155*, 156
Eggplant caviar 153, *155*
tomato butter with potato-crusted red mullet *85*, 88
Eight-spice powder 382

Fish stock 243, *247*
Fish velouté 244, *247*

garlic, sage and pine mushroom sauce with roast veal fillet 122–123, *124*
Fois gras
baked in brioche *179,* 182
butter and parfait of chicken livers *179*, 180–181
caramelised apple, poached walnuts and grapes with Sauternes emulsion 173–174, *178*
crayfish, sauce Nantua and braised winter vegetables with *179*, 183
duck à l'orange *281*, 285–286
extravagant burger *304*, 306
hare pâté 273, *276*
pan-fried, with apricots and tobacco sauce 177, *178*
parfait of chicken livers and *179*, 180–181
terrine of foie gras, ox tongue and lentils du Puy 172, *178*
twice-cooked duck leg with foie gras and orange sauce 175–176, *178*
Frangipane or almond cream 382
Fricassee
mushroom 112, *116*
spinach and wild mushroom fricassee with John Dory fillets *124*, 125

Goat's cheese fromage blanc, *365*, 366
tomato soup, cold-pressed, with profiteroles and 79, 80, *84*
Goat's cheese wrapped in puff pastry *365*, 367
Glace de viande 295, *297*
Grand Marnier, grilled marron with *233*, 239
Grouper with confit potatoes and onions *262*, 263

Ham, green asparagus wrapped in *163*, 167
Hare
assiette of wild hare 270–271, *276*
pâté 273, *276*
twice-cooked hare leg 272, *280*
Haricot blanc and white truffle soup *131*, 133
Hazelnut and watercress salad *163*, 167
Hazelnut vinaigrette 396
ceviche of scallops 193, *196*
duck galette *276*, 283–284
goat's cheese wrapped in puff pastry *365*, 367
salmon tartare *233*, 237
scallops wrapped in smoked salmon with blini and salmon roe 190, *196*
smoked salmon paupiettes *233*, 234–235
snapper with smoked baby potatoes and caviar *220*, 221–222
terrine of foie gras, ox tongue and lentils du Puy 172, *178*
watercress and hazelnut salad *163*, 167
Hollandaise sauce 385
mornay sauce 389

Ice cream
vanilla 327
variations 328, *329*
white truffle *131*, 135

Jaconde sponge, 352
biscuit glace savoy *329*, 332–333
chocolate truffle mousse *351*, 355–56
opera cake, classic *351*, 352–354
pêche Melba *329*, 331–332
Jerusalem artichokes *see* Topinambour
Jelly, Madeira 386–387
John Dory
fillets with spinach and wild mushroom fricassee *124*, 125
lobster mousse 251, *254*
Jus gras 299, *304*
filet de bœuf et pommes mille-feuille au jus gras *304*, 305
lamb with basil mousse and ratatouille *309*, 312–313
stuffed spring lamb with 309, 310

Index

Lamb
hogget in soy sauce *309*, 311
jus gras with stuffed spring lamb 309, 310
provençal *309*, 314–315
ratatouille and basil mousse with poached *309*, 312–313
selle de pré-salé aux laities 307, *309*
spicy lamb samosas 308, *309*
sweetbread and white asparagus vol-au-vent *162*, 164
Langoustine stock 245, *247*
Lemon tart *32*, 34–35
Lentils de Puy 386
partridge with Calvados and apple 278–279, *280*
spicy lamb samosas 308, *309*
terrine of foie gras, ox tongue and lentils du Puy 172, *178*
Lime and coconut sauce, pheasant with 274–275, *276*
Lobster bisque 249, *254*
lobster mousse 251, *254*
Lobster mousse 251, *254*
poached trout royale with sauce Normande 229, *232*
wild oysters and puff pastry with *207*, 212
Lobster sauce 244

Macaroons *341*, 342
Madeira jelly 386–387
Madeira sauce *297*, 298
Madeleines *341*, 343
Marinade, gaille espice 383
Marinade, snail 393
kipfler potatoes filled with *96*, 98
Marron
á la parisienne *233*, 238
grilled, with Grand Marnier *233*, 239
Mary Rose sauce 388
Tomato stuffed with crab and avocado 82, *84*
Mayonnaise 388
marron á la parisienne *233*, 238
salad beaucaire 160, *162*
variations 388
Mayonnaise, green 388
tomato stuffed with crab and avocado 82, *84*
Mayonnaise, truffle 394
ceviche of scallops 193, *196*
roast scallop, pork belly, pig's ear and truffle salad 191–192, *196*
Melba toast 54, *57*
Meringue, Italian 336
basic soufflé 334
biscuit glace savoy *329*, 332–333
sorbet au clicquot rosé 324, *329*
Mornay sauce 389
Mousse, asparagus *see* Asparagus mousse
Mousse, basil *see* Basil mousse
Mousse, chicken *see* Chicken mousse
Mousse, chocolate truffle *351*, 355–56
Mousse, lobster 251, *254*
poached trout royale with sauce Normande 229, *232*
wild oysters and puff pastry with *207*, 212
Mousse, pheasant 277, *280*
quail pasties *281*, 289
Mousse, smoked salmon 234
Mousseline
pheasant, à l'anglaise 277, *280*
pommes, and caviar with baby potatoes *220*, 222
scallop *196*, 197
Mushrooms
cappuccino *117*, 119
fricassee 112, *116*
John Dory fillets with spinach and wild mushroom fricassee *124*, 125
morels stuffed with chicken and tarragon mousse *117*, 118–119
pine mushroom, garlic and sage sauce, roast veal fillet with 122–123, *124*
potato ravioli with mushroom essence 114–115, *117*
purée 111, *116*
risotto 113–114, *117*
sauce 110, *116*
slippery jack mushrooms and asparagus purée filling duck egg omelettes 121–122, *124*
stock 109, *116*

supremes de volaille chimay 279, *280*
truffle broth baked in puff pastry 120, *124*
Mussels
marinière of Spring Bay 250, *254*
risotto au fruits de mer 260–261, *262*
stock 389
Mussel velouté 244
grouper with confit potatoes and onions *262*, 263
tomato jelly with sea urchin and basil velouté 80–81, *84*
trout royale with sauce Normande 229, *232*

Nantua sauce *247*, 248
crayfish, with foie gras, braised winter vegetables and *179*, 183
Normande sauce, poached trout royale with 229, *232*

Omelettes, duck egg, filled with asparagus purée and slippery jack mushrooms 121–122, *124*
Olive tapenade 375
lamb provençal *309*, 314–315
stuffed spring lamb with jus gras 309, 310
Onion
confit potatoes and onions with steamed grouper *262*, 263
purée *145*, 148
Orange, duck à la *281*, 285–286
Orange sauce and fois gras with twice cooked duck leg 175–176, *178*
Osso bucco jus with confit of salmon *233*, 236–237
Oysters
chicken pie *207*, 213
crumbed, with brandade and bouillabaisse *207*, 210
cucumber relish and caviar with 205, *206*
poached, with scrambled duck eggs *207*, 211
smoked salmon and citrus jelly with 202–203, *206*
tempura-battered, with crispy black pudding and quail eggs 204–205, *206*
warmed, with linguine and Champagne velouté *206*, 208–209
wild, with lobster mousse and puff pastry *207*, 212

Pancakes, blini *63*, 64
Pancetta
extravagant burger *304*, 306
pea soup with roasted scallops wrapped in *145*, 146
salmon infused with, 21, *32*
Parmesan, Grana Padano
à la florentine soufflé d'ecrevisses *262*, 264
black truffle risotto 129, *131*
mushroom risotto 113–114, *117*
risotto au fruits de mer 260–261, *262*
velouté de champignons a l'Italienne *145*, 147
white truffle risotto *131*, 134
Parsley purée 303
beef with crispy snails and anchovy butter 302–303, *304*
grouper with confit potatoes and onions *262*, 263
Parsley sauce 277
pheasant mousseline à l'anglaise 277, *280*
Partridge with Calvados and apple 278–279, *280*
Pasta *see also* Ravioli
dough 114, 285
duck à l'orange *281*, 285–286
marinière of Spring Bay mussels 250, *254*
warmed oysters with linguine and Champagne velouté *206*, 208–209
velouté de champignons a l'Italienne *145*, 147
Pastries *see also* Biscuits, Quiches, Tarts
anchovy sticks, *69,* 73
choux 62, 100,
croissants 66–67, *68*
croissants, chocolate *68*, 70
Danish *69*, 71–72
pâte sel (short crust pastry) *see* Pâte sel
profiteroles *see* Profiteroles
puff *see* Puff pastry

Pâté
hare 273, *276*
quail *179*, 184–185
smoked trout and salmon 228, *232*
Pâte sel (short crust pastry) *69*, 74
beef pies, miniature 300, *304*
chicken and oyster pie *207*, 213
quail pasties *281*, 289
Peaches,
pêche Melba *329*, 331–332
quail with vanilla and white *276*, 288
Pears
apple chutney 370
apple crème brûlée with poire William sorbet 321, *322*
poached 390
Peas
à la Française 98, 141, *144*
bonne femme 143, *145*
soup with roasted scallops wrapped in pancetta *145*, 146
Pea purée 142
assiette of wild hare 270–271, *276*
duck galette 276, 283–284
sea urchin and quail eggs with 142–143, *144*
wild barramundi with vanilla sauce *233*, 235
Percierge 390
Petits pois *see* Peas
Pheasant
marinated, with lime and coconut sauce 274–275, *276*
mousseline à l'anglaise 277, *280*
supremes de volaille chimay 279, *280*
Pies
beef 300, *304*
chicken and oyster *207*, 213
Pistachio soufflé with a soft chocolate centre 338–339, *350*
Pizza dough *69*, 72–73
Pommes Anna 95, *96*
filet de bœuf et pommes mille-feuille au jus gras *304*, 305
hogget in soy sauce *309*, 311
quail with vanilla and white peaches *276*, 288
Pommes Beaucaire 103, *104*, 123
Pommes à la boulangere *97*, 102
Pommes Dauphine *97*, 100
Pommes fondantes 94, *96*
Pommes Gaufrette *104*, 105
venison with sautéed cabbage and chocolate and raspberry sauce *281*, 287
Pommes Maxim 95, *96*
Pommes mille-feuille *97*, 101
beef with crispy snails and anchovy butter 302–303, *304*
filet de bœuf et pommes mille-feuille au jus gras *304*, 305
partridge, with Calvados and apple 278–279, *280*
Pommes mousseline *97*, 102
baby potatoes filled with caviar and *220*, 222
brandade 230, *232*
stuffed spring lamb with jus gras 309, 310
twice-cooked hare leg 272, *280*
Pommes paille 104, 105
Pommes Pont Neuf *97*, 99
extravagant burger *304*, 306
Pommes sauté 103, *104*
Pommes soufflées *96*, 98
wild duck with cherries *281*, 282–283
Pork belly, roast scallop, pig's ear and truffle salad 191–192, *196*
Potatoes *see also* Pommes
baby, filled with pommes mousseline and caviar *220*, 222
confit *97*, 99
filet de daurade et pommes de terre au crabe *255*, 257
grouper with confit of onions and *262*, 263
kipfler, filled with snails *96*, 98
poached snapper with caviar and smoked baby *220*, 221–222
potato-crusted red mullet with eggplant caviar and tomato butter *85*, 88

ravioli with mushroom essence 114–115, *117*
saffron 88, 93, *96*
Praline 391
Profiteroles 62, *63*
tomato soup, cold-pressed with fromage blanc and 79, 80, *84*
Provençal sauce 314
lamb provençal *309,* 314–315
Prunes
apple and prune croustillant *322*, 323
armagnac ice cream 328
Puff pastry 54–55, *57*
assiette of wild hare 270–271, *276*
coquilles Saint Jacques voilées 194–195, *196*
duck galette *276*, 283–284
goat's cheese wrapped in *365*, 367
pizza dough *69,* 72–73
tarte aux pommes à la tatin 319, *322*
truffle broth baked in 120, *124*
vol-au-vent 396–397
wild oysters with lobster mousse and *207*, 212
Pumpkin purée, 395
poached lamb with basil mousse and ratatouille *309*, 312–313
Purée, asparagus
duck egg omelettes filled with slippery jack mushrooms and 121–122, *124*
Purée, basil 372
Purée, cauliflower
hogget in soy sauce *309*, 311
venison carpaccio with cauliflower and caviar 219, *220*
Purée, mushroom 111, *116*
Purée, onion *145*, 148
Purée, parsley 303
beef with crispy snails and anchovy butter 302–303, *304*
grouper with confit potatoes and onions *262*, 263
Purée, pea 142
assiette of wild hare 270–271, *276*
duck galette 276, 283–284
sea urchin and quail eggs with 142–143, *144*
wild barramundi with vanilla sauce *233*, 235
Purée, pumpkin 395
poached lamb with basil mousse and ratatouille *309*, 312–313
Purée, vegetable 395 *see also* Cauliflower purée

Quail *see also* Quail eggs
gaille espice marinade 383
pasties *281*, 289
pâté *179*, 184–185
with vanilla and white peaches *276*, 288
Quail eggs
beef tartare with *301*, 304
extravagant burger *304*, 306
pea purée with sea urchin and 142–143, *144*
salmon tartare *233*, 237
tempura-battered oysters with crispy black pudding and 204–205, *206*
Quiche Lorraine *69*, 75

Rabbit
wild rabbit stew à la bourguignonne 4–5, *32*
Raspberry and chocolate sauce and sautéed cabbage with venison *281*, 287
Raspberry coulis 331–332
chocolate truffle mousse *351*, 355–56
pêche Melba *329*, 331–332
Ratatouille and basil mousse with poached lamb *309*, 312–313
Ravioli
apple, with star anise and white pepper 320, *321*
dough 392
potato, with mushroom essence 114–115, *117*
Red mullet
bouillabaisse *255*, 258–259
potato-crusted, with eggplant caviar and tomato butter *85*, 88
Red wine sauce 296, *297*
Duck galette *276*, 283–284
filet de bœuf et pommes mille-feuille au jus gras *304*, 305

grouper with confit potatoes and onions *262*, 263
selle de pré-salé aux laities 307, *309*
truffle mayonnaise 394
venison with sautéed cabbage and chocolate and raspberry sauce *281*, 287
wild duck with cherries *281*, 282–283
Risotto
au fruits de mer 260–261, *262*
black truffle 129, *131*
mushroom 113–114, *117*
white truffle *131*, 134
Rouille 259
Rum babas 60–61, *63*

Sable biscuits *32*, 36
Salads
Beaucaire 160, *162*
roast scallop, pork belly, pig's ear and truffle 191–192, *196*
Russian 238
watercress and hazelnut *163*, 167
zucchini 151, *154*
Salmon
lightly steamed, infused with pancetta 21, *32*
osso bucco jus with confit of *233*, 236–237
pâté, smoked trout and 228, *232*
tartare *233*, 237
Salmon, smoked
blini and salmon roe with scallops wrapped in 190, *196*
crab rillette *255*, 256
mousse 234
oysters and citrus jelly with 202–203, *206*
paupiettes *233*, 234–235
Samosas
dough 64, *68*
spicy lamb 308, *309*
Sauces *see also* Aioli, Beurre Blanc, Mayonnaise, Velouté
béarnaise *see* Béarnaise sauce
béchamel *see* Béchamel sauce
beurre blanc 374
Bois Boudran 205
caramel Calvados *see* Caramel Calvados sauce
chocolate and raspberry 287
hollandaise *see* Hollandaise sauce
lime and coconut 274–275
lobster 244
madeira *297*, 298
Mary Rose 388
mornay 389
mushroom 110, *116*
Nantua *247*, 248
Normande 229
orange 175–176
parsley 277
provençal 314
red wine 296, *297*
sauternes 174
vanilla, wild barramundi with *233*, 235
vierge 392
Sauternes sauce 174
grilled fois gras, caramelised apple, poached walnuts and grapes with 173–174, *178*
partridge with calvados and apple 278–279, *280*
Scallops
ceviche of scallops 193, *196*
coquilles Saint Jacques voilées 194–195, *196*
mousseline *196* 197
roast, pork belly, pig's ear and truffle salad 191–192, *196*
roasted, wrapped in pancetta, with pea soup *145*, 146
wrapped in smoked salmon with blini and salmon roe 190, *196*
Sea urchins
pea purée with quail eggs and 142–143, *144*
tomato jelly with sea urchin and basil velouté 80–81, *84*
Shallotts, confit of 149, *154*
Shellfish vinaigrette 246, *247*
Shrimp butter *see* Butter, shrimp
Snails
beef and anchovy butter with crispy 302–303, *304*
kipfler potatoes filled with *96*, 98
hazelnut vinaigrette with 234
marinade 393

Snapper
filet de daurade et pommes de terre au crabe *255*, 257
with smoked baby potatoes and caviar *220*, 221–222
Soda bread 50, *56*
Sorbet 330
almond gazpacho, with tomato tarts and crispy anchovies 86–87
apple crème brûlée with poire William sorbet 321, *322*
sorbet au clicquot rosé 324, *329*
Soufflé
à la florentine soufflé d'ecrevisses *262*, 264
basic 334
cheese, twice-cooked 364, *365*
demoulded pistachio soufflé with a soft chocolate centre 336–337, *350*
pommes *96*, 98
variations 338, *339*
Soups
bouillabaisse *see* Bouillabaisse
cappuccino of mushroom *117*, 119
chestnut *155*, 158
consommé à la Française *163*, 166
duck consommé XXX
mushroom and truffle broth baked in puff pastry 120, *124*
pea, with roasted scallops wrapped in pancetta *145*, 146
tomato, cold-pressed 79, *84*
tomato gazpacho, classic 83, *85*
Topinambour 161, *162*
vichyssoise of white asparagus *163*, 165
white truffle and haricot blanc *131*, 133
Sourdough bread 52–53, *56*
salmon tartare *233*, 237
tomato gazpacho, classic 83, *85*
tomato tarts with almond gazpacho sorbet and crispy anchovies 86–87,
Spinach
John Dory fillets with spinach and wild mushroom fricassee *124*, 125
Squid, risotto au fruits de mer 260–261, *262*
Stew, rabbit à la bourguignonne 4–5, *32*
Stock
artichokes, for cooking 159, 160, *162*
chicken 378
double chicken 381
fish 243, *247*
Langoustine 245, *247*
mushroom 109, *116*
mussel 389
veal 294, *297*
vegetable 140, *144*
Syrups
orange sugar 324
soaking 60
sugar 393
syrup 30 330

Tapenade, black olive 375
lamb provençal *309*, 314–315
stuffed spring lamb with jus gras 309, 310
Tarts
aux pommes à la tatin 319, *322*
chocolate robuchon 347, *350*
lemon *32*, 34–35
tomato *85*, 86–87,
Tempura batter 87, 204
barramundi and zucchini flowers stuffed with brandade 231, *232*
beef with crispy snails and anchovy butter 302–303, *304*
oysters with crispy black pudding and quail eggs 204–205, *206*
Tomato butter, potato-crusted red mullet with eggplant caviar and *85*, 88
Tomato coulis *85*, 89
Tomato fondue (paste) 81, *84*,
eggplant caviar 153, *155*
Tomato gazpacho, classic 83, *85*
Tomato jelly with sea urchin and basil velouté 80–81, *84*
Tomato soup, cold-pressed 79, *84*
fromage blanc and profiteroles 79

tomato jelly with sea urchin and basil velouté 80–81, *84*

Tomato stuffed with crab and avocado 82, *84*

Tomato tarts with almond gazpacho sorbet and crispy anchovies 86–87

Tomato vinaigrette 257

filet de daurade et pommes de terre au crabe *255*, 257

Tomatoes, confit 86

extravagant burger *304*, 306

stuffed spring lamb with jus gras 309, 310

lamb provençal *309*, 314–315

Topinambour soup 161, *162*

Trout

poached trout royale with sauce Normande 229, *232*

smoked, and salmon pâté 228, *232*

Truffles

black, risotto 129, *131*

mayonnaise *see* Mayonnaise, truffle

mushroom and truffle broth baked in puff pastry 120, *124*

preserved black 130, *131*

white, and haricot blanc soup *131*, 133

white, ice cream *131*, 135

white, risotto *131*, 134

white truffle and asparagus custard, scrambled duck eggs with *131*, 132–133

Tuiles 340, *341*

Vanilla

butter 288

chestnuts combined with vanilla beans and dried apricots 157

ice cream 327

quail with vanilla and white peaches *276*, 288

sauce with wild barramundi with *233*, 235

Veal

glace de viande 295, *297*

roast fillet with garlic, sage and pine mushroom sauce 122–123, *124*

stock 294, *297*

Vegetable bouillon 395

Vegetable emulsion 141, *144*

Vegetable purée 395

Vegetable stock 140, *144*

Velouté de champignons a l'Italienne *145*, 147

Velouté, Champagne 208

poached oysters with scrambled duck eggs *207*, 211

warmed oysters with linguine and *206*, 208–209

Velouté, fish 244, *247*

garlic, sage and pine mushroom sauce with roast veal fillet 122–123, *124*

Velouté, mussel 244

grouper with confit potatoes and onions *262*, 263

tomato jelly with sea urchin and basil velouté 80–81, *84*

trout royale with sauce Normande 229, *232*

Venison

carpaccio with cauliflower and caviar 219, *220*

sautéed cabbage and chocolate and raspberry sauce *281*, 287

Vichyssoise of white asparagus *163*, 165

Vierge sauce 392

hogget in soy sauce *309*, 311

Vinaigrette, French 396

filet de daurade et pommes de terre au crabe *255*, 257

salad beaucaire 160, *162*

tempura-battered oysters with crispy black pudding and quail eggs 204, *206*

Vinaigrette, hazelnut *see* Hazelnut vinaigrette

Vinaigrette, shellfish 246, *247*

Vinaigrette, tomato 257

filet de daurade et pommes de terre au crabe *255*, 257

Vinaigrette, walnut 396

foie gras baked in brioche *179*, 182

Vol-au-vent 396–397

white asparagus and lamb sweetbread *162*, 164

Walnuts, peeled 391

White truffle *see* Truffles

Yabbies
- à la florentine soufflé d'ecrevisses *262*, 264
- shrimp butter *262*, 265

Yeast, converting fresh to dry 49

Yeast batter 65, *68*

Zucchini
- barramundi and zucchini flowers stuffed with brandade 231, *232*
- salad 151, *154*
- tian 152, *154*